The Independent Hostel Guide 2009

United Kingdom

Ed
Sam
Bob

The Backpackers Press

ISBN 978-0-9536185-8-3

Independent Hostel Guide 2009: United Kingdom

18th Edition
Editors : Sam Dalley and Bob Oldfield (AKA Sam & Peter Oldfield)

Briitish Library Cataloguing in Publication Data
A Catalogue record for this book is available from the British Library
ISBN   978-0-9536185-8-3

ISBN 978-0-9536185-8-3

9 780953 618583 >

Published by: The Backpackers Press, Speedwell House,
Upperwood, Matlock Bath, Derbyshire, DE4 3PE
www.independenthostelguide.co.uk
Tel: +44 (0) 1629 580427

Printed by: Pindar, Preston (01772) 620999
Cover Artwork : Just 30 Ltd www.just30.co.uk
Cover photography : Robert Morris www.robertmorrisimages.co.uk
Back cover photo : Comrie Croft Fishing Loch (pg 340)
Internal photographs: Provided by the Independent Hostels

Distributed in the UK by:-
        Cordee Books and Maps, 3a De Montfort Street.
        Leicester, LE1 7HD, Tel: (0116) 2543579

Distributed overseas by:-
        Global Exchange, Australia, Tel: (02) 4929 4688

CONTENTS

Symbols   4
Independent Hostels   5

Maps :
    England   6
    Wales   206
    Scotland   286
    Northern Ireland   444

Hostels :
    England   10
    Wales   210
    Scotland   290
    Scottish Independent Hostels   317
    Northern Ireland   445
    Other Countries   448

Hostel Networks and Associations   453
Index (hostels by name)   462

Printed on paper manufactured from
100% recycled materials.

SYMBOLS

👫	Mixed dormitories
👫	Single sex dormitories
P	Private rooms
	Blankets or duvets provided
	Sheets required
	Sleeping bags required
	Hostel fully heated (including common room)
	Common room only heated
	Drying room available
	Showers available
	Cooking facilities available
	Shop at hostel
	Meals provided at hostel (with notice)
	Breakfast only at hostel (with notice)
	Meals available locally
	Clothes washing facilities available
♿	Facilities for less-able people.
	Internet facilities
1m	Within 1 mile of a Sustrans cycle route
3m	Within 3 miles of a Sustrans cycle route
5m	Within 5 miles of a Sustrans cycle route
	Affiliated to Hostelling International
	Member of Scottoish Independent Hostels
GROUPS ONLY	Accommodation only for groups

INDEPENDENT HOSTELS[5]

- ▲ No membership requirements
- ▲ Self catering facilities
- ▲ Dorms, private bedrooms and en-suite rooms
- ▲ Groups, individuals and families welcome
- ▲ Great locations for outdoor activities
- ▲ Central city locations for independent travellers
- ▲ Can be booked completely (sole-use) for get-togethers
- ▲ Available for individual nights, weekends or weeks
- ▲ Privately owned
- ▲ Can be YHA affiliated, but are always privately run
- ▲ Eco-conscious
- ▲ Great value
- ▲ Updated daily on **www.Independenthostelguide.co.uk**

pp	per person
GR	Ordnance Survey grid reference
C$	Canadian Dollars

 VisitScotland Quality Assured

 VisitWales Quality Assured · Wales Cymru

 NI Tourist Board Q.Assured · Northern Ireland Tourist Board

 VisitEngland Quality Assured

Liverpool
Manchester
122 124 125,126
121
100
Shrewsbury
96 97,98 99
89
92 90
Cheltenham
W A L E S
46 Bristol
44
Minehead 43
38 40 41 42
51
25
26
Bude
24
37
Exeter
47
33,34
30
28,29
32
Newquay 35,36
21,22 27
12 20 Plymouth
10 11 23
16 18,19
13,14
Penzance

| 0 | miles | 50 |
| 0 | kilometres | 80 |

South England/Midlands

Sheffield
128
Lincoln
116
118 120
114 112
119 115
108 110
Derby
Nottingham
106
101,102
104
Norwich
Leicester
Peterborough
Birmingham
94,95
Coventry
Northampton
Cambridge
81
Luton
Colchester
87,88
82
Oxford
86
84
London
Reading
65 to 80
58 60 62
Canterbury
Dover
55
Salisbury
64
54
Southampton
52
56
57
53
Brighton
Bournemouth
48,50

KEY

45 - **Hostel page number**

45 - **Page number of group only accomodation**

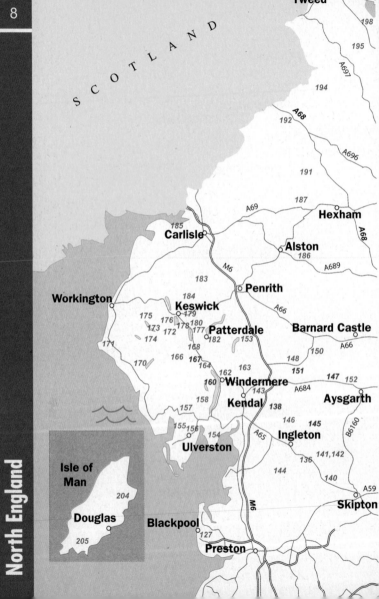

Berwick
Upon
Tweed

202,200

198

195

SCOTLAND

194

A697

A68

192

A696

191

187

A69

Hexham

185

Carlisle

Alston

A68

186

M6

A689

183

Penrith

Workington

184

A66

Keswick

179

Barnard Castle

175

176

178

180

Patterdale

A66

173

172

177

150

174

182

153

168

148

151

171

166

167

164

163

147

152

170

162

Windermere

A684

160

143

Aysgarth

158

Kendal

138

157

146

145

B6160

155

156

154

Ingleton

Ulverston

A65

141,142

136

144

140

M6

A59

Skipton

Isle of
Man

204

Douglas

205

Blackpool

127

Preston

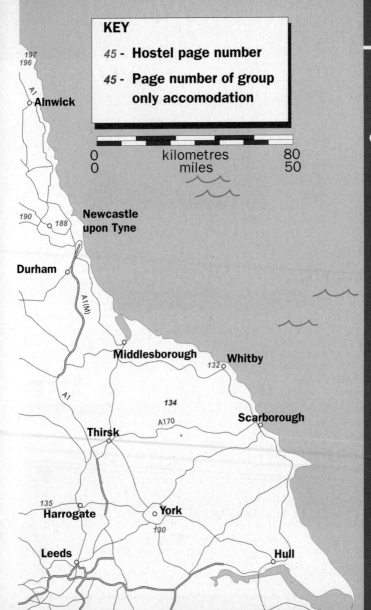

KEY

45 - **Hostel page number**

45 - **Page number of group only accomodation**

0   kilometres   80
0   miles   50

197
196

A1

○ **Alnwick**

190   ○ *188*   **Newcastle upon Tyne**

Durham ○

A1(M)

Middlesborough   *132* ○ **Whitby**

A1

134

A170

Scarborough ○

Thirsk ○

135
○ **Harrogate**

○ **York**

130

Leeds ○

Hull ○

KELYNACK
BUNKBARN

Kelynack Bunkbarn nestles in the secluded Cot Valley, one mile from the Atlantic Coast in the heart of the Land's End Peninsula Area of Outstanding Natural Beauty.
The Barn has one twin room, two two-bedded and one four-bedded bunkroom. Blankets and pillows are provided. There is a toilet/shower room and communal kitchen with full cooking facilities. Adjacent is the bike store and a laundry/drying room shared with the campers on site.
We also have a small shop for essentials.

St Just, a mile away, has plenty of food shops and a selection of pubs and take-aways. Kelynack is ideal for coast and moorland walking, spending time on the beaches, birdwatching, rock climbing and exploring the ancient villages, standing stones and tin mining heritage of unspoilt West Penwith.

DETAILS

- **Open** - All year, arrive after 2pm, vacate by 10am. 24 hr access.
- **Number of beds** - 10: 1 x 4 : 3 x 2.
- **Booking** - Booking is advised (25% deposit)
- **Price per night** - £12 per bed. Exclusive use £110 per night. No meters.
- **Public Transport** - There is a frequent bus from Penzance Rail Station to St Just. The hostel is one mile south of St Just. Free transport from St Just by prior arrangement.
- **Directions** - GR 373 301. The hostel is 200 yards east of the B3306, 1 mile south of St Just, 5 miles north of Land's End and 20 mins walk from coastal path.

CONTACT: Francis or Wendy Grose
Kelynack Camping Park, Kelynack, St Just, Penzance, Cornwall, TR19 7RE
Tel: 01736 787633
kelynackholidays@tiscali.co.uk www.kelynackholidays.co.uk

Zennor is a small picturesque village situated between St Ives and Land's End and is a haven for walkers, bird watchers and anyone who wants a taste of the rural way of life or just simply to relax! The hostel is located very close to the pub and St Ives is nearby for shopping, clubbing, cinemas, restaurants and some of the finest beaches in Cornwall.

The Old Chapel Backpackers has been converted to a very high standard and is perfectly situated for clear views over the sea and moorland. We have four rooms that sleep six people, one room that sleeps four and a family room with double bed. There are washbasins in every room and the hostel is centrally heated throughout. We can offer self-catering and we can provide breakfast, packed lunches and evening meals if required. There is also a café on the premises serving delicious soup, rolls and cakes

DETAILS

- **Open** - All year, winter by prior arrangement, all day
- **Number of beds** - 32: 4 x 6 : 1 x 4 : 1 x family room
- **Booking** - Booking is advisable, 20% deposit
- **Price per night** - From £15 per person all year
- **Public Transport** - There are train stations at St Ives (4 miles) and Penzance (10 miles). Local buses run to/from St Ives every few hours. The taxi fare from St Ives is approximately £5.
- **Directions** - Approximately 4 miles from St Ives on Coastal Road heading towards Land's End.

CONTACT: Paul or Hetty
Zennor, St Ives, Cornwall, TR26 3BY
Tel: 01736 798307
zennorbackpackers@btinternet.com www.backpackers.co.uk/zennor

ST IVES
BACKPACKERS

St Ives is the jewel in the crown of the beautiful Cornish Riviera, famous for its artistic community, Tate Gallery, picturesque town, harbour, surf beaches and bay. An ideal location for relaxing, surfing (5 minutes walk to Porthmeor Beach), climbing, scuba diving, walking the coast path, fishing, great restaurants, shopping or just relaxing in a quaint Cornish seaside town

St Ives Backpackers was originally a Wesleyan Chapel School built in 1845. The building is based around a central courtyard - ideal for barbecues and socialising. Clean and comfortable surroundings, friendly and informal atmosphere, internet hotspot! Discounts for local cafés, restaurants and nightclubs. NO CURFEW!!!

Fully equipped kitchen. Bedding provided. Surfboard/wetsuit storage. Regular barbecues. Pool table and football table.

DETAILS

- **Open** - All year, 24 hours
- **Number of beds** - 62: 8 x 3,6 x 3,5 x 1,3 x 4, 2 x twin, 2 x double.
- **Booking** - Advisable, groups require deposit.
- **Price per night** - Oct-Apr from £11.95, May from £13.95, Sept from £15.95, June from £15.95, Jul-Aug from £17.95. Extra for bank holidays and special events.
- **Public Transport** - Bus: National Express; Train: Mon - Sun 12 per day (change at St Erth); Five minutes walk from bus and train stations.
- **Directions** - Car: Signposted off the A30

CONTACT: Reception
Town Centre, St Ives, Cornwall, TR26 1SG
Tel: (01736) 799444
st.ives@backpackers.co.uk www.backpackers.co.uk/st-ives/index.html

West Cornwall is famous for it's rugged coastlines, secret coves and long sandy beaches. It offers the chance to relax and unwind, to surf, walk, deep sea dive, horse ride and to visit galleries, small harbours and villages. There are many attractions such as the famous Minack open air theatre.

The YMCA is more than just a hostel, we offer sporting and conference facilities as well as an internet café. Our facilities provide the ideal location for school/youth groups of any size, for short weekends or for longer holidays. The YMCA has been serving the community of Penwith since 1893, providing an ideal base for you to discover all the area has to offer.

Now available: Isle of Scilly parking from just £2.50 a day!!

DETAILS

- **Open** - All year, 8am to 10pm (except by prior arrangement)
- **Number of beds** - 52: 6x5, 5x4, 1x2
- **Booking** - booking not essential but advisable in Summer
- **Price per night** - Dorm £16.40pp, single £21.75, twin £19.40pp, family rooms £51.50. From 3/09/08 dorm £15.40, single £19.75. Discount for parties of 15+. 10% discount for students in dormitories.
- **Public Transport** - Penzance Train Station 15 min walk. Penzance Bus Station bus service numbers 6A and 6B. Taxi from Penzance centre approx £3.
- **Directions** - From the train / bus stations, turn left towards the centre of town onto Market Jew Street. Turn left and follow Market Jew Street until it becomes Alverton Road. Go straight over the roundabout until you see our sign on the left (approx 200m).

CONTACT: Reception Team
International House, The Orchard, Alverton, Penzance, TR18 4TE
Tel: 01736 334820
admin@cornwall.ymca.org.uk www.cornwall.ymca.org.uk

PENZANCE
BACKPACKERS

Penzance, with its mild climate, its wonderful location looking across to spectacular St Michael's Mount, with all the coach and rail services terminating here, is the ideal base for exploring the far SW of England and the Scilly Isles. Whether you are looking for sandy beaches and sheltered coves; the storm lashed cliffs of Land's End; sub-tropical gardens; internationally acclaimed artists; the remains of ancient cultures; or simply somewhere to relax and take time out, Penzance Backpackers is for you. We are situated in a lovely tree-lined road close to the sea front, with the town centre, bus station and railway station only a short walk away. Accommodation is mostly in small bunk-bedded rooms with bed-linen. Fully equipped self-catering kitchen, hot showers, comfortable lounge, lots of local information and a warm welcome all included.

DETAILS

- **Open** - All year, 24 hours
- **Number of beds** - 30: 2 double, 1x 4 (double+2bunks), 3x6, 1x7.
- **Booking** - It's best to phone.
- **Price per night** - From £15 per person. Discount for long stays.
- **Public Transport** -   Penzance has a train station and National Express service. 15 mins walk from train/bus station or catch buses 1, 1a, 5a or 6a from Tourist Information/bus/train station. Ask for top of Alexandra Road.
- **Directions** - From Tourist Information/bus/train station either follow Quay and Promenade to mini-roundabout, turn right up Alexandra Rd, we are a short way up on the left; or follow main road through town centre until second mini-roundabout, turn left down Alexandra Rd; we are on right.

CONTACT:
The Blue Dolphin, Alexandra Road, Penzance, TR18 4LZ
Tel: 01736 363836
info@pzbackpack.com www.pzbackpack.com

GRANARY
BARN / BACKPACKERS

Granary Barn is a new camping barn forming an important link in the Cornwall camping barn and backpackers network. It is situated up a lovely tree lined lane off the B3302 road. The barn consists of a main hall equipped with 8 beds with mattresses (blankets & sleeping bags required). There is heating, toilet with H&C basin, shower room (hot showers-metered) and communal kitchen with dining area/lounge. There is also a surf-board/bike store, laundry/drying room, ample parking and BBQ area. The farm is surrounded by a network of public footpaths, bridle ways and byways.

Nearby is the traditional Cornish village of Sithney featuring a beautiful 15th century church, tea room and open farmland. Porthleven, with its distinctive harbour, sheltered beach, excellent places to surf, eat and drink, galleries and shops is 10 mins drive. A few miles west is the mile long sweep of white sand, surf and golf course of Praa Sands. St Michael's Mount and the Lizard Peninsula are all within 30 mins drive. An ideal location if you are seeking to combine rural setting with access to the south Cornish coastline and its golden sands, hidden coves and picturesque fishing villages.

DETAILS

- **Open** - All year, all day
- **Number of beds** - 8
- **Booking** - Essential - call to check availability (24 hrs)
- **Price per night** - £7.50 per person
- **Public Transport** - Train & bus stations; Camborne, Redruth and Penzance.
- **Directions** - GR OS Map 103 SW 638 298 on the B3302

CONTACT: Tom
Sithney, Helston, TR13 0AE
Tel: Mobile 07740 514 188 (24hrs)
thomas-martin1@sky.com

TREGEDNA
LODGE

Tregedna lodge is a recently converted barn, offering comfortable, spacious and flexible accommodation.
Located in the picturesque Maen valley, close to Maenporth beach - a safe, clean, sandy beach with watersports.

Near to Falmouth with a wide range of restaurants, pubs, places of interest. Tregedna is ideally situated to enjoy the many sights and activities that Cornwall has to offer.

4-star graded by English tourist board.

DETAILS

- **Open** - All year, all day (please phone between 9am-8pm)
- **Number of beds** - 24: 1x8,1x6,1x2, 2x4 / family (double bed and bunk bed)
- **Booking** - Booking essential. 25% deposit.
- **Price per night** - £18pp (low season) £20pp (July/August). Family rooms £50 per room.
- **Public Transport** - Nearest train stations are within Falmouth, approx 1.5 miles. Nearest bus depot Falmouth. Buses run past Tregedna hourly during summer months, less frequently during winter months.
- **Directions** - By car from Truro take the A39 to Falmouth. Go straight over the double roundabout at Treluswell and straight on (bearing right) at the first of the two roundabouts ahead. At the 2nd, turn left, at the ASDA roundabout go straight across. At the Hillhead roundabout turn right, go straight over the next two roundabouts and continue on this road for approx 2 miles.Tregedna is on your right.

CONTACT: Liz
Tregedna farm, Maenporth, Falmouth, Cornwall, TR11 5HL
Tel: 01326 250529
tregednafarm@btinternet.com www.tregednafarmholidays.co.uk/lodge.html

FALMOUTH
BACKPACKERS
ENGLAND

Falmouth's beautiful natural harbour provides a picturesque background to the main street of charming shops, restaurants, cafés and pubs; good opportunity to sample Cornish cream teas, pasties, local seafood and real ales. Voted the 2nd best coastal town, Falmouth is renowned for it's sandy beaches, Pendennis Castle, exotic gardens, the Falmouth Arts Centre and the Princess Pavilion. Go sightseeing on passenger ferries to St Mawes, Truro, Flushing and the Helford Passage. On a rainy day visit Ships and Castle leisure pool and the National Maritime Museum. Take advantage of watersports, fishing trips, sailing, diving, with tuition and equipment hire. Falmouth Backpackers is conveniently situated next to Princess Pavilion, 200 metres from main beach, coastal footpath and minutes to town, harbour and castle. Relax in a friendly, clean, homely atmosphere. Owner managed, by experienced world traveller. Guests have use of a well-equipped kitchen and TV lounge; games, frisbee and boogie board.

DETAILS

- **Open** - Closed December. 9am to 12pm and 5pm to 10pm
- **Number of beds** - 20: 1 x 2, 1 x 3, 2 x 4, 1 x 5, 1 double ensuite (some seaviews)
- **Booking** - Telephone or email in advance
- **Price per night** - From £19 per person
- **Public Transport** - Train - change at Truro for Falmouth Town Station 250 mtrs. National Express to Falmouth. By air - London Stansted/Gatwick to Newquay
- **Directions** - From M5, A30 over Bodmin Moor to Truro, A39 to Falmouth, stay on A39 until Gyllyngvase Road on right, left into Gyllyngvase Terrace.

CONTACT: Charlotte
9 Gyllyngvase Terrace, Falmouth, Cornwall, TR11 4DL
Tel: 01326 319996, mobile 07940 390072
charlotte@mitchell999.fsworld.co.uk www.falmouthbackpackers.co.uk

PORTHTOWAN
BACKPACKERS

Looking for low budget accommodation near Porthtowan, Cornwall? You've found it! Porthtowan Backpackers is small, friendly and family-run and is ideal for surfers, body boarders, walkers, backpackers and students. Situated on Cornwall's North Coast and only 300 yds from a blue flag beach, one of the best surfing beaches in Cornwall. At high tide there's plenty of sand and at low tide it is possible to walk to Chapel Porth, St. Agnes. If the tide comes up while at Chapel Porth there is a really nice cliff walk to get back to Porthtowan. A post office with convience store, surf shop, and bars are within close walking distance. Accommodation comprises a 6 bed room, 4 bed room, and a double room, all ensuite; communal lounge with 42" TV and kitchenette; storage for surf boards and wetsuits; car parking; a roof deck for sunbathing and a barbeque area in the back garden. All major credit/debit cards accepted. We can pick you up from train station (if arranged before your stay) for £5.00 per group.

DETAILS

- **Open** - All year, all day
- **Number of beds** - 12: 1x6, 1x4, 1x2
- **Booking** - Booking is advised by phone or email, with booking fee.
- **Price per night** - Shared room: £20.50pp, off peak (4th April to 30 Sept) £18.50pp. 4 nights Mon to Fri £75pp (£66 off peak). Double room: £25pp (£20.50 off peak); 4 nights Mon to Fri £90 (£75 off peak). Continental breakfast inc.
- **Public Transport** - Trains at Redruth (4 miles). Buses to village from Truro (Hopleys). Airport at Newquay (Ryan Air, Fly-be, Air South West). Taxis available.
- **Directions** - In the centre of Porthtowan village, between Newquay and St Ives.

CONTACT:
Porthtowan Backpackers, Seamyst, Beach Road, Porthtowan, TR4 8AA
Tel: (01209) 891697, Fax: (01209) 891697
info@sicklamelazy.co.uk www.sicklamelazy.co.uk

ORIGINAL
BACKPACKERS

Overlooking one of Newquay's finest beaches, we offer low cost accommodation in the heart of town for international travellers and surfers.

We offer mainly dorm style accommodation, however two twin rooms are available. We have hot showers and board / bike storage can be arranged. There is no curfew, just come and go as you please.

Being centrally based, The Original Backpackers is ideally located for the beaches, the town's many pubs and clubs.

A relaxed atmosphere is guaranteed.

DETAILS

- **Open** - All year (low season group bookings only), all day
- **Number of beds** - 32: 3 x 6 : 2 x 5 : 2 x 2
- **Booking** - Booking is usually essential due to high demand.
- **Price per night** - Off peak from £15.00 pp, peak times from £20.00 pp. Group discounts available off peak.
- **Public Transport** - Newquay has a train station and is served by National Express and an airport
- **Directions** - If driving, head towards Fistral Beach, turn right at Tower Garages. Follow this road following outbound traffic, take the second left, signposted Beachfield Ave & The Crescent. Pass in front of The Central, turn right, Beachfield Ave is at the bottom of this road, the hostel is on the right.

CONTACT: Manager
Towan Beach, Beachfield Ave, Newquay, Cornwall, TR7 1DR
Tel: 01637 874668
originalbp@hotmail.com www.originalbackpackers.co.uk

MATTS
SURF LODGE

Newquay is about having fun - and the fun starts here! The Lodge has been open for twelve years and still offers the same easygoing relaxed atmosphere. Newquay is an all year round mecca for surfers, students and travellers, with dramatic cliffs, idyllic beaches and attractions galore.

The backpackers is situated at the highest point of the town, only five minutes walk from Central Square with its nightlife and shops. Fistral Beach and the Town beaches are all within ten minutes walk. All the rooms are clean and comfortable, many with seaview or en-suite facilities. Rates include breakfast, tea/coffee all day and unlimited hot showers. There is a fully equipped kitchen, no curfews, a licensed bar which has good music and 100s of DVDs, plus a games room with library, games and pool table. Free car park and secure surfboard and bike storage.

DETAILS

- **Open** - All year, 24 hours
- **Number of beds** - 49: 4 x 6 : 3 x 4 : 1 x 3 : 5 x twin/double
- **Booking** - Recommended for weekends and peak season, but not essential. First night's fee required as deposit.
- **Price per night** - From £8pp (or £10 for en-suite seaview). From £15pp July, August and bank holidays. £45 per week available from September to June.
- **Public Transport** - Local train and bus station. Free pickup when available.
- **Directions** - From coach station walk up St George's Rd, turn right at top. From Train Station turn left and left again opposite Victoria Hotel onto Berry Rd which leads onto Mount Wise

CONTACT: Matt
110 Mount Wise, Newquay, Cornwall, TR7 1QP
Tel: 01637 874651
matt@surflodge.co.uk www.surflodge.co.uk

Truro Backpackers Lodge provides welcoming, family-run accommodation in the heart of Cornwall. Here you will find a comfortable environment and ideal base for your visit to this wonderful county. The house is a rambling 1840's building with many original features and great period charm.
There is a large fully equipped kitchen with an Aga for residents' use. Tea and coffee making facilities are available all day and there is a large comfy lounge with Sky TV to relax in.

The city of Truro provides many attractions and facilities, plus rail and bus links to many other parts of Cornwall. Truro is the capital city of Cornwall and has excellent transport links with the rest of the county, making it a good base for touring. The bus station is just a 5 minute walk away. In addition to the historic Cathedral and popular Theatre the City boasts many bars and restaurants.

Because the hostel is small advanced booking is essential.

DETAILS

- **Open** - All year, all day
- **Number of beds** - 15: 1x5, 1x4, 1x3, 1x2, 1x1)
- **Booking** - Book in advance by phone.
- **Price per night** - Dorm from £15pp, Double Room £35, Single Room from £20pp
- **Public Transport** -   Truro has a train station. Bus station is 5 mins walk. Bus links to many parts of Cornwall.
- **Directions** - See map on website.

CONTACT: Robert Nolan
10 The Parade, Truro, Cornwall, TR1 1QE
Tel: 01872 260857 or 07813 755210
trurobackpackers@aol.com www.trurobackpackers.co.uk

NORTHSHOREBUDE

ENGLAND

You can make your stay whatever you want it to be. A relaxed place with a variety of bedrooms, large garden, close to town, beaches and South West Coastal path.

An ideal base to see the South West's attractions: The Eden Project, Tintagel Castle, The Tamar Lakes, Dartmoor, Bodmin Moor and the South West Coastal Path. There are competition standard surfing beaches nearby. Families with children aged over 5 welcome. Meet old friends or make new ones, on the deck, in the lounge or around the dining room table after cooking up a storm in the fully fitted kitchen.

DETAILS

- **Open** - All year except Christmas week, 8.30am to 1pm and 4.30pm to 10.30pm
- **Number of beds** - 43: 2x6 : 5x4 : 1x3 : 1x2 : 3xdbl
- **Booking** - Advisable, credit card secures booking. Photo ID at check in. (Groups 6 or more by prior booking)
- **Price per night** - From £12pp dorm rooms (single night supplement)
- **Public Transport** - To Bude: From Exeter Via Okehampton X9. From Plymouth X8. From Newquay X10 (changing at Okehampton). From Bideford 85. All buses-First Bus Company. There are train and bus links from London to Exeter.
- **Directions** - From A39, head into Bude down Stratton Rd past Morrisons on your right, follow the road down past Esso garage. Take the second road on the right, Killerton Road (before the Bencollen Pub). Continue up to the top of the road and Northshorebude is on the corner on your left. Turn into Redwood Grove and parking is the first on the left.

CONTACT: Sean or Janine
57 Killerton Road, Bude, Cornwall, EX23 8EW
Tel: 01288 354256 or 07970 149486
info@northshorebude.com www.northshorebude.com

A former Victorian school, Elmscott is surrounded by unspoilt coastline with sea views of Lundy Island. This property offers a next-to-nature retreat. Great for walking, cycling, surfing and bird watching. There are amazing rock formations and many quiet lanes to explore. The famous fishing village of Clovelly is a few miles away with its cobbled streets and pretty harbour. Also nearby is Harland Abbey where Sense and Sensibility was filmed. Elmscott is located a few minutes walk from the South West Coast Path which passes many spectacular coves and river mouths. The accommodation is in one unit of 20 beds and another of 12. It has mixed dorms, single sex dorms and private rooms. In winter it is only available for groups (of up to 35 people). There is a kitchen, a well stocked shop in summer and a games room close by. Self catering only.

DETAILS

- **Open** - All year (groups only in winter), 24 hours
- **Number of beds** - 32 (35 in winter): 1 unit of 20: 2x6, 2x4; 1 unit of 12: 1x6, 1x4, 1x2. Extra 3 bed room available for sole use bookings in winter.
- **Booking** - In summer book direct with the hostel by phone or email. In winter book via the YHA website, or for last minute sole use bookings call the owners.
- **Price per night** - Adult £15 to £20, under 16's £12.50 to £15.50 (discounts for YHA members). Enquire for special prices for groups or longer stays.
- **Public Transport** - Nearest trains Barnstaple (25 miles). Buses from Barnstaple to Hartland (4 miles from hostel). Phone hostel for taxi service.
- **Directions** - The hostel is in the small hamlet of Elmscott 4 miles from the village of Hartland. Grid Ref 231 217.

CONTACT: John & Thirza Goaman
Elmscott, Hartland, Bideford, Devon, EX39 6ES
Tel: 01237 441276, Hostel 01237 441367
john.goa@virgin.net www.elmscott.org.uk

YARDE ORCHARD
CAFÉ AND BUNKHOUSE

If you're walking the Tarka Trail or cycling the Devon coast-to-coast, don't miss Yarde Orchard. Sited at the highest point on the trail, there is a cafe with local freshly prepared food and a green bunkhouse offering overnight accommodation in summer and group accommodation in the winter. The Tarka Trail has some real gems for those inclined to linger. It passes through woodland carpeted with wild daffodil and wood anemone in spring, through coniferous forests where glowworms display on summer nights and through the grass lands of the Marland basin rich in wild flowers. The bunkhouse is right on the trail, in a green building with rain water harvesting, reedbed water treatment, warmcel insulation, solar panels and wood-fuel heating. There is a lounge with a wood fueled range, a galleried landing and a self catering kitchen with gas hob, fridge and utensils. There are two upstairs dorms with 6 and 4 bunks and a family room downstairs with private facilities, double bed, bunk bed and cot.

DETAILS

■ **Open** - All year, all day
■ **Number of beds** - 14: 1x6, 1x4, 1x4 (family) + cot
■ **Booking** - Book by phone or email
■ **Price per night** - bunk/sleeping bag £12 per night (£8 under 18), family room £40 per night, exclusive use £140 1st night, £120 subsequent nights.
■ **Public Transport** - 118 bus (Tavistock-Barnstaple), alight at Gribble. Trains: Barnstaple station (with cycle hire) then 18 miles along Tarka Trail to Yarde.
■ **Directions** - By car: From Great Torrington take A386 towards Hatherleigh. After 2 miles at Gribble (118 bus stops here), take minor right turn signed Petersmarland, Petrockstowe. By bike: Yarde Orchard is located on NCN routes 3 & 27 at East Yarde

CONTACT: David Job
Yarde Orchard, East Yarde, Petersmarland, Torrington, Devon, EX38 8QA
Tel: 01805 624007 Mob: 07972 786306
info@yarde-orchard.co.uk www.yarde-orchard.co.uk

Globe Backpackers Plymouth is located just five minutes walk from the ferry port, where boats leave for Roscoff and Santander. The hostel is close to all amenities and a short stroll to the famous Barbican waterfront, Mayflower Steps and city centre. Also near to the bus and railway stations. Excursions to Dartmoor, canoeing on the Tamar River, local boat trips, sailing and walking the coastal paths can be arranged from Plymouth. The theatre, sports/leisure centre, ice-skating rink and National Aquarium are a short walk from the hostel. Globe Backpackers Plymouth has 4, 6 and 8 bedded dorms, plus 4 double rooms. Bedding and linen included in the price. Fully equipped self-catering kitchen, TV lounge, separate social room and courtyard garden. NO ID. NO STAY (Brits and Overseas all need to produce valid ID to be able to stay.)

DETAILS

- **Open** - All year, reception 8am-11pm, less in winter. No curfew.
- **Number of beds** - 48
- **Booking** - Phone ahead to secure booking
- **Price per night** - From £15.00pp, weekly rates available. 50p surcharge for card payments.
- **Public Transport** - National Express, local buses and various rail networks.
- **Directions** - From train station walk up Saltash Road to North Croft roundabout. Turn right along Western Approach to Pavilions on your left. From bus station walk up Exeter Street, across roundabout to Royal Parade. Cross road to Union Street, Pavilions on your left. From Plymouth Pavilions walk towards the Hoe, turn left up Citadel Road, the hostel is in 100 metres on the right hand side.

CONTACT:
172 Citadel Road, The Hoe, Plymouth, PL1 3BD
Tel: 01752 225158, Fax: 01752 207847
info@plymouthbackpackers.co.uk www.plymouthbackpackers.co.uk

The Plume of Feathers Inn is situated in the moorland village of Princetown which is the main village in Dartmoor National Park. The park covers 368 square miles and is famous for it's rugged beauty, quaint villages, prehistoric remains, and its many peaks, such as High Willhays (2039ft) and Yes Tor (2030ft). The Plume is a traditional, family-run Inn dating from 1785, it has log fires, real ale and plenty of atmosphere. The Alpine Bunkhouse and New Bunkhouse provide comfortable low cost accommodation. The Inn also has B&B en-suite accommodation and a 75 tent camping area with toilets and showers. There is a wide range of activities available in the Dartmoor area including sailing, fishing, riding, abseiling, white water canoeing, climbing, pony trekking and walking. PLEASE CONTACT THIS HOSTEL BY PHONE OR POST.

DETAILS

- **Open** - All year, all day
- **Number of beds** - 42: 2 x 10 5 x 4 1 x 2 1x4
- **Booking** - To secure beds, book in advance with 50% deposit. For weekends 3 to 4 months in advance is advised.
- **Price per night** - From £12pp (Bunkhouse), £6.50pp (Camping), B&B from £45pp.
- **Public Transport** - Nearest train and National Express services are in Plymouth (17 miles) and Exeter (26 miles). The Transmoor Link bus service between Plymouth and Exeter stops at Princetown, bus fare is £5 - £6. Taxi fare from Plymouth approx £18, from Exeter approx £25.
- **Directions** - The Plume of Feathers Inn is in Princetown village square, next to the Dartmoor National Park High Moorland Centre.

CONTACT:
Princetown, Yelverton, Devon, PL20 6QQ
Tel: 01822 890240, Fax: 01882 890780
sam@backpackerspress.com

FOX TOR
CAFÉ AND BUNKHOUSE ENGLAND

Princetown on Dartmoor is an ideal base for anyone wishing to spend time on Dartmoor whether it is to walk, climb, cycle, kayak or just relax and enjoy the spectacular scenery. Fox Tor Café and Bunkhouse is situated near the centre of the village of Princetown - famous for the prison !

The bunkhouse offers self-catering accommodation for up to 12 in 3 rooms of 4. It is newly decorated, has central heating and a kitchen equipped with microwave, fridge, kettle, toaster and sink. There are separate male and female showers and toilets with underfloor heating. Bunkhouse guests also have the option to use the drying room / store room (big enough for bicycles).

Bunkhouse users can book packed lunches and breakfasts for an early start. No smoking inside.

DETAILS

■ **Open** - All year, all day. Arrive from 4pm, leave by 10.30am.
■ **Number of beds** - 12: 3x4
■ **Booking** - Advisable with 50% deposit.
■ **Price per night** - From £9.50 per person. Sole use £100.
■ **Public Transport** - Trains at Exeter and Plymouth. DevonBus 98 Tavistock-Princetown. Devon Bus 82 Exeter-Plymouth. First 272 Gunnislake-Newton Abbot.
■ **Directions** - GR 591 735. Just off the mini roundabout in the centre of Princetown on the Two Bridges road (B3212). 20 mins drive from Tavistock, 15 mins Yelverton, 35 mins Ashburton.

CONTACT: Sam Rockey
Two Bridges Road, Princetown, Yelverton, Devon, PL20 6QS
Tel: 01822 890238
foxtorcafe@aol.com www.foxtorcafe.co.uk

DARTMOOR
EXPEDITION CENTRE

Great for walking, climbing, canoeing, caving, archaeology, painting or visiting places of interest nearby. Dartmoor Expedition Centre has two 300-year-old barn bunkhouses with cobbled floors and thick granite walls. Simple but comfortable accommodation for groups of 4+ only, with bunk beds and a wood burning stove. Radiant heaters (two in each area) and night storage heating (one in each barn). Kitchen area equipped with fridge, water heater, electric stoves and kettles. All crockery and pans provided, and there is freezer space available. Electric appliances are coin operated (£1 coins). Solar hot water system for free showers in wash rooms. House Barn has the living area downstairs and upstairs sleeps 9 plus 5 in an inner cubicle. Gate Barn sleeps 11 downstairs and 10 upstairs. There are two upgraded rooms (1 double, 1 twin). Beds provided with sheet/pillow/pillowcase, sleeping bags needed.

DETAILS

- **Open** - All year, 7.30 am to 10.30 pm
- **Number of beds** - 37: 1 x 1 : 1 x 2 : 1 x 8 : 1 x 5 : 1 x 11 : 1 x 10
- **Booking** - Book in advance with 25% deposit.
- **Price per night** - £14.00pp (£16.00 per person in upgraded room). Minimum of 4 people.
- **Public Transport** - Newton Abbot is the nearest train station. In summer there are buses to Widecombe (1.5 miles from hostel). Taxi fare from station £25.
- **Directions** - GR 700 764. Come down Widecombe Hill into the village. Turn right 200yds after school and travel up a steep hill past Southcombe onto the open moor. Continue for one mile until you reach crossroads. Turn right and take first left after 400yds. Hostel is 200yds on left.

CONTACT: John Earle
Widecombe-in-the-Moor, Newton Abbot, Devon, TQ13 7TX
Tel: 01364 621249
earle@clara.co.uk www.dartmoorbase.co.uk

South Dartmoor Bunkhouse is situated in the centre of Buckfastleigh, on the southern flanks of the Dartmoor National Park. This magnificent area of 360 sq. miles offers a range of outdoor pursuits including walking, climbing, caving, canoeing, mountain biking and horse riding. Within short walking distance of the bunkhouse are five pubs, shops, cash point, fish & chip shop / restaurant, pizza, kebabs, Chinese and tea shop. The non-smoking bunkhouse has a common room with open plan newly refurbished fully equipped kitchen. A separate area contains the shower, toilet, and washbasin. There is a store / changing area and a drying room. Upstairs has wooden bunks for 16 people in a refurbished area. Electricity is by a £1 slot meter.

DETAILS

- **Open** - All year, keys available by prior arrangement
- **Number of beds** - 16 : 1 x 12, 1 x 4
- **Booking** - Booking with £20 per night non-refundable deposit (payable to Devon Speleo Society) is essential.
- **Price per night** - £6.00 per person, £72.00 sole use.
- **Public Transport** - Trains: Newton Abbot or Totnes. Local Buses and Taxis.
- **Directions** - GR 735 660. Enter Buckfastleigh at the A38/A384 junc. at mini roundabout, turn left, past garage on right. Pass 2 turns to Buckfastleigh, (first is NO ENTRY). Continue for 500m taking next right into town, signposted 'Town Centre'. Continue past car park on right. At junction immediately ahead turn left (signed Town Hall), straight on is NO ENTRY. Pass the Town Hall on left & school on right, after 300m turn right at "T" junc. into Crest Hill. Bunkhouse is approx 85m on the left.

CONTACT: Jon (8am - 8pm)
11 Crest Hill, Buckfastleigh, Devon, TQ11 0AN
Tel: 01626 859005 or 07748 762580
bunkhousewarden@southdartmoorbunkhouse.co.uk www.
southdartmoorbunkhouse.co.uk

Sparrowhawk is a small, friendly eco-hostel located within the breathtaking Dartmoor National Park. The hostel is situated in the village centre of Moretonhampstead, 14 miles west of Exeter and can be reached easily by frequent direct bus. Accommodation is in a beautifully converted, fully equipped stable. High open moorland is close by for great hiking, cycling and off-road mountain biking, while the rocky tors rising up on the hilltops offer climbers a challenge. Wild swims in the rivers amongst woodlands or out on the moor is a must for the adventurous traveller. Magnificent stone circles, dwellings and burial sites of ancient civilizations together with wild ponies, buzzards, flora and fauna are all here to be explored. Moretonhampstead has shops, cafés, pubs, good food, live music, and an outdoor heated swimming pool. Dartmoor Way and CTC End2End cycle routes are on the doorstep. Sparrowhawk has solar-heated showers, waste recycling, secure bike shed and a bus stop nearby.

DETAILS

- **Open** - All year, all day
- **Number of beds** - 18: 1 x 14 plus double / family room
- **Booking** - Book ahead if possible by phone or email.
- **Price per night** - Adults £15. Under 14 £6. Double/family room £35/£42 for 4.
- **Public Transport** - Direct from Exeter Bus 359 or 82. Direct from Plymouth Bus 82. From Okehampton or Newton Abbot Bus 173 or 179. Enquires Tel 0870 6082608.
- **Directions** - From Exeter, take the B3212 signposted on the one-way system at Exe Bridges. From Plymouth head towards Yelverton and then B3212. The hostel is on Ford Street (A382) 100 metres from tourist office.

CONTACT: Alison
45 Ford Street, Moretonhampstead, Dartmoor, Devon, TQ13 8LN
Tel: 01647 440318 - 07870 513570
ali@sparrwohawkbackpackers.co.uk www.sparrowhawkbackpackers.co.uk

BLYTHESWOOD
HOSTEL

Blytheswood Hostel is a detached wooden chalet in secluded woodland overlooking the Teign Valley on the eastern edge of Dartmoor. It is an ideal base for exploring rugged high Dartmoor and the delightful lower slopes rich in wild flowers, butterflies and birds. The surrounding native woodland and nature reserve are home to badgers, deer and otters. There are walks straight from the door (come and see the daffodils in spring) and fishing, golf and cycling nearby. Local attractions include Castle Drogo, The Miniature Pony Centre, Canonteign Falls and picturesque thatched villages. The cathedral city of Exeter is 8 miles away and the beaches of South Devon are 40 minutes drive. Blytheswood Hostel provides flexible accommodation in cosy rooms sleeping between 2 and 8 people in bunks. It is ideal for use by families and groups who can book sole use of the whole hostel. There is a fully equipped self catering kitchen, lounge/dining room, drying room and picnic areas. Duvets and linen provided.

DETAILS

■ **Open** - All year, Reception open 8 to 10.30am and 5 to 8pm (The hostel is closed between 10.30am and 5pm, unless prior arrangement.
■ **Number of beds** - 24: 1x2, 2x4,1x6,1x8
■ **Booking** - Booking is essential. Deposit required.
■ **Price per night** - £14.00pp. Children under 18 £8.00.
■ **Public Transport** - Trains Exeter. Bus 359 from Exeter + 82 on summer wknds
■ **Directions** - On the B3212 between Exeter and Moretonhampstead, 1 mile outside of Dunsford. Approx 100m from Steps Bridge, opposite car park. Please use car park when staying at the hostel.

CONTACT: Patrick and Tracey
Steps Bridge, Dunsford, Exeter, Devon, EX6 7EQ
Tel: 01647 252435
blytheswood@blueyonder.co.uk www.blytheswood.co.uk

Torquay is on the English Riviera, famous for warm weather and Mediterranean atmosphere. Turquoise sea, red cliffs, long sandy beaches and secret shingle coves combine to create one of the UK's most beautiful coastlines. It is renowned as a watersport mecca with sailing, water-skiing, windsurfing, diving etc and nightlife with pubs, clubs and restaurants a mere stagger from the hostel which is in the heart of Torquay.

Hostel activities include beach barbecues, jam nights, international food nights and video evenings. There are also trips to Dartmoor exploring emerald river valleys where pixies dwell and the open tor-dotted moors. The hostel offers travellers a friendly, almost family atmosphere. Those who find it hard to leave can easily find work.

DETAILS

- **Open** - All year, 24 hrs. Check in 9-11am and 5-9pm.
- **Number of beds** - 45: 1 x double, 3 x 4, 1 x 5, 3 x 6 , 1 x 8.
- **Booking** - Advised at all times.
- **Price per night** - £8 to £14 per night. £60 to £85 per week.
- **Public Transport** - Torquay can be reached by coach or train from all major towns. From London take a train from Paddington/Waterloo or a coach from Victoria/Heathrow.
- **Directions** - Drivers: follow signs to sea front. Turn left. At junction with lights and Belgrave Hotel, bear left up Sheddon Hill. Next T junction is Abbey Road. Turn left. Hostel is 200m on right.

CONTACT: The Manager
119 Abbey Road, Torquay, Devon, TQ2 5NP
Tel: 01803 299924
jane@torquaybackpackers.co.uk www.torquaybackpackers.co.uk

LE PAPILLON
BACKPACKERS

Le Papillon is a three storey Victorian villa set in a quarter of an acre with a large car park and a south facing garden. The property has been newly refurbished and all the rooms have wooden floors, wash basins and comfortable beds. The dorm is a light and sunny room with large windows overlooking the garden. The TV lounge has comfortable armchairs to rest after a busy day and free wireless internet access. The breakfast room leads onto the garden (with BBQ area) and the kitchen is large and well equipped. There are plenty of shower rooms and toilets.

From Le Papillon it is an easy walk to the sandy beaches around the bay. As the English Riviera has one of the mildest climates in Britain, sitting around the cafes, restaurants and pubs gives a near Mediterranean feel. You can indulge in many water sports including, sailing, diving, wind surfing, water skiing or a ride on the large Banana! Or take the Balloon on the seafront to dazzling heights with breathtaking views over the South West. The harbour, close by, is famous for its many pubs and clubs.

DETAILS

- **Open** - All year , all day
- **Number of beds** - 26: 1x12, 1x6, 1x4, 2x dbl
- **Booking** - Book by phone or email with payment in advance (non refundable).
- **Price per night** - £15.00 per person. Minimum of two nights stay for individuals.
- **Public Transport** - Torre Station (5 mins walk), Torquay Station (10 mins drive). Coach Station (5 mins drive). Airports at Exeter, Plymouth and Bristol
- **Directions** - Behind the police station in the centre of Torquay.

CONTACT: Marga Collins
18 Vansittart Road, Torquay, Devon, TQ2 5BW
Tel: 01803 290173, mobile 07530 006897
info@backpackerstorquay.co.uk www.backpackerstorquay.co.uk

A city centre hostel within easy walking of everything: the beautiful old port, Cathedral, shopping district and wonderful mix of pubs, clubs, live music, restaurants and café scene. We therefore attract the young and "young at heart" and have the comings and goings reflecting a vibrant city centre. We will not suit those requiring a guaranteed quiet location, or young families. We are 20 minutes drive to Exmouth with its 2 miles sandy beach, great for all sail sports, and the same to Dartmoor National Park: great for walking, rock climbing, cycling and horse riding.

Exeter is also an excellent place to find work and just 2½ hours by train to London. All nationalities must produce identification – NO ID NO STAY! We do not permit the following to stay: DSS, hens and stags, unaccompanied under 18's and families with children under 16.

DETAILS

- **Open** - All year, 8am - 11pm only. No curfew once checked in.
- **Number of beds** - 57: 1 x 2/4 : 3 x 6 : 2 x 8 : 2 x 10
- **Booking** - To secure booking phone ahead.
- **Price per night** - From £16.50 pp, weekly rates from £75 available. 50p surcharge for cards.
- **Public Transport** - National Express, local bus companies and rail networks.
- **Directions** - Bus Station: Cross road, take side turning Southernhay East. Stay on LH side until Southgate Hotel. We are diagonally opposite on other side of junction. From Central rail station go down Queen St to High St, turn right and at 1st set of lights, turn left South St, continue to junction at bottom of hill. Cross at lights, we are on right.

CONTACT:
71 Holloway Street, Exeter, EX2 4JD
Tel: 01392 215521, Fax: 01392 215531
info@exeterbackpackers.co.uk www.exeterbackpackers.co.uk

OCEAN
BACKPACKERS

Ocean Backpackers is a homely hostel with a laid back atmosphere and no curfew. Situated in a quaint North Devon town built around an ancient fishing harbour. Central to the harbour itself, the bus station, high street, pubs, restaurants and many beaches including surfers favourites: Croyde, Saunton and Woolacombe. If the surf is down, don't despair, just try the other activities available; quad biking, paint balling, kayaking, adventure swimming, mountain biking, horse riding and microlighting. Adrenalin not your thing? Then take a trip to Lundy Island, spot rare birds, seals, basking sharks and dolphins. Wonderful walking country, the coastal path between Woolacombe and Lynton is breathtaking and Exmoor has an abundance of walks through Britain's most spectacular scenery. The hostel facilities include lounge, free internet access, self-catering kitchen, surf board storage and a car park. Ilfracombe has plenty of summer work so why not come and hang out here for a while?

DETAILS

- **Open** - All year, reception 9am-12 & 4.30-10pm. No curfew.
- **Number of beds** - 44:- 1x8, 5x6, 1 x double, 1 x double & bunk.
- **Booking** - Booking advised but not essential.
- **Price per night** - From £10-14 in dorm. Double/Twin £35 per room.
- **Public Transport** - Direct coaches from London Victoria/Heathrow/Plymouth/Exeter. By train take the Tarka line to Barnstaple then bus to Ilfracombe.
- **Directions** - From M5 take A361. From Cornwall take A39 to Barnstaple then follow the signs to Ilfracombe. Ocean Backpackers is by the harbour opposite the bus station. For more detailed directions go to our website and click on directions.

CONTACT: Chris and Abby
29 St James Place, Ilfracombe, Devon, EX34 9BJ
Tel: 01271 867835
info@oceanbackpackers.co.uk www.oceanbackpackers.co.uk

EXMOOR
BASECAMP

Exmoor Basecamp is a converted barn giving comfortable, high standard bunkhouse accommodation. There are 2 large dormitories each sleeping 8 in bunkbeds and a 2 bedded leaders' room. There are excellent hot showers, drying room, lounge/eating area, fully equipped kitchen and a barbecue. The Basecamp is situated at Countisbury on the North Devon coast. The surrounding countryside includes the dramatic Watersmeet Valleys, moors of Exmoor and coastal paths. Lynton and Lynmouth are the nearest villages and the Atlantic surf beaches are within easy reach.The Basecamp is owned and managed by The National Trust and a free night's accommodation can be earned for each day's conservation work arranged with local wardens. Other local activities are walking, horse riding, boat trips, fishing and cycling. However you spend your time the basecamp is ideal for getting away from it all.

            GROUPS ONLY

DETAILS

- **Open** - All year, 24 hours
- **Number of beds** - 18: 2x8, 1x2
- **Booking** - Booking essential with £50 deposit
- **Price per night** - £120 winter, £160 summer. 10% discount for 4+ nights (except Easter, Christmas & New Year).
- **Public Transport** - The nearest train and coach stations are in Barnstaple (approx. 20 miles), from there take a local bus to Lynton. Buses to Countisbury are very limited and summer only. Taxis from Lynton approx £5.
- **Directions** - From Minehead follow A39 to Countisbury. We are on the left after the Sandpiper Inn. From Lynmouth we are first building on right. Car Park is opposite.

CONTACT: Karen
Countisbury, Lynton, Devon, EX35 6NE
Tel: 01598 741101 / 07974 829171
Karen.elkin@nationaltrust.org.uk www.nationaltrust.org.uk/basecamps

The Campbell Room offers self-catering group accommodation for training courses, youth groups and schools, or groups of walkers, cyclists, families and friends. Sheltered at the mouth of a rural valley on the edge of the Quantock Hills Area of Outstanding Natural Beauty, the building offers a main activity hall which can also sleep 18 on comfortable mattresses, 2 bedrooms each sleeping 3, a fully equipped kitchen, washrooms, showers, drying room, a campfire area and space for 1 or 2 tents.

Many routes for walking, hiking and mountain biking pass close to the centre and a swimming pool is nearby. Groups with transport can access many attractions and activities including beaches with rock pools and fossils, the coastal resort of Minehead, the West Somerset Railway, Wells Cathedral, Glastonbury Tor, Wookey Hole, Cheddar Gorge, Dunster Castle, Cricket St Thomas Wildlife Park, Exmoor, and the county town of Taunton.

DETAILS

- **Open** - All year, by arrangement
- **Number of beds** - 24: 1 x 18 : 2 x 3
- **Booking** - Essential, one month with deposit.
- **Price per night** - £3.95pp (2 leaders free for groups over 12), min £48 per night
- **Public Transport** - Train and bus stations at Bridgwater. Take the bus to Nether Stowey, just over 1 mile from the Campbell Room.
- **Directions** - GR ST 187381. M5 junction 23 or 24 Bridgwater. A39 west to Nether Stowey, follow signs to Over Stowey. From church follow road 300m east, then 400m south (toward Forest Trail Ramscombe). Centre at T junction (W of Aley, TA5 1HB)

CONTACT: Pat Briggs
36 Old Rd, North Petherton, Bridgwater, Somerset, TA6 6TG
Tel: 01278 662537
info@campbellroom.org.uk www.campbellroom.org.uk

GLASTONBURY
BACKPACKERS

Glastonbury Backpackers is the place for budget accommodation in Glastonbury. Shrouded in legend and myth, the burial place of Arthur and Guinevere. Now famous for it's religious, cultural and musical events including the Glastonbury Music Festival.

The hostel is a 16th-century coaching inn which has been renovated to provide a unique and lively place to stay. Accommodation is in backpackers' dorms and twin and double rooms, most with en-suite. There is free bed linen, self-catering kitchen, TV and video lounge, and adjacent parking. There is a café bar and public bar with happy hours and live music on most Friday nights. The town centre boasts many shops and restaurants, all with the unique style and atmosphere that is Glastonbury.

DETAILS

- **Open** - All year, 24 hours
- **Number of beds** - 42
- **Booking** - Phone with credit card
- **Price per night** - From £15 (dorm), £35-£50 (double/ twin/ ensuites
- **Public Transport** - National Express and the cheaper Bakers Dolphin coaches do daily returns to London Victoria, dropping outside the hostel. Nearest train stations are Castle Cary and Bristol. From Bristol catch 376 bus from end of Station Drive to outside of hostel.
- **Directions** - At the bottom of Glastonbury High Street, adjacent to the market cross. The hostel is painted bright blue.

CONTACT: Reception
4 Market Place, Glastonbury, Somerset, BA6 9HD
Tel: 01458 833353, Fax: 01458 835988
info@GlastonburyBackpackers.co.uk www.GlastonburyBackpackers.co.uk

Larkshall is the Cerberus Spelaeological Society's headquarters and offers excellent modern facilities. It is available for use not only by members, but also guest individuals or groups wanting accommodation on Mendip. It makes an ideal base for caving, as well as many other outdoor activities including walking, cycling, climbing etc. It is also a good base for anyone wanting to explore the Somerset countryside and within very easy reach are the famous tourist attractions of Wells, Wookey Hole, Cheddar Gorge and Caves, and the city of Bath. The accommodation provides all the home comforts with a kitchen/dining room, large lounge, and showers and changing facilities. For anyone so inclined the central corridor can be traversed using the climbing holds fitted along the wall. The guests communal bunkroom has ample space and can sleep large groups in comfort. For those that prefer, it is possible to camp, and there is a large car park.

DETAILS

- **Open** - All year, 24 hours. Key available by prior arrangement.
- **Number of beds** - 1 x 28. Unlimited camping available.
- **Booking** - Advisable. Email preferred via website, or phone or write. Non refundable deposit of £20 a night required.
- **Price per night** - £5. Sole use of bunkroom £140. Min 2 nights at wknds.
- **Public Transport** - There is a bus stop near the crossroads in Oakhill on the A367. Taxis are available in Shepton Mallet, Wells and Frome
- **Directions** - Larkshall is 4 miles north of Shepton Mallet and 15 miles south of Bath off the A367. At crossroads in Oakhill take road to Stoke St Michael. Larkshall is about one mile from Oakhill on the right (ST 6505 4720).

CONTACT:
Larkshall, Midway, Stoke St Michael, Somerset, BA3 5JE
Tel: 0845 475 0954
hostelbookings@cerberusspeleo.org.uk www.cerberusspeleo.org.uk

BATH
YMCA

Bath YMCA offers a warm welcome and the best value accommodation. From its central location all the sights of this World Heritage City are easily reached on foot. Bath is also an ideal base for the explorer. Staying longer brings Stonehenge, Wookey Hole Caves, Cheddar Gorge, the southern reaches of the Cotswolds, and more exciting destinations all within reach. With a total of 202 beds, we have a great deal of experience in making all our guests feel comfortable. We have a fully air conditioned lounge area, colour TV and restaurant which offers a varied lunch menu at special YMCA subsidised prices. Laundry, lockers, pool and football table, telephone fax and internet facilities are available. The Health and Fitness suite provides a steam and sauna room and new equipment with a qualified staff team who have worked hard to create a club atmosphere. 'Fitness with Fun' is our motto. Couples, families, groups and backpackers' are all welcome, you don't have to be young or male. All these facilities and the YMCA's traditional sense of community will make your stay a truly memorable one.

DETAILS

- **Open** - All year, 24-hour reception
- **Number of beds** - 202: 1x20, 1x14, 1x12, 2x10, 7x3, 38x2, 26x1
- **Booking** - Credit card guarantees.
- **Price per night** - From £15pp dorm bed, inc. light breakfast.
- **Public Transport** - Bath has a train station and is served by National Express.
- **Directions** - Located approximately ½ mile from rail and bus station. Broad Street is located near the Podium Shopping Centre off Walcott Street.

CONTACT: Reception
International House, Broad Street Place, Bath, BA1 5LH
Tel: 01225 325900, Fax: 01225 462065
stay@bathymca.co.uk www.bathymca.co.uk

BRISTOL
ENGLAND BACKPACKERS HOSTEL

  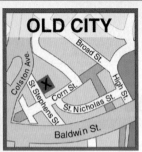

City Centre hostel

Clean & comfy beds - free linen & hot showers - big kitchen - free tea, coffee & hot choc - indoor bicycle storage.

Late night basement bar - piano & guitar room - dvd lounge - cheap internet machines - free laptop wireless access - luggage storage room - laundrette.

Run by backpackers for backpackers - mixed/single sex dorms - private rooms - no curfew after check in

DETAILS

■ **Open** - All year, reception hours 0900 - 2330 (No curfew)
■ **Number of beds** - 90: Bunk bed accommodation in private twin, private triple or 6, 8 and 10 bed dorms.
■ **Booking** - Most cards, phone or walk in.
■ **Price per night** - £16pp. Private rooms from £36. See website for discounts.
■ **Public Transport** - See below.
■ **Directions** - Located in 'Old City', the historic centre of Bristol. From 'Bristol Central Bus Station (Marlborough St) 7 mins walk. Follow pedestrian signs to 'Old City' then see map above. From 'Bristol Temple Meads Train Station' 12 mins walk. Follow pedestrian signs to 'Old City' then see map above. Or take bus number 8 or 9 (£1.30) to the 'Centre Promenade'. Disembark at The Bristol Hippodrome. From Airport take the 'Shuttle' to the Central Bus Station. By road follow signs for Baldwin Street in the city centre.

CONTACT:
17 St Stephen's Street, Bristol, BS1 1EQ
Tel: 0117 9257900
info@bristolbackpackers.co.uk www.bristolbackpackers.co.uk

The David Donald Field Studies Base offers accommodation for educational, family and other groups in a converted 1940 RAF radar station, renovated with central heating and double glazing. It sleeps 24 but up to 30 if some wish to camp and share the indoor facilities. There is a well equipped kitchen, a spacious community room, a drying room, picnic area, BBQ / campsite area, a games area and lots of parking. There are ramps to the main building and adapted toilets for wheelchair users, but for these the lane to the centre is very difficult without a car. This is an outstanding area for environmental studies and is also popular with groups or families enjoying a relaxing break, reunions, walking, outdoor actvities and other social events. It is within an SSSI, and has Lulworth Cove, Durdle Door, The Arne Nature Reserve, Purbeck Marine Reserve, Corfe Castle, Poole Harbour and lots of other interesting sites nearby.

DETAILS

■ **Open** - All year
■ **Number of beds** - 24: 1x2, 1x2 ensuite, 1x9, 1x11 plus limited camping.
■ **Booking** - Booking required with £200 deposit. Phone for availability. Forms can be downloaded from website and returned to P&D Adv Centre, Recreation Road, Parkstone, Poole, BH12 2EA,
■ **Price per night** - Prices for 2009: Whole centre from £300 per night. £5 per person for numbers exceeding 24, up to a maximum of 30. Bed linen £5 per person.
■ **Public Transport** - Train to Wareham. Wilts & Dorset Buses to Worth Matravers.
■ **Directions** - Arriving in Worth Matravers from Kingston bear right by duck pond into Pikes Lane. After Renscombe Farm road turns sharp right then left onto Renscombe Rd. 200m further the driveway to the base is on the right. OS SY967777

CONTACT: David Donald Field Studies Base
Off Renscombe Rd, Worth Matravers, Isle of Purbeck, Dorset BH19 3LL
Tel: 01202 710701
enquiries@dorsetadventure.co.uk www.dorsetadventure.co.uk

SWANAGE AUBERGE
BUNKHOUSE

ENGLAND

Swanage Auberge, the bunkhouse that cares, is a refuge for climbers, walkers and divers. Situated at the eastern end of the Jurassic Coast with excellent walking, diving and rock climbing on the doorstep. The bunkhouse is in the centre of Swanage town, a stones throw from the South West Coast Path and all local amenities - pubs, shops, restaurants etc. Swanage Auberge is totally self contained with central heating, fully equipped self catering kitchen, drying and laundry facilities and a meals service if required. There are two bunk rooms, one with 4 standard bunks and the other with 6 alpine style places (3 and 3). There is also accommodation for 4 and a family room in the adjoining house. Pillow and towel provided and bedding is available for hire. There are two showers, loos and washrooms and an area to hang and wash wetsuits. There is a rucksack and boot rack in the entrance corridor. Sandals are provided. Parking for 2 vehicles is usually available when booking (first come first served basis). Price includes cereal breakfast and beverages. Packed lunches available (see website for further details).

DETAILS
- **Open** - All year, opens 5.30pm (all day once booked in)
- **Number of beds** - 17: 1x6, 2x4, Family room (dbl + single)
- **Booking** - Book by phone or email. Booking form online. 20% deposit required.
- **Price per night** - £16 pp including cereal breakfast and free tea or coffee. Group rates available. Hire of duvet with sheets £2.50 per week. Credit cards not accepted.
- **Public Transport** - Bus from Poole or Wareham. Train service to Wareham.
- **Directions** - At the end of the first left hand alley off Mount Pleasant Lane.

CONTACT: Pete or Pam
45 High Street, Swanage, Dorset, BH19 2LX
Tel: 01929 424368, mobile 07711117668 , Fax: 01929 424368
bookings@swanageauberge.co.uk www.swanageauberge.co.uk

The Townsend Centre is located on Dorset's World Heritage coastline overlooking Swanage Bay. The beach and surrounding coastal paths are within 10 mins walk. Swanage is a thriving seaside town with a safe sandy beach and activities for all ages. Open countryside and the steam railway are within easy walking access. Accommodation is in 3 sections, with each section containing a number of bunk bed rooms and some ensuite private bedrooms. Facilities include football pitch, volleyball, table tennis, pool table, TV and internet access. There's a small sitting room with microwave, fridge and tea making facilities and a dining room with a fridge. Large groups have access to self-catering facilities.

DETAILS

- **Open** - July 24th–Aug 30th 2009 (not all weeks), Office: 9am – 4pm Mon to Fri
- **Number of beds** - 89: Section 1 = 27: 2x12,3x1   Section 2 = 31: 2x14,3x1
Section 3 = 30: 6x4,2x2,1x2,2x1 and 2 room flat.
- **Booking** - Book with a deposit of 20% or the cost of first night if this is greater.
- **Price per night** - Individuals: £20pp (U16 £15pp). Bed and Breakfast £24.00pp (U16 £19pp). Groups of 60 plus get sole use with Self catering at £19pp (U16 £14pp), Bed and Breakfast £23.00pp, (U16 £18pp).
- **Public Transport** - Mainline trains at Wareham (10m). Buses to Swanage from Wareham, Poole (no.40) and Bournemouth (no.50). Get off at Swanage Steam Railway Stn. Walk to the R past Co-op, cross the road, turn L. After 50 yds turn right up a path. Turn R at top of path. After shop turn L, go uphill 100m and Centre's on R.
- **Directions** - A351 head to town centre. At traffic lights, turn R then L at roundabout. Follow road to R then fork L just before zebra crossing. Go up hill and turn L just before the Black Swan. Go uphill 100m. As it turns left carry on up road.

CONTACT: Katy, administrator
Cobblers Lane, Swanage, Dorset, BH19 2PX
Tel: 01929 422448
townsend@widehorizons.org.uk www.widehorizons.org.uk/t_home.aspx

Base Lodge is ideally situated for exploring Exmoor, The Quantocks and The North Devon Coast by mountain bike or foot. Excellent off and on road mountain biking for all levels. Guided mountain biking and secure lock up facilities.

Exmoor affords excellent scenic moor and coastal views and the 600+ mile-long South West Coastal Path starts here in Minehead. Other activities can be arranged including mountain biking, navigational training, climbing, surfing, pony-trekking and natural history walks and talks. Base Lodge is clean, comfortable and friendly, providing a shared fully equipped kitchen and dining room. Local pubs and restaurants are all within walking distance.

DETAILS

■ **Open** - All day access once booked, bookings taken by e-mail or phone or take a chance and call in, all day access, reception open from 3pm
■ **Number of beds** - 25: 2x7: 1x5: 1x3: 1x2 :1x1
■ **Booking** - Advisable. Deposit required for groups or exclusive use.
■ **Price per night** - Dorms £12.50, private twin or single £15pp, private double £16pp. Exclusive use of Base Lodge from £250.
■ **Public Transport** - Coach station 5 min walk. Buses from Taunton, Exeter and Tiverton. Train station: Taunton (26 miles). Steam railway from Taunton to Minehead.
■ **Directions** - With the sea behind you, drive/walk up The Parade until you reach Park Street, continue straight on until you reach a fork. Take the right hand into The Parks (Baptist Church on your right). Only limited parking is available.

CONTACT: Wendy or Graham
16 The Parks, Minehead, Somerset, TA24 8BS
Tel: 01643 703520 or 0773 1651536
togooutdoors@hotmail.com www.togooutdoors.com

AVON TYRRELL
ACTIVITY CENTRE

Avon Tyrrell Activity Centre is set in 65 acres of private grounds in the heart of the New Forest National Park. The centre is committed to providing fun, educational and activity holidays and breaks to all groups of people regardless of age and ability in a secure and safe environment.

Our Grade 1 listed house can provide full board for groups of between 15 and 110, mostly in dormitory style bedrooms. There are also twin rooms, some with ensuite facilities. Our self catering wooden lodges range from 6, to 12, to the largest 14 berth lodge. Groups can also stay on our camp site nestled amongst the pine trees. The campsite is open between April and October. Families and day visit groups are also welcomed. All our accommodation has disabled access and disabled equipment is available to guests in both the House and lodges at no extra cost.

DETAILS

- **Open** - All year, All day
- **Number of beds** - 110 in Main House 6,12 and 14 berth lodges, large campsite
- **Booking** - Booking essential.
- **Price per night** - Please visit our website for 2009 prices, special offers and late deals.
- **Public Transport** - Trains at Christchurch, New Milton and Brockenhurst (6,7 & 10 miles).
- **Directions** - GR SU 185 003. The Centre is half way between the villages of Burley and Bransgore.

CONTACT:
Bransgore, Hampshire, BH23 8EE
Tel: 01425 672347, Fax: 01425 675108
info@ukyouth.org   www.avontyrrell.org.uk

Britain's only island city, Portsmouth is a unique blend of seaside resort and naval heritage. Portsmouth and Southsea Backpackers is the city's only independent hostel for travellers. It offers a friendly cosmopolitan atmosphere within easy reach of the major tourist attractions including the ships (Victory, Mary Rose and Warrior), the D Day museum, and the new Gunwharf Quays. It is only 150m from the beach and in an area containing an excellent variety of pubs, restaurants and clubs. The accommodation is mostly in small dorms for 4 people, but there are also twins, doubles and family rooms, some with en-suite facilities. All hot showers are free. We have a large social area which has Freeview TV, an internet facility, pool, darts and a dining area. There is a fully equipped kitchen, BBQ, seating in the garden area and secure cycle storage.

DETAILS

- **Open** - All year, service: 8am to 11pm
- **Number of beds** - 68: 1x8, 1x6, 10x4, 7x2
- **Booking** - Advisable, groups require deposit
- **Price per night** - From £15pp, £34 per room (double/twin), £38 (double ensuite)
- **Public Transport** - From any bus or train station catch a bus to Southsea and get off at the Strand. Walk back the way the bus has come and Florence Road is 2nd left. If there are 2+ people get a taxi. Ferries from Portsmouth go to France, Spain, the Channel Islands, and the Isle of Wight.
- **Directions** - From the M27 take the M275 to Portsmouth and follow signs to the seafront. Drive along the seafront until blue glass building (The Pyramids) and turn left. Turn right at mini roundabout and Florence Road is then 1st on the left.

CONTACT: Sammi
4 Florence Road, Southsea, Portsmouth, Hants, P05 2NE
Tel: 023 92832495, Fax: 023 92832495
info@portsmouthbackpackers.co.uk www.portsmouthbackpackers.co.uk

WETHERDOWN
HOSTEL

The Weatherdown Hostel is part of Sustainability Centre, which promotes environmental awareness and low impact living. On top of the South Downs, it is an award-winning example of an eco-renovation and a comfortable place to stay, just a few steps from the South Downs National Trail. A clean, bright, friendly hostel, open to all. Ideal for family get-togethers, walkers, cyclists, business away-days and wedding parties.

The hostel has spacious communal areas, comfortable bedrooms with hand basins & all linen provided & separate bathrooms / toilets throughout. A 'help yourself' breakfast is included in the price, available from 8am. There is a small fully equipped self-catering kitchen. Packed lunches available by order. Within 2 miles of the hostel are 4 country pubs, local shops, Chinese, Indian & Pizza takeaways.

DETAILS

- **Open** - All year, all day
- **Number of beds** - 34: 10 x 3, 2 x 2
- **Booking** - Book by telephone or online.
- **Price per night** - Shared rooms (twin/triple) £22pp Group booking (8+) £19.50pp. All prices include linen & breakfast.
- **Public Transport** - Trains at Petersfield, 6 miles (£10 by taxi). From station 38 bus to Clanfield or the 52 or 67 to East Meon.
- **Directions** - GR 676 189. From A3 take Clanfield turn (brown sign). Turn right after Rising Sun in Clanfield. At top of hill, turn left signed Droxford.

CONTACT: Tori
The Sustainability Centre, Droxford Road, East Meon, Hampshire, GU32 1HR
Tel: 01730 823 549, Mob: 07884 258713, Fax: 01730 823 168
hostel@sustainability-centre.org www.sustainability-centre.org

The Camping Barn is a traditional Surrey timber barn in Puttenham village on the North Downs Way and Sustrans NCN22 cycle route. It is located in the Surrey Hills Area of Outstanding Natural Beauty with delightful cycling and walking routes all around. There is a fully equipped self-catering kitchen, a shower, toilets and foam covered sleeping platforms, all to a high standard. Electricity and hot water included but bring your own towel and sleeping bag (or hire one - £2.50 a stay). Evening meals are available in the village. The Barn has many sustainable features including solar panels and rainwater collection for flushing toilets. The Barn is wardened. NO CARS ON SITE. Excellent cycle shed. Young people under 18 are welcome but must be accompanied by a responsible adult.

DETAILS

- **Open** - Easter to October, 1700 to 1000
- **Number of beds** - sleeping platforms for 11
- **Booking** - booking is essential
- **Price per night** - £12 adults, £10 under 18. Sole use negotiable. £2 'green' discount if arriving by foot, bicycle or public transport.
- **Public Transport** - Trains (08457 484950) at Wanborough (3.5 km), Guildford (7 km) and Farnham (9 km). The X65 Stagecoach bus (0845 1210180) from Guildford and Farnham drops you within 1 km of the barn. Alight at Puttenham turn (Hogs Back) and walk south to village.
- **Directions** - GR SU 933 479. Turn off A31 south onto B3000 then take first right into village. The Camping Barn is signposted immediately opposite the church.

CONTACT: Sarah Hart
The Street, Puttenham, Nr Guildford, Surrey, GU3 1AR
Tel: 01306 877 964, Fax: 01306 877964
tanners@yha.org.uk   www.puttenhamcampingbarn.co.uk

GUMBER
BOTHY

Gumber Bothy is a converted traditional Sussex barn on the National Trust's Slindon Estate in the heart of the South Downs. It provides simple overnight accommodation or camping for walkers, riders and cyclists, just off the South Downs Way.

The bothy forms part of Gumber Farm and is 5 minutes walk from Stane Street, the Roman Road that crosses the South Downs Way at Bignor Hill.

Facilities include platforms in 3 dorms sleeping up to 30, good hot showers and basins, kitchen/diner with gas hob and washing up facilities, a few pots and pans provided. Paddock for friendly horses and racks for bikes. Wheelchair accessible (please phone for details).

Sorry, but as we're a sheep farm, no dogs and most definitely NO CARS. Not suitable for under fives.

DETAILS

- **Open** - March to October (inclusive), flexible
- **Number of beds** - 30: 1 x 16 : 1 x 6 : 1 x 4 plus overflow area
- **Booking** - Booking by telephone. Booking required for groups with 50% deposit.
- **Price per night** - £10.00 (adult), £5.00 (under 16s).
- **Public Transport** - Train stations, Arundel (urban) 5 miles, Amberley (rural) 4 miles, Chichester (8 miles). National Express stop at Chichester. Buses 84 and 85 from Chichester, stop at Fontwell and then it is a 3 mile walk to the Bothy. Taxi fare from Arundel to Northwood Farm is approx £10, followed by a 2 mile country walk.
- **Directions** - OS Map LR197 or E121 GR 961 119, Nearest car park GR 973 129. No vehicular access. One mile off South Downs Way on Stane Street bridleway

CONTACT: Basecamp Warden
Slindon Estate Yard, Slindon, Arundel, West Sussex, BN18 0RG
Tel: 01243 814730
katie.archer@nationaltrust.org.uk

BRIGHTON ROYAL
HOTEL
ENGLAND

Kipps Hostel - Canterbury, one of the highest rated hostels in Britain, now has a hotel in Brighton.

There are 10 quality, well equipped bedrooms all featuring TV, clock radio, CD player and wash basin with free Wi-Fi Internet access throughout.

Guests can relax on the roof terrace or in the lounge area and enjoy a continental breakfast in the dining area or a drink at the bar.

Friendly Staff.

Close to all attractions and shopping.

DETAILS

- **Open** - All year, reception 8am-11pm – No Curfew
- **Number of beds** - 28: 1x1, 7xDouble, 1xTwin, 1x3 Bedded, 1x8 Bedded
- **Booking** - Please book by phone or email
- **Price per night** - From £17.50 per person per night
- **Public Transport** - We are close to Brighton Train Station and Bus Station, From Train Station: exit and walk ahead down the main street for a few minutes, Turn into Church Street (on your left) and walk along Church Street until the end, The Hotel is opposite. From Bus Station: Exit onto Old Steine Road and turn left towards the Grand Pavillion. At the far end of the Pavillion and opposite is the hotel.
- **Directions** - Take the M23, then A23 towards Brighton Town Centre. The Hotel is opposite the Royal Pavillion on Grand Parade.

CONTACT: Reception
76 Grand Parade, Brighton, BN2 9JA
Tel: 01273 604182
brightonroyalhotel@gmail.com

COLDBLOW FARM
BUNKBARNS

Coldblow Farm is situated on the Kent Downs just north east of Maidstone. The farm today provides a range of self-catering accommodation for both people and horses! The long distance trail, the North Downs Way, runs along the southern boundary of the farm and the Pilgrims Way is just a short distance away. The farm is surrounded by a network of public footpaths, bridleways and byways. The accommodation comprises: two Bunkhouse Barns, sleeping 10 (3 rooms, 2, 4 & 4) or 41 (7 rooms, 4 x 8 bunks, 3, 2 & 4 beds); Camping Barn sleeping 15 on sleeping platforms; Flint Cottage (studio style, sleeping two); a Camping Paddock and 18 Stables for horses and ponies. All barns have fully equipped kitchen/dining rooms and central heating. Log burners in the Camping Barn and Flint Cottage. Toilets and showers (on meters) in all barns and for Camping Paddock, but the Camping Barn shares washing facilities of small bunk barn. New for summer 2009 - Eco and Disabled Friendly Lodge.

DETAILS

- **Open** - All year, reception 9am till 6pm
- **Number of beds** - New Barn 41: 4x8, 1x4, 1x3, 1x2; Old Barn 10: 2x4, 1x2 ; Camping Barn 15: 1x15; Cottage 2; Eco Lodge 8: (available from summer 2009)
- **Booking** - Advanced booking essential, with full payment.
- **Price per night** - Camping Barn £8, Bunkhouses £12.50, Cottage £60 (for 2).
- **Public Transport** - Bearsted is the nearest train station (2 miles by road or path).
- **Directions** - From Thurnham at the Black Horse Pub crossroads take the Pilgrims Way signposted to Hucking. Turn next left at staggered crossroads into Coldblow Lane, Coldblow Farm is half a mile up hill on right. If towing or in large vehicle ring us

CONTACT: Booking Office,
Coldblow Lane,Thurnham, Maidstone, Kent, ME14 3LR
Tel: 01622 730439
coldblowfarm@homecall.co.uk www.coldblow-camping.co.uk

PALACE FARM
HOSTEL

Palace Farm Hostel is a relaxing and flexible hostel on a family run arable and fruit farm. It is situated in the village of Doddington, which has a pub, in the North Kent Downs Area of Outstanding Natural Beauty. The area is great for walking, cycling (cycle hire available £5 a day) and wildlife. The location is central for exploring Canterbury, Rochester, Chatham, Leeds Castle and the many other historic towns, villages and castles in Kent. The accommodation in converted farm buildings, consists of six fully heated en-suite rooms sleeping up to 30 guests. The rooms surround an attractive courtyard garden with lawns, patio and barbecue area, ideal for families and groups. The en-suite rooms cater for all age groups and those with disabilities. There are quality double beds & 3ft bunk beds. Duvets, linen and continental breakfast included. Small tent only campsite. Green Tourism Business Scheme GOLD Award winner.

DETAILS

- **Open** - All year, 8am to 10pm flexible, please ask
- **Number of beds** - 30: 1x8, 1x6, 2x5, 1x4, and 1x2
- **Booking** - Advised, not essential mid week.
- **Price per night** - From £14 child, £18 adult (private rooms). Reduction for groups staying for 3 or more nights, please ask.
- **Public Transport** - Trains at Sittingbourne (London Victoria to Dover). Buses from Sittingbourne station to Doddington two hourly (Mon-Sat), last buses 16.30 & 17.30.
- **Directions** - From A2 between Sittingbourne and Faversham turn south at Teynham, signed to Lynsted. Go through Lynsted and over M2 bridge, take 2nd turning right into Down Court Rd. Farm is 90 metres on left.

CONTACT: Graham and Liz Cuthbert
Down Court Road, Doddington, Sittingbourne / Faversham, Kent, ME9 0AU
Tel: 01795 886200
info@palacefarm.com   www.palacefarm.com

KIPPS
INDEPENDENT HOSTEL

Kipps is an ideal home from home for backpackers, visitors or small groups looking for self-catering budget accommodation in Canterbury. It is a short walk to the town centre and the historic attractions including the renowned Canterbury Cathedral. Canterbury also makes an ideal base for day trips to Dover, Leeds Castle and the many local beaches. Facilities include dining room, TV lounge with digital TV, a garden, a fully equipped kitchen, a small shop offering breakfast and other food items, bicycle hire. Free WIFI & broadband access. Rooms include single/double/twin/family & dorms of up to 8 beds (most en-suite). Camping available in summer. Free on-street parking.

Kipps have now opened a hostel/hotel in Brighton, opposite the Royal Pavilion and close to town. For further information visit www.brightonroyalhotel.com.

DETAILS

- **Open** - All year, no curfew, reception 7.30am to 11pm
- **Number of beds** - 50:- 2 x 1, 2 x 2, 1 x 3,1 x 5, 1 x 7, 3 x 8, 1 x 10
- **Booking** - Advance booking recommended.
- **Price per night** - Dorms £15pp, Singles £20pp, Doubles £35, Quads £45. Weekly and winter rates available. Credit cards accepted.
- **Public Transport** - Canterbury East train station on London Victoria to Dover line, is ½ mile by footpath (phone hostel for directions). The local C4 bus stops by the door of the hostel. Taxi from coach/rail stations is £3.
- **Directions** - By car :- Take B2068 to Hythe from City Ring Road (A28). Turn right at first traffic lights by church. KiPPS is 300 yds on left.

CONTACT: Lee Parsons
40 Nunnery Fields, Canterbury, Kent, CT1 3JT
Tel: 01227 786121
info@kipps-hostel.com www.kipps-hostel.com

THE GLADE
AT BLACKBOYS

The Glade is a quiet retreat in the heart of rural East Sussex, only an hour's drive from central London and 25 mins from the south coast. This former YHA hostel is set in an acre of its own grounds close to the intersection of the Weald and Vanguard Ways and 20 mins drive from the climbing crags at Harrisons Rocks and Bowles outdoor centre. The small dorms and private location make it ideal for sole-use, for family re-unions, parties or corporate team-building groups. When the hostel is open to all, the pleasant lounge/dining room makes a great place to socialise. The Glade has recently been refurbished with new showers and wet-rooms (one of which is disabled-friendly), and a make-over on the lounge/dining room including a new wood burning stove. Kitchen facilities include cooker with oven and additional hob and grill, fridges, freezer, toasters and microwaves. All bedding is provided. Outside there is a spacious secure bike shed and picnic benches which are great for al-fresco eating. There is also woodland parking space for several cars.

DETAILS

- **Open** - All year, closed between 10am and 5pm (when not in sole use)
- **Number of beds** - 30:1x6,1x5, 2x4,3x3, 2x1
- **Booking** - Please enquire by phone or email.
- **Price per night** - Sole use £390 per night. At all other times, £15 per adult and £10 for under 16s. Family room discounts available.
- **Public Transport** - Stagecoach Bus 318 stops at Blackboys Village 0.5 miles from hostel. Trains at Buxted 2.5 miles away. National Express at Uckfield 4 miles away.
- **Directions** - From Blackboys village take Gun Road and look for signs.

CONTACT: Alan
The Glade, YHABlackboys, Gun Road, Blackboys, Uckfield, Sussex, TN22 5HU
Tel: 01825 890607
blackboys@yha.org.uk www.the-glade.co.uk

ALL STAR HOSTEL is a new hostel very close to Kilburn Tube Station (only 15 mins from Central London) and the 24 hour bus routes. Completely refurbished for 2008 with brand new facilities including pressure showers, fully fitted kitchens, wooden floors, lounge room with Sky TV, free internet, laundry facilities (free soap powder), and security lockers in all the rooms. Choose from 6 bed dorms and 4 bed dorms, female only rooms, mixed rooms and double rooms with TV/DVD. Free tea and coffee all day and free toast and jam breakfast. The All Star Hostel will offer you a comfortable homely stay with a friendly atmosphere at great prices for your trip to London. AccommodationLondon also operates over 300 apartments and shared antipodean houses in North West London, with secure private rooms. They provide a great atmosphere with other working holidaymakers to give you that feel for London living.

DETAILS

■ **Open** - All year, office hours 8am 6pm Mon-Sat. Sundays 9am-5pm .
■ **Number of beds** - 100+ beds plus apartments and houses.
■ **Booking** - Book online.
■ **Price per night** - Minimum of 4 nights stay. Dorms from £15, private rooms from £20pp. Long term from £10 a night. £15 check-in fee on Sundays.
■ **Public Transport** - Close to Kilburn Tube Station on the Jubliee Line (zone 2). Free pick up from tube station (office hours only). Frequent bus services including a night bus from the city .
■ **Directions** - Located a short distance from the main arterial roads through the city.

CONTACT: Reception
39 Chatsworth Road, London, NW2 4BL
Tel: 0208 459 6203 , Fax: 0208 451 3258
info@accommodationlondon.net www.accommodationlondon.net

PALMERS
LODGE

Palmers Lodge is a unique Grade II listed building. A three million pound refurbishment has turned this house, the former home of Samuel Palmer (Huntley & Palmers) into a stunning hostel. Guests can enjoy modern facilities, such as FREE internet, whilst admiring the beautiful oak flooring, fireplaces and ceilings! The Lodge has a 24hr reception, bar, restaurant, large lounge, full security card access, generous car park and plenty of showers! With Swiss Cottage tube just across the road the heart of the city is just minutes away whilst, if you fancy a really late night, we are also on the Night Bus route from Trafalgar Square. Winner Silver Award, Visit London best hostel 2006. Nominated for Visit London best hostel 2007. Constantly in Hostels.com top 10 hostels worldwide since July 2006.

DETAILS

- **Open** - All year, 365 days, 24 hours
- **Number of beds** - 273 : 3x2 6x4,4x6,4x8,2x10,3x12,3x14,1x19,1x18,1x24,1x28
- **Booking** - Booking is advised but not essential. Deposit for first night is preferred. Photo ID is required at check in.
- **Price per night** - £14.00 to £24.00 per person, including breakfast.
- **Public Transport** - Next to Swiss Cottage and Finchley Road stations. Leave Swiss Cottage tube exit 2, At the top of the stairs turn to face the main road. College Crescent goes up on your right. Also on bus routes for Stansted and Luton airports.
- **Directions** - Palmers Lodge is located just off the A41 which can be accessed from the M1, M25 or A1. Simply stay on the A41 towards central London and turn left just before Swiss Cottage tube; drive round to the left along College Crescent.

CONTACT: Reception
40 College Crescent, Swiss Cottage, London, NW3 5LB
Tel: 0207 483 8470, Fax: 0207 483 8471
reception@palmerslodge.co.uk www.palmerslodge.co.uk

DOVER CASTLE
HOSTEL AND FLATSHARES

The Dover Castle Hostel is a friendly, privately run hostel offering the best value accommodation for backpackers in central London. We have 65 beds in bright dormitory style rooms which range in size from 4 to 12 persons. We offer daily and weekly rates and prices include breakfast, taxes and free luggage lock-up. The hostel has great facilities, including it's own late licensed bar, free WiFi internet, kitchen, lockers and a laundry service. There is no curfew - you may party all night, sleep all day! Hostel guests get a discount card for cheap food and drink. For longer term guests, we offer house/flatshares in central London, zones 1 & 2. Single rooms are from £95 a week and twin rooms from £75 per person per week. The apartments are clean, furnished and with free WiFi internet. More information and booking online at www.london99.com. Hope to meet you soon !

DETAILS

- **Open** - All year, 24 hours
- **Number of beds** - 65: 1x3 : 1x4 : 2x6 : 3x8 : 1x10 : 1x12
- **Booking** - Booking advisable in summer. Credit card secures bed.
- **Price per night** - £10-£15 per person including breakfast
- **Public Transport** - Nearest main line station is London Bridge. Take underground Northern (black) Line to Borough. The hostel is opposite Borough underground station between London Bridge and Elephant and Castle. We are located 10 mins from Waterloo International Station.
- **Directions** - From Borough Underground Station cross the road to Great Dover Street, we are 1 minute walk and located on the right hand side.

CONTACT: Martin
6 Great Dover Street, Borough, London, SE1 4XW
Tel: 020 74037773, Fax: 020 77878654
dovercastle@hotmail.com www.dovercastlehostel.co.uk

GENERATOR
LONDON

The Generator is London's largest, liveliest and funkiest hostel with over 800 beds and is famous for its party atmosphere. We are open 24 hours a day, 365 days a year with friendly staff who are always on hand to help. Just minutes from Covent Garden and Leicester Square The Generator is located in the heart of Bloomsbury. There is a late bar (open 6.00 pm to 2.00 am) which provides the perfect environment to meet young travellers from all over the world. Other facilities include a laundry, chill out room, games room with pool tables and satellite TV, internet café, safety deposit boxes and free luggage storage on departure. Continental Breakfast is free for everyone, as are bed sheets & 24hour hot showers and a walking tour of London. Accommodation is available in singles, twins, triples, quads plus both small and large dorms.The hostel is generally suitable for 18-35s. It is a must-stay hostel for all backpackers if you want to meet loads of people from all over the world and party the night away.

DETAILS

- **Open** - All year, 24 hours
- **Number of beds** - 840
- **Booking** - With credit card- 48 hr cancellation.
- **Price per night** - From £15 per person in a dorm room.
- **Public Transport** - Kings Cross/Euston Station are both approx 5 minutes walk from the hostel. The nearest National Express station is Victoria and the closest tube station is Russell Square.
- **Directions** - From Russell Square Tube cross onto Marchmont Street, walk to traffic lights and turn right onto Tavistock Place - the hostel is at number 37.

CONTACT:
Compton Place, (off 37 Tavistock Place), Russell Square London, WC1H 9SE
Tel: 0207 388 7666
res@generatorhostels.com www.generatorhostels.com

CLINK
HOSTEL

Clink is all about reinvention. Not only have we restored a 200 year old courthouse to create a stylish backpackers, we have also changed the traditional perception of youth hostels. With its utterly cool interior, modern facilities and high-tech pod beds, Clink is a far cry from the generic hostel. What makes us exceptional:

The Courtroom Lounge… chill out where The Clash were on trial.

The Prison Cells…sleep it all off in an authentic prison cell; whether in solitary confinement or with your partner in crime.

The Internet Lounge/TV Lounge… write your own story from the place that inspired Charles Dickens to create Oliver Twist.

Each pod bed has a personal light, a safety locker and a storage box combining comfort, security and privacy.

Stylish in-house Bar: happy hours and entertainment every night!

Stay and judge for yourself…

DETAILS

- **Open** - All year, 24 hours - no curfew or lockouts
- **Number of beds** - 600: 4-16 bedded, triple, twin, single, ensuite, cell rooms(for 2).
- **Booking** - Book online, by email or by phone.
- **Price per night** - From £10pp including FREE breakfast. Group discounts.
- **Public Transport** - Just around the corner from King's Cross Station with direct links to Heathrow, Luton, Gatwick, Victoria, the Eurostar and one change to Stansted.
- **Directions** - King's Cross station is 5 mins away by foot. Exit the station, walk down King's Cross Road for 500m and you'll find us on your left.

CONTACT: Reception
78 Kings Cross Road, King's Cross, London, WC1X 9QG
Tel: 020 7183 9400, Fax: 020 7713 0735
info@clinkhostel.com   www.clinkhostel.com

PICCADILLY
BACKPACKERS HOSTEL

Piccadilly Backpackers Hostel is literally a hop, skip and a jump from Piccadilly Circus. London's most central hostel for travellers on a budget! Soak up the atmosphere from this vibrant area, as famous as the capital itself. Our award winning hostel, spread over 5 colourful floors, is surrounded with London's attractions, including the famous nightspot Leicester Square, the trendy area of Soho, shops of Oxford Street, and London's renowned Theatre Land.

Heaps of free facilities include wide screen TV, lockers, luggage storage and the all important breakfast, with access to high speed internet and a dedicated Travel shop and more! Come join us for a cheap drink in our funky bar - and nightly party events are organised daily. You're sure to have an awesome time! Overall, Piccadilly Backpackers offers an unbeatable blend of value, comfort and security, and is undeniably the greatest portal for visitors to London!

DETAILS

- **Open** - All year, 24 hours
- **Number of beds** - 700
- **Booking** - Advisable, groups require deposit
- **Price per night** - From £12
- **Public Transport** - One minutes walk from Piccadilly Circus Tube station.
- **Directions** - Take exit 1 from Piccadilly Circus tube station, head down Sherwood Street, Piccadilly Backpackers is on your right just after Piccadilly Theatre. By car follow signs for central London, then to Piccadilly Circus, then follow signs to nearby NCP car park.

CONTACT: Reception
12 Sherwood Street, Piccadilly, London, W1F 7BR
Tel: 0207 434 9009, Fax: 0207 434 9010
bookings@piccadillybackpackers.com www.piccadillybackpackers.com

SMART
HYDE PARK INN
ENGLAND

Smart Hyde Park Inn is London's award winning Hostel which consistently is voted in the top ten hostels in the WORLD! It has also been voted best located hostel in LONDON, so stay with us and your journey to London will start with an experience that you won't forget.

The hostel is located in London's buzzing Bayswater and is set in a stunning grade I listed building. Hyde Park Inn is a clean, safe and secure place to stay with 24-hour access to the hostel facilities and your room. Each of our staff is highly trained, so they know what you are looking for and are there to assist you during your stay.

DETAILS

- **Open** - All year, 24 hours (no curfew or lockouts)
- **Number of beds** - 223: 3x1, 5x2, 1x3, 6x4, 7x6, 9x8, 3x10, 2x12
- **Booking** - Book by phone, fax, email or online www.smartbackpackers.com
- **Price per night** - From £9 per person (inclusive of breakfast and linen)
- **Public Transport** - Tube Stations: Bayswater (Circle and District line) and Queensway (Central line). Train Stations: Victoria, Paddington, Kings Cross, and Euston. Bus station: Victoria. Easy links from all major airports - Heathrow, Gatwick, Luton, City & Stansted.
- **Directions** - From Bayswater Station cross the road and walk down Inverness Place, at the end of the road is Hyde Park Inn. From Queensway Station turn left onto Bayswater Road, cross the road and take the first right into Inverness Place. At the end of the road is Hyde Park Inn.

CONTACT:
48-50 Inverness Terrace, Bayswater, London, W2 3JA
Tel: 020 7229 0000, Fax: 020 7229 8333
hpibookings@smartbackpackers.com www.smartbackpackers.com

SMART RUSSELL SQ.
HOSTEL
ENGLAND

Smart Russell Square London Hostel is situated in the heart of Bloomsbury in Central London.
Ideally located between the City, the Law Courts and West End, the hostel is also a short walk from the British Museum, Covent Garden, Oxford Street and University College London.

Facilities include common room, games room, kitchen, pool table, fridge, towel hire, jobs board, currency exchange, luggage storage and 24 hour security. Access is by key card. There is local on-street car parking.

DETAILS

- **Open** - All year, 24 hours
- **Number of beds** - 65: dorms form 6 to 24 beds; 3x2
- **Booking** - Booking required with 10% deposit at time of booking for individuals / 30% deposit for groups
- **Price per night** - From £8.50 (inclusive of breakfast).
- **Public Transport** - Underground: Russell Square station on the Piccadilly Line is close to Smart Russell Square and stops at Heathrow Airport, Covent Garden, Leicester Square, and Knightsbridge (Harrods).Bus: London Buses stop near the hostel at Russell Square. Airport transfers are available from our hostel through the porters (payable locally).Train: King's Cross, Euston and St. Pancras Stations are a short walk from the hostel.
- **Directions** - Smart Russell Square is a just behind Russell Square Tube Station. Just turn left out of the station then 2nd left into Guildford Street, walk down Guildford Street 20m to number 71.

CONTACT: Receptionist
70-72 Guildford Street, London, WC1N 1DF
Tel: 020 7833 8818 Fax: 020 7278 7309
srsbookings@smartbackpackers.com www.smartbackpackers.com

SMART
CAMDEN INN

Smart Camden Inn is one of London's premier hostels and is located in London's legendary Camden Town area, set in a stunning building.

Smart Camden Inn is a clean, safe and secure place to stay with 24-hour access to the hostel facilities and your room. All the rooms have washing facilities en-suite. There are many bath and shower rooms in our building with unlimited piping hot water.

We cater for all travellers, from groups to backpackers and provide the perfect place to meet and mix with like-minded people from all over the world. Camden Inn's staff are highly trained, so they know what you are looking for and are there to assist you during your stay.

DETAILS

■ **Open** - All year, 24 hours (no curfew or lockouts)
■ **Number of beds** - 108: 1x14 : 9x6 : 10x4
■ **Booking** - Book by phone, fax or email or online www.smartbackpackers.com
■ **Price per night** - From £9 per person including breakfast
■ **Public Transport** - Tube Stations: Camden Town (Northern Line). Train Stations: Euston, Kings Cross, Liverpool Street & Paddington. Bus station: Victoria. Easy links from all major airports - Heathrow, Gatwick, Luton, City & Stansted.
■ **Directions** - From Camden Town take the left exit. Walk down Bayham Street, which is opposite the station. We are on the right side of the street approx. 2 min from the station.

CONTACT:
55-57 Bayham Street, London, NW1 0AA
Tel: 020 7388 8900, Fax: 020 7388 2008
scibookings@smartbackpackers.com www.smartbackpackers.com

SMART
HYDE PARK VIEW

Hyde Park View is our newest hostel located in the buzzing area of Bayswater and a stone's throw away from Hyde Park and lots of other tourist attractions.

It has also been voted in the top ten hostels in the WORLD! So stay with us and your journey to London will start with an experience that you won't forget. Hyde Park View is a stunning listed building. It is a clean, safe and secure place to stay with 24-hour access to the hostel facilities and your room. Each of our staff is highly trained, so they know what you are looking for and are there to assist you during your stay.

DETAILS

- **Open** - All year, 24 hours
- **Number of beds** - 104: 2 x 4, 16 x 6
- **Booking** - www.smartbackpackers.com online booking or phone. Deposit required for groups.
- **Price per night** - From £9.00 per night per bed (inclusive of breakfast and linen).
- **Public Transport** - Tube stations: Bayswater (Circle and District line) and Queensway (Central line). Train stations: Victoria, Paddington, Kings Cross, and Euston. Bus station: Victoria. Easy links from all major airports - Heathrow, Gatwick, Luton, City & Stansted.
- **Directions** - From Bayswater Tube Station cross the road (Queensway Road) and turn right. Walk for 2 minutes till you hit the Bayswater road. Turn left and walk for 5 min and turn left into Leinster Gardens Road. Keep walking and you will see Craven (Gardens) Hotel on your right. Take the turn just after the hotel and you will see Hyde Park View Hostel.

CONTACT: Reception
11 Craven Hill Gardens, Bayswater, London, W2 3EU
Tel: 020 7402 4101, Fax: 020 7262 2083
hpvbookings@smartbackpackers.com www.smartbackpackers.com

ASHLEE HOUSE

Stay in stylish, modern cheap accommodation with great facilities and relaxing lounge areas. Feel right at home with a diverse mixture of international travellers. You'll also find yourself a stone's throw from the British Museum, Covent Garden, Bloomsbury and Camden Market or just minutes away from the bright lights of Piccadilly Circus and Leicester Square. Security is excellent with coded entrances to the building and the rooms.

There is also a fully equipped self-catering kitchen. And we can even get you on the guest list of some of London's hottest nightclubs! So if it's the real London experience you're looking for come to Ashlee House and start living it!

DETAILS

- **Open** - All year, 24 hours - no curfew or lockouts
- **Number of beds** - 3 large dorms, 6 dorms, 12 small dorms and 4 private rooms
- **Booking** - Advanced booking recommended.
- **Price per night** - From £9pp including FREE breakfast. Group discounts.
- **Public Transport** - Kings Cross has excellent public transport: underground, local buses and direct links with all major airports - Heathrow, Gatwick, Luton and Stansted. Only 20 mins from Waterloo International and Victoria.
- **Directions** - King's Cross station is 2 mins away by foot. From the station take the exit for Grays Inn Road, departing the exit McDonald's will be on right. Keep McDonald's right, walk straight ahead, passing an exchange bureau, the police station and KFC. The road curves to the right - this is Grays Inn Road - the hostel is 200 metres up the road on the right, opposite The Royal Throat Nose and Ear Hospital.

CONTACT:
261-265 Gray's Inn Road, King's Cross, London, WC1X 8QT
Tel: 020 7833 9400, Fax: 020 7833 9677
info@ashleehouse.co.uk www.ashleehouse.co.uk

THE 1912 CENTRE
GROUP HOSTEL
ENGLAND

The 1912 Centre is a 26 Bed Hostel in the heart of Harwich heritage area, only 50 metres from the sandy beach, promenade and harbour. It was built in 1912 as the Town Fire Station and the old engine garage now forms the central dining and recreational area. The upper floor has access to four cabin style sleeping areas, two with two berths and two with six berths. The ground floor has two cabins, one six berth, and one four berth with ensuite facilities. All cabins have bunk beds. The Centre is centrally heated and has a fully equipped kitchen, showers, a drying room and ground floor facilities for the disabled. Bring sleeping bags or hire duvets. The housekeeper can provide booked meals, or you can self-cater.

The 1912 Centre is situated within the Harwich conservation area. The town is built on a narrow spit of land between the sea and two rivers and owes much of its charm to medieval origins.

DETAILS

- **Open** - All year, all day
- **Number of beds** - 26: 3x6, 1x4, 2x2
- **Booking** - Book by phone or email. Enquiry form online.
- **Price per night** - £194 sole use. Weekly £984. Mon to Fri £774. Fri to Sun £380. Duvet hire £6.50 per person.
- **Public Transport** - Harwich Town train and bus station are a few minutes walk away. Follow signs to Electric Palace cinema which is next door to hostel.
- **Directions** - Follow A120 to Harwich. Follow signs past Harwich Quay until you come to a large painted wall mural then take 1st right and the centre is on your right

CONTACT:
Cow Lane, Off Wellington Road, Harwich, Essex, C012 3ES
Tel: 01255 552010, Fax: 01255 552010
1912@harwichconnexions.co.uk www.harwichconnexions.co.uk

HARLOW
ENGLAND INTERNATIONAL HOSTEL

Harlow International Hostel is situated in the centre of a landscaped park and is one of the oldest buildings in Harlow. The town of Harlow is the ideal base from which to explore London, Cambridge and the best of the South East of England. The journey time to central London is only 35 minutes from the hostel. National Cycle Route One passes our front door. We are the closest hostel to Stansted Airport. There is a range of room sizes from single to eight bedded, many with their own washing facilities. Self-catering facilities, refreshments and a small shop are all available. During your visit you can relax with a book from our large collection or enjoy a board game with other guests. A children's zoo, assault course, swimming and outdoor pursuit centre are available in the park. Meals provided for groups.

DETAILS

- **Open** - All year, 08:00 - 24:00 (check in 16:00 - 22:30)
- **Number of beds** - 36: 2x1 : 2x2 : 3x4 : 3x6
- **Booking** - Advance booking (can be taken 18 months in advance) is recommended. Deposit of £1pppn of stay.
- **Price per night** - £12.50 per adults, Family rooms £44 (sleeps 4), £55 (sleep 5), £66 (sleep 6). Please check our website for latest prices and discounts.
- **Public Transport** - The rail station is only 800m from hostel with links to London, Cambridge & Stansted Airport. Buses connect to London and airports.
- **Directions** - J7 of M11 take A414 into Harlow. At the 4th roundabout take 1st exit (First Ave). Drive to 4th set of traffic lights. Immediately after lights turn right (School Lane). Hostel is on left opp Greyhound Pub.

CONTACT: Richard or Iku
13 School Lane Harlow, Essex, CM20 2QD
Tel: 01279 421702
mail@h-i-h.co.uk www.h-i-h.co.uk

COURT HILL
CENTRE

Just 2 miles south of Wantage, and only a few steps from the historic Ridgeway National Trail, The Court Hill Centre enjoys breathtaking views over the Vale of the White Horse. Reclaimed barns surround a pretty courtyard garden, on the site of a disused rubbish dump! Offering accommodation to families, groups and individuals, a popular year-round destination. we offer evening meals, breakfasts, and picnic lunches, all prepared using as much local produce as possible. Meals are served in the beautiful high-roofed dining room which retains the impressive proportions and atmosphere of the old barn. Before and after your meal relax in the cosy sunken lounge with a log fire when it's chilly. We offer a limited number of pitches for small tents, and can accommodate small groups by arrangement. Our 2 tipis sleeping 5/6 each are available from April to the end of August. A meeting/classroom and bike hire are also available.

DETAILS

■ **Open** - From Good Friday to the end of October. Bookings accepted 48 hours in advance at all other times if possible, Office 08:00-11:00 & 17:00-22:00
■ **Number of beds** - 59: 1x10+, 1x9, 1x6, 1x5, 7x4
■ **Booking** - Essential 48 hours in advance. Payment required to guarantee booking
■ **Price per night** - Adult £17, Under 18 £13.00
■ **Public Transport** - Train, Didcot Parkway 10 Miles. Stagecoach, 32/A, X35,36 from Didcot Parkway to Wantage 2 Miles. There is no direct connection to the centre.
■ **Directions** - From the M4 Jct 14, follow signs to Wantage. From Oxford A420 and A338 through Wantage. The Courthill Ridgeway Centre is accessed from the A338 close to Letcombe Regis

CONTACT: Reception
Courthill, Letcombe Regis, Wantage, OX12 9NE
Tel: 01235 760253
info@Courthill.org.uk www.Courthill.org.uk

RAMBLERS' RETREAT
WENDOVER HOUSE
ENGLAND

Wendover House is a residential school set in the heart of the Chiltern Hills, right on the Ridgeway Path. At weekends and school holidays the Ramblers' Retreat welcomes walkers and holiday makers into the school. The retreat has one dormitory with five curtained bedspaces, a private room for one, a well-equipped kitchen and plenty of washing facilities. The school is situated around an 18th Century Manor House with 22 acres of land. It is easily accessible by road and there is a direct rail link to London Marylebone only a few minutes walk away. Wendover Village is an old market town set in an area of Outstanding Natural Beauty. It has lots of historic buildings with excellent pubs and restaurants only 5 minutes walk from the school. As well as the Ridgeway Path there are 33 miles of public rights of way crisscrossing the parish

DETAILS

- **Open** - Weekends and school holidays, all day
- **Number of beds** - 6: 1 x 5, 1 x 1
- **Booking** - Book minimum of 24 hours in advance. No deposit required (payment by cash or cheque only).
- **Price per night** - £12 per person. Optional bedding pack (inc towel) £3
- **Public Transport** - Wendover station on the Marylebone to Aylesbury line is 6 mins walk. Trains run approximately twice an hour. Local bus service from Aylesbury runs twice an hour and hourly at weekends.
- **Directions** - Wendover House is just off the A413 in the centre of Wendover. If arriving from Aylesbury, travel through Wendover in the direction of Amersham. Look for turning signed "St Mary's Church". Drive past the church and look for school.

CONTACT:
Wendover House School, Church Lane, Wendover, Bucks, HP22 6NL
Tel: 01296 622157 (school hours), 01296 626065 or (01296) 625319
office@wendoverhouse.bucks.sch.uk www.wendoverhouse.bucks.sch.uk

UNDER NEW MANAGEMENT. Oxford Backpackers is a purpose built hostel, in the heart of Oxford, the leading university town of England. The hostel is two minutes walk from the train and bus stations and close to the Tourist Information Centre and all the City's attractions. It is safe, clean and friendly. Small dorms with individual pin code locks, fully equipped kitchen, well supplied bar, laundry, games room, internet access and organised activities add to the experience.

Oxford City is steeped in history and culture. You can explore Christ Church, Magdalen and New College of the University, the Bodleian Library, the Oxford Story and Britain's oldest museum the Ashmolean Museum. Or explore the canals and quiet villages of the Cotswolds.

DETAILS

■ **Open** - All year, 24 hour access, service 8am until 11.30pm.
■ **Number of beds** - 120
■ **Booking** - Booking is advised in summer (April to Sept), 7 days in advance with deposit by credit card.
■ **Price per night** - From £13 per person. Discounts for longer stays and groups. Discounts when you book ahead to Bath Backpackers hostel (01225) 446787.
■ **Public Transport** - Oxford has train and National Express services. Hostel is 100m from train station and easy walking distance from the coach station.
■ **Directions** - From train station turn left and walk 100 metres, hostel is on your right. From Oxford coach station turn right, hostel is over the bridge 100 metres on your left. By road follow signs to the train station.

CONTACT:
9a Hythe Bridge Street, Oxford, OX1 2EW
Tel: 01865 721761, Fax: 01865 203293
oxford@hostels.co.uk www.hostels.co.uk

Central Backpackers is conveniently situated right downtown on one of Oxford's liveliest streets, lined with 8 bars, 3 clubs and 5 restaurants! Just a few minutes walk away are tourist information, universities, museums, tour bus pick up, supermarkets, cinemas, theatres, canal walks and the recently refurbished Oxford Castle and Prison Complex. Oxford is also a great start for touring nearby Cotswold villages and Blenheim Palace. This newly opened, smoke free hostel offers clean, new beds and a helpful team with advice and local knowledge. The hostel is equipped with a self-catered kitchen (offering free tea and coffee), dining room, cosy TV lounge (with satellite TV and DVDs), outdoor deck and BBQ. There are also lockers for all guests, swipe card access to dorms, free map, free internet and wireless access and a laundry service. Families and groups welcome. ID required. Free continental breakfast.

DETAILS

- **Open** - All year, 24 hours. No curfew
- **Number of beds** - 50: 1x12, 3x8, 1x6, 2x4
- **Booking** - Advisable, essential in high season.
- **Price per night** - From £14 per person.
- **Public Transport** - Oxford Tube bus company leaves London every 12 mins and costs £12-15 return. Oxford Express buses offer direct services to and from Heathrow, Gatwick and London Airports. Trains from Paddington every 10-20 mins.
- **Directions** - Bus: (3 mins) turn right onto George St, follow the road around to the left. Take first right onto Park End St. Train: (3 mins) Look to your left and see Royal Oxford Hotel. Park End St runs down the right side of the hotel. Give us a call if lost.

CONTACT: Reception
13 Park End Street, Oxford, OX1 1HH
Tel: 01865 242288
oxford@centralbackpackers.co.uk www.centralbackpackers.co.uk

BISHOP MASCALL
CENTRE
ENGLAND

The Bishop Mascall Centre has developed from a former church school and provides hostel-style accommodation for up to 48 people. The residential area has sixteen single and four twin rooms, plus two dormitories each sleeping twelve people in bunk beds. Rooms have wash-hand basins. Showers, toilets and a bathroom are located on each floor. A range of good home-cooked food is available in the Centre's dining room. Other facilities include a licensed bar, free internet connection, TV / video, audio-visual equipment, library and chapel.

A short walk away is the centre of the ancient market town of Ludlow, where you can wander medieval streets to the Norman Castle and the splendid church of St Laurence . The surrounding excellent walking country and varied geology make it an ideal base for outdoor enthusiasts. The Centre offers flexible meeting spaces, good food, simple, comfortable accommodation and a personal service. It is a Christian charitable foundation, but it is open to all.

DETAILS

- **Open** - All year, all day
- **Number of beds** - 48: 2x12 + singles and twins.
- **Booking** - Book by phone or email.
- **Price per night** - B&B £16pp (dorm), £19pp (twin) and £20 pp (single). Packages with full catering are also available. Prices are based on group sizes over 5.
- **Public Transport** - Ludlow train station is on the Cardiff to Manchester route. Buses operate from Birmingham, Shrewsbury and Hereford.
- **Directions** - We are in the heart of Ludlow, about 5 minutes' walk from the station

CONTACT: House Manager
Lower Galdeford, Ludlow, Shropshire, SY8 1RZ
Tel: 01584 873882, Fax: 01584 877945
info@thebmc.org.uk www.thebmc.org.uk/

BERROW HOUSE
ENGLAND BUNKHOUSE & CAMP SITE

Berrow House is situated in Hollybush between Rugged Stone Hill and Midsummer Hill in the Malvern Range. It is ideally suited for families, groups and individuals (including those with special needs) who want easy access to the countryside. The Forest of Dean, the Welsh border and the start of the Worcestershire Way Walk are near, with the towns of Malvern, Ledbury, Tewkesbury, Worcester, and Gloucester, all within a half hour drive. The Bunkhouse has sleeping accommodation for 5 in the main room and 3 more beds on the upper floor. The main room has heating and easy chairs. The adjacent kitchen/dining room has hot water, cooker, cutlery, crockery and cooking utensils. Toilets, dryer and shower are adjacent. The Fold is a separate building which has sleeping accommodation for 4 in two rooms, a fully equipped kitchen, heating, toilet, shower and a cloakroom. The Nook (caravan) has a double and single bed and uses the bunkhouse facilities. Camping, picnic area, water garden and car park are also available.

DETAILS

- **Open** - All year, 24 hours
- **Number of beds** - 8 (Bunkhouse), 4 (The Fold), 3 (The Nook) and 8 tents.
- **Booking** - Not required for individuals
- **Price per night** - £10 per person.
- **Public Transport** - Nearest train station and National Express service are in Ledbury, which is 3 miles from the hostel and would cost approx. £3 in a taxi.
- **Directions** - Take A449 from Ledbury towards Malvern. Turn right on to A438 through Eastnor. Berrow House is behind phone box in Hollybush (yellow sign).

CONTACT: Bill or Mary Cole
Hollybush, Ledbury, Herefordshire, HR8 1ET
Tel: 01531 635845, Fax: 635845
berrowhouse@tiscali.co.uk www.berrowhouse.co.uk

BERROW HOUSE

CAMPING

CARAVANS

BUNKHOUSE

The bunkhouse, a specially adapted barn, is specifically designed to cater for individuals or larger parties of walkers and cyclists, some of whom may be exploring the Herefordshire Trail, the Malvern Hills or the Forest of Dean. There are 4 twin bedded units and 1 sleeping 4 (2 singles and a bunk). Each room is furnished with a wardrobe, dining area and cooking area. The cooking area has a kettle, toaster, microwave, 2 ring table top cooker, fridge, basic utensils and crockery. Electric is by coin meter. Bedding can be provided for an extra charge. There are two toilet blocks with showers, washing-up and laundry facilities.
With a backcloth of mixed woodland, the surrounding environment has been enhanced by a wild flower and natural woodland area complementing the pools and waterfalls where fishing or a relaxing picnic can be enjoyed. The nearby town of Ledbury is famous for its black and white buildings, cobbled streets, Poetry Festival, and was recently winner of the Britain in Bloom Competition.

DETAILS

- **Open** - All year, All day
- **Number of beds** - 12 : 4x2, 1x4
- **Booking** - Booking in advance advised.
- **Price per night** - Telephone for prices
- **Public Transport** - Public transport is available within 1/2mile.
- **Directions** - From Junction 2, M50 take the A417 to Ledbury. At the first roundabout turn left following Leadon Way (the by-pass). At the third roundabout turn left into Little Marcle Road. Go past the factory and take the right turn signposted Falcon Lane & Baregains Lane. Woodside Lodges is the sixth entrance on the right.

CONTACT:
Woodside Lodges, Falcon Lane, Ledbury, Herefordshire, HR8 2JN
Tel: 01531 670 269
info@woodsidelodges.co.uk www.woodsidelodges.co.uk

HATTERS HOSTEL
BIRMINGHAM

We've upped the norm in hostel accommodation in Birmingham with our latest cosy and gorgeous addition, offering hotel style facilities while maintaining the fun and character of a hostel. Our talents include clean, secure ensuite rooms ranging from 1 to 10 beds, fluffy pillows and sparkling funky surroundings.
We've picked our staff from the obsessed-about-Birmingham tree and now they're here waiting, bursting with insider information and desperate to help you discover everything that make us fall in love with it. Located in the vibrant Jewellery Quarter in the heart of the city, the hostel is within walking distance of tons of places to eat, drink, shop and experience the heart of England!
Local and national transport is just a stone's throw away as well as all of the undiscovered gems that Birmingham has to offer.
Perfect for a one night stay to explore the city better or great as a temporary stop while you find your own place.

DETAILS

- **Open** - all year , 24 hours
- **Number of beds** - 100 (all ensuite): 8 private rooms, 2 x 12 bed, 1 x 10 bed, 7 x 6 bed, 2 x 4 bed
- **Booking** - Booking not essential but recommended, especially on weekends. Photo ID (ie passport, ID card, driving license) required at check in.
- **Price per night** - From £14.50 Please contact the hostel directly for groups
- **Public Transport** - 20 minutes walk northwards from New St Train station, 30 mins from Digbeth Coach Station. Nearest trains at Snow Hill Stn (5 mins).
- **Directions** - From New St. Station go left onto New St, take 5th right onto Bennett's Hill, then 2nd right onto Colmore Row and finally 2nd left, Livery St.

CONTACT:
92-97 Livery Street, Birmingham, B3 1RJ
Tel: 0121 236 4031
birmingham@hattersgroup.com www.hattersgroup.com/birmingham

Birmingham Central Backpackers is Birmingham's first and best independent backpackers' hostel and THE place to stay while exploring the brilliance of Birmingham. Located a minute's walk from the National Express coach station, 1 minute from the buses to the NEC and Airport and a mere 7 minute walk to New Street train station, our location can't be beaten for convenience. Rooms include 4-8 person dorms, a pod dorm and singles and privates. Friendly international staff, two cosy common rooms for relaxation, guest kitchen, free breakfast and nightly snack buffet, free Wi-Fi and budget computer stations, gigantic cinema screen with over 600 movies to choose from, Playstation 3, Nintendo Wii, pool, travel information centre, outdoor patio and guest-only bar. So when in Birmingham make us your place to stay, you won't regret it!

DETAILS

- **Open** - All year, check-in from 2pm-11pm. Common area open 8am-12am
- **Number of beds** - 80: 11 rooms of 4-8 beds 1x3, 3x2, 2x1 + pod dorm
- **Booking** - Book by phone, email or online. 2% credit card fee, 40p debit card fee for bookings of £50 or more.
- **Price per night** - £16 weekdays, £17 Fri and Sat, inc. linen, light breakfast and nightly snack buffet.
- **Public Transport** - Digbeth coach station and New Street train station near by.
- **Directions** - From Digbeth Coach Station take Milk Street (Big Bulls Head on corner). Hostel located above Billy's Bar, one block down. From New Street Station, walk down New Street through the Bull Ring and down the steps to the markets. Take a left at the markets and go to the traffic light. Cross over the light to the Digbeth High Street. Walk 4 blocks, and turn left onto Milk Street.

CONTACT: Ian and Jen Randall
58 Coventry Street, Digbeth, Birmingham, B5 5NH
Tel: 0121 643-0033, Mobile: 0775-682-9970
info@birminghamcentralbackpackers.com www.birminghamcentralbackpackers.com

This small hostel, once the old village school, is tucked away in the Shropshire hills with the Long Mynd to the east and Stiperstones to the west. It is an ideal spot for ramblers with the Shropshire Way passing close by and a great network of uncrowded paths to explore. Walkers on the Shropshire Way may see wild poinies, woodpeckers, skylarks, ravens and various birds of prey. Small towns nearby worthy of a visit include Ludlow, Much Wenlock, Bishops Castle and sleepy Montgomery. There's also the Acton Scott working farm museum and The Bog former mining centre close by, and a pub next door serving food.

The hostel has a good kitchen, a lounge with wood fire, books and games, a drying room, a food shop and a large garden. One ensuite room has some facilities for the disabled, phone to discuss your requirements. Meals are available and camping is allowed.

DETAILS

- **Open** - All year, Reception 8-10 am, 5-10 pm. Hostel closes at 11pm.
- **Number of beds** - 37: 1x4 ensuite, 1x2 ensuite,1x8, 1x10, 1x12
- **Booking** - Telephone to book. No credit or debit cards accepted. Cheques must be made payable to Bridges Youth Hostel not YHA.
- **Price per night** - Adults £14. Under 18's £10.
- **Public Transport** - Trains at Church Stretton (5 miles).
- **Directions** - From Church Stretton, take 'The Burway' road uphill. Take right fork at top of Long Mynd. From Shrewsbury take road via Longden and Pulverbatch, then left by Horseshoe Inn. Access from Church Stretton over the Long Mynd Hill is not advisable in bad weather during winter

CONTACT: Bridges Youth Hostel
Ratlinghope, Shrewsbury, Shropshire, SY5 0SP
Tel: 01588 650656, Fax: 01588 650531
sam@backpackerspress.com   www.yha.org.uk

All Stretton Bunkhouse offers comfortable self-catering accommodation with underfloor heating for small groups of up to 10 people. It has easy access to the Long Mynd which offers walks and bike rides for all levels of fitness. There are local stables where you can book horse riding by the hour or day. It is within easy reach of the busy town of Church Stretton and all its facilities, and just 10 minutes walk from the local pub (but please always book meals as they are not very big). Takeaway food can be ordered from Church Stretton.

There are three bedrooms in the bunkhouse: Synalds and Cardoc have two bunks (sleeping 4) and Novers has two singles. A cot is also available.The well equipped kitchen has cooker, microwave, toaster, kettle and fridge. There is a shower, two toilets and a tumble dryer.
The track up to the property is steep and rough so wheelchair access is difficult.

DETAILS

- **Open** - All year, 5pm to 10.30pm. Reception 5pm to 9pm.
- **Number of beds** - 10 plus 1 cot.
- **Booking** - Book by phone, post or online.
- **Price per night** - £16.50, £14 under 18's. £3 discount for all YHA members.
- **Public Transport** - Trains to Church Stretton from Shrewsbury, Hereford and Cardiff. Station 1.2 miles walk (or taxi) from Bunkhouse. National Express buses to Shrewsbury, hourly local buses from Shrewsbury to Church Stretton via All Stretton.
- **Directions** - 300m on right going up Batch Valley road (which joins B4370 a mile north of Church Stretton).

CONTACT:
Meadow Green, Batch Valley, All Stretton, Shrops, SY6 6JW
Tel: 01694 722593   Mob: 0781 551 7482
info@allstrettonbunkhouse.co.uk www.allstrettonbunkhouse.co.uk

Womerton Farm Bunkhouse is situated right next to the Longmynd, an AONB, in the heart of the Shropshire Hills. Our bunkhouse offers a small select accommodation to sleep 8, 6 in bunks downstairs and a double fold-down sofa bed upstairs. There is a fully equipped kitchen and living area upstairs. We are 3 miles from Church Stretton, 12 miles from historic Shrewsbury and 15 miles from Ludlow, food capital of Shropshire. There are many local attractions such as Acton Scott Working Farm Museum, Stokesay Castle, Museum of Lost Content and Discovery Centre. The Longmynd is fantastic for walking, mountain biking and horse riding. Horses can be field accommodated if arranged in advance. Well behaved dogs that are not moulting allowed. For photo gallery, directions and details please visit our website at www.womerton-farm.co.uk

DETAILS

- **Open** - All year, all day. Closed from 11 am to 4pm on change over days.
- **Number of beds** - 9: 1x6, 1x1 + double sofa bed in living area
- **Booking** - Booking recommended to guarantee a place. Last minute phone bookings are welcomed, but could be disappointed. Deposit of £10 required.
- **Price per night** - £80 Christmas/ New Year, £80 Easter to Sept. £60 off peak
- **Public Transport** - Nearest train and bus station is Church Stretton (3 miles). Taxi fare is about £10. We can usually arrange transport from Church Stretton if contacted in advance.
- **Directions** - From Church Stretton follow A49 north. Past coffee shop and craft centre take a left turn signed Lower Wood. From Shrewsbury on A49 south, pass though Leebotwood then take the right turn signed Lower Wood. Follow this road for 1 mile, cross a cattle grid onto the Longmynd and we are the first farm on the right.

CONTACT: Ruth or Tony
Womerton Farm, All Stretton, Church Stretton, Shropshire, SY6 6LJ
Tel: 01694 751 260
ruth@womerton-farm.co.uk www.womerton-farm.co.uk

Stokes Barn is located on top of Wenlock Edge, an Area of Outstanding Natural Beauty and in the heart of Shropshire countryside. The barn offers comfortable, centrally heated, dormitory accommodation for a wide range of groups.

Stokes Barn is an ideal base for field study groups, universities, schools, walkers or just a relaxing reunion with friends. The Ironbridge World Heritage Site is only 6 miles away and is a great attraction. Walk to the historic town of Much Wenlock to visit shops, pubs and sports facilities. Situated only a few miles from Church Stretton and the Long Mynd the barn is in a walking / cycling haven. Many activities available.

Have a relaxing and enjoyable stay.

DETAILS

- **Open** - All year, all day
- **Number of beds** - 27: 1x12,1x10,1x5
- **Booking** - Deposit required.
- **Price per night** - £12 pp plus £4 duvet charge.
- **Public Transport** - Trains at Telford (10 miles) and in Shrewsbury (10 miles). National Express coaches call at Shrewsbury from London, call 0839 142348 for information. Midland Red buses stop in Much Wenlock, enquires 01952 223766.
- **Directions** - GR 609 999. From the M6 take M54 Telford following Ironbridge Gorge signs. A4169 to Much Wenlock, joining A458 for Shrewsbury. The Barn is signed at Newton House Farm (TF13 6DB) on the Much Wenlock to Shrewsbury Rd.

CONTACT:
Stokes Barn, Newtown Farm, Much Wenlock, Shropshire, TF13 6DB
Tel: 01952 727491 ext 2, Mob: 07973 329889, Fax: 728130
info@stokesbarn.co.uk www.stokesbarn.co.uk

Springhill is a hill farm at 1475ft above sea level, near the Shropshire / Wales border with beautiful views over the Ceiriog Valley and Berwyn Mountains.

Great for walking and activity breaks or just to relax. We have cycle hire and horse riding for all, from 1 hour to holidays on site.

The main bunkhouse can sleep around 20, with 2 smaller self catering cotages, up to 10 more. Underfloor heating, entrance hall with w/c and drying room. Large kitchen, dining and sitting rooms, 5 bedrooms sleeping 1-8. Also outside is a large patio and lawn, BBQ and hot tub and a large room for meetings and recreation. Your own horse and pets welcome on request.

DETAILS

- **Open** - All year, all day (please don't phone after 9pm)
- **Number of beds** - 30: 20 (bunkhouse) + two cottages
- **Booking** - Advisable, deposit required
- **Price per night** - £17pp (including bedding but not towels)
- **Public Transport** - Nearest train station Chirk (8 miles). Nearest bus service is in the village Glyn Ceiriog (2.5 miles). Transfer can be arranged.
- **Directions** - GR SJ 210 346. On the A483 from Wrexham, take the third exit on the first roundabout (Macdonalds). At the next roundabout take the first exit, continue into Chirk, and then turn right for Glyn Ceiriog. After 6 miles you will arrive at Glyn Ceiriog. At the mini roundabout turn left, go over the bridge, and then straight away turn right into a small lane. Continue up the hill for about two miles, do not turn off.

CONTACT: Sue Sopwith
Springhill Farm, Selattyn, Oswestry, Shropshire, SY10 7NZ
Tel: 01691 718406
sue@springhillfarm.co.uk www.atspringhill.co.uk

DEEPDALE GRANARY[101]
GROUP HOSTEL
ENGLAND

A perfect base for groups to stay, explore and absorb the stunning North Norfolk coast. Deepdale Granary is a self-contained 17th century building sleeping 18 in four bedrooms with a fully fitted kitchen and dining/sitting room. Part of the award winning Deepdale Farm, right on the coast in the heart of an Area of Outstanding Natural Beauty. We have excellent pubs nearby, both traditional and chic. Great restaurants and miles of unspoilt beaches and dunes. The Norfolk coast is perfect for walking and cycling with miles of coast path and picturesque villages. Take time to discover our heritage sties including the Sandringham and Holkham estates or enjoy birdwatching in the tranquil beauty of the unique saltmarsh. The Granary is fully heated, has showers, a drying room and solar water heating. Next-door Dalegate Market has shops, a supermarket, and a brilliant café serving locally sourced food. Camping and Tipis also available.

DETAILS

- **Open** - All year, all day. Collect key from Deepdale Information.
- **Number of beds** - 18: 2 x 6 : 1 x 4 : 1 x 2.
- **Booking** - Essential, 20% deposit, balance in advance. See website for details
- **Price per night** - From £144 per night, for up to 18 people.
- **Public Transport** - Trains / coaches at King's Lynn (25 miles) then excellent Coastal Hopper bus to Burnham Deepdale. Coastal Hopper services the coast from King's Lynn to Cromer, including Sandringham. Traveline 0870 608 2 608.
- **Directions** - GR 803443. On A149 coast road, halfway between Hunstanton and Wells-next-the-Sea. Beside Deepdale Garage & opposite Deepdale Church.

CONTACT:
Deepdale Farm, Burnham Deepdale, Norfolk, PE31 8DD
Tel: 01485 210256
info@deepdalefarm.co.uk www.deepdalebackpackers.co.uk

DEEPDALE
BACKPACKERS

Eco friendly award winning backpackers hostel on the beautiful north Norfolk coast. Escape the smog of the cities to this stunning part of the world. We offer private ensuite rooms (double, twin, triple, quad and family), single sex and mixed dorms. There's so much to do here, adrenaline sports, great pubs and restaurants, miles of sandy beaches. Deepdale is a perfect base for walking and cycling with miles of coast path, the famous big skies and quaint fishing harbours. Or just come and chill. Our facilities are second to none, all rooms are en-suite, we have a fully equipped farmhouse kitchen and a really cosy lounge with a TV and a woodburner for cooler nights. There's a lovely courtyard with barbeques for summer evenings. Deepdale is a working farm and eco-friendly with recycling, underfloor heating and solar water. Next-door Dalegate Market has shops, a supermarket, and a brilliant café serving locally sourced food. Camping and Tipis also available

DETAILS

- **Open** - All day every day, collect key from Deepdale Information.
- **Number of beds** - 50
- **Booking** - Pre-booking recommended. Max group size 12. See website.
- **Price per night** - From £9.50 (£63 per week) dorm room. £28 twin/double room.
- **Public Transport** - Train and coaches at Kings Lynn (25 Miles). Coast Hopper bus to Burnham Deepdale on the coast road from Kings Lynn to Cromer, stops at Sandringham, Holkham and Titchwell Bird Reserve. Travelline 0870 6082608
- **Directions** - GR 803443 On A149 Coast road halfway between Hunstanton and Wells-next-the-Sea. Beside Dalegate Market, opposite Deepdale Church.

CONTACT:
Deepdale Farm, Burnham Deepdale, Norfolk, PE31 8DD
Tel: 01485 210256
info@deepdalefarm.co.uk www.deepdalebackpackers.co.uk

Visitors to Castle Acre are entranced by the special atmosphere of this medieval walled town which lies within the outer bailey of an 11th-century castle. Castle Acre is on the Peddars Way, an ancient track now a long distance path. The Old Red Lion, a former pub, is centrally situated and carries on the tradition of serving travellers who seek refreshment and repose.

Guests can stay in private rooms or dormitories, where bedding and linen are provided free of charge. There are quiet areas (with wood burning stoves) for reading, meeting other guests and playing. There are two large areas and studio space (one with kitchen and toilet) which are ideal for group use, courses and retreats. There is a ground floor double room with disabled use toilet. Sole occupancy of entire premises may be hired; rates negotiable. Drying facilities. Good local shops, pubs etc. Tourism concern supporter. No smoking.

DETAILS

- **Open** - All year, all day access. Arrival times by arrangement.
- **Number of beds** - 24: 1x10, 1x6, 2 x double (1 en-suite), 2 x twin
- **Booking** - Useful but not essential
- **Price per night** - £17.50 - £25, en-suite £30 (inc. bedding and breakfast). One night supplements.
- **Public Transport** - Train stations at King's Lynn & Downham Market (14 miles). Buses from King's Lynn to Swaffham. Daily National Express coach between Victoria Coach Station & Swaffham. Norfolk Bus info 0500 626116. Taxi from Swaffham £7.
- **Directions** - GR 818151. Castle Acre is 3.5 miles north of Swaffham (A47) on the A1065. The hostel is on left, 75yds down from Bailey Gate in village centre.

CONTACT: Alison Loughlin
Bailey Street, Castle Acre, Norfolk, PE32 2AG
Tel: 01760 755557
oldredlion@yahoo.co.uk www.oldredlion.here2stay.org.uk

THE IGLOO
ENGLAND BACKPACKERS HOSTEL

Within walking distance of the city's historical sights and entertaining sounds, the Igloo is Nottingham's most popular choice for the budget-minded traveller. On offer to overseas jobseekers, backpackers and youth groups is a clean, safe and warm overnight stay in a large, listed Victorian house. Just £15 per night buys a whole host of homely comforts; bunk bed dorms, hot power showers, lounge with TV, films and WiFi, games room with pool table, fully-equipped kitchen, free tea & coffee, laundry facilities and good company. Open in outlook and open all day all year, it is the ideal home-from-home for hostellers seeking rest and recuperation before pursuing the exploits of Robin Hood or enjoying the energetic nightlife of this popular university city. Check out our web site.

DETAILS

- **Open** - All year, all day
- **Number of beds** - 36: 1x6; 1x8; 1x10; 1x12
- **Booking** - Essential during Summer months. Groups must confirm by email or by phone with deposit.
- **Price per night** - £15.00 pp. £60 per week after 7 nights stay. Seasonal discounts available.
- **Public Transport** - Direct, regular trains from London etc. National Express to Broadmarsh bus station. From bus/train stations 20mins walk, £4 taxi ride or catch tram to Trent Uni (4th stop), take next R (Peel St), follow to Golden Fleece pub.
- **Directions** - From the Tourist Information Centre (Market Square) turn right out of TIC, take next left onto Cumber Street, keep walking straight on for ten mins, past the Victoria Shopping centre, untill you reach the Golden Fleece Pub. The igloo is directly opposite. Entry is on the side of the buidling.

CONTACT: Igloo
110 Mansfield Road, Nottingham, NG1 3HL
Tel: 0115 9475250
reception@igloohostel.co.uk www.igloohostel.co.uk

SHEEN
BUNKHOUSE

Sheen Bunkhouse is a newly converted barn in a quiet corner of the Peak District, close to the beautiful Dove and Manifold valleys. Comprehensively equipped, it offers a large TV lounge, well-equipped self-catering facilities and two bunkrooms with wash basins. Toilets and showers are conveniently located for both rooms.

Passing close by the barn, the Manifold Valley Track, Tissington Trail and High Peak Trail provide easy access to beautiful countryside, ideal for families and cyclists. Dovedale, the Upper Dove Valley and the remote and mysterious moorlands around Flash and Longnor offer stunning scenery for walkers. Visit the markets and parks at Buxton (8 miles), Leek (10 miles) and Bakewell (12 miles) for a great day out. Other attractions include Alton Towers (35mins by car) and the famous Opera House and show caves at Buxton.

DETAILS

- **Open** - All year, 24 hours access, reception 8-10am, 5-9pm
- **Number of beds** - 14: 1x8, 1x6
- **Booking** - Book by phone or email
- **Price per night** - From: Adults £14.00, Under 16's £9.50.
- **Public Transport** - Train station at Buxton. Daily bus operated by Bowers from Buxton to Hartington passes close to bunkhouse.
- **Directions** - On the B5054 between Hartington and Hulme End take the turning to Sheen (also signposted for 'Staffordshire Knott'). The bunkhouse is on the right 200yds after the pub.

CONTACT: Graham Belfield
Peakstones, Sheen, Derbyshire, SK17 0ES
Tel: 01298 84501, Fax: 01298 84501
grahambelfield@fsmail.net

BARN FARM
BARNS AND CAMPSITE

Barn Farm is a working farm in the village of Birchover with fine views over the Derwent valley. Nearby are Stanton Moor with Victorian stone carvings and Nine Ladies stone circle; Robin Hood's Stride and other bouldering and climbing areas; the Limestone Way; a village shop and two pubs which serve food. Four camping barns are available: Sabine Hay has 15 bunkbeds arranged around a communal space with fully fitted kitchen; Hill Carr and Warren Carr have a similar arrangement with 15 and 12 single beds respectively. Stables Barn has 6 bunkbeds. All bunkhouses have self-catering facilities, are heated and have private bathroom and shower facilities in adjacent barns. Also available: two ensuite double-bed units, the Garden Room and the Gatehouse Barn. There's also space for camping (no single sex groups), caravans and campervans with good showers, toilets and laundry facilities. Barn farm also offers indoor or outdoor storage for caravans and campervans.

DETAILS

- **Open** - All year, accommodation available all day.
- **Number of beds** - 52: 1x15, 1x15, 1x12, 1x6, 1x2, 1x2 plus camping.
- **Booking** - Booking advisable 50% deposit.
- **Price per night** - Hill Carr £150, Sabine Hay £140, Warren Carr £240, Stables Barn £100. Garden Room £40/ night; Gatehouse Barn £85/night (min.2 nights) Weekly rates available. Camping £7.50pp (£5pp DofE groups).
- **Public Transport** - The 172 bus from Bakewell to Matlock runs approx. hourly.
- **Directions** - From the A6 between Matlock and Bakewell take the B5056. Follow signs for Birchover, continue past the Druid Inn to farm sign at the top of the village.

CONTACT:
Birchover, Matlock, Derbyshire, DE4 2BL
Tel: 01629 650245
gilberthh@msn.com www.peakdistrictonline.co.uk

PEAK DISTRICT
HOLIDAY BARN

Situated in the heart of the Peak District, 15 miles from Sheffield and 8 miles from Buxton, within some of England's most spectacular landscapes Peak District Holiday Barn is an impressively large barn recently converted to a very high standard while retaining many of the original features. It is fully insulated with double glazing and central heating. Suitable for reunions, family gatherings and team building courses, it is a great base for large groups to experience the numerous activities on the doorstep: walking, cycling, caving, climbing, mountain biking, hang gliding, off roading, green laning, abseiling and sleeping. With 6 bedrooms (including 2 king sized and 3 doubles + 14 large bunk beds) + 4 bathrooms on 2 floors the barn comfortably sleeps up to 26. All bedding is included but please bring towels. There is plenty of parking, a lawned garden and BBQ area with plenty of seating. A cosy pub next door opens Fri-Sun with good food and live music, and a cafe is just opposite. Please respect nearby residents and neighbouring working farm regarding late night noise levels.

DETAILS

- **Open** - All year, all day.
- **Number of beds** - 26 : 2x2, 2x4, 2x6 plus 2 ZBeds
- **Booking** - Booking required with £200 bond.
- **Price per night** - Weekends: 2 nights £1200 (£1400 June-Aug); 3nights £1800 (£2000). Weekdays £475 (£550). Full week £2700 (£3000)
- **Public Transport** - Stations on Sheffield to Manchester railway within 7 miles. Transpeak bus Nottingham to Manchester stops at Ashford (4 miles).
- **Directions** - Situated on the A623 in Wardlow Mires, next to the pub. OS 182757

CONTACT: Amanda Gregory
Wardlow Mires, near Tideswell, Buxton, Derbyshire, SK17 8RW
Tel: Booking enquiries: 07525 051 226 (Amanda), 07791667027 (Mark)
bookings@peakdistrictholidaybarn.co.uk   www.peakdistrictholidaybarn.co.uk

BUSHEY HEATH
FARM BARNS

Bushey Heath Farm is a family run smallholding in the heart of the Peak District, central to all the popular visitor centres, but just off the beaten track. Offering a summer campsite, self-catering static caravan and 'top of the range' bunkbarns for up to 14 people. Incorporating a Ground Source Heat Pump, a wind turbine for electricity and rainwater harvesting for wc flushing. We have developed the farm in an environmentally sensitive way so visitors can experience practical sustainable ideas. The static caravan has two bedrooms and shower/wc and can sleep up to 6. The Hen House Bunk Barn has two bedrooms with bunks for 4 in each. The Little Barn has a large single bedroom with bunks for 6 people. Both barns have luxury shower rooms and a combined fully equipped kitchen/diner open area downstairs. Sleeping bags required. Good dogs accepted.

DETAILS

- **Open** - All year. Campsite May till October, opening hours by arrangement
- **Number of beds** - 8: Hen House, 6: Little Barn, 6: Static caravan, 80 Pitches.
- **Booking** - Camping at Bank Hols only. Bunkhouse early with deposit advisable.
- **Price per night** - Camping Adult £4, Child £2, Vehicle £2. Static Caravan £160-£285 per week, short breaks available. Hen House - sole use £120pn. Little Barn – sole use £90pn. Weekends sole use only.
- **Public Transport** - Nearest trains at Hope (4 miles), Nearest buses in Tideswell (2 miles). Bus numbers 65, 66, x67, 173, 177, 197, 202.
- **Directions** - GR SK 146 785. From Tideswell take Manchester Road past Star Pub and cross over A623, road stops at farm. Going west along A623, 11/2 mile past the Anchor Pub turn right at cross roads in 's' bends..

CONTACT: Rod Baraona or Lisa Thomas
Tideswell Moor,Tideswell, Buxton, Derbyshire, SK17 8JE
Tel: 01298 873007, Mobile: 07710 163376
rod@baraona.freeserve.co.uk www.busheyheathfarm.co.uk

The Reckoning House camping barn has been renovated to a high standard including double glazing and insulation. It is situated on the edge of Lathkill Dale, 3 miles from Bakewell. Lathkill Dale is a nature reserve managed by English Nature to protect a variety of flora and fauna as well as some outstanding geological features. Horse riding, fishing, golf and cycle hire are all available locally. There are also many local walks including the Limestone Way.

It has a cooking area, 4 calor gas rings (gas supplied) a washing up sink with hot water, a toilet, wash basin, storage heaters in all rooms and shower inside the barn. The sleeping area is upstairs and has two separate sleeping floors.

DETAILS

- **Open** - All year, by arrangement
- **Number of beds** - 12
- **Booking** - Sole use bookings only, in advance (min 2 nights at weekends). 10% deposit, balance 2 weeks before arrival.
- **Price per night** - £8.50 per person. Sole use £85 per night, Reduction for sole use on Sun (excluding bank holidays), Mon, Tue, Wed or Thurs nights.
- **Public Transport** - Train stations at Buxton (10 miles) and Matlock (13 miles). National Express drop at Bakewell. Local buses (enquiries 01332 292200) go to Bakewell from Monyash, Over Haddon, Matlock and Buxton.
- **Directions** - GR 184 666. Take the B5055 out of Bakewell towards Monyash. Continue for 3 miles. After passing Haddon Grove Farm holiday cottages (the second set of cottages on right), take the first turn left at the signpost to Haddon Grove. Bear left at the bottom of the lane. The camping barn is the first on the left in a half mile.

CONTACT:
Mandale Farm, Haddon Grove, Bakewell, Derbyshire, DE45 1JF
Tel: 01629 812416
julia.finney@virgin.net www.mandalehouse.co.uk

HOMESTEAD
AND CHEESEHOUSE

The Bunkhouses are situated on a small mixed farm in the middle of Bamford, just 3 miles from Stanage Edge. The Derwent Dams are between 1.5 and 7 miles further up the valley. Castleton is 5 miles to the north, Chatsworth 10 miles to the south west.
Both bunkhouses have individual bunks each with mattress, fitted sheets and pillow, gas central heating and drying facilities.

Homestead has 22 beds in 3 rooms, and 2 bathrooms with 2 toilets and showers in each, a large dayroom with oak seating and a fully equipped kitchen with gas cooker. Cheesehouse is a self-contained bunkhouse with four bunks, ideal for a small family or group. It has a shower and toilet and is equipped with a kitchen having cooking rings, a microwave oven, toaster and kettle. The Bunkhouses are 2 minutes walk from two pubs. No dogs.

DETAILS

- **Open** - All year, no restriction
- **Number of beds** - Homestead 22: 1x10, 2x6. Cheesehouse 4: 1x4.
- **Booking** - Recommended for weekends.
- **Price per night** - £10 per person. Sole use: Homestead £175, Cheesehouse £36.
- **Public Transport** - Nearest train station Bamford, 10 mins walk. Bus 274 & 275 operates Sundays Bamford/Sheffield or to Castleton. Bus 272 Bamford to Sheffield and Castleton. Bus 175 Bamford/Bakewell.
- **Directions** - The farm is in the centre of Bamford on South View Lane (turn off A6013 at the 'Country Stores').

CONTACT: Helena Platts
The Farm, Bamford, Hope Valley, S33 0BL
Tel: 01433 651298
sam@backpackerspress.com

PINDALE FARM
OUTDOOR CENTRE

The Centre is situated one mile from Castleton in the heart of the Peak District. It comprises a farmhouse pre-dating 1340 and lead mine buildings from the 1850s, which have been completely rebuilt from a near derelict condition. The Centre now offers 5 different kinds of accommodation. The farmhouse offers traditional bed and (an AGA cooked) breakfast. The Barn has 6 independent self-catering units, the lower 3 of these can accommodate people with certain physical disabilities. The old Lead Mine Engine House, our logo, is a self-catering unit sleeping 8. The Powder House, originally the mine's explosive store, is a small camping barn with basic facilities for up to 4 people. A campsite, adjacent to the Centre, has showers, hot water, and toilet facilities. The Centre is the ideal base for walking, climbing, caving, horse riding etc. Instruction is available if required. Well behaved pets welcome.

DETAILS

■ **Open** - All year (Camping March-October), 24 hours
■ **Number of beds** - 64 bunkbeds plus camping and B&B
■ **Booking** -   Early booking (deposit) is best.
■ **Price per night** - Camping £4 pp, Powder House £5 pp, Engine House and Barn £8 pp, B&B £25 pp with four poster bed and an AGA breakfast.
■ **Public Transport** - Hope has a train station. The nearest National Express service is in Sheffield. Approximate taxi fare to Sheffield is £15-£20. On local buses ask for Hope. Hope is 15 minutes walk from the hostel.
■ **Directions** - GR 163 825   From Hope follow cement works signs, turn off main road between church and Woodroffe Arms.

CONTACT:
Pindale Lane, Hope, Hope Valley, Derbyshire, S33 6RN
Tel: 01433 620111, Fax: 01433 620729
pindalefarm@btconnect.com www.pindale.fsbusiness.co.uk

Moorside Farm is a 300-year-old farmhouse set 1200 feet up in the beautiful Peak District National Park on the Derbyshire/Staffordshire border and approximately five miles from the historic town of Buxton.

Sleeping accommodation is provided in two areas, one for 14 - this is alpine style with pine clad ceiling and a pine floor with bunk beds. The second area has 6 beds, also in bunks and is an ideal room for a small group or family. Downstairs there are showers, toilets and a large dining / general room. The farmhouse has full central heating and drying facilities are available. We provide a three course breakfast, a packed lunch and a substantial dinner in the evening, vegetarians are catered for. A small kitchen is available for making tea and coffee. Ample parking space is provided. All bookings have sole use of the accommodation.

DETAILS

- **Open** - All year, 24 hours
- **Number of beds** - 20: 1 x 14 : 1 x 6
- **Booking** - Booking with deposit required with two weeks' notice
- **Price per night** - £27.00 per person, bed, breakfast and evening meal included. £18.00 per person bed and breakfast. (min 4 persons)
- **Public Transport** - Nearest train station Buxton. Take bus to Longnor or Travellers Rest. Bus enquiries 01332 292200.
- **Directions** - GR SK 055 670. Leave A53, Buxton to Leek road, at Travellers Rest, take 4th lane on left, down to T junction, take first left, Moorside Farm is first right entrance.

CONTACT: Charlie
Hollinsclough, Longnor, Buxton, Derbyshire, SK17 0RF
Tel: 01298 83406
moorsidefarm@yahoo.co.uk www.moorsidefarm.com

THORPE FARM
BUNKHOUSES

Thorpe Farm Bunkhouses are situated a mile northeast of Hathersage, on a family run mixed / dairy farm. It is 2 miles from Stanage Edge and other popular climbing and walking areas are nearby. Castleton is 6 miles up the Hope Valley and Eyam is 6 miles southwest.

Each bunkhouse has dormitories with individual bunks each with mattress and pillow. There is some sleeping space in the sitting rooms and room for camping outside. The bunkhouses have heating, drying facilities, hot showers, toilets, electric/gas cooking, fridges, freezers, electric kettles, toasters etc. The Byre is all on one level with disabled facilities.

DETAILS

- **Open** - All year, no restrictions
- **Number of beds** - Old Shippon 32: 2x12, 2x4. Byre 14: 1x6, 2x4. Old Stables 14: 1x8, 1x6. Pondside 14: 1x8, 1x6
- **Booking** - Highly recommended for weekends.
- **Price per night** - From £10pp. Sole use from £100 per night.
- **Public Transport** - Train station at Hathersage, 10 mins walk from bunkhouse. Bus service 272 operates from Sheffield to Hathersage. Weekends only bus service 257 operates from Sheffield via Stanage & Snake Pass to Hathersage. Details phone Busline 01298 230980 or 01246 250450.
- **Directions** - GR 223 824. If walking from A6187/A625 in Hathersage turn right (just past the George Hotel) up Jaggers Lane, turn second right up Coggers Lane and fifth turning on left (signed Thorpe Farm). If driving follow the road from Hathersage towards Hope for ¾ mile, then turn right into private drive (signposted Thorpe Farm).

CONTACT: Jane Marsden
Thorpe Farm, Hathersage, Peak District, Via Sheffield, S32 1BQ
Tel: 01433 650659
marsdenhathersage@surfree.co.uk www.thorpe-bunk.co.uk

CHESTER
BACKPACKERS

Chester Backpackers is located just a few minutes walk from the ancient heart of the historic city of Chester in an original Tudor coaching inn (formally the Waterloo Inn). We offer clean, comfortable rooms most of which have en-suite facilities, with freshly laundered linen provided as standard. Free tea and coffee, free left luggage facilities and well-equipped rooms make Chester Backpackers an ideal base for walking the Roman walls of Chester, exploring the nearby Welsh mountains and dramatic coastline or day trips to Liverpool and Manchester. We can also assist with finding work for longer-term travellers and our attractive long-term rates make it an ideal location to spend time in this beautiful city. We are open 24 hours with no curfew, and our friendly well-trained staff (travellers themselves) are on hand to offer help and advice.

DETAILS

- **Open** - All year, 24 hours , no curfew
- **Number of beds** - 32: 1 x 18 : 1 x 8 : 2 x 2 : 2 x 1
- **Booking** - Book by phone or email. Strongly recommended at weekends, 2 to 4 days notice advisable at other times
- **Price per night** - Dorm £15pp (£17 at weekend), Single £25pp (£30 at weekend). Dbl/ twin £40 per room (£45 at weekend). Long term rates available.
- **Public Transport** - Hostel is 10 mins walk from train station and National Express coach station. Liverpool and Manchester airports are 30 mins drive away.
- **Directions** - From train walk up City Rd. At ring road (nr Last Orders) bear left into Boughton (A41). Hostel 100 metres on left. From National Express walk up Union St with park on right, turn right at major junction. Hostel 100m on left. Car park at rear.

CONTACT:
67 Boughton, Chester, CH3 5AF
Tel: 01244 400185
sales@chesterbackpackers.co.uk www.chesterbackpackers.co.uk

The International Inn is a multi award-winning hostel in a converted Victorian warehouse, located in the heart of Liverpool City Centre's cultural quarter.

Liverpool has a wealth of attractions for visitors and you will find theatres, heritage, two Cathedrals as well as the City's renowned nightlife venues just a stone's throw away. The Hostel is also ideally located for visiting students, being opposite the University. The International Inn provides fully heated accommodation in en-suite dormitories of 2, 4, 6, 8 and 10 beds. Private fully furnished apartments also available and newly opened cocoon pod hotel rooms. Facilities include a café, fully equipped kitchen, TV/DVD/games lounge, laundry, baggage store, internet access and information desk. There are no curfews to curtail your evening's fun.

DETAILS

- **Open** - All year, all day
- **Number of beds** - 103: 4x2, 5x4, 2x5, 1x6, 1x7, 4x8, 2x10 plus apartments
- **Booking** - Advisable at the weekend
- **Price per night** - From £15 (dorm) or £18 per person in twin room. Price includes tea, coffee, toast'n'jam 24hrs.
- **Public Transport** - Liverpool Lime Street Station 10 minutes walk away. National Express Station 10-15 minutes walk.
- **Directions** - From Lime St Station take the Skelhorn St exit. Turn left up hill and continue along Copperas Hill. At Main Road jnct. turn right along Russell St, continuing along Clarence St then Rodney St. At jnct. of Hardman St (HSBC bank on corner) turn left. South Hunter St is 2nd on left. The hostel is 20m up on the right.

CONTACT:
South Hunter Street, (off Hardman Street), Liverpool, L1 9JG
Tel: 0151 709 8135
info@internationalinn.co.uk www.internationalinn.co.uk

EMBASSIE
HOSTEL

The Embassie is a terrace house in an unspoilt Georgian square used in the filming of 'In the Name of the Father'. The house was built in 1820 and until 1986 it was the Consulate of Venezuela. Only 15 minutes walk from city centre.

Liverpool is known for it's nightlife, a student population of 70,000 ensures a lively scene, bands start playing at 11pm and bars are regularly open till 2am.

Hostellers have a key to come and go, the hostel is clean, safe and staffed 24 hours. Bedding is provided (including sheets) and free coffee, tea, toast and jam are available 24 hours, eat as much as you want. International, or UK regional travellers only, NO LOCALS.

DETAILS

- **Open** - All year, 24 hr access with key.
- **Number of beds** - 40
- **Booking** - Booking is not essential for individuals. Groups larger than 6 should book (20% deposit).
- **Price per night** - £15 (Sunday to Thursday), £17.50 (Friday), £20 (Saturday).
- **Public Transport** - Liverpool has a train station and is served by National Express Coaches. A £3.50 taxi fare will bring you from the train or bus station to the hostel door, (good idea if you have a heavy rucksack).
- **Directions** - From the Anglican Cathedral (the third largest in the world) continue uphill along Canning Street away from the city centre. This will bring you into Falkner Square (15-20 mins). The hostel has a red door and is by a phone box.

CONTACT: Kevin
1 Falkner Square, Liverpool, L8 7NU
Tel: 0151 7071089
embassie@gmail.com www.embassie.com

Recently refurbished to it's 100 year old splendour and winner of the Manchester Tourism Customer Care award, The Hatters has firmly established itself as the city's favourite funky hostel. Located in the Northern Quarter in the heart of the city centre, this is an ideal spot to start exploring the north west of England.

Hatters caters for independent travellers and groups. It has a fully serviced kitchen with seating for groups of up to 50 and free all-day continental breakfast. There is an internet cafe and free wireless connection. Let the knowledgeable and friendly staff guide you to the best that this great city has to offer, from live music and football to restaurants, shopping, museums, pubs and clubs.

Three star graded with Visit Britain.

DETAILS

- **Open** - All year, 24 hours
- **Number of beds** - 150: 1x18, 7x10, 6x8, 1x6, 2x4, 2x2, 3x1
- **Booking** - Booking recommended, essential for groups with deposit. ID is required at check in. Booking not essential for individuals.
- **Price per night** - From £14.50
- **Public Transport** - We are located only 5 minutes from Piccadilly railway station which is in the city centre. The main bus and tram station is on Piccadilly Gardens which is literally around the corner.
- **Directions** - Coming into Manchester follow signs for Piccadilly Station. Newton Street is at the top of Portland and London Piccadilly Road.

CONTACT:
50 Newton Street, Manchester, M1 2EA
Tel: 0161) 236 9500
Manchester@hattersgroup.com www.hattersgroup.com

Welcome to Hilton Chambers - Manchester's introduction to posh hostels.

Located in the Manchester's bohemian Northern Quarter in the city centre, this fresh and airy hostel offers hotel-style facilities while maintaining the fun and character of a hostel. We boast ensuite dormitories, internet access, a self-catering kitchen, a free, light, all-day breakfast, free luggage storage and much much more! Let our welcome be your guide as we give you insider hints and tips so you can experience the real Manchester and all it is famous for. We are just a stone's throw from live music, entertainment, nightclubs, bars, museums, and shops too. The famous Manchester United Stadium "Old Trafford" is just 15 minutes away by tram and City of Manchester Stadium is a short bus trip away (or a brisk walk). Come and pay us a visit soon.

DETAILS

- **Open** - All year, 24 hours
- **Number of beds** - 155 = 3 x triple ensuite, 3 x double ensuite, 4 x twin ensuite, 1 x 10 bed ensuite, 3 x 8 bed ensuite, 7 x 6 bed ensuite, 1 x 4 ensuite, 1 x 8 standard, 4 x 6 standard, 2 x 4 standard
- **Booking** - Booking not essential but recommended, especially on weekends. Photo ID (ie passport, ID card, driving license, etc) is required on check in
- **Price per night** - From £15. Please contact the hostel directly for groups
- **Public Transport** - Only 5 minutes from main train and coach stations.
- **Directions** - From Piccadilly Square follow Oldham St. At third crossroads turn right onto Hilton St. Hostel is on left after a few more steps.

CONTACT: Reception
15 Hilton Street, Manchester, M1 1JJ
Tel: 0161 236 4414
Hilton@hattersgroup.com www.hattersgroup.com/hilton

The Fylde is a centrally located Backpackers hostel ideal for walkers, cyclists and travellers looking for budget accommodation within Lancashire, the Wyre and the Fylde. Blackpool is famed for its tower, beaches, piers, trams and fairgrounds, but it has lots more to offer: cinemas, nightclubs, galleries, parks.....

Recently refurbished, The Fylde has a variety of modern, spacious and clean rooms. Facilities include a comfortable sun lounge, a spacious dining room, a games room with full sized pool table, a bar, and free parking for guests. For further information on our accommodation see website.

DETAILS

- **Open** - All year, all day. Reception open 8.00am until 10pm. Check out by 12noon.
- **Number of beds** - 28: 3x4, 1x3, 4x dbl, 2x twin, 1x1
- **Booking** - Not essential, but advisable for weekends, school holidays and Blackpool Illuminations. Credit card no. secures booking.
- **Price per night** - Midweek £15-£20pp, weekends (minimum of 2 night stay) £20-£25pp. All prices include breakfast. Reductions for longer stays.
- **Public Transport** - Trains at Blackpool North (1 mile, £4 by taxi). Talbot Road Coach Station (20 mins walk, £4 by taxi). Blackpool airport (3 miles, £8 by taxi or local bus).
- **Directions** - Turn off M55 at junction 4. Turn right at the roundabout and keep straight for about 3 miles. After four sets of traffic lights you will see CSL furniture shop. Continue along Park Road, passing Coin Age Laundry and some small B&B's. At the next set of lights on Park Road you will see Kingsley Court. Turn left at the lights on to Palatine Road and we are on the left side.

CONTACT: Vicky or Kate Easley
93 Palatine Road, Blackpool, Lancashire, FY1 4BX
Tel: 01253 623735
enquiries@fyldehotel.com   www.fyldehotel.com

BROOK HOUSE
BARN

Brook House Barn provides comfortable, self-catering accommodation ideally suited for families, groups or individuals. This high standard barn conversion has a fully equipped kitchen/dining area, drying room, utility, and a large lounge with panoramic views over the Wolds countryside. There are 2 bedrooms on the ground floor and 3 bedrooms and a small lounge on the first floor. The bedrooms have a mix of beds and bunks, bed linen is provided and all have en-suite shower rooms. A two bedroom (4/5 person) cottage converted to a similar standard (graded Visit Britain 4 *) is also available. The village of Scamblesby, at the heart of the Lincolnshire Wolds and on the Viking Way, has footpaths, bridle ways and meandering country lanes. The historic market towns of Louth and Horncastle are 10 mins drive, Lincoln, Boston and the Coastal Beaches are 1/2 hour away. Cadwell Park racing circuit, Market Rasen racecourse and the Battle of Britain and Aviation Heritage centres are nearby.

DETAILS

- **Open** - All year, flexible accesss.
- **Number of beds** - 22
- **Booking** - Booking advisable, 20% deposit, balance 1 month prior to visit.
- **Price per night** - From £20pp, family and group rates available. Whole barn hire Fri Sat Sun, 2 nights £300 per night, 3 nights £270 per night. Mon to Thurs, 2 nights £250 per night, 3 or 4 nights £220 per night. Whole barn £1500-00 per week.
- **Public Transport** - Trains: Lincoln, Grimsby. Coaches: Louth, Horncastle. Interconnect 6 (0845 234 3344) calls at Scamblesby and other villages in the Wolds.
- **Directions** - Scamblesby village is just off the main A153 Horncastle to Louth rd.

CONTACT: The Strawsons
Watery Lane, Scamblesby, Nr Louth, Lincolnshire, LN11 9XL
Tel: 01507 343266
enquiry@brookhousefarm.com   www.barnbreaks.co.uk

NABURN STATION

ENGLAND

Naburn Station is a converted railway station situated on the Trans Pennine Trail and Sustrans cycle route 65. It offers high quality accommodation ideal for cyclists and walkers. It also provides the perfect base for exploring the many delights of York and North Yorkshire with easy access to the city, the moors, the dales and the coast. The local village pub provides basic groceries and good food and there are other pubs and shops within easy walking and cycling distance. Cycle and boat hire are available locally and there are riding stables in the village. Facilities include a well equipped kitchen, a laundry and drying room, off road parking, secure bike storage and internet access. All bedding and towels are provided. No smoking. Pets and children welcome.

DETAILS

- **Open** - All year, 24 hours
- **Number of beds** - Singles/twins/double and up to 4 beds
- **Booking** - Advised in summer + bank holidays
- **Price per night** - £15pp,under 14 yrs £10. Inc:bedding, towels,tea and coffee. Camping £5 per person. 10% discount for cyclists.
- **Public Transport** - Trains at York (5 miles) and Selby (10 miles). Arriva bus 42 between Selby and York stops at bottom of the drive. Collection can be arranged from either station and local bike hire is available.
- **Directions** - On A19 from York turn right at sign to Naburn just before A64 ring road junction. From A64 Selby junction follow A19 towards York. Take first left signed Naburn. Just before the village go under the old railway bridge and turn immediately left. On Sustrans cycle route 65, 5mins walk from Naburn.

CONTACT: Ann
Station House, Naburn, York, YO19 4RW
Tel: 01904 647528 mob:07775 572 130
Saturn65@btinternet.com

Harbour Grange is Whitby's long established, friendly backpackers hostel. It is beautifully situated on the River Esk, in Whitby itself, and only 5 minutes walk from train and bus stations. The hostel is all on the ground floor and has good facilities for self-catering with a dining area and a separate lounge area, both big enough to seat 24 people. There are 5 dormitories and family rooms are available on request. The hostel is open all day but so that everyone can have a chance of a good night's sleep, there is a curfew at 11.30 (quiet at midnight). The premises are non-smoking.

Whitby is a beautiful little fishing town surrounded by beaches and moorland. Here you can find stunning views from cliff walks and visit lovely villages like Grosmont where steam trains run from Whitby to Pickering and Goathland where Heartbeat is filmed. Take a look at where Captain Cook lived and the Abbey that has stood as a landmark for 800 years.

DETAILS

- **Open** - 1st April - 31st Oct. Open all year for groups booked in advance. Hostel open all day. Check in 5pm-9pm.
- **Number of beds** - 24: 1 x 2 : 2 x 4 : 1 x 6 : 1 x 8.
- **Booking** - Booking advised for weekends and for groups, 10% deposit.
- **Price per night** - From £17 per person. Sole use £290 a night.
- **Public Transport** - Whitby has a train station and a bus station.
- **Directions** - From Whitby train and bus stations: cross the bridge and turn right. Follow the river. First right after 'The Bottom House' pub.

CONTACT: Birgitta Ward-Foxton
Spital Bridge, Whitby, North Yorkshire, YO22 4EF
Tel: 01947 600817, Mobile 0777 9798611
backpackers@harbourgrange.co.uk www.whitbybackpackers.co.uk

BRANSDALE MILL

Bransdale Mill is a converted Water Mill at the head of an unspoiled and hidden valley in the North York Moors. Accommodation is basic, but comfortable. It is an ideal base from which to get away from it all and to enjoy peace and tranquillity in beautiful countryside. There are many fine walks in the surrounding area, which is rich in wildlife. The nearest towns are Kirkbymoorside and Helmsley, both 10 miles away, and the North Yorkshire coast can be reached within an hour. The local pubs are 8 miles away, both of which serve food. Local attractions include the North Yorkshire Moors Railway; Heartbeat Country; National Trust properties at Nunnington, Rievaulx, Bridestones, and the Yorkshire Coast; Pickering and Helmsley Castles and Duncombe Park. The surrounding farmland is owned by the National Trust and let to tenant farmers; please respect the working life of the Dale.

         GROUPS ONLY

DETAILS

- **Open** - All year, All day
- **Number of beds** - 13: 1 x 7 : 1 x 6.
- **Booking** - Essential, min. 2 weeks in advance.
- **Price per night** - £120 per group (discounts may be available for small groups - please contact for details)
- **Public Transport** - National Express to Pickering. Local buses Malton (18 miles) and Kirkbymoorside. Taxi Kirkbymoorside approx £10.
- **Directions** - From Kirkbymoorside Market Place left at the mini roundabout take left fork to Fadmoor continue 9 miles. Just before the head of Bransdale see a gate with sign 'Basecamp', follow track to Mill.

CONTACT: Anne Deebank
Bransdale, Fadmoor, York, YO62 7JL
Tel: 01751 431693
anne.deebank@nationaltrust.org.uk

Situated in the Yorkshire Dales amidst stunning landscape overlooking Thruscross Reservoir in a designated Area of Outstanding Natural Beauty on the edge of the Dales National Park, this self-catering accommodation centre offers excellent facilities for up to 30 people in 9 bedrooms with bunk beds. Leaders' en-suite accommodation has private catering, dining and lounge facilities. The centre is fully centrally heated. There are 4 showers, 4 hand basins and 4 toilets. There are no extra charges for heating, lighting and hot water. The well-equipped kitchen includes a 4-oven Aga cooker, two fridges and a freezer, together with all the cooking utensils and equipment. 3 star Hostel. Ideal for Team Building Courses, Schools, Scouts, Guides and family parties etc. Located only 12 miles from Harrogate and Skipton, 30 miles from the City of York. Tourist Board inspected and managed by the owners. All groups must be accompanied by an adult (25+).

DETAILS

- **Open** - All year, flexible
- **Number of beds** - 30 :- 4 x 2 : 3 x 4 : 1 x 6 : 1 x 4 en-suite
- **Booking** - Advisable at weekends
- **Price per night** - £12.50 pp. Sole use £260 (Sat/Sun/Bank Hol), £200 any other night, £600 for 4 nights midweek. Sunday night, if staying for 2+ nights £150.
- **Public Transport** - Nearest train stations are at Harrogate and Skipton, both 12 miles from the hostel. Taxi fare from either station would be approximately £22.
- **Directions** - GR 146 575. Leave A59 at Blubberhouses, signed West End 2.5 miles. Do not turn off, centre is on left side.

CONTACT:
West End, Summerbridge, Harrogate, HG3 4BA
Tel: 01943 880207
m.verity@virgin.net www.westendoutdoorcentre.co.uk

Dalesbridge is located on the A65 at Austwick, on the edge of the Yorkshire Dales National Park, just five miles from both Ingleton and Settle. It is a comfortable venue for those visiting the Yorkshire Dales, whether you are a family, a group or an individual. The six bed units have a kitchen area with a cooker, fridge, washing up sink, shower and toilet. Crockery, cutlery and cooking pots are provided and there is a seating area in the middle of the room. The four bed units have a shower and toilet, small seating area with kettle, toaster, microwave, crockery and cutlery. These rooms are ideal for the smaller group not requiring full self-catering facilities. Utilising all the units provides group accommodation for up to 40. You will need to bring your own sleeping bag and pillow, alternatively bedding is available to hire. We have a great deal to offer: bar, drying room, functions, B&B, and campsite.

DETAILS

- **Open** - All year, reception open 9:00-17:00
- **Number of beds** - 40
- **Booking** - Advance booking with deposit
- **Price per night** - £14 per person. ~ £78 - 6 bed unit ~ £52 - 4 bed unit.
- **Public Transport** - Settle railway station is 5 miles away and Clapham station 1.5 miles. There are infrequent buses but if you would like collection from either railway station please give us a call.
- **Directions** - GR 762 676. The hostel is on the main A65. When travelling from Settle towards Ingleton we are situated on the left hand side between the two turnings into Austwick.

CONTACT: Jon
Austwick, Nr Settle, LA2 8AZ
Tel: 015242 51021
info@dalesbridge.co.uk www.dalesbridge.co.uk

LONGRIGG
RESIDENTIAL CENTRE

Longrigg Residential Centre is within walking distance of Sedbergh, only 10 miles from Kendal and less than 10 minutes from the M6, an ideal location for exploring the Lakes and the Yorkshire Dales. The centre stands in its own grounds and overlooks the unspoilt splendour of the Howgill Fells. Perfect for mixed groups or families. Walking cycling, canoeing, and caving are nearby. The centre has recently been refurbished. It has two dormitories each sleeping 6 in the main building and a larger separate building sleeping 20 in dormitories of 2,4,6 and 8. There are ample shower and toilet facilities. Sleeping bags and pillowcase are required. The large kitchen is equipped for group catering. The lounge has easy chairs and gives access to the patio area. A separate games room has pool table TV and table football. There is a drying room and tumble dryer. The Centre holds an Adventure Activity Licence and can offer instruction and equipment. Entry is by a touch lock system. The centre is owned by an Education Authority and complies with relevant Health and Safety requirements.

DETAILS

- **Open** - All year, all day
- **Number of beds** - 32: 1x8, 3x6, 1x4, 1x2
- **Booking** - Book by phone or email
- **Price per night** - £14.50, minimum of 10 people.
- **Public Transport** - Trains at Oxenholme on the West Coast Line.
- **Directions** - Longrigg Centre is located near the village of Sedbergh, which lies on the edge of the Yorkshire Dales and is just 30 minutes from the Lake District. Easy access via M6 junction 37.

CONTACT: Rob Gregory
Frostrow Lane, Sedbergh, Cumbria, LA10 5SW
Tel: 01539 621161
longrigg.centre@kencomp.net www.longrigg.org.uk

Airton Quaker Meeting house was built in 1690 by William Ellis and the adjoining hostel was originally a stable for the Quakers attending the meetings. The stable was converted into a wartime evacuee hostel in 1940 and used as a holiday hostel from 1943 with a modernisation in 1983. The meeting house is still used for worship. The hostel is situated in the centre of Airton, a typical Yorkshire Dales village on the banks of the River Aire. The Pennine Way passes the village and Malham Cove, Janet's Foss and Gordale Scar are in walking distance. The hostel has a self-catering kitchen / common area and 3 rooms, 2 with 4 bunks, 1 with 6. Blankets and pillows are provided but you must bring your own sleeping bag. There is a farm shop and café at Airton (closed Mondays) and more facilities in Gargrave. Parties of children (except families) must be accompanied by two adults. No animals permitted except guide dogs.

DETAILS

- **Open** - All year, no restrictions
- **Number of beds** - 14: 2 x 4 ; 1 x 6
- **Booking** - Advance booking is recommended with a deposit of 10%.
- **Price per night** - £10 (adults) £5 (Children under 12). Exclusive use of the hostel is available for a supplement charge.
- **Public Transport** - Nearest train stations Gargrave (4.5miles), Skipton (8.5miles). Buses from Skipton to Malham pass through Airton. Approx taxi fare from Skipton £12.
- **Directions** - GR 904 592 Block of buildings in Airton Village, on the right hand side of the road, leading down to the river bridge.

CONTACT: Mr or Mrs Parker
The Nook, Airton, Skipton, North Yorkshire, BD23 4AE
Tel: 01729 830263
bobminor@aol.com

The Golden Lion Bunkroom is part of the hotel and is situated in the Yorkshire Dales overlooking Pen-y-ghent. A newly-opened bunkhouse provides an extra 40 beds. These make an ideal base for the adventurous who are tackling the 'Three Peaks' or a welcome break for Pennine Way Walkers. It is believed that The Golden Lion was a coaching inn during the sixteenth century and the old coach highway can still be followed on foot. Three public bars provide a good selection of real ales and The Flag Floored Tap Room makes an ideal place for people who enjoy outdoor activities - even in wet weather there is no need to remove boots to enjoy a refreshing drink. Singing sessions are not uncommon. Visitors with musical instruments and plenty of enthusiasm are welcome! A variety of food can provide anything from a beefburger to an à la carte menu. Vegetarian meals are also available. There is also a 40 bed bunkhouse available close by, see entry for 3 Peaks Bunkhouse.

DETAILS

- **Open** - All year (except Christmas Day), 11am to 11pm
- **Number of beds** - 15: (Hotel Bunkroom)
- **Booking** - Booking recommended with deposit of full amount £10 pp per night.
- **Price per night** - £10pp
- **Public Transport** - Nearest train stations are Settle (6 miles) and Horton (½ mile). Three buses a day stop near to the Golden Lion Hotel. Taxi fare to Settle is approximately £5-£6.
- **Directions** - Follow signs from Settle to Horton-in-Ribblesdale. We are opposite the church.

CONTACT: Michael Johnson
Horton-in-Ribblesdale, Nr. Settle, North Yorkshire, BD24 0HB
Tel: 01729 860206, Fax: 860206
tricia@goldenlionhotel.co.uk www.goldenlionhotel.co.uk/

3 PEAKS
BUNK BARN

This newly-built bunkroom situated close to the Golden Lion Hotel in the idyllic village of Horton in Ribblesdale is available either for groups or individuals. It is in an ideal location for walking the Pennine Way, climbing the 3 Peaks (Pen-y-ghent, Ingleborough & Whernside), caving in the many potholes, exploring the Settle to Carlisle Railway, fishing at the nearby Helwith Bridge, clay pigeon shooting at Coniston Cold or for a relaxing weekend away with friends.

The bunkroom consists of 2 large bedrooms each with at least 20 beds, 4 shower rooms (1 having disabled facilities) and a drying room. There is plenty of parking space and a ¾ acre field for recreation (ideal for BBQs or picnics). Any bookings are welcome small or large: schools, colleges, universities, 4x4 groups, cyclists, hen/stag parties, all are welcome. The Golden Lion Hotel and other cafes are close-by if you require cooked breakfasts, packed lunches or bar snacks. The village has a Post Office/Stores, Cafe/Tourist Information Centre, two hotels and a useful rail link to Leeds & Carlisle.

DETAILS

- **Open** - All day. Please arrive before 10pm, let us know if this is a problem. Check out by 10am.
- **Number of beds** - 40 : 2 x 20
- **Booking** - Bookings only confirmed by payment
- **Price per night** - £12pp. Discounts for group bookings and charities.
- **Public Transport** - The Settle to Carlisle train stops in the village.
- **Directions** - In the village of Horton on the B6479 to the north of Settle.

CONTACT: Carl & Susan Johnson
1 Chapel Lane, Horton in Ribblesdale, Settle, North Yorkshire, BD24 0HA
Tel: 01729 860380 Mob: 0787 0849419
susanjohnson75@tiscali.co.uk www.3peaksbunkroom.co.uk

Wythmoor Camping Barn is on the Walney to Wear coast to coast cycle route and a few hundred metres from the Dales Way long distance footpath. It enjoys great views of the Howgill fells and the distant mountains of the Central Lakes. Being only 4.5 miles from Kendal and less than 10 mins from the M6 this is an ideal location for exploring the Lake District and the Yorkshire Dales. The 19th century barn has hot water provided by solar panels, underfloor heating powered by ground source heat pump and mains electricity supplemented by wind turbine. The barn is generously sized for twelve people and includes facilities for wheelchair users, two separate heated shower rooms and a food preparation area with sinks and cooking slabs (bring your own camping stove). Kettle and microwave are provided. Local taxis available for transport to Kendal and Sedburgh. Holmescales Farm Outdoor Centre is close by.

DETAILS

- **Open** - All year, all day
- **Number of beds** - 12: 1x12 (10 single beds, 1 double)
- **Booking** - Book online, by phone or email. Booking not always required
- **Price per night** - £7 per person.
- **Public Transport** - Oxenholme (6.5 miles) and Kendal (4.5 miles) have stations.
- **Directions** - Take Appleby Road (A685) from Kendal. After 2.5 miles turn right signed 'Docker' (single track). Opposite Docker Hall farm take left fork signed Lambrigg. Follow for 2 miles, barn is on left. From M6 Junction 37 take A684 towards Sedburgh; then direct left signed Lambrigg/Beck Foot. After 1.5 miles take left signed Lambrigg and Docker (single track). Barn is on right in half a mile.

CONTACT: Bruce Withington
Wythmoor Farm, Lambrigg, Kendal, LA8 0DH
Tel: Booking office 01946 758198, Farm mobile 07971 018567
info@lakelandcampingbarns.co.uk www.lakelandcampingbarns.co.uk

ROEBURNDALE
CAMPING BARN

Roeburndale Camping Barn is situated in a secluded meadow on the banks of the River Roeburn, and surrounded by native woodlands. It is a mile walk from the car park through woods and over a swing bridge. It is ideal for walkers, study groups or as a quiet retreat.

There are two floors and a balcony overlooking the river. The upstairs has bunk beds for 16 people. Some double and some single beds. Downstairs there are table and chairs, gas cooker and wood burning stove (wood available at £3 per bag). Plenty of eating utensils are provided. There are simple washing and compost toilet facilities. Outside there is a field and a small fireplace. There is also a yurt and a 10 bed study centre for hire - ring (015242) 21880. No dogs.

DETAILS

- **Open** - March to November (inclusive), 24 hours
- **Number of beds** - 16: 1x16 + camping
- **Booking** - At weekends sole use bookings for 2+ nights get priority. Individuals and single night bookings are only available at short notice. Pay sole use rates to secure booking in advance.
- **Price per night** - Sole use: £100 for 3 night weekend (Fri,Sat,Sun); £210 for a week; £40 for a single night. Individuals £4.50 per person (only available at short notice).
- **Public Transport** - Trains at Lancaster (12 miles) and Wennington (3 miles). Hourly buses from Lancaster bus station to Hornby or Wray, then 1 hour walk to barn.
- **Directions** - GR SD 611 650. 12 miles east of Lancaster, Junction 34 on M6. Take A683 then B6480 to Wray or Hornby.

CONTACT: Jane McArthur
Backs Bottom Farm, Roeburndale West, nr Wray, Lancaster, LA2 9LL
Tel: 08454 585795 or 015242 22214
roeburndalecampingbarn@phonecoop.coop www.middlewood.org.uk

Situated 4.5 miles from Ingleton in Yorkshire Dales limestone country. Located between Ingleborough and Whernside with superb views of both, the bunkhouse makes an ideal base for sporting or nature holidays. The area is well known for it's scenery including the Three Peaks walk, (Ingleborough, Pen-y-ghent and Whernside), the waterfalls walk and for having some of the best caves and potholes in the country including the famous Gaping Ghyll system and the White Scar show cave.

This is a stone property, which has been converted from an old school, with much of the character remaining and provides self-catering accommodation for up to 30 people. The property comprises lounge, drying room, 3 shower rooms with hand basins and toilets, well equipped kitchen / dining room with industrial cooker, toaster, fridge, freezer, dishwasher, microwave, and payphone. Nearest pub 100 yds.

            GROUPS ONLY

DETAILS

- **Open** - All year, 24 hours
- **Number of beds** - 30 (5 x 6)
- **Booking** - Early booking advised for popular times. £100 deposit for 2 nights. 25% for 3 nights or over.
- **Price per night** - Minimum of 20 people £190 per night. £9.50 per person over 20 and up to maximum of 30. Minimum of 2 nights at weekend.
- **Public Transport** - Ribblehead station 1 mile. Buses run from Ingleton 4.5 miles.
- **Directions** - 4.5 miles on the B6255 Ingleton to Hawes Road, just after Chapel-Le-Dale village on left hand side. 11 miles from Hawes on B6255.

CONTACT: Clare and Peter Fox
Chapel-le-Dale, Ingleton, Carnforth, Lancs, LA6 3AR
Tel: 01729 823835, Fax: 42327
hyginbarwick@aol.com www.oldschoolbunkhouse.co.uk

The beautiful Dentdale Valley is the ideal place for walking, caving, climbing or just enjoying the stunning views.   Three good pubs, 3 cafés and a shop just a stroll away give you the best of both worlds.

The bunkhouse is set in the grounds of historic Whernside Manor, a grade 2 listed building. This is an English Tourist Board approved bunkhouse, well equipped with cooker, microwave, b/w TV, crockery and pans. All you need is food and sleeping bags (these can be hired). Everyone loves the hot shower rooms and drying rooms.

Barbeque and outdoor eating area for hot days, cosy and heated for colder ones. The perfect place for a get together.

DETAILS

- **Open** - All year, 24 hours
- **Number of beds** - 12: 1 x 12
- **Booking** - Booking essential with 25% deposit
- **Price per night** - £10pp   Group use £90.
- **Public Transport** - Dent Station 3 miles. Coach station Kendal 15 miles. Local bus Wednesdays and Saturdays to and from Kendal and Dent.
- **Directions** - Leave M6, junction 37. Follow Sedburgh Road for approx 5 miles, then Dent road for 3 miles. Whernside Manor is approx 1.25 miles along the road past Dent Post Office.

CONTACT: Angela Johnson
Whernside Manor, Dent, Sedburgh, Cumbria, LA10 5RE
Tel: 015396 25213
whernsidemanor@aol.com www.whernsidemanor.com

Harris House is the outdoor pursuits centre of the William Hulme's Grammar School (Manchester). The centre occupies an old village school, with attached headmaster's house, on the edge of the hamlet of Hardraw. It is a grade II listed building built in 1875 in attractive Dales stone. Ample parking is available in the old playground and the large schoolroom is used for communal activities. The well appointed and practical accommodation is centrally heated throughout and can accommodate groups of up to 34. Hardraw has a camp site, a café and the Green Dragon Inn (adjacent to Hardraw Force waterfall). Many groups use these facilities to complement their visit. The café offers good value, substantial home cooking for groups. In the locality are opportunities for caving, rock climbing, fell walking and cycling (secure storage). The Pennine Way passes the centre. The local town of Hawes has a full range of shops. Harris House is an ideal base for Duke of Edinburgh's award expedition training or educational visits.

DETAILS

- **Open** - All year, 24 hours
- **Number of beds** - 32: 3x8, 2x3, 1x2
- **Booking** - Essential (20% deposit) but short notice bookings are often available.
- **Price per night** - £14 per person, min £140.
- **Public Transport** - Garsdale Station is 8 miles away, connected by infrequent buses. Hawes, a pleasant one and a half mile walk away, has more frequent buses.
- **Directions** - Turn north off A684 1 mile to the west of Hawes and proceed for ½ mile. Harris House is at the west end of the hamlet of Hardraw.

CONTACT: Warden
The Old School, Hardraw, near Hawes, Wensleydale, North Yorkshire, DL8 3LZ
Tel: 0161 226 2054
john.hardy@whgs-academy.org www.whgs.co.uk

BENTS
CAMPING BARN

Bents Camping Barn was formerly a shepherds' cottage in the 1600s. You will need sleeping bags, walking boots and warm clothes. There are 2 sleeping rooms on the first floor with bunk beds. On the ground floor there is a kitchen with cooking area, a dining area with tables and benches and a WC with washbasins. Other facilities include electric lighting and power points throughout (£1 coin meter), crockery, cutlery, toaster, microwave, 3 electric cooking rings, 2 electric kettles, 2 electric convector heaters, parking. The barn is accessible from the Coast to Coast path and there is good fell walking in the Howgill Fells, Wild Boar Fell and Crosby Garrett Common. Smardale Gill Nature Reserve and Sunbiggin Tarn are nearby. The area is ideal for mountain biking and the Settle to Carlisle Railway is 5 miles away at Kirkby Stephen.

DETAILS

■ **Open** - All year, all day
■ **Number of beds** - 12 to 14: 1x10, 1x6
■ **Booking** - Booking is essential for groups (2 weeks in advance with deposit). Individuals are advised to phone.
■ **Price per night** - £7 per person.   Sole use £72 per night.
■ **Public Transport** - Train station at Kirkby Stephen (5 miles).   Local buses to village of Newbiggin-on-Lune.
■ **Directions** - GR MY 708 065 OS map 91. From Junction 38 of the M6 take the A685 to Newbiggin-on-Lune. Take Great Asby Road on left then first right through tall gate. Follow tarmac road past Tower House and follow signs to Bents Farm up farm track.

CONTACT: Dorothy Ousby
Newbiggin-on-Lune, Kirkby-Stephen, Cumbria, CA17 4NX
Tel: Booking 01946 758198 Dorothy 01768 371760
info@lakelandcampingbarns.co.uk www.bentscampingbarn.co.uk

KIRKBY STEPHEN
HOSTEL

UNDER NEW OWNERSHIP SINCE APRIL 2008. Kirkby Stephen Hostel is a former Methodist church with substantial additions. The old chapel now accommodates a large dining room and kitchens, with a lounge/reading room in the gallery. The bedrooms and dormitories are in a building at the rear, with ample lavatories and showers. The hostel features the original stained glass windows, pews, pulpit and organ.

Kirkby Stephen is a pleasant market town in the upper Eden valley, situated 15 miles from Kendal, 15 miles from Hawes and on Wainwright's coast to coast path and the W2W cycle path. It also enjoys easy access to Lady Anne's Walk, the Howgill Hills, the Dales National Park and the Lake District. The hostel stands prominently on the main street, with a range of restaurants, cafes, pubs, fish and chip shops and food shops on the doorstep. Paragliding is also available in Kirkby Stephen.

DETAILS

- **Open** - All year, please arrive after 5pm
- **Number of beds** - 40: 1x8, 3x6, 2x4, 2x2, 1x2 ensuite
- **Booking** - Book by phone. Booking advised but not essential.
- **Price per night** - £18pp. Reductions for groups.
- **Public Transport** - One mile from Kirkby Stephen train station on the Leeds-Carlisle line. Regular buses from Penrith, Kendal and Appleby stop outside hostel.
- **Directions** - In the centre of town on main road. From M6 leave at junction 38 and follow signs towards Appleby.

CONTACT: Denise
Market Street, Kirkby Stephen, Yorkshire, CA17 4QQ
Tel: 0870 770 5904 or 01768 371793 or 07812 558 525
sam@backpackerspress.com www.IndependentHostelsUK.co.uk

Fell End, overlooking the unspoilt Howgill Fells, consists of two 18th-century buildings providing comfortable bunk-house accommodation for people wishing to explore this beautiful area. Perfect for mixed groups, families and people with special needs or mobility difficulties. Walking, cycling, canoeing and caving nearby and the Lake District only 1 hour away. The Schoolhouse (white building) sleeps 8 people in bunks in the central area with an extra bed in an adjoining room. There is a fully equipped kitchen with fridge/freezer and cooker. The bathroom has two toilets, one shower and 4 wash basins. Greenslack has a further 2 bunks and 1 single bed plus a bathroom designed for people with mobility problems, but has no kitchen so can't be booked separately. The living room has a multi-fuel stove, which also heats the radiators. Entry is by a touch lock system. Dogs allowed under strict supervision. Fell End is owned by the Bendrigg Trust, a charity offering outdoor activities for disabled people. To discuss the facilities available please contact Lynne Irish.

DETAILS

- **Open** - All year, 24 hours
- **Number of beds** - 14: 1 x 8 : 1 x 5 : 1 x 1.
- **Booking** - Advance booking with 20% deposit
- **Price per night** - £9pp + VAT. Minimum booking: 6 for Schoolhouse only, 8 for both buildings.
- **Public Transport** - Trains at Kirkby Stephen (6 miles) on the Carlisle/Settle/Leeds line. Then take bus 564 Mon to Sat (4 per day). Tel 0870 6082 608 for times.
- **Directions** - GR:723983(Postcode CA17 4LN). Directions given on booking.

CONTACT: Lynne Irish
Bendrigg Trust, Old Hutton, Kendal LA8 0NR
Tel: 01539 723766, Fax: 01539 722446
Lynne@bendrigg.org.uk www.fellend-bunkhouse.org.uk

MARSETT
BARN

Marsett Barn is a back to nature experience, it is an old barn in an old landscape. The barn is basic but full of character and charm and has been sympathetically restored to retain its special place in this dales setting.

On the ground floor there is an entrance area with living and dining space, a wood burning stove, a fully fitted kitchen, a drying area, and a toilet for people with disabilities.
Upstairs there are two sleeping areas, each with platform to sleep 20 people. Also toilets with handbasins and showers.

Activities may be available at Low Mill Outdoor Centre from £100 per session.

A list of activities is available on request.

DETAILS

- **Open** - All year,
- **Number of beds** - Sleeps approx 20 people
- **Booking** - Booking is essential
- **Price per night** - £9 per person (minimum of £36 per night) includes gas.
- **Public Transport** - The nearest bus stop is Bainbridge (4 miles) and nearest train station Garsdale (11 miles).
- **Directions** - From Marsett Green, access is normally on foot or cycle.   From the green, follow the track on left towards Stalling Busk. The Barn is in a field on the right, approximately ½ kilometre from the green.

CONTACT:
c/o Low Mill Outdoor Centre, Askrigg, Leyburn, North Yorkshire, DL8 3HZ
Tel: 01969 650432
info@lowmill.com www.lowmill.com

New Ing Lodge offers comfort and tranquillity at an affordable price, in the beautiful Lake District National Park. The Wainwright Coast to Coast walk passes the building and some of the best mountain biking routes in Britain are on the doorstep. Maps and guides are available for walkers, mountain bikes can be hired (with a special rate for residents), and there is an orienteering course outside the back door. Kayaking, climbing, wilderness camping and bushcraft skill courses can be arranged.

New Ing Lodge is at the north-east of the Lake District National Park. Ideal for hiking on High Street Roman Road, the Haweswater Valley, the Eden Valley and the less-visited Howgill Fells. For a more relaxed day, there is Shap Abbey, or the Rheged Discovery Centre with an Imax cinema and the National Mountain Exhibition. New Ing is ideal for individuals, groups or a families. Activity breaks for children (with out without their parents) are run by the owner, who is a school Head of Sports teacher.

DETAILS

- **Open** - All year, all day, contact between 7am & 11pm
- **Number of beds** - 20: 1x8, 1x6, 1x4, 1x2
- **Booking** - Not essential. As soon as possible in advance. Deposit 10%.
- **Price per night** - £12.50 per person without bedding, £14 with bedding. Discounts for larger groups, and longer stays – please request.
- **Public Transport** - By bus from Penrith station. Pick-up from station is possible.
- **Directions** - at the north end of Shap Village, just 20 metres off the A6 opposite the supermarket. Kendal 17 miles, Penrith 12 miles. M6 Junction 39 2 miles.

CONTACT: Andy or Scott
New Ing Lodge, Shap, Penrith, Cumbria, CA10 3LX
Tel: 01931 716719 or 07792 222881
andy@newinglodge.co.uk www.newinglodge.co.uk

STABLES
LODGE

Cartmel is a picturesque village located at the southern end of the Lake District Peninsula, close to the northern shore of Morecambe Bay. Cartmel is an ideal base for exploring the Lake District and surrounding areas. It is popular with families, walkers and cyclists, who appreciate a friendly relaxed environment, wonderful scenery and easy access to both mountains and the coast.

The hostel provides affordable self-catering accommodation, with shower and toilet facilities, a common room and a fully equipped kitchen. All you need to bring is a sleeping bag. There is ample free parking, secure bike storage, and both children and dogs are welcome.

DETAILS

- **Open** - All year, by arrangement (office Mon -Fri 9am-4.45pm)
- **Number of beds** - 19: 3 x 2, 1 x 3, 1 x 4, 1 x 6
- **Booking** - Give 24 hours notice at weekends.
- **Price per night** - £10 per person
- **Public Transport** - Trains at Grange-over-Sands and Cark, both approximately 3 miles away, and an hourly bus service operates Monday – Saturday from each. Bus links to Grange-over-Sands are also available from Kendal and Barrow-in-Furness. Information is available from Traveline on 0870 6082608
- **Directions** - Stables Lodge is located in the grounds of Cartmel Racecourse. From the village square, turn right at the Sticky Toffee Pudding shop, and the entrance to Stables Lodge is located on your right hand side past the last house (approx 400 metres). Registration is at the Racecourse Office at the Grandstand on the opposite side of the road.

CONTACT:
The Racecourse, Cartmel, Cumbria, LA11 6QF
Tel: 015395 36340
info@cartmel-racecourse.co.uk www.cartmel-racecourse.co.uk

DUDDON SANDS
HOSTEL
ENGLAND

The purpose built Duddon Sands Hostel, overlooking the Duddon Estuary, stands in the grounds of The Ship, a cosy village inn built in 1691 and known for its friendly atmosphere, good ales and ghost story. The pub has a beautiful beer garden with estuary views, barbecue and brazier which guests can use. The pub is open Thurs (Quiz night), Fri and Sat evenings, and Sun on request for large groups. It does not serve meals but there are two other pubs in the village which do and several take-aways in nearby villages. The hostel has a kitchen/diner for self catering and groups who hire the whole hostel can use a large kitchen and dining/sitting room (with large screen TV) in the pub. A cook/chef can be hired by arrangement. All bedding is provided (not towels) and a cot is available. There are many tourist attactions nearby, and outdoor activities can be arranged through the hostel. Bike wash & storage is available. Come and celebrate any event, summer solstice, a big birthday or just Friday again!

DETAILS

- **Open** - All year, all day (phone to arrange arrival)
- **Number of beds** - 19 : 2x4, 1x8 + cot + 2-3 air beds (half price)
- **Booking** - Recommended, especially for large groups. A deposit required.
- **Price per night** - From £13 per person. Special rates 4 nights sole use Mon to Thurs £550, 3 nights sole use Fri to Sun £550.
- **Public Transport** - Train: request stop at Kirkby. Bus: Take X7 (Barrow-in-Furness to Millom) and get off at Moorland Stores in Kirkby, follow signs for hostel.
- **Directions** - At Moorland Stores crossroads on A595 in centre of Kirkby take turn for Sandside and Train Station. Hostel is at bottom of hill.

CONTACT:
The Ship Inn, Askewgate Brow, Kirkby-in-Furness, Cumbria, LA17 7TE
Tel: 01229 889454
theship1691@googlemail.com www.theship1691.co.uk

THE WALKERS HOSTEL

On the edge of the Lake District, the Walkers Hostel has 30 beds with between 2 and 9 beds to a room. Light Breakfast is included in the price which includes cereals, toast, fruit juice and tea or coffee. We have a reasonably well stocked book shelf with guide books, maps and books of general interest. There is a no smoking policy in the house and grounds, a cycle lockup, a drying room and an open fire. We enjoy the company of our guests. WiFi available. Ulverston is an old market town with plenty of good pubs. The Cumbria Way starts at Ulverston and there are street markets on Thursdays and Saturdays as well as other attractions. The lighthouse on Hoad Hill is a famous landmark and is adjacent to the Walkers Hostel, which is ideally suited for long and short walks. We are happy to give advice on how to get the most from your visit and scenery. Whole hostel booking enquiries welcome for walkers or corporate groups.

DETAILS

- **Open** - All year except a couple of days at Christmas., flexible hours.
- **Number of beds** - 30: 1x9, 1x8 1x6, 1x5 1x2
- **Booking** - Booking is advisable, not essential.
- **Price per night** - £16.50 per person.
- **Public Transport** - Ulverston has a good train service. National Express Coaches and local Stage Coach buses also come to Ulverston - Enquires tel 0870 608 2608.
- **Directions** - From M6 Jn 36 take the A590. On the edge of Ulverston there is a roundabout. Turn left, and left again. From the bus or train station, walk towards town. Turn right down A590. We are just beyond the second roundabout.

CONTACT: Derek or Jocelynne Bigland
Oubas House, 1 Oubas Hill, Ulverston, Cumbria, LA12 7LB
Tel: 01229 480511
info@thewalkershostel.co.uk www.thewalkershostel.co.uk

Fell End is a traditional 18th Century Lakeland stone barn, located within its own grass courtyard approximately ½ mile from the farm. It is in the centre of a 500 acre estate in the western fells with easy access to some spectacular scenery, ideal for walkers, cyclists and wildlife enthusiasts. It is a short drive from Coniston (6 miles) and the Duddon Valley (5 miles). There are magnificent views, star-filled skies (a truly breathtaking sight) and the tranquil 'sound of silence'. Fell End Barn is lit by chandeliers and tea lights (provided) and heated by woodburing stove (a gas heater is also available for hire). There is no electricity and you will need to bring your own cooking and lighting equipment and bedding with mat. There are 2 picnic style tables, a wash basin and WC. Ideal for campfires or BBQs. Wood is available from the farm. Check the website www.lakelandcampingbarns.co.uk and book online..

DETAILS

- **Open** - All year, all day
- **Number of beds** - 12: 1x12
- **Booking** - Book online. Booking in advance is essential.
- **Price per night** - £7.00 per person
- **Public Transport** - Trains: Foxfield (3 miles). Buses: Grizebeck (3 miles).
- **Directions** - Leave M6 at J36, follow the A590 towards Barrow. Near Greenodd Estuary take A5092 signed to Broughton-in-Furness. Follow this road until you reach Grizebeck. Just before Grizebeck garage take lane on right signposted 'Woodland'. Follow for 2 miles, over a cattle grid, until road becomes level. Take lane on left signed 'Woodland Hall' and follow for 1 mile.

CONTACT: Booking office / Jean
Thornthwaite farm, Woodland, Broughton in Furness, Cumbria, LA20 6DF
Tel: Booking office 01946 758198, Farm 01229 716 340
info@lakelandcampingbarns.co.uk www.lakelandcampingbarns.co.uk

ROOKHOW
CENTRE

Perhaps the best situated small hostel in the Lake District. Peaceful, in 12 acres of its own woodland, but close to the heart of the Lakes, ten minutes from Coniston Water and Windermere, and on the edge of the famous Grizedale Forest Park with its trails and sculptures.   Superb area for walking, cycling and all outdoor activities. Also for quiet retreat, relaxation, study and artistic pursuits. The Rookhow Centre is within the former stables of the nearby historic Quaker meeting house which is also available for conferences and group sessions.
Guests find the centre warm, comfortable and well equipped. It has electric heating and an optional wood burning stove. There are three sleeping areas, a self-catering kitchen/dining area and picnic tables and barbecue for warm days.
There is a bonfire area within the centre's private woodand.

DETAILS

- **Open** - All year, all day
- **Number of beds** - 20: 1x9 : 1x8 : plus extra on bed settees. Also camping.
- **Booking** - Booking is essential (deposit).
- **Price per night** - From :- Adult £14.00, £7.00 for under 16's. Sole use £150
- **Public Transport** - Trains at Grange-over-Sands (11 miles, approx £20 by taxi). A seasonal bus service sometimes operates to the hostel - check with the warden
- **Directions** - GR 332 896. From A590 leave at Greenodd (A5092) junction and follow sign for Workington for ¼ mile. Take minor road to right signed Oxen Park. Continue through Oxen Park for a further 2 miles, Rookhow is on left. From Ambleside : to Hawkshead, then to Grizedale. Continue beyond Grizedale for 3.5 miles (Satterthwaite to Ulverston Road). Rookhow is on the right.

CONTACT: Warden
Rusland, Grizedale, Cumbria, South Lakeland, LA12 8LA
Tel: 01229 860231 Mob: 0794 350 8100
straughton@btinternet.com

HIGH WRAY
BASECAMP

Situated in the heart of South Lakeland in secluded woodland, 4 miles from the village of Ambleside, High Wray Basecamp provides an ideal base for groups wishing to explore and take part in activities in the Lake District Area. Local attractions include rambling, fell walking, climbing and water sports, with the Basecamp Warden being happy to assist with information on local walks and activities. The Longland Block has two separate fully centrally heated dormitories each sleeping 8, with a separate washing and living area/kitchen block. The comfortable living area is heated by a central wood burning stove and the kitchen has a commercial gas cooker, fridge freezer, microwave and utensils. The Acland block has two separate centrally heated dormitories sleeping 8 each, with toilet and shower room attached. The kitchen/lounge area is fitted with commercial gas cooker, fridges, microwave and utensils.

       GROUPS ONLY

DETAILS

- **Open** - All year, 24 hours
- **Number of beds** - 16 + 20
- **Booking** - Booking with deposit of £50
- **Price per night** - Longland £9.25pp (Mon-Thur), £11pp (Fri-Sun). Acland £9.75pp (Mon-Thur), £11.50pp (Fri-Sun).
- **Public Transport** - Nearest train station Windermere 8 miles. Local bus (505 'Coniston Rambler' Windermere - Hawkshead) stops 2 miles away at turning to Wray Castle (Cumbria travel-line 0870 6082608)
- **Directions** - GR: 373 995 Take A593 from Ambleside towards Coniston, bear left onto the B5286 signed Hawkshead, fork left for High Wray village, signed Wray Castle. Basecamp is ¼ mile up dirt road on the left at the end of High Wray village.

CONTACT:
High Wray, Ambleside, Cumbria, LA22 0JE
Tel: 015394 34633
paul.kear@nationaltrust.org.uk

LAKE DISTRICT
BACKPACKERS

Situated in the heart of Windermere and central Lakeland, you will find our cosy, friendly hostel ideally situated for exploring the surrounding area. We can advise you on routes for walks and cycle rides and provide you with maps. We are often asked to help organise abseiling, canoeing, sailing, windsurfing, even caving! There is easy access to the lake and fells from our door and we are adjacent to the main 555 bus route through Lakeland.

The hostel with its small dormitories provides you with every comfort but at a budget price. We are right next to a number of pubs, restaurants and take-aways and only minutes away from the rail and bus stations. Lockers are available and internet access and Sky keep you in touch!
A well equipped kitchen and comfortable common room make your stay one to remember.

DETAILS

- **Open** - All year, 24 hours
- **Number of beds** - 20:- 1x7, 2 x 4, 1x 3, 1 x2
- **Booking** - Essential, 24 hours in advance.
- **Price per night** - £14.50 (£12.50 per night for 3 nts or more). Price includes self service continental breakfast and free tea/coffee.
- **Public Transport** - Windermere train station is 2 minutes walk. National Express Coach stop 2 minutes walk.
- **Directions** - Turn left out of station, walk to information centre, hostel is opposite, next to Simpson and Parsons Insurance Company.

CONTACT: Paul
High Street, Windermere, Cumbria, LA23 1AF
Tel: 015394 46374, Fax: 015394 88611
fletcher_recruitment@yahoo.co.uk www.lakedistrictbackpackers.co.uk

Kentmere is a quiet, unspoilt valley within the Lake District National Park. It's a ramblers' paradise with woods, fields, lanes, a scattering of traditional lakeland farms and dwellings, and of course the fells with their walks so favoured by Wainwright. The Lakeland to Lindisfarne Long Distance path passes this way as well as the mountain bikers' and horse riders' Coast to Coast. Kentmere offers plenty of activities which include biking, riding and fishing, but most of all quiet enjoyment. A pleasant day's visit can be found at the market town of Kendal and Lake Windermere which are only 20 minutes away. The recently converted Barn has two sleeping areas, fully fitted kitchen, two showers and toilets. All you need is your sleeping bag, mattresses provided. Breakfasts and suppers are available next door at the B&B.

DETAILS

- **Open** - All year, 24 hours
- **Number of beds** - 14:   1 x 4   1 x 10
- **Booking** - Recommended with 50% deposit for groups. Individuals can book but not essential
- **Price per night** - £10.00 per person or £100 sole use. There will be a surcharge for a single night booking on a Friday or Saturday night.
- **Public Transport** - Staveley 4 miles with train and bus service. Oxenholme train station is 10 miles. Kendal/Windermere National Express 8 miles.
- **Directions** - GR 462 041, MAP OS English Lakes South East. Green Quarter. Leave the A591 and come into Staveley, proceed to Kentmere for 4 miles, then take right fork to Green Quarter keeping right until you reach Maggs Howe.

CONTACT: Christine Hevey
Maggs Howe, Kentmere, Kendal, Cumbria, LA8 9JP
Tel: 01539 821689
enquiry@maggshowe.co.uk   www.maggshowe.co.uk

AMBLESIDE
BACKPACKERS

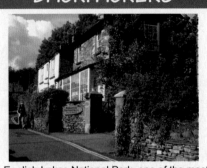

Get away to The English Lakes National Park, one of the most beautiful scenic areas in the UK. The hostel is in a marvellous location with fell and mountain walks, boating, scenic drives, cycle touring, mountain biking and outdoor activities practically from the doorstep. Set just 4 minutes walking from the centre of Ambleside it is also a great centre for visiting places made famous by Wordsworth, Ruskin and Beatrix Potter. Ambleside is excellent for shopping and eating out with many outdoor equipment shops, restaurants and pubs. With 66 beds Ambleside Backpackers can accommodate groups as well as individuals in either single sex or mixed dorms. A large, traditional Lakeland cottage featuring a great lounge with a fire and piano, dining room, large well equipped kitchen for your use - not to mention central heating, showers and washing/drying facilities. Reasonably priced light breakfast, free internet access, free tea/coffee, friendly helpful staff, and good bus links to most fell walk starts and lakes makes this hostel the ideal base.

DETAILS

- **Open** - Open most of the year, all day
- **Number of beds** - 66: 1x14, 1x12, 2x7, 2x6, 3x4, 1x2
- **Booking** - Recommended, essential for groups, deposit required.
- **Price per night** - £18pp. £15pp for three or more nights. Special winter breaks.
- **Public Transport** - Windermere train station 4 miles then 555 bus to Ambleside.
- **Directions** - From Ambleside bus stop: up hill to T junction, across road to Old Lake Rd, 200m up on left.– By road : A591 Windermere to Ambleside. At 2nd Hayes Garden Ctr. sign. turn right into Old Lake Rd. 300m on right.

CONTACT:
Ambleside BP's, Iveing Cottage, Old Lake Rd, Ambleside Cumbria, LA22 0DJ
Tel: 015394 32340
bookings@amblesidebackpackers.com www.amblesidebackpackers.com

STICKLEBARN
BUNKHOUSE

The Sticklebarn is beautifully situated amidst some of the finest mountain scenery in England. It is at the very foot of the famous Langdale Pikes and Dungeon Ghyll waterfalls and seven miles north west of Ambleside. The Sticklebarn is privately owned and is available to the general outdoor public and traveller on foot.

The bunkhouse has no common room or self-catering facilities but meals are provided in the pub. Sorry no pets are allowed in the bunkhouse. A brochure is available on request. Food served 12noon to 2.30pm and 6pm to 9.30pm. Saturdays, Sundays and bank holidays: 12noon to 9.30pm. Breakfasts available between 8.30am and 11.00am weekends, 9am and 10.30am during week. Live music every weekend from March to end of October. Check out the weather via our webcam on the Langdale Website.

DETAILS

- **Open** - All year, all day
- **Number of beds** - Winter 20, Summer 8
- **Booking** - Pre-booking is advised for weekends and groups and requires a 50% deposit.
- **Price per night** - £12.00 per person
- **Public Transport** - Bus service 516 to Great Langdale from Ambleside, ask for New Dungeon Ghyll Hotel, walk 2 mins (timetable 01946 632222).
- **Directions** - From the A591 Windermere to Keswick road at Ambleside take the A593 turn to Coniston / Torver. After two miles take the B5343 to Great Langdale via Chapel Stile. The Bunkhouse is adjacent to the Sticklebarn Tavern.

CONTACT: Terry or Lorna Graham
Sticklebarn Tavern, Great Langdale, LA22 9JU
Tel: 015394 37356
sticklebarn@aol.com www.langdaleweb.co.uk

RYDAL HALL
BUNKHOUSE
ENGLAND

The Bunkhouse is situated in the centre of Rydal Hall estate, sheltered on three sides by the Fairfield Horseshoe and offering access to the best of Lakeland's activities. Facilities inside provide the necessities for groups of up to 36. There are 2 dormitories sleeping 14 and 18 in bunk beds and 2 leader rooms each sleeping 2. There is a large common room which can be used for dining or recreation. A welcoming log burner provides additional warmth to the ample heating powered by our nearby water turbine. The kitchen is fully furnished for cooking en masse and there are 2 separate toilet facilities with showers. Laundry and drying facilities are close by and a games room with table tennis and pool is available on request. Users need to bring sleeping bags, pillow cases and extra blankets during winter. Rydal Hall also offers camping to organised groups and there is comfortable residential accommodation for up to 56 at the Hall in single, twin, double and family rooms.

DETAILS

- **Open** - All year, 24 hours
- **Number of beds** - Bunkhouse 36: 1x14, 1x18, 2x2
- **Booking** - Required with deposit. No bookings by email please.
- **Price per night** - Sole use Nov-Mar (excl.Xmas & New Year) £180, Apr-Oct £270 10% discount for youth groups + midweek. Individual bookings by arrangement.
- **Public Transport** - Trains at Windermere. National Express at Ambleside. Local stagecoach service (555) from Lancaster to Keswick stops 200 yards from Hall.
- **Directions** - GR 366 064. Take the A561 from Ambleside to Grasmere, Rydal is reached after 2 miles. By the church turn right and go up lane for 200m.

CONTACT:
Rydal Hall, Ambleside, Cumbria, LA22 9LX
Tel: 01539 432 050, Fax: 01539 434 887
mail@rydalhall.org www.rydalhall.org

GRASMERE
INDEPENDENT HOSTEL

This small deluxe hostel is situated on a farm right at the heart of the Lakes. See the best of Lakeland right from our doorstep. Give the car a holiday. Take the Wordsworth walk around Grasmere and Rydal Lake, or do a mountain classic, climb Helvellyn or Fairfield from our door. The Coast to Coast footpath goes right through the farm. Over 101 other local attractions and activities, including a good pub with fine bar meals just 300 yds down the road. Our English Tourism Council 4 star graded hostel has en-suite bedrooms with made up beds (sheets & duvets), lockers, bedside lights, a coin operated sauna, commercial laundry, drying room, dining room, 2 self-catering kitchens with microwaves, fridges, toasters etc. A stunning common room with large TV, a lockable bike/luggage store and private parking. We are resident proprietors. Cleanliness and friendliness assured. Totally non-smoking. Individuals, families and groups all welcome. Please always check availability by phone.

DETAILS

- **Open** - All year (winter, subject to minimum numbers), 8am to 10pm, (keys issued)
- **Number of beds** - 24: 1 x 3 : 1 x 4 : 1 x 5 : 2 x 6.
- **Booking** - Advisable, credit card confirms bed.
- **Price per night** - From £18.50pp (bedding inc). Groups please apply.
- **Public Transport** - Train to Windermere (11 miles from hostel), catch 555 bus from Windermere or Keswick, ask for Travellers Rest Pub. There is also a National Express coach that runs between London/Grasmere daily.
- **Directions** - GR 336 094. 1.25 miles north of village. Stay on main A591 right to our drive, 400m north of Travellers Rest Pub on the right hand side.

CONTACT: Mr Bev Dennison
Broadrayne Farm, Keswick Road, Grasmere, Cumbria, LA22 9RU
Tel: 015394 35055
Bev@grasmerehostel.co.uk www.grasmerehostel.co.uk

MURT BARN
CAMPING BARN

Murt is a traditional farm, dating from 1728, situated in the Wasdale valley. The camping barn is a converted stone hayloft and byre, attached to the farmhouse, with stunning views to the Scafell Massif, and the surrounding fells. Sleeping accommodation and cooking area are on the first floor, reached by an internal wooden staircase. The shower, toilet and washing up facilities are downstairs. Electricity is metered (£1 coins) and provides light, water heater, hot shower, electric heater and a power point. Car parking is adjacent to the barn. You need to bring a sleeping bag/mat and stove and eating utensils if you wish to self cater. Murt is 3/4 mile from Wastwater and is an ideal base for high fell walks including Scafell Pike, Mosedale Horseshoe, Great Gable etc. There is direct access to footpaths and bridle-ways. For those interested in flora and fauna, the Wasdale valley has great variety, and coastal dune walks, Muncaster Castle and Ravensglass (for the Eskdale railway) are all only a stones throw away. There are 2 pubs in the village, 10 minutes walk from the Barn.

DETAILS

- **Open** - All year, arrive after 4pm.
- **Number of beds** - 8: 1x8
- **Booking** - Booking recommended. Book online.
- **Price per night** - £7 per person. Sole use w/ends and bank/hols £56 per night.
- **Public Transport** - Seascale station, then taxi to Wasdale.
- **Directions** - From the A595, follow signs to Santon Bridge and Wasdale. After approx. 2 miles, bear sharp left over bridge, and sharp right immediately afterwards. At junction turn right, to Wasdale Head, and Murt is the 2nd gate on left.

CONTACT:
Murt, Nether Wasdale, Seascale, Cumbria, CA20 1ET
Tel: Booking office 01946 758198
info@lakelandcampingbarns.co.uk www.wasdaleweb.co.uk

TARN FLATT
CAMPING BARN
ENGLAND

Tarn Flatt Camping Barn is a traditional sandstone barn on St Bees Head overlooking the Scottish coastline and the Isle of Man. It is on a working farm which also includes a lighthouse, RSPB bird reserve on 100 metre cliffs and access to Fleswick Bay - a secluded shingle cove. There is canoeing and fishing in the area and the rock climbing and boulders at the base of the cliff are superb. There are several local circular walks with panoramic views of the coast and the fells and easy access to the quieter western Lakeland fells and lakes. The award-winning historic Georgian town and harbour of Whitehaven is only 3 miles away and St Bees (the starting point of the Coast to Coast walk) is 2 miles via the coastal path. The barn has a raised wooden sleeping area on the ground floor. There is electric light, a cooking slab (please bring your own stove and utensils) and an open fire (wood available from the farm). Toilets, wash-basin and showers are in adjacent buildings. Meals are available by arrangement. Children welcome. Dogs are accepted in sole use only.

DETAILS

- **Open** - All year, 24 hours
- **Number of beds** - 12 bed spaces.
- **Booking** - Booking in advance is advised.
- **Price per night** - £7 per person.
- **Public Transport** - Trains at Whitehaven (4 miles) and St Bees (3 miles). Buses also at Whitehaven.
- **Directions** - GR 947 146. With Sandwith village green on right, pass row of houses and turn right, at phone box take private road for 1 mile.

CONTACT: Janice Telfer
Tarn Flatt Hall, Sandwith, Whitehaven, Cumbria, CA28 9UX
Tel: Detail 01946 692162, Booking 01946 758198
stay@tarnflattfarm.co.uk www.tarnflattfarm.co.uk

DINAH HOGGUS
CAMPING BARN

Dinah Hoggus Camping Barn is situated on the old Packhorse route to Watendlath. It is right on the Cumbria Way and Coast to Coast routes.

The sleeping area is on the first floor and 12 mattresses are provided. There is a cooking and eating area on the ground floor with tables and benches. There is mains electricity and water, a small electric ring cooker, micro-wave, electric kettle, toaster, clothes dryer and electric heaters. The toliet/shower room is at the end of the building and has a hot electric shower and washbasin. Electricity is charged extra. Meter reading at start and end of stay. The pub is 300yds away and village shop 200yds.

Check the website www.lakelandcampingbarns.co.uk and book on line.

DETAILS

- **Open** - All year, all day
- **Number of beds** - 12
- **Booking** - Book online
- **Price per night** - £7 per person
- **Public Transport** - The local bus service out of Keswick stops at Hazel Bank Lane End (Rosthwaite), just 100yds from the barn.
- **Directions** - The camping barn is situated on the outskirts of the village of Rosthwaite in Borrowdale. Take the B5289 road out of Keswick up the Borrowdale Valley for approx 6 miles. When you see the Rosthwaite village sign take first left (Hazel Bank Lane) over the hump bridge and into the left. Park beside the barn.

CONTACT:
Thorneythwaite Farm, Borrowdale, Keswick, Cumbria, CA12 5XQ
Tel: Booking office 01946 758198, Farm 017687 77237
info@lakelandcampingbarns.co.uk www.lakelandcampingbarns.co.uk

Cragg Barn Camping Barn is a traditional stone-built barn with stunning views of Buttermere fells. It has a kitchen and seating area with a sink and cold running water. There is a hot shower on a meter and a toilet and washbasin with hot and cold water. The sleeping area has 8 mattresses, bring your own sleeping bag. You need a stove and eating utensils if you wish to self cater. Cragg Barn is a great base for walkers of all abilities. It is also ideal for climbing, fishing and wildlife/bird-watching. There are many local tourist attractions within a short drive. Cragg House Farm also has a holiday cottage sleeping 2. Check the websites www.buttermerecottage.co.uk or www.lakelandcampingbarns.co.uk and book on line.

DETAILS

- **Open** - All year, all day, late arrivals by arrangement.
- **Number of beds** - 8: 1 x 8
- **Booking** - Booking essential at least 24 hrs in advance. Book online.
- **Price per night** - £7 per person.
- **Public Transport** - Train stations at Penrith / Workington. Bus links from Penrith station and Workington town centre to Keswick. Bus runs seasonally from Keswick.
- **Directions** - GR NY 173 171. From Keswick follow signs to Borrowdale, continue through Rosthwaite, Seatoller and over Honister Pass. Continue past Buttermere lake into Buttermere village. Keep on main road. Cragg House Farm is on the left on the brow of the hill before you get to NT carpark. In icy conditions approach from Cockermouth town centre and continue through Lorton. Turn left to Buttermere following road signs. Cragg Farm is 1st on the right past the Buttermere village sign.

CONTACT:
Cragg House Farm, Buttermere, Cockermouth, Cumbria, CA13 9XA
Tel: Camping Barn 01946 758198. Holiday Cottage 017687 70204
info@lakelandcampingbarns.co.uk www.buttermerecottage.co.uk

Towards the head of Ennerdale valley, one of the most beautiful, least spoilt and quietest valleys in the Lake District, sitting at the foot of Pillar and Red Pike you will find Low Gillerthwaite. An ideal base for fell walking, classic rock climbs, bird and wildlife watching, mountain biking, orienteering (we have our own permanent beginners course), canoeing (instruction available for groups) and environmental studies. Originally a 15th-century farmhouse, the Centre has group self-catering facilities, drying room, a library of environmental books, a group lecture room and two lounges with log burning fires. Due to its remoteness the Centre generates its own electricity. Vehicle access is by forest track and a BT payphone is on site (most mobiles do not work here).

Low Gillerthwaite is an ideal base for clubs, extended family groups, school and youth groups. More information can be found on our website.

DETAILS

- **Open** - All year, except Christmas and Boxing Day, 24 hours
- **Number of beds** - 40: 2x4 : 1x8 : 1x10 : 1x14
- **Booking** - Always phone to check availability
- **Price per night** - From £9.50 per person, camping is £4.00.
- **Public Transport** - Whitehaven Station 12 miles. Buses to Ennerdale Bridge from Cleator Moor or Cockermouth (5miles).
- **Directions** - GR NY 139 141. From Ennerdale Bridge take road east, via Croasdale, 3.5 miles to Ennerdale Forest. Continue on forest track 3 miles. Hostel is the first building below the RH road, 200m before the YHA.

CONTACT:
Ennerdale, Cleator, CA23 3AX
Tel: 01946 861229
Warden@lgfc.org.uk www.lgfc.org.uk

Lying in the picturesque Loweswater Valley, Swallow Barn is part of a traditional set of buildings dating back to 1670 on a working beef and sheep farm. The barn accommodates 18 people on mattresses in 4 sleeping areas. There is a cooking and eating area with tables and chairs, 2 coin-operated showers and 2 toilets.

Swallow Barn is an excellent base for exploring the western fells with both high and low level walks and spectacular views, or you can enjoy the peace and tranquillity of the valley. Boat hire and fishing permits are available from the farm. The coast to coast cycle route is right on the doorstep. The Kirkstyle Pub provides excellent food, just over a mile away and the market town of Cockermouth is only 8 miles. Check the website www.lakelandcampingbarns. co.uk and book online.

DETAILS

- **Open** - All year, all day
- **Number of beds** - 18: 1x9, 3x3
- **Booking** - Book online in advance, especially for school and bank holidays.
- **Price per night** - £7 per person.
- **Public Transport** - The nearest train station is Penrith with a bus to Cockermouth, then a taxi costing approximately £25.
- **Directions** - Leave the M6 at junct. 40 and follow the A66 to the Egremont turn off at Cockermouth. Follow the A5086,Egremont road for 6 miles. Turn left at Mockerkin and follow road to Loweswater. Farm is just past the Grange Hotel on the left .

CONTACT:
Waterend Farm, Loweswater, Cockermouth, Cumbria, CA13 0SU
Tel: Booking office 01946 758198, Farm 01946 861465
info@lakelandcampingbarns.co.uk www.lakelandcampingbarns.co.uk

CATBELLS
CAMPING BARN

Catbells Camping Barn is part of a traditional set of farm buildings dating back to the 14th century.   The barn is on the slopes of Catbells in the tranquil Newlands Valley, with magnificent views over the Lake District. The Cumberland Way passes through the farmyard. Keswick is only 4 miles away and both Borrowdale and Buttermere are in walking distance. The camping barn is on the ground floor and has sleeping accommodation for 12, with mattresses provided. Bring your own sleeping bags. The barn is heated with a multi-fuel stove (not suitable for cooking) and coal can be bought at the farm. In the adjacent building is a toilet and a cooking area suitable for a camping stove. Bring your own stove, cutlery, crockery and cooking utensils.   It is possible to walk to a pub which serves food.   Breakfast can be provided with notice.

DETAILS

- **Open** - All year, 24 hours
- **Number of beds** - 12: 1x12
- **Booking** - Advisable, groups require deposit.
- **Price per night** - £7 per person
- **Public Transport** - Trains at Penrith (20 miles). Regular buses (meet the trains) from Penrith to Keswick.   Summer bus from Keswick to Buttermere stops ¾ mile from Barn. Summer ferry from Keswick to Hawes End (3/4 mile from barn).
- **Directions** - GR 245211 Leave the M6 at Junction 40 and follow the A66 past Keswick. At Portinscale turn left, follow the Buttermere road for 3 miles. Turn sharp left at Stair, follow the sign for Skelgill, up the road for 1/2 mile and right into farmyard. Please follow these directions and not those from 'sat-nav'.

CONTACT: Mrs Grave
Low Skelgill, Newlands, Keswick, Cumbria, CA12 5UE
Tel: 01946 758198 or 0709 2031363
info@lakelandcampingbarns.co.uk www.lakelandcampingbarns.co.uk

Situated in Thirlmere at the foot of the Helvellyn range of mountains, close to Sticks Pass and spectacular Fisher-gill waterfall, with numerous walks, hill and rock climbing from the barn. It's an ideal place for touring the Lake District being just off the A591 road with local and national bus stops at the end of the lane.

Accommodation consists of two rooms: a kitchen/diner with fridge, 4 ring calor gas stove, kettle, toaster, tables and chairs, and all pots, pans etc; and a sleeping area consisting of 10 bunk beds with mattresses, pillows, blankets and duvets (sleeping bags/liners are required). Both rooms have a woodburning stove with a daily allowance of wood included (extra is available from the farm). There's also a shower cubicle (metered), toilet, wash basin and a small seating area. Outside there is ample parking with a small patio area with barbeque, tables and chairs. A pub serving meals is nearby (approx 1/4 mile). Keswick is 5 miles, Grasmere 7 miles. Open all year. Pets by arrangement.

DETAILS

- **Open** - All year., all day
- **Number of beds** - 10
- **Booking** - Advanced booking recommended.
- **Price per night** - £10 to £11. Sole use £100-£110.
- **Public Transport** - Local and national buses stop at the end of the lane on the A591
- **Directions** - Travelling on the A591 SE from Keswick, after about 5 miles take 1st lane on left after junction with B5322. Barn is after about 100m.

CONTACT: Mrs Jean Hodgson
Stybeck farm, Thirlmere, Keswick, Cumbria CA12 4TN
Tel: 017687 73232 or 017687 74391
stybeckfarm@farming.co.uk www.stybeckfarm.co.uk

CAUSEWAY FOOT
CAMPING BARN

Causeway Foot Farm Camping Barn is on a small family-run sheep and dairy farm set in the magnificent scenery of the Naddle Valley, just outside Keswick. The two storey barn enjoys a detached location with good access and parking. The ground floor has 8 bunkbeds, electric heaters and storage space. The upper floor has 12 bunkbeds, electric heaters, folding dining tables with bench seats and a well fitted kitchen with 6 burner gas cooker, fridge, microwave, electric kettle and toaster. The sink has hot & cold running water and there is a selection of pans, crockery and cutlery. The bunks have mattresses & pillows. There is a toilet/shower block 50 metres from the barn.
The farm also has a 3 bedroomed bungalow and three holiday caravans.

With glorious views over the Lakeland fells of Skiddaw, Latrigg, Blencathra and Helvellyn, this is a popular location for those wishing to relax, whilst also making an excellent and convenient base for walkers and families.

DETAILS

- **Open** - All year, 24 hours
- **Number of beds** - 20: 1x8, 1x12
- **Booking** - Deposit, balance on arrival.
- **Price per night** - Sole use of whole barn:- Fri or Sat £100, Sun-Thur £60 per night. Price includes gas, electricity by £1 meter.
- **Public Transport** - Trains at Penrith (16 miles). Hourly buses Penrith to Keswick.
- **Directions** - On the A591 between Keswick and Windermere, about 2.5 miles from Keswick opposite a lay-by and phone box.

CONTACT: Greg Nicholson
Causeway Foot Farm, Naddle, Keswick, Cumbria, CA12 4TF
Tel: 017687 72290
jackie@causewayfoot.co.uk www.causewayfoot.co.uk

Denton House is a purpose built hostel and outdoor centre in the heart of the Lake District. The hostel is designed for group use so has plenty of hot water for showers, central heating throughout, a commercial kitchen, a large dining room and solid bunkbeds! Denton House now welcomes individuals too with upgraded facilities designed to be homely as well as functional. Denton House Outdoor Centre can provide traditional activities for groups of all ages. The centre is particularly suitable for those wanting to explore the great outdoors; we have storage for kayaks and bikes and there's access/egress to the River Greta just across the road. Qualified instructors are available to provide advice as well as to run trips and help organise expeditions.

Denton House is primarily an adult hostel; under 16s are welcome in supervised groups or in exclusive use dorms with parents. Dogs welcome in some rooms if pre-booked. Due to the large number of school, youth and military groups, corporate teambuilds and celebration weekends, early booking is advised.

DETAILS

- **Open** - All year, 24 hours
- **Number of beds** - 56: 1x4 : 2x6 : 1x8 : 2x10 : 1x12.
- **Booking** - Preferred (25% deposit for groups)
- **Price per night** - £13 midweek, £14 weekends
- **Public Transport** - Nearest train station Penrith, buses hourly to Keswick.
- **Directions** - From centre out of town towards Windermere, keep the park on your left (approx 10mins). We are on the right after post sorting office.

CONTACT:
Penrith Road, Keswick, Cumbria, CA12 4JW
Tel: 017687 75351
sales@vividevents.co.uk www.vividevents.co.uk

St John's-in-the-Vale Camping Barn is adapted from an 18th Century stable and hayloft, in an idyllic setting overlooking St John's Beck on a peaceful hill farm, with stunning views to Blencathra, Helvellyn and Castle Rock.
The Barn has a sleeping area upstairs (mattress provided) with a sitting and dining area below. Seperate toilet, shower and cooking area (bring your own equipment) are within the building. A wood-burning fire provides a focal point and warmth! There is a BBQ and seating area outside, magical on a star-filled night as we have no light pollution.

Low Bridge End Farm has a tea garden - all home baking. Breakfasts and packed lunches can be ordered in advance from the farm. To get the full picture see our virtual tour, complete details then book online at.
www.lakelandcampingbarns.co.uk

DETAILS

- **Open** - All year, 24 hours
- **Number of beds** - 8 : 1x8
- **Booking** - Advised in advance. Credit card booking available on (01946) 758198.
- **Price per night** - £7 per person
- **Public Transport** - Trains terminate at Windermere. From there take a 555 bus towards Keswick. Get off at Thirlmere Dam Road End (Smaithwaite). Climb over ladder stile and we are ½ mile north along a footpath.
- **Directions** - Leave M6 at junction 40. Take A66 towards Keswick for 14 miles. Turn left onto B5322 St Johns in the Vale Road. 3 miles along the road on the right.

CONTACT: Graham or Sarah
Low Bridge End Farm, St Johns-in-the-Vale, Keswick, CA12 4TS
Tel: 017687 79242 (Bookings 01946 758198)
info@campingbarn.com www.campingbarn.com

SWIRRAL
CAMPING BARN

Swirral Barn is one of a group of mine buildings, situated at 1,000ft on the flank of the Helvellyn Mountain Range. It offers the basic necessities: hot water, toilet, tables, benches and a sleeping platform with mattresses. You will need to bring a stove and utensils if you wish to cook, a torch and a sleeping bag. The location is perfect for walking over the fells. Popular routes to Striding Edge and Swirral Edge pass the door, and there is quick access to Ullswater and the Eastern Fells. Enjoy a hike up Helvellyn and the surrounding peaks or, for less strenuous walking, try the scenic lake shore paths around Ullswater. Rowing, sailing and steam boats trips are available on Ullswater, where you can relax by the waterside. There are so many thing to do in this beautiful area. The barns facilities are: Sleeping platform on the first floor. Slate cooking area, cold tap and toilet, plus electric lighting. Nearest pub is only 1 mile away, with the nearest village store only 1.5 miles away.

DETAILS

- **Open** - All year, all day
- **Number of beds** - 8: 1x8
- **Booking** - Book online. Booking in advance is essential.
- **Price per night** - £7.00 per person
- **Public Transport** - Buses run every 2 hours from Penrith to Glenridding. It is just over 1 mile walk from bus stop to barn.
- **Directions** - From Pooley Bridge take A592 to Glenridding then to main car park. Follow the sign post to Helvellyn Youth Hostel. Swirrel Barn is 100 metres past the hostel on the left.

CONTACT: Jeanette
Striding Edge, Glenridding, Cumbria, CA11 0NR
Tel: Booking office 01946 758198, Farm mobile 07775561512
info@lakelandcampingbarns.co.uk www.lakelandcampingbarns.co.uk

Hudscales Camping Barn is part of a group of traditional farm buildings, situated at 1000ft on the northern-most flank of the Lakeland Fells. It overlooks the villages of Caldbeck and Hesket Newmarket and is in an ideal position for exploring the northern fells. It is situated right on the Cumbria Way.

Sleeping accommodation is on the ground floor along with a separate cooking and eating area. You will need to bring sleeping bags and mats. If you wish to cook bring a camping stove and all utensils / crockery. There is a separate toilet and washbasin and a metered shower. A woodburning stove is provided for added comfort (logs extra) and there is electric lighting plus metered power points.

Check the website www.lakelandcampingbarns.co.uk and book on line.

DETAILS

- **Open** - All year, all day
- **Number of beds** - 12: 1x12
- **Booking** - Book online. Bookings preferred but not essential.
- **Price per night** - £7 per person
- **Public Transport** - Penrith station 12 miles. Carlisle station 15 miles. No buses from Penrith. Limited service from Carlisle. Taxi fare from Carlisle approx £20.
- **Directions** - Leave M6 at J41 and take B5305 for Wigton. After approx 9 miles take left turn for Hesket Newmarket. Drive to top end of village and take left turn for Fellside. Hudscales Camping Barn is approx 1 mile on left up a lane.

CONTACT: Booking office / William or Judith
Hudscales, Hesket Newmarket, Wigton, Cumbria, CA7 8JZ
Tel: Booking office 01946 758198, Farm 016974 78637
info@lakelandcampingbarns.co.uk www.lakelandcampingbarns.co.uk

SKIDDAW HOUSE

ENGLAND

At 1550 feet, Skiddaw House is the highest YHA affiliated hostel in Britain. A former shooting lodge and shepherd's bothy on the Cumbria Way, it is an ideal base for exploring the little used and quiet northern fells. This is a remote and isolated place in which to reflect on the wilderness, with no sign of the 21st Century in any direction. With no electricity, phones ringing or TV to distract from the vista of a clear unpolluted starry night. This is simple accommodation with log and coal fires the only heating. No noise pollution from traffic as the nearest road is 3½ miles away, yet only an hour or so's walk from civilisation. Walkers and cyclists are advised to bring a map and torch. Campers welcome.

DETAILS

- **Open** - 1st March (to be confirmed) to 31st Oct. Groups only Nov-Dec, mornings till 10am, 5pm to 11pm
- **Number of beds** - 21: 1x7, 2x5, 1x4
- **Booking** - Book in advance for groups of 5 or more, by email, text, phone or post (postal service is slow). 50% deposit required for advance bookings.
- **Price per night** - £15pp (over 21), £11.50pp (16-21), £7.50pp (under 16). YHA members £1.50-£3 discount. Camping £7.50. Credit / debit cards not accepted.
- **Public Transport** - Nearest trains and National express coaches at Penrith. From Penrith take X4 or X5 bus towards Keswick and Workington. Alight at the Horse and Farrier (Threlkeld). From Carlisle take 554 bus to Keswick (only 3 per day). Alight at Castle Inn (Bassenthwaite) and then walk 6 miles.
- **Directions** - No access for cars, nearest tarmac road 3½ miles. Vehicles can be left at Fell Car Park by Blencathra Centre above Threlkeld, at Lattrigg Car Park (end of Gale Rd near Applethwaite) or at Whitewater Dash Falls south of Bassenthwaite.

CONTACT: Martin or Marie
Bassenthwaite, Keswick, Cumbria, CA12 4QX
Tel: 07747 174293
skiddawhouse@yahoo.co.uk www.skiddawhouse.co.uk

Hillside Farm is a Georgian farmstead in a conservation area just steps away from Hadrian's Wall. It is located in the small village of Boustead Hill, near the Solway Coast Area of Outstanding Natural Beauty and RSPB nature reserve. The farm has stunning views over the Solway Firth Marshes towards Scotland. Hadrian's Wall National Trail and Hadrian's Cycleway pass right by. Hillside farm is a working farm and the fourth generation of a farming family welcomes you to stay in the bunkbarn or in the B&B rooms in the farmhouse. The Bunkbarn is a recent conversion of the farm's Georgian stable block. It has cooking slabs, cutlery and crockery and a 2 ring gas stove. There are hot showers and towels and sleeping bags can be hired if required. There is no heating in the barn. You can arrange delivery of shopping via the farmhouse and with notice you can eat a full english breakfast at the farmhouse. Walking, cycling and family groups are most welcome.

DETAILS

- **Open** - All year, all day
- **Number of beds** - 12
- **Booking** - Book by phone.
- **Price per night** - £8 per person. £1 shower. £6 full English breakfast.
- **Public Transport** -
- **Directions** - From M6 junction 43 follow signs for A595 past the castle, turn at small rundabout onto B5307. After 1 mile turn right following signs for Burgh-by-Sands. Pass through town and cross the cattle grid onto Marsh Road. Take next left into village of Boustead Hill, then 2nd turning on left under arches into farmyard.

CONTACT: Mrs Sandra Rudd
Hillside Farm, Boustead Hill, Burgh-by-Sands, Carlisle, Cumbria, CA5 6AA
Tel: 01228 576398
ruddshillside1@btinternet.com   www.hadrianswalkbnb.co.uk

NENTHEAD MINES
BUNKHOUSES

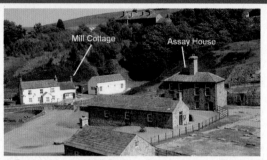

Mill Cottage   Assay House

Assay House Bunkhouse and Mill Cottage Bunkhouse are situated at Nenthead Mines, a Scheduled Ancient Monument. In the 19th century it was part of the largest lead and silver mining and processing area in the country. Nenthead is in the North Pennines Area of Outstanding Natural Beauty, and is one of the highest villages in England. An ideal location for people wishing to explore the dramatic North Pennine area, with walks and the C2C cycle route passing the door, as well as the opportunity to visit the Heritage Centre. The Assay House was the laboratory of the Assay Master, who analysed ore samples and set the prices paid to the miners. Now converted to a bunkhouse it sleeps up to 12 people in two upstairs bedrooms. There is a kitchen / dining room downstairs. Mill Cottage was part of the home of the Smelt Mill manager. The Bunkhouse sleeps six in the upstairs bunkroom. Each bed is styled like a ship's cabin bunk with curtains for privacy, a light and shelf. Either bunkhouse is available for groups. Cafe on site and pub in the village.

DETAILS

- **Open** - All year. (Heritage Centre Apr-Oct.), Heritage Centre open 11am-5pm.
- **Number of beds** - Mill Cottage 6: 1 x 6, Assay House 12: 2 x 6
- **Booking** - Preferred but not essential. Deposit is required.
- **Price per night** - £12.50
- **Public Transport** - Trains at Hexham (24 miles) and Penrith (25 miles). Limited bus service (Wright Bros Buses 01434 381200) from Hexham and Penrith to Alston.
- **Directions** - In Nenthead village off the A689 Alston to Stanhope road. The bunkhouse is on the Nenthead Mines site.

CONTACT: Paul Mercer/ Tim Haldon
Nenthead Mines, Nenthead, Alston, Cumbria, CA9 3PD
Tel: 01434 382037 or 01434 382726
bunkhouse@npht.com www.npht.com/nentheadmines

Gibbs Hill Farm Hostel is a new conversion of a Barn on a traditional working hill farm. The hostel is designed to reduce energy consumption and is centrally heated throughout. There are 3 bunkrooms, 2 shower rooms, 2 toilets, a well equipped kitchen, comfortable sitting and dining area and a large deck where guests may enjoy the evening sun. The hostel has a drying room, lockers, laundry facilities and safe cycle storage. Ideal for families who may take a whole room with private facilities. Study groups welcome and evening meals can be provided. Situated near Hadrians Wall it is an excellent base for exploring the Roman sites, Hadrians Wall Trail and Northumberland National Park. Basic items of food may be purchased and meals can be ordered in the evening for the next day. Continental Breakfast is £4, Packed Lunches £5.

DETAILS

- **Open** - All year, flexible, but no check in after 9pm
- **Number of beds** - 18: 3x6
- **Booking** - Advisable, groups require deposit.
- **Price per night** - £12pp week, £14pp wk/end. Bring sleeping bag or hire linen £3.
- **Public Transport** - Trains at Haltwhistle 6 miles. Regular Bus Service along A69 between Newcastle and Carlisle, and in summer the Hadrians Wall Bus runs between Newcastle and Carlisle. Alight at Once Brewed Information Centre and walk north to farm. Last bus 5.30pm from Haltwhistle.
- **Directions** - From the A69, turn north at Bardon Mill, signed 'Once Brewed'. Follow the signs towards 'Housesteads'. At the B6318, turn right and then immediately left towards 'Steel Rigg'. Follow for 1 mile, turn right to 'Gibbs Hill'.

CONTACT: Valerie Gibson
Gibbs Hill Farm, Bardon Mill, Nr Hexham, Northumberland, NE47 7AP
Tel: 01434 344030, Fax: 01434 344030
val@gibbshillfarm.co.uk www.gibbshillfarm.co.uk

ALBATROSS
BACKPACKERS IN!

Fly high with the award winning Albatross! This clean and modern backpackers hostel is located in Newcastle's City Centre. In walking distance are sporting, musical and conference venues, art galleries, historical attractions, food markets and public transport facilities. So come discover the North East, and get ready for Newcastle's highly acclaimed night life. The Albatross provides rooms of 12, 10, 8, 6, 5, 4 or 2 beds and has a total capacity of 177 beds. The overnight price includes: bedding; 24hr reception; fully fitted self-catering kitchen with tea, coffee and toast; free WiFi access and computer terminals; pool table; satellite TV; 150-year old cellar; outside sitting/ barbeque area; free first come first served car parking; free baggage storage; laundry facilities; CCTV; and electronic key card system. The Albatross has been awarded for Outstanding Customer Service in 2008 and voted by Hostelworld customers as " No 1 Hostel in England 2007 ".

DETAILS

- **Open** - All year, 24 hours
- **Number of beds** - 177
- **Booking** - Recommended. Photo ID at check-in (passport or driver licence).
- **Price per night** - From £16.50pp (dorm) to £22.50pp (2 bed room)
- **Public Transport** - Five minutes walk from central train, bus and metro stations.
- **Directions** - Central Station / Megabus drop off point: from main entrance, head right, take the first street on your left (Grainger St), you'll find us on your left 200m uphill. From National Express coach station: head down Scotswood Rd to Central Station. From Airport: take Metro to Central Station (20 mins travel). From Port (Ferry): buses travel between the port and Central Station and take 20 mins.

CONTACT: Reception
51 Grainger Street, Newcastle Upon Tyne, NE1 5JE
Tel: 0191 2331330, Fax: 0191 2603389
info@albatrossnewcastle.co.uk www.albatrossnewcastle.com

HOUGHTON NORTH
FARM ACCOMMODATION

Houghton North Farm, partly built with stones from Hadrian's Wall, has been in the Laws Family for five generations. It is situated in the beautiful Northumberland countryside right on the Heritage trail and 15 miles from the start of the Hadrian's Wall Trail. Within the region walkers can enjoy marked woodland trails, rugged moorland and hills, and some of the most beautiful deserted beaches in the UK. The newly built spacious accommodation can take a group of up to 23 and is also ideal for individuals and families. It is a 4*Hostel with Visit Britain. The bunk style rooms (some en-suite) are located around the central courtyard and include the use of a self-catering kitchen where a light breakfast is served. There is also a well appointed TV lounge with log fire and internet access, barbecue, secure cycle storage and parking. Long-term parking, baggage transfer and packed lunches are available on request. Within 10 mins walk are pubs, a restaurant and shops in Heddon-on-the-Wall.

DETAILS

- **Open** - All year, All day
- **Number of beds** - 22: 1x5, 3x4, 1x3, 1x2
- **Booking** - Book with a non refundable deposit of £10 per person per night
- **Price per night** - From £25 (adult), £15 (under 12) inc breakfast. Group discounts.
- **Public Transport** - Trains at Wylam (2 miles) and Newcastle (7 miles). The 685 Newcastle-Carlisle bus stops right outside the farm. Baggage transfer is available.
- **Directions** - From Newcastle take the Heddon turn off the A69 to the B6528, farm is 1/4 mile outside of the village of Heddon. From Carlisle take Horsley junction and continue approx 3 miles beyond Horsley. Farm on the left at the top of a hill

CONTACT: Mrs Paula Laws
Houghton North Farm, Heddon-on-the-Wall, Northumberland, NE15 0EZ
Tel: 01661 854364
wjlaws@btconnect.com   www.houghtonnorthfarm.co.uk

Demesne Farm Bunkhouse is a self-catering unit which was converted in 2004 from a barn on a working hill farm. The farm is situated on the Pennine Way, Route 68 cycle route, Reivers cycle route and is within 100 metres of the centre of the North Tyne village of Bellingham on the edge of the Northumberland National Park. The bunkhouse provides an ideal base for exploring Northumberland, Hadrian's Wall, Kielder Water and many climbing crags. It accommodates 15 and is perfect for smaller groups, individuals and families. The bedrooms are fitted with hand crafted oak man-sized bunk beds, high quality mattresses, pillows and curtains with cushion flooring. The communal living area with potbelly stove and fitted kitchen includes cooker, microwave, fridge, kettle, toaster, crockery, cutlery, cooking utensils, farmhouse tables, chairs and easy chairs. It has 2 bathrooms with hot showers, hand basins, toilets and under floor heating. Outside in the courtyard there is ample parking, bike lock up and a gravelled area with picnic tables. Linen can be hired.

DETAILS

- **Open** - All year, flexible, but no check in after 9pm
- **Number of beds** - 15: 1 x 8, 1 x 4, 1 x 3
- **Booking** - Please book in advance.
- **Price per night** - £15 per person (including linen).
- **Public Transport** - Trains at Hexham (17 miles), regular bus service from Hexham to Bellingham. Bellingham bus stop 100 metres from Bunkhouse. By car: Newcastle 45 mins, Scottish Border 20 mins, Kielder Water 10 mins.
- **Directions** - 100 metres from centre of village, located next to Northern Garage.

CONTACT: Robert Telfer
Demesne Farm, Bellingham, Hexham, Northumberland, NE48 2BS
Tel: 01434 220258 Mobile 07967 396345
stay@demesnefarmcampsite.co.uk www.demesnefarmcampsite.co.uk

FOREST VIEW
WALKERS HOSTEL

Forest View is set in the hamlet of Byrness on the edge of Keilder Forest and Northumberland National Park. An ideal stopover on the A68 England to Scotland route. The Pennine Way runs just a few hundred yards from the hostel.

The building has just undergone a major refurbishment with new beds, curtains and carpets. The central heating is supplied by an eco-friendly wood pellet boiler and the hot water by solar panels. The log burning stoves in the quiet room and dining room keep the hostel cosy all year round. The beds are arranged in 2, 3 & 4 bedded rooms and bed linen is supplied. Secure storage is provided for up to 10 bikes.

There is a large selection of bottled beers and wines, meals can be provided or guests can use the well equipped self catering kitchen.

DETAILS

- **Open** - All year, 24hrs (coded entry system)
- **Number of beds** - 20: 2x4, 2x3, 3x2
- **Booking** - Booking is recommended
- **Price per night** - Adult £16, Under 16s £14
- **Public Transport** - Nearest rail station Newcastle-Upon-Tyne 40 miles then National Express to lay-by 200yds from hostel.
- **Directions** - Forest View is just off the A68, 4 miles from the Scottish Border, 16 miles south of Jedburgh and 10 miles north of Otterburn. The National Express bus drops off 200yds from the Hostel.

CONTACT: Colin or Joyce
7 Otterburn Green, Byrness Village, Northumberland, NE19 1TS
Tel: 01830 520425
joycetaylor1703@hotmail.co.uk

BARROWBURN
CAMPING BARN

Barrowburn is an unspoilt valley in the heart of the Cheviot Hills. This "get away from it all" location will refresh and relax. There's no electricity or mobile phone coverage. Lighting is provided by modern gas lamps, heat by real fires (coal provided) and there is a phone box nearby. Surrounded by the beauty and ruggedness of the Northumberland National Park this is a playground for outdoor enthusiasts with footpaths, bridle ways and challenging mountain bike trails. Nature lovers will enjoy the skylarks, deer and badgers.

The old school camping barn provides basic accommodation for up to 17. The large main room has an open fire and sleeping is on raised wooden platforms. The kitchen has 4 burners and a sink with hot water. There are WCs and wash areas. To stay here you will need a sleeping bag and mat, matches, firelighters, bin bag and a torch. Nearby is the Deer Hut, a basic bungalow with two twin-bedded rooms, bathroom, basically equipped kitchen and cosy living room with fire and sofa-bed. Parking for 3 cars. Camping available.

DETAILS

- **Open** - All year, all day
- **Number of beds** - Camping Barn 17: 1x17, Deer Hut 4: 2x2 + 6 tents.
- **Booking** - Book by phone or email
- **Price per night** - £10pp or £80 for barn (all bookings get sole use). Deer Hut £60.
- **Public Transport** - Trains at Alnmouth (30 miles).
- **Directions** - GR NT 869108. 5 miles west of Alwinton on the Coquet Valley rd, turn right by phone box and pass the farm, over a little ford, and up hill for 150m.

CONTACT: Ian and Eunice Tait
Barrowburn, Harbottle, Morpeth, Northumberland, NE65 7BP
Tel: 01669 621176
stay@barrowburn.com www.barrowburn.com

Chatton Park Bunkhouse started life as a Smithy and has been converted into self-catering accommodation. It is situated on a mixed working farm which nestles around the river Till, ½ mile from Chatton village.
Eight miles from the coast and 5miles from the Cheviot Hills, Chatton Park is an ideal base for exploring Northumberland's vast empty beaches, heather clad hills & historic castles. Walking, watersports, climbing, fishing, golf and cycling are all available nearby.

Accommodating 12, the bunkhouse is perfect for smaller groups, families & individuals. The 2 bedrooms are fitted with large custom made bunks and can be rented separately as secure units. Bedding can be provided at a small extra fee. The living area has a fully equipped kitchen & seating around the original blacksmith's fire. Wash & drying room with hot showers. Secure storage, ample parking. Room for camping. DIY livery. Dog kennels provided.

DETAILS

- **Open** - All year, flexible but no check in after 9pm
- **Number of beds** - 12: 2x6
- **Booking** - Booking recommended but not essential
- **Price per night** - £12 pp. Group bookings negotiable
- **Public Transport** - Nearest train station Berwick upon Tweed. Buses to Chatton from Alnwick / Berwick.
- **Directions** - From A1 take B6348 to Chatton. 4 miles at bottom of hill on right is Chatton Park Farm

CONTACT: Jane or Duncan
Chatton Park Farm, Chatton, Alnwick, Northumberland, NE66 5RA
Tel: 01668 215247
ord@chattonpk.fsnet.co.uk www.chattonparkfarm.co.uk

JOINERS SHOP
BUNKHOUSE

The Joiners Shop Bunkhouse is an attractive 17th-century building retaining much of its historical charm and character. It is situated in a quiet hamlet only 7 miles from Alnwick, the seat of the Duke of Northumberland, 5 miles from the beautiful Northumberland Coast and 10 miles from Wooler and the Cheviot Hills. The area offers opportunities for walking, climbing, mountain biking, golfing, all water sports or simply sightseeing.

The Joiners Shop Bunkhouse has full cooking facilities and a dining area along with a log fire and cosy sitting area. The 18 large pine beds are in heated dormitories of twos and threes. Indoor space is available for bikes and other equipment and there is ample parking.
Dogs welcome. NB There are dogs on site!

DETAILS

- **Open** - All year, no restrictions
- **Number of beds** - 18
- **Booking** - Advised for weekends and holidays.
- **Price per night** - £12.00 per person.
- **Public Transport** - There are train stations at Chathill (1.5 miles) limited service and Alnmouth (10 miles). There are National Express services at Alnwick (7 miles) and Berwick (24 miles). The local bus company is called ARRIVA and the nearest stop is Brownieside on the A1 (1.5 miles).
- **Directions** - GR 183 254 Seven miles north of Alnwick on the A1 to Brownieside. Turn off A1 at sign for Preston Tower, hostel is 1.5 miles on the left

CONTACT: Wal Wallace
Preston, Chathill, Northumberland, NE67 5ES
Tel: 01665 589245 or 07745 373729
bunkhouse.wal@btinternet.com www.bunkhousenorthumberland.co.uk

The Tackroom Bunkhouse is situated on a mixed working farm between the seaside villages of Beadnell and Seahouses, yards from a beautiful sandy beach on the spectacular Northumberland Coast. The area is ideal for walking, watersports, climbing, cycling, diving or just sightseeing. Accommodating 12, the bunkhouse is ideal for smaller groups, individuals and couples. The two bedrooms are each fitted with 6 man sized bunk-beds and a locker for each visitor. Sleeping bags are essential.

The communal area has a mini kitchen with hob, microwave, fridge, toaster etc, a dining table to seat 12 and colour TV. All crockery, cutlery and cooking utensils are supplied but there is no oven.

Adjoining the bunkhouse is a shared shower/toilet block complete with washing machine and tumble drier. Also available is a lock-up and off road parking. The Tackroom Bunkhouse is heated.

DETAILS

■ **Open** - All year, flexible, but no check-in after 10pm.

■ **Number of beds** - 12: 2 x 6.

■ **Booking** - Recommended but not essential

■ **Price per night** - £12 per person or £120 sole use.

■ **Public Transport** - Nearest train station is Berwick upon Tweed. There are intermittent local buses to Seahouses and Beadnell, passing ½ mile away from the hostel.

■ **Directions** - From A1 take the B1340, follow road to Beadnell (signed Seahouses/Beadnell). Annstead farm is approx ½ mile past Beadnell on the left.

CONTACT: Sue Mellor
Annstead Farm, Beadnell, Northumberland, NE67 5BT
Tel: 01665 720387, Fax: 01665 721494
stay@annstead.co.uk www.annstead.co.uk

BLUEBELL FARM
BUNKBARN

Bluebell Farm Bunkbarn is situated on a family-owned caravan park and campsite. The Bunkbarn sleeps 14, and there is also a wooden ark which sleeps 6 and five self-catering cottages. The bunkbarn has a family room for 6 and an 8 bed dorm. The bunks are equipped with blankets and pillows. Linen and towels can be hired or bring your own sleeping bag. There is a fully equipped self-catering kitchen and a bike store. Packed lunches available by arrangement. Hot showers, electricity and gas are all included in the price.

Bluebell Farm is in the centre of the village within walking distance of shops and pubs. It is ideally located for exploring Nothumberland's Heritage Coast Route to the east, the Cheviot Hills National Park to the west and the historic Scottish Borders. Many outdoor pursuits are available including golf, climbing, canoeing, diving, horse riding, fishing, cycling and walking. Dogs welcome by arrangement. Duke of Edinburgh groups welcome. Exclusive use available.

DETAILS

- **Open** - All year, check in by 9 pm, departure by 10 am.
- **Number of beds** - 14 : 1 x 8, 1 x 6
- **Booking** - Not essential
- **Price per night** - Adults £10, under 14s £5. Linen and towel hire £5 per person.
- **Public Transport** - Trains at Berwick upon Tweed. Buses from Berwick to Belford. National Express coaches stop in Belford. Local bus from Newcastle.
- **Directions** - From the A1 take B1342 into the village. Turn onto B6349 signposted for Wooler. Bluebell Farm is first main driveway on right, almost opposite the Co-op.

CONTACT: Phyl
Bluebell Farm Caravan Park, Belford, Northumberland, NE70 7QE
Tel: 01668 213362
corillas@tiscali.co.uk www.bluebellfarmbelford.co.uk

THE HIDEAWAY
HOSTEL

Centuries old, The Hideaway is conveniently situated in the heart of picturesque Old Berwick, yet is amazingly secluded, set behind high stone walls. Admire the magnificent stone fireplace as you toast yourself by the multi fuel stove. Enjoy a barbecue on the verandah or in the delightful tiny courtyard garden as you relax in the cool summer night air, heavy with the scent of honeysuckle and jasmine.

Shared facilities include a well equipped kitchen, sitting room with TV and dining room. Berwick is an ideal base for exploring Northumberland, Lindisfarne and the Scottish Borders. It is also close to an amazing number of cycle routes. We have excellent secure cycle storage and drying facilities. Well behaved dogs by prior arrangement. No smoking.

DETAILS

- **Open** - All year, all day, check in 4pm-10pm
- **Number of beds** - 11: 1x3, 4x2 (1 twin ensuite, 2 double, 1 double ensuite)
- **Booking** - Booking advisable. 33% deposit. Beds held till 6pm without deposit.
- **Price per night** - £10pppn (2008), £15pppn (2009). New price includes Continental Breakfast! Single supp £5. Sleeping bag FREE. Other bedding £5 ppp stay.
- **Public Transport** - 10 mins walk from Berwick Station and long distance buses.
- **Directions** - Look for Church Street by the Guildhall. The Hideaway can be found between "The Sporran" giftshop and "Hair at 11". Look for the cycle logos in the passageway through the wrought iron gate! For a detailed location map, go to Google Maps, and type Hideaway plus our postcode.

CONTACT: J Morton
1 The Courtyard, Church Street, Berwick-upon-Tweed, TD15 1EE
Tel: 01289 308737, Mobile 07989 468008
patmosphere@yahoo.co.uk

Berwick-on-Tweed Backpackers has the perfect location inside the Elizabethan walls of this ancient market town and only a short walk from the bus and train stations. Berwick is an ideal stop-off on the train and road route from London to Edinburgh. Stop for a last taste of England just 50 miles from Scotland's capital or stay longer and explore the bracing Northumberland Coast.

Berwick-on-Tweed Backpackers is in a quiet courtyard and has an informal come and go as you please atmosphere. The hostel has self-catering facilities and there is a covered area for dry secure storage of bicycles. The hostel is next to Berwick Quayside, the Maltings Art Centre, Barrels Ale House, Brilliant Bikes and the Green Shop.
Four Star Tourist Board Graded

DETAILS

■ **Open** - All year, 11am to 7pm - summer. 4pm to 7pm - winter.
■ **Number of beds** - 20: Lots of twins and doubles
■ **Booking** - Advisable in summer but not essential
■ **Price per night** - from £16.95 to £29.95 inc continental breakfast
■ **Public Transport** - Berwick-on-Tweed railway station is 10 minutes walk away and the bus station is 5 minutes walk away.
■ **Directions** - In Berwick town centre, follow the main street towards the town hall. Take first right turn after the town hall, down Hide Hill, turn first right at the bottom of the hill into Bridge Street. The hostel is half way along Bridge Street on the right opposite the bookshop.

CONTACT: Angela Chappell
56 Bridge Street, Berwick-on-Tweed, Northumberland, TD15 1AQ
Tel: (01289) 331481
bkbackpacker@aol.com www.berwickbackpackers.co.uk

Maughold Venture Centre Bunkhouse is built of Manx stone, overlooking farmland with views in the distance to the sea. It offers self-catering facilities with the option of purchasing meals from the neighbouring adventure centre if required (subject to availability). All bedrooms are en-suite with full central heating. Facilities include a basic but functional games room and kitchen The number of beds in each room can be altered to suit your requirements.

The local beach of Port e Vullen, 10 mins walk away, is popular with our visitors and the Bunkhouse is adjacent to the Venture Centre where you may arrange sessions of kayaking, abseiling, air rifle shooting, archery, gorge walking, dinghy sailing, power boating and team events. We have our own stop, Lewaigue Halt, on the Manx Electric Railway giving access to Douglas, Ramsay and to mountain walks and tranquil glens. Ideal for groups, families and individuals.

DETAILS

■ **Open** - February to November, 24 hours
■ **Number of beds** - 52   2x2 : 1x6 : 4x8 : 1x10
■ **Booking** - Telephone reservation essential
■ **Price per night** - £10-£15 per person
■ **Public Transport** - No 3 Bus or Manx Electric Railway from Douglas or Ramsey. Get off bus at Dreemskerry (5 mins walk); get off railway at Lewaigue Halt (nearby). Taxi from Ramsey £5. Taxi from Douglas £25.
■ **Directions** - GR 469922. From Douglas take the A2 coast road. When the road begins to descend into Ramsey the Venture Centre is signposted on the right hand side. Follow the signs - it is the first building on the left.

CONTACT: Simon Read
The Venture Centre, Maughold, Isle of Man, IM7 1AW
Tel: 01624 814240
Contact@adventure-centre.co.uk www.adventure-centre.co.uk

King William's College is the only independent school in the Isle of Man and is located on Castletown Bay in the south of the island. The Isle of Man has lots to offer, including an interesting transport system, great beaches, mountainous heathland, historic sites, charming villages and numerous walks.   Junior House, formerly used for junior boarding, is set in the expansive College grounds and provides a mix of accommodation options ranging from twin rooms to dormitories. The building has recently been refurbished and all the bathroom facilities upgraded. There is a lounge, laundry room, TV room, drying room and a limited kitchen area.

Junior House is an ideal location for all the attractions in the south of the island and the facilities are well matched to those looking for outdoor activity holidays. Catering can be provided at most times although guests should check at the time of booking. Junior House is a relaxed, clean and well maintained property.

DETAILS

- **Open** - All year (except Christmas and New Year), all day
- **Number of beds** - 60: 1x14 : 2x12 : 1x 8: 7x2
- **Booking** - Groups, TT races book with deposit.
- **Price per night** - From £15.00 per person. Breakfast extra.
- **Public Transport** -   The airport is located next to the College. Ferries dock at Douglas from Liverpool, Heysham, Dublin and Belfast.
- **Directions** - From Douglas follow signs to Castletown and the Airport. Bus stop is located opposite the entrance to King William's College.

CONTACT: Ruth Watterson
King William's College, Castletown, Isle of Man, IM9 1TP
Tel: 01624 820470 / 820400, Fax: 01624 820402
rooms@kwc.sch.im www.kwc.sch.im

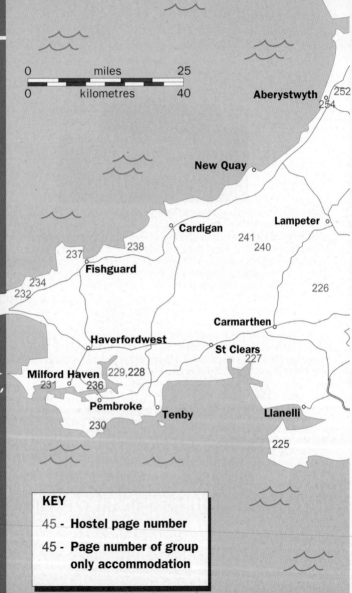

South Wales

miles 0 — 25
kilometres 0 — 40

Aberystwyth 252
254

New Quay

Cardigan
241
240
Lampeter

238
237

Fishguard

234
232

226

Carmarthen

Haverfordwest

St Clears
227

Milford Haven 229, 228
231 236

Pembroke
230

Tenby

Llanelli

225

KEY

45 - Hostel page number

45 - Page number of group only accommodation

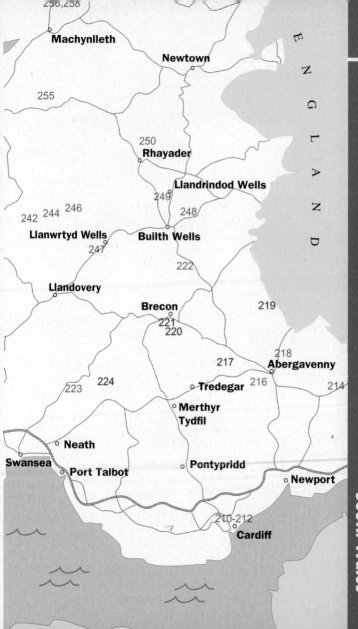

256,258

Machynlleth

Newtown

E
N
G
L
A
N
D

255

250
Rhayader

Llandrindod Wells

249

248

242 244 246

Llanwrtyd Wells

247

Builth Wells

222

Llandovery

219

Brecon

221

220

218

217

Abergavenny

216

214

223 224

Tredegar

Merthyr Tydfil

Neath

Swansea

Port Talbot

Pontypridd

Newport

210-212

Cardiff

South Wales

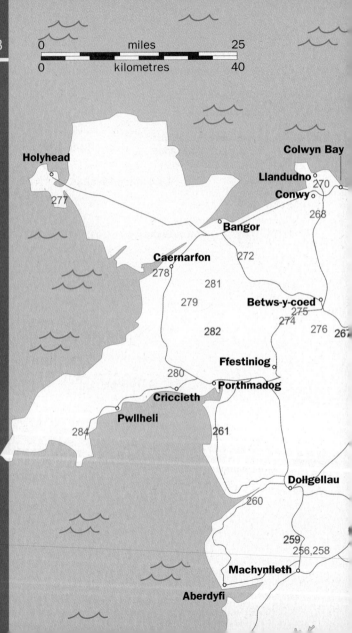

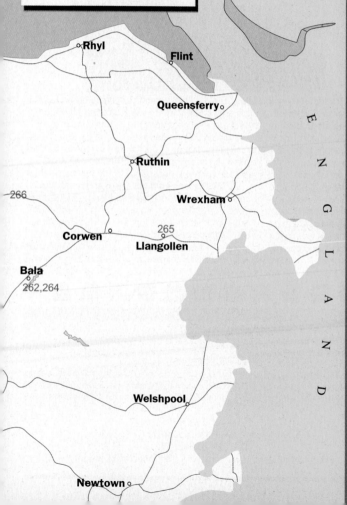

KEY

45 - Hostel page number

45 - Page number of group only accommodation

Rhyl

Flint

Queensferry

Ruthin

Wrexham

266

Corwen

265

Llangollen

Bala
262,264

Welshpool

Newtown

ENGLAND

North Wales

CARDIFF
BACKPACKER CAERDYDD

Voted Number 1 hostel in Wales 2007 by Hostelworld.com customers. Cardiff Backpacker Caerdydd, the original independent hostel, has recently been redesigned to become perfect group accommodation. With a choice of different sized dormitories and a number of private rooms we cater perfectly for schools, colleges, sports teams or large groups of friends looking to visit Cardiff. With secure access throughout, a superb self catering kitchen and a bar available on request your group can have sole occupancy of the building with no need to keep the noise down. During the weekend we are open to individuals and with just 40 beds we are small enough to feel cosy and friendly whilst large enough to accommodate a good mix of people from all over the world. Our bar is a great place to get to know your fellow travellers and have a few drinks before hitting town which is only a 10 minute walk away. All the staff are well travelled and would love to offer tips on the coolest things to do whilst in Cardiff and share travelling tales with you! "Cardiff Backpacker is a dream and a strong favourite with independent travellers" Lonely Planet Europe & Britain 2007.

DETAILS

- **Open** - Fri-Sat only unless booked by a group. 24 hours. 7.30am-2.30pm in week.
- **Number of beds** - 39 , 1 x 4, 1 x 5, 1 x 6, 2 x 8, 4 x 2
- **Booking** - Booking recommended and essential (with deposit) for groups.
- **Price per night** - From £17 per person, including light breakfast.
- **Public Transport** - Train, coach and bus stations 5 to 10 minutes walk away.
- **Directions** - From Cardiff Central Station, turn left crossing the River Taff. Follow river upstream, turn left past NosDa Studio Hostel. Hostel on roundabout ahead.

CONTACT:
98 Neville Street, Riverside, Cardiff, CF11 6LS
Tel: 029 20 345577
info@cardiffbackpacker.com www.cardiffbackpacker.com

NOSDA STUDIO
HOSTEL

NosDa means "Good night" in Welsh and that is exactly what we promise. NosDa Studio Hostel is a hostel/hotel hybrid, a new concept of stylish budget accommodation. There's a choice of secure mixed and single sex dormitories and also a number of private rooms, each with their own pod style bathrooms, mini kitchens, TV's and even balconies. "NosDa is redefining the hostelling genre" Lonely Planet 2007. Uniquely situated along the banks of the river Taff, NosDa occupies a newly refurbished 19th century building with superb views of the iconic Millennium Stadium. Our lively bar has a selection of Welsh beers, ciders and spirits and the affordable menu lets you taste some delicious local produce. There is an in house gym and nightclub, and if that wears you out why not chill in our new funky TV lounge? With the castle, stadium and train station all within sight, NosDa Studio Hostel is the most centrally located hostel with a view to die for and the facilities to match!

DETAILS

- **Open** - All year, 24 hours
- **Number of beds** - 138: 4 x 4, 6 x 6, 2 x 8, 1 x 10 + 52 beds in private rooms.
- **Booking** - Essential for groups, advisable for individuals. Book online.
- **Price per night** - From £17.50, Double/Twin from £55
- **Public Transport** - Train, coach and bus stations 5 minutes walk from the hostel.
- **Directions** - By car: From the M4, take junction 32 and follow signs for city centre. Approaching the centre follow the road around the castle then straight ahead over the bridge crossing the river Taff. Take the next left into Lower Cathedral Road, then 1st left at into Despenser Street, By foot from Cardiff Central Station, turn left across the river and follow the embankment upstream, with the stadium opposite. Look ahead.

CONTACT: Reception
53-59, Despenser Street, Riverside, Cardiff, CF11 6AG
Tel: 029 20378866
info@nosda.co.uk www.nosda.co.uk

Cardiff University provides holiday accommodation at a number of sites all with easy access to the heart of one of Europe's most vibrant capital cities.
Close to the city centre, Senghennydd Hall provides en-suite single rooms with access to shared kitchen/dining rooms.
A short walk from the city centre and with limited parking is Colum Hall, providing self-catering accommodation arranged in flats for eight people.

Ten minutes drive from the city centre, close to the grounds of Cardiff's Castle is Talybont. Located on the banks of the river Taff, this accommodation was host to the Special Olympics and has a number of sports facilities, a large social centre and up to 1200 single en-suite self-catering bedrooms and extensive free parking. Talybont is an excellent venue for groups, sporting associations and large events.

DETAILS

- **Open** - 19 June to 11 September 2009, , reception open 8am-5pm
- **Number of beds** - 1200+ bedrooms (en-suite)
- **Booking** - Telephone or email to enquire
- **Price per night** - Self Catering £26.05pp, or £159.85pp per week. B&B (if available) £34.25pp. All prices inc VAT, bed linen and towels.
- **Public Transport** - Cardiff Central Station: trains, coaches, connections to airports. Buses from city centre.
- **Directions** - From junction 29 of M4, follow the A48(M)/A48, signpost Cardiff East and South, to the A470, signpost City Centre, into the Cathays area of the city.

CONTACT: Cardiff University Conference Office
Southgate House, PO Box 533, Cardiff, CF14 3X2
Tel: 029 2087 4702 / 4616, Fax: 029 2087 4990
Groupaccom@cardiff.ac.uk www.cardiff.ac.uk/resid

RICKYARD
BUNKHOUSE

Welcome to Rickyard Bunkhouse set amidst idyllic countryside and well away form the hustle and bustle. Offa's Dyke footpath passes the entrance. We are within 25 mins of Wye Valley, Symonds Yat, and the Forest of Dean. Many outdoor pursuits can be enjoyed, canoeing, rafting, potholing, quad biking, rock climbing, paint balling to name but a few. The river Trothy borders our land, kingfishers and otters enjoy the peace and tranquillity of the Trothy valley. Buzzards circle high above, easily recognised by their distinctive call. The Bunkhouse holds 20 easily, has an excellent, very well equipped kitchen, separate dining/relaxing area with tv, background heating and sleeping accommodation split into several areas. It is totally self contained, ideal for re-unions, groups and families. Please come and enjoy our tranquil surroundings but we don't welcome loud music or wild parties. There is a large secure area for camping where children can safely play and ample parking with hard standing. Luggage transfer, breakfasts and pack lunches can be arranged. Bedding can be supplied. Exclusive use available, please enquire.

DETAILS

- **Open** - All year, all day
- **Number of beds** - 20: + camping
- **Booking** - Deposit required, no credit cards. Notice not always required.
- **Price per night** - £13pp. Private en-suite room for 4 persons £16pp. Can be booked for sole use. Tents £5pp.
- **Public Transport** - Trains at Abergavenny (11m). Buses Monmouth (3m).
- **Directions** - Next to the Hendre Farm House on the same side of the road.

CONTACT: Graham Edwards
Wonastow, Monmouth, NP25 4DJ
Tel: 01600 740128
rickyardbunkhouse@googlemail.com www.rickyardbunkhouse.co.uk

MIDDLE NINFA
BUNKHOUSE/COTTAGE

Middle Ninfa Farm, situated in the Brecon Beacons on the edge of the Blaenavon Industrial Landscape World Heritage Site, offers bunkhouse/cottage accommodation, camping and hands-on training in coracle making and willow sculpture. The farm has fine views over the Usk Valley, of the Skirrid and rural Monmouthshire. The Bunkhouse provides comfortable self-catering accommodation for up to 6 people. The rustic charm of the old stone building has been retained whilst ensuring modern comforts. The ground floor has lounge/dining area with double divan and TV, well-equipped kitchen and toilet/shower room.   Upstairs (Mezzanine Floor) there are 4 single beds, accessed by a spiral staircase. Guests should bring food, sleeping bags, towels & pillowcases.   Home grown fruit, veg and local produce available. Sauna available. Walking and Cycling Welcome and Green Dragon Level 2 environmental award.

DETAILS

- **Open** - All year, all day
- **Number of beds** - 6: 1x4, 1x2
- **Booking** - Book by phone or email
- **Price per night** - Sun to Thur £10pp or £50 sole use. Fri, Sat and Bank Holidays £12pp or £60 sole use. Sole use per week £220-£300. Camping £3pp.
- **Public Transport** - The nearest bus is at Llanfoist (1.5 miles). The train station is at Abergavenny (3.5 miles). Taxis from the station cost approximately £7.00
- **Directions** - Approx. 2 miles from A465 (Hereford/Neath), A40 (Brecon/Monmouth and M50) and A4042 (Newport, M4). See website for map. The farm is reached by a steep winding road from Llanfoist, crossing the Monmouthshire and Brecon Canal.

CONTACT: Richard and Rohan Lewis
Middle Ninfa Farm, Llanellen, Abergavenny, NP7 9LE
Tel: 01873 854662
richard@middleninfa.co.uk www.middleninfa.co.uk

Wern Watkin Bunkhouse is located in the Brecon Beacons National Park, high up on Mynnedd Llangattock. It is also known as YHA Llangattock Mountain. There is direct access on foot to the mountainside and a flat mountain road to a National Cycle Route. The Bunkhouse is a converted stone barn with bunks for 30 people in 7 mainly en-suite bedrooms. The massive dining room and seating area opens out onto ancient woodlands. There is under-floor heating throughout, excellent drying facilities and ample hot water. The location is ideal for caving, rock climbing, canoeing, abseiling, orienteering, pony trekking and mountain biking. Outdoor pursuit training can be arranged from local qualified instructors. The bunkhouse is within easy walking distance of Llangattock cave complex (one of Europe's most elaborate cave systems) as well as climbing crags and open moorland. A short drive away are the rest of Brecon Beacons, the scenic Wye and Usk river valleys and a wealth of industrial heritage at the World Heritage site of Blaenavon. Catering can be provided for groups.

DETAILS

- **Open** - All year, all day
- **Number of beds** - 30: 4x6, 1x4, 2x2. All rooms but one en-suite
- **Booking** - Availability shown online. 10% deposit, balance two weeks in advance.
- **Price per night** - Sole use £450 week nights, £555 weekend nights. Smaller groups by negotiation £16pp weeknights, £18.50 pp weekend.
- **Public Transport** - Trains Abergavenny (8miles). Nearest buses Crickhowell.
- **Directions** - Access can be either from Crickhowell or Brynmawr on small mountain roads. Detailed instructions will be sent with your booking.

CONTACT: Andrew Fryer
Wern Watkin, Hillside, Llangattock, Crickhowell, NP8 1LG
Tel: 01873 812307
enquiries@wernwatkin.co.uk   www.wernwatkin.co.uk

SMITHY'S
BUNKHOUSE

Located on a working hill farm, Smithy's Bunkhouse lies in the Black Mountains within the Brecon Beacons National Park, two and a half miles from the historic market town of Abergavenny. Designed to accommodate 24 persons in two dormitories of 12 bunks, additional space is available above the common room if required. The bunkhouse is equipped with showers, toilets, fully equipped kitchen, drying area, coin operated washer and dryer and a common room with a wood burning stove. It is heated during the winter by night storage heaters, hot water and electricity are supplied at no extra cost, some firewood is provided and extra may be purchased. A 16th-century coaching inn is located at the top of the farm drive which serves bar snacks, restaurant meals and traditional ales. The area is ideal for walking, climbing, caving, mountain biking, canoeing, water sports, pony trekking.

DETAILS

- **Open** - All year, 24 hours by arrangement
- **Number of beds** - 24 : 2 x 12
- **Booking** - Booking is advised. £150 deposit required for groups. Cheques payable to Smithy's Bunkhouse.
- **Price per night** - £13.50pp for individuals & small groups. £11pp for groups of 7+.
- **Public Transport** - Nearest train station Abergavenny (2 miles). Taxi fare from station approximately £5. No local buses.
- **Directions** - GR 304 178. Pantygelli village is located two and a half miles north of Abergavenny on the old Hereford Road. Access to the bunkhouse is down the farm drive opposite the Crown Inn.

CONTACT: Neil or Katy Smith
Lower House Farm, Pantygelli, Abergavenny, Monmouthshire, NP7 7HR
Tel: 01873 853432
info@smithysbunkhouse.com www.smithysbunkhouse.com

This old stone barn continues the tradition of 900 years when Llanthony Priory provided shelter and accommodation. Surrounded by the Black Mountains in the Brecon Beacons National Park, this spectacular setting is a superb base for walking, riding, pony trekking and other mountain activities.

Sixteen bunks are split into three separate areas for sleeping; there is a fully equipped kitchen, hot water for showers, heating throughout and a wood burning stove in the eating area. Small or large groups are welcome, but there is a minimum charge at weekends. Two pubs offer real beer and bar food.

Just 50 minutes from the M4 Severn Bridge and 1 hour from the M5/M50 Junction, this must be one of the easiest bunkbarns to reach from the motorways - and yet you feel you are miles from anywhere.

DETAILS

- **Open** - All year, 24 hours no restrictions
- **Number of beds** - 16: 1 x 8 : 1 x 4 : 1 x 6
- **Booking** - Booking and deposit required.
- **Price per night** - £10.00 per person. Minimum charge of £240 at weekends (2 nights).
- **Public Transport** - Abergavenny railway station 12 miles.
- **Directions** - GR SO 288 278 Map on website. Turn west off A465 Abergavenny to Hereford road at Llanvihangel Crucorney (5 miles north of Abergavenny). Llanthony is 6 miles along country lane - follow signs to Priory. On cycle route 42.

CONTACT:
Court Farm, Llanthony, Abergavenny, Monmouthshire, NP7 7NN
Tel: 01873 890359
courtfarm@llanthony.co.uk www.llanthony.co.uk

CANTREF FARM
BUNKHOUSES

The Upper Cantref Farm Bunkhouses are on a working farm situated in the heart of the Brecon Beacons National Park within walking distance of the main peaks and four miles from the town of Brecon. Two farm buildings have been converted to top quality bunkhouse accommodation.

The large bunkhouse accommodates groups up to 24 people. On the ground floor 6 bedrooms and 4 shower/toilet rooms are provided whilst on the 1st floor a fully equipped kitchen/dining area combines with a large common room. There is disabled access throughout lower floor.

The smaller bunkhouse accommodates up to 10 people. The building is single story and contains 3 bedrooms, 2 showers/toilet rooms and a fully equipped kitchen and eating area.

Both bunkhouses are fully heated and have plenty of hot water at all times and the use of coin operated tumble dryer. The bunkhouses may be used independently or together. We offer pony/horse riding on site.

DETAILS

- **Open** - All year, By arrangement
- **Number of beds** - Large 24: 2x6, 2x4,1x2, 1x2 ensuite. Small 10: 2x4,1x2.
- **Booking** - Advanced booking with deposit
- **Price per night** - From £13.50 pp. See website for up-dated prices.
- **Public Transport** - Trains: Abergavenny 20 miles. Buses: Brecon 4 miles.
- **Directions** - GR 057 258. From Brecon take the A40 east, after 2 miles turn left onto B4558, see Cantref Riding Centre sign, follow brown & white signs.

CONTACT:
Cantref, BreconPowys. LD3 8LR
Tel: (01874) 665223
info@cantref.com   www.cantref.com

Nestling between the river Usk and the Canal, Canal Barn Bunkhouse has a superb setting and yet is near Brecon town centre. The Bunkhouse is at the centre of activity in the Brecon Beacons National Park with easy access to the numerous exciting outdoor activities available in this beautiful part of Wales. Brecon town has a range of pubs, restaurants, takeaways and entertainments to satisfy most tastes and pockets, and all nearby in a safe walking distance. Sleeping up to 24 people, the Bunkhouse offers award winning environmentally friendly, competitively priced, group accommodation of exceptional quality that is accessible by disabled people.

Specifically designed as a base for your outdoor activities club, the Bunkhouse is equipped to a very high standard indeed and is an excellent venue for team building and residential training courses, or the place for an action packed get together with friends and family.

DETAILS

- **Open** - All year, all day
- **Number of beds** - 24 (in 6 rooms)
- **Booking** - Booking essential (minimum group of 6 people)
- **Price per night** - From £12.50
- **Public Transport** - Train/bus to Merthyr Tydfil or Abergavenny, then bus to Brecon.
- **Directions** - GR 052 279. On the canal towpath close to Brecon town centre. Vehicular access is via the canal bridge next to the Morrison Petrol Station on the nearby Abergavenny to Brecon road (B4601).

CONTACT: Ralph or Liz
Ty Camlas, Canal Bank, Brecon, Powys, LD3 7HH
Tel: 01874 625361
ihg@canal-barn.co.uk www.canal-barn.co.uk

TRERICKET MILL
BUNKHOUSE

Across the stream from Trericket Corn Mill this stone bunkhouse in an old cider orchard overlooks the River Wye. It is particularly suitable for small groups and individuals with two rooms sleeping four people each and an additional en-suite bunkroom for two in the mill. The bunkhouse is clean and cosy; heating, hot water and showers are all inclusive. Limited self-catering facilities are provided in a covered outdoor kitchen. Alternatively breakfasts and packed lunches can be provided and good pub meals are available locally. There are heated drying and common rooms in the mill and camping is also available.

Trericket Mill is situated on the Wye Valley Walk and National Cycle Route 8. An ideal stop-over for walkers, cyclists and for others wishing to relax in the beautiful countryside of Mid Wales. Canoeing, pony trekking, gliding, mountain bikes, rope centre and white water rafting all available locally.

DETAILS

- **Open** - All year, 24 hour access
- **Number of beds** - 10: 2 x 4, 1 x 2 en-suite, plus 6 veggie B&B beds
- **Booking** - Advanced booking advised.
- **Price per night** - From £12.50 per person
- **Public Transport** - Train stations at Builth Wells (10 miles) Hereford (30 miles) Merthyr Tydfil (30 miles). Daily bus service - ask to be dropped at Trericket Mill. National Express coaches drop off at Hereford and Brecon (13 miles). For transport enquiries call 0870 6082608.
- **Directions** - GR SO 112 414. We are set back from the A470 Brecon to Builth Wells road between the villages of Llyswen and Erwood.

CONTACT: Alistair/Nicky Legge
Erwood, Builth Wells, Powys, LD2 3TQ
Tel: 01982 560312
mail@trericket.co.uk www.trericket.co.uk

Exciting, untamed, & beautiful - do you see yourself in Wales? Ko Samui, Goa, London, Dublin, Merlins Ystradgynlais - what never heard of us? You will be describing us to your friends as a 'must go' place. Merlins offers basic but comfortable rooms the majority of which have en-suite facilities. Merlins has a warm and welcoming atmosphere and we pride ourselves on our Welsh hospitality. We have a bar and café. We are Wales Tourist board accredited, they say 'very comfortable hostel accommodation presented to a very good overall standard and very worthy of the 3 star quality rating awarded'. Being on the very edge of the Brecon Beacons National Park the area has lots of castles and historic sites to visit, is steeped in folklore and is famous for it's natural beauty. Merlins is well placed to offer a range of 'in your face' high adrenalin adventure activities such as canyoning, caving, climbing, abseiling, coasteering, hill walking, kayaking, canoeing, quad biking, paintballing, adventure days, and nearby Swansea has excellent nightlife.

DETAILS

- **Open** - All year, 24 hours
- **Number of beds** - 40: 1 x 13 : 1 x double : 2 x 2 : 1 x 5 : 4 x 4
- **Booking** - Booking essential
- **Price per night** - £15pp Monday to Thursday. £20pp Friday to Sunday.
- **Public Transport** - Hourly train services from London Paddington to Neath & Swansea, buses connect. Regular ferry between Swansea and Cork.
- **Directions** - M4 Junc.45. North on A4067 for 10 miles, right for Ystradgynlais, left at mini roundabout, over bridge, left after pedestrian crossing, 50 mtrs down on right.

CONTACT: Connie
44-46 Commercial Street, Ystradgynlais, Swansea, SA9 1JH
Tel: 01639 845670
info@callofthewild.co.uk www.backpackerwales.com

CLYNGWYN
BUNKHOUSE

Clyngwyn Bunkhouse is situated in the Brecon Beacons, in the heart of waterfall country, very near to the caves & waterfalls of Ystradfellte and close to the famous Sgwd Yr Eira waterfalls where you can walk behind the falling water. The location has ideal terrain for mountain biking, gorge walking, canyoning, caving, abseiling, climbing, quad biking, photography and painting. Clyngwyn Bunkhouse is ideal for groups of friends or family. It sleeps up to 15 with camping for 5 people available to larger groups. There is a fully equipped kitchen, central heating and a drying area which ensure a cosy stay. There is a relaxation area with TV, DVD and CD player and outside there is a fire-pit and BBQ which make a great place to relax in the evenings enjoying the mountain views. There is also 4 acres of land ideal for ball games and team building exercises and a separate function room for hire. The local villages of Ystradfellte and Pontneddfechan (2½ miles away) have pubs with restaurants and are accessible via a local mini bus taxi service. Dogs by arrangement.

DETAILS

- **Open** - All year, all day
- **Number of beds** - 19: 1x11, 2x4
- **Booking** - Booking essential. Credit/Debit cards not accepted
- **Price per night** - Weekdays sole use for up to 15 £150pn, up to 19 £190pn, £15pp for small groups, £52 for a 4 bed room. Weekends up to 15 £180pn, or £228pn.
- **Public Transport** - Trains Neath or Merthyr (11 miles). Mini bus can be arranged.
- **Directions** - From A465 leave at Glenneath drive-through and take signs for Pontneddfechan. Then 2.5 miles up Ystradfellte road, turn right down small track.

CONTACT: Julie Hurst
Clyngwyn Farm, Ystradfellte Rd, Pontneddfechan, Powys, SA11 5US
Tel: 01639 722930
enquiries@bunkhouse-south-wales.co.uk www.bunkhouse-south-wales.co.uk

Hardingsdown Bunkhouse is a tastefully restored stone barn situated on an organic farm. It provides comfortable self-catering accommodation for families or groups. The ground floor consists of a fully equipped kitchen, 2 shower/toilet rooms, a living room with 2 single sofa-beds and comfy chairs. Off the living room is a bedroom with a bunkbed sleeping 2 people. A spiral staircase leads upstairs where there are 3 bedrooms sleeping 5, 3 and 2 in bunks and single beds. A separate drying room is available for outdoor gear and a lock-up for storing bikes, surfboards, canoes etc. There is ample parking and a patio area which catches the evening sun. The Gower has national nature reserves, outstanding coastal scenery, family beaches, castles and ancient monuments. Llangennith beach is one of the best surfing beaches in the south west and Mewslade Bay and Fall Bay are used by climbers. Walkers and bikers can use the local network of footpaths and bridleways. Shops and pubs nearby.

DETAILS

- **Open** - All year, 24 hours
- **Number of beds** - 14: 1x5, 1x3, 3x2
- **Booking** - Non-returnable deposit of 30%, balance 1 month before arrival.
- **Price per night** - Sole use £180, £1100 per week. Smaller groups sharing the bunkhouse with other users, £15 per person.
- **Public Transport** - Regular bus (No16) from Swansea 0870 6082608.
- **Directions** - Turn left off the B4295 ½ mile after Burry Green (by bus shelter and post box). Follow lane till it changes into a rough track and turn right into Lower Hardingsdown Farm. Bunkhouse is on left of farmyard.

CONTACT: Allison or Andrew Tyrrell
Lower Hardingsdown Farm,Llangennith, Gower,Swansea, SA3 1HT
Tel: 01792 386222
bunkhousegower@tiscali.co.uk www.bunkhousegower.co.uk

Gilfach Wen Barn has been converted to provide competitively priced self-catering accommodation for individuals, extended families or groups on a working farm adjacent to Brechfa Forest. Graded as a 4 star bunkhouse it sleeps up to 32 in 7 bedrooms and has a large kitchen/dining room, lounge and drying room. There is a downstairs bedroom and shower room for disabled visitors. The facilities are purpose designed to be walker, cyclist and equestrian friendly for those taking advantage of the benefits of being adjacent to Brechfa Forest - the largest man made forest in Europe.

Gilfach Wen Barn is a perfect venue for a holiday or weekend away – if you do not want to drive you need never leave the valley. The barn is fully equipped and the village is within walking distance (1mile).
This is a stunningly beautiful area close to Brecon Beacons National Park, in the foothills of the Cambrian Mountains but only a short drive to Cefn Sidan Sands - an award winning 7 mile long beach.

DETAILS

- **Open** - Open all year, all day
- **Number of beds** - 32: 3x6, 1x5, 1x4,1x3,1x2 in 10 double beds and 12 singles.
- **Booking** - Advance booking required.
- **Price per night** - £15 per person. Sole use is £325 per night.
- **Public Transport** - Trains and coaches at Carmarthen. Daily bus from Carmarthen to Brechfa passes gate. Bus stop at Horeb crossroads but may drop at gate,
- **Directions** - GR SN 513 292 On the B4310 between Horeb and Brechfa.

CONTACT: Jillie
Gilfach Wen, Brechfa, Carmarthenshire, SA32 7QL
Tel: 07970 629726
GilfachWenBarn@aol.com www.brechfa-bunkhouse.com

PANTYRATHRO
INTERNATIONAL HOSTEL

Llansteffan is a beautiful quaint village set at the tip of the Towi River and Carmarthen Bay. The sandy beaches nestled below the castle offer swimming and relaxation. The virtually traffic free country lanes make this area ideal for cycling. For the walker Carmarthenshire offers coastal walks and country walks. Carmarthen (Wales' oldest city) and ancestral home to Merlin of King Arthur's Legends, offers most social and cultural activities. The Pantyrathro International Hostel provides dorm and double room accommodation and also 3 new ensuite units of 6, 8 and 12 beds. Facilities include self-catering kitchen, dining area, TV lounge and showers. Our two Mexican bars offer pool, darts, TV, weekly drink specials and food (eat-in or take-out). Horse riding, cycle hire and excursions for trekking, canoeing and surfing offered. Take a day trip or relax on the beaches or have a drink in our bars - something for everyone.

DETAILS

- **Open** - March to Jan, 24 hours
- **Number of beds** - 51: 1 x 12, 1 x 8, 2 x 6, 4 x 4, 1 x 3
- **Booking** - Booking recommended. 50% depost required in advance for groups.
- **Price per night** - £13pp dorm, £14pp ensuite. Group discounts.
- **Public Transport** - Carmarthen has both coach and train stations servicing South Wales, SW England and London. Local bus runs 6 times a day to Llansteffan. Ask driver to let you off at Pantyrathro.
- **Directions** - Pantyrathro is 6 miles from Carmarthen on the B4312, midway between Llangain and Llansteffan. Two miles from Llangain you will see the hostel signposted, turn right and follow signs to top of lane.

CONTACT: Ken Knuckles
Pantyrathro Country Inn, Llansteffan, Carmarthen, SA33 5AJ
Tel: 01267 241014, Fax: 241014
kenknuckles@hotmail.com www.backpackershostelwales.co.uk

PENQUOIT
CENTRE

Penquoit was an ancient half croft where the human inhabitants originally lived above the animals.   It has been converted into hostel accommodation for groups of between 10 and 25.   The centre is adjacent to the Pembrokeshire National Park and within 8-20 miles of over twenty beautiful beaches and the Preseli Hills, castles, Tenby and Caldy, riding and canoeing.   The area is rich in bird life, river, sea and wildfowl but the focus is for group activities/workshops/ creativity.   There is a courtyard, a long room, also a range of fields (one with sauna), woodland and estuary. The centre is ideal for drama, healing, plant studies, yoga, art work and family get-to-gethers.

The hostel consists of two dormitories, (one on the ground floor), communal showers and toilet block. There are also two private rooms. There is a large dining room with wood burning stove.   The kitchen is fully equipped and the centre is fully centrally heated.

DETAILS

- **Open** - All year, all day
- **Number of beds** - 25+: 1 x 10, 1 x 15, plus 2 private rooms.
- **Booking** - Booking essential, deposit 25%.
- **Price per night** - £10 per person
- **Public Transport** - Trains and National Express stop at Kilgetty or Tenby (7miles). Irish Ferry and Pembroke (6 miles). We can collect if necessary
- **Directions** - M4 to Carmarthen, A40 towards Haverfordwest. At Canaston Bridge (just after Robeston Wathem) take A4075 for Pembroke, at Cresselly (6 miles) turn right, then right again at T junction.   After small bridge turn left uphill towards Lawrenny, the Centre is on right (½ mile).

CONTACT: Joan Carlisle
Lawrenny, Kilgetty, Pembrokeshire, SA68 0PL
Tel: (01646) 651666
joan@penquoit.plus.com

Millennium hostel is a refurbished Victorian school situated in an attractive village on the upper reaches of the Cleddau River with almost direct access to river and woodland areas. The hostel is centrally heated thoughout, it has a modern kitchen/dining area, a good-sized common room and access to a large hall for activities (hire separate). There are 2 showers, 3 WCs and all rooms have wash hand basins. The kitchen area is equipped with a large oven, 3 four-ring hobs, 2 microwaves, 2 large toasters, 2 fridges and a freezer. There is a good drying room, a large car park, cycle shelter and a patio with picnic tables. The hostel has a 15-seater mini-bus, which can be hired by the day. Community shop in village open 7 days a week. Pub and tearoom within walking distance. There is 24 hour contact by freephone with the Warden who lives in the village.

DETAILS

■ **Open** - All year for groups. Easter to 31st Oct for individuals/ families, from 5pm.
■ **Number of beds** - 23. 1x3, 3x4, 1x8. All can be used as family rooms.
■ **Booking** - Required with deposit of 50%, balance payable on arrival. No deposit required if booking less than 7 days in advance.
■ **Price per night** - Adult £13.50, under 18 £9, under 3 years free. Sole use by group £225 per night (groups must bring their own sleeping bags).
■ **Public Transport** - Coachs/trains at Kilgetty (8m). Get 381 bus (Tenby to Pembroke Dock) at Kilgetty, ask for Cresswell Quay, 2½m (40 min walk) from hostel.
■ **Directions** - From A40 St Clears to Haverfordwest take A4075 signed Tenby and Oakwood Leisure Park. Just past turning to Oakwood, turn right and follow signs to Lawrenny. Bear right in front of church. Car park is on left behind Village Hall.

CONTACT: Admin
Lawrenny, Pembrokeshire, SA68 0PN
Tel: 01646 651270 / 651856
lawrenny.hostel@xifos.co.uk

The Stackpole Centre provides fully accessible holiday and conference accommodation, only a mile from Broadhaven and Barafundle beaches in the Pembrokeshire Coast National Park.

The Stackpole estate of countryside and coast includes a nature reserve, ancient settlements, stunning cliffs and wild woodlands.

The accommodation has been developed from a range of stone farm buildings. It comprises three large houses and five cottages, which sleep between 5 and 19 people in single and twin rooms. Facilities include a leisure pool, sauna, theatre and covered arena. Contacts are available for activities such as canoeing, rock climbing, abseiling, cycling, horseriding, music and drama.

DETAILS

■ **Open** - All year, all day, Reception 9am - 8 pm
■ **Number of beds** - Kingfisher House 17/19: 2x2, 13x1. Swan House 14: 2x2, 10x1. Heron House 16: in ten bedrooms. Swift Cottage:7. Swallow Cottage 6: 3x2, two more cottages of 6: 3x2, 1 cottage 4 : 2x2
■ **Booking** - Bookings are made through reception.
■ **Price per night** - Minimum of two nights stay. Please contact bookings team for a quote. There are low and high season tariffs.
■ **Public Transport** - Trains Pembroke (5 miles). Bus from Pembroke: Silcox 387 Coastal Cruiser.
■ **Directions** - On the B4319 from Pembroke to Stackpole and Bosherton (various entry points onto estate).

CONTACT: Stackpole Reception
Old Home Farm Yard, Stackpole, nr Pembroke, Pembrokeshire, SA71 5DQ
Tel: 01646 661425
stackpole.receptionc@nationaltrust.org.uk www.stackpolecentre.org.uk

Upper Neeston Lodges are energy-efficient barn conversions on a family run sheep farm. Close to the Milford Haven Waterway in the Pembrokeshire Coast Park they are ideal for divers, climbers and walkers. There are two independent units, one accommodating 10 people and one accommodating 8. Shared between the units are a laundry/drying room, wash-down area, secure storage areas and ample parking. THE COWSHED is single storey with disabled access. It has a large sitting room and kitchen/dining area, and two bedrooms, each with a large en-suite shower room and sleeping 6 and 4 in bunks. THE BARN has two storeys with an upstairs sitting room and kitchen/dining area. The bedrooms are downstairs sleeping 6 and 2 in bunks each with en-suite shower room. Each unit has a TV, CD player and wood burning stove, both have access to garden/patio areas. Graded as a 5 Star bunkhouse by the WTB.

DETAILS

- **Open** - All year, check in from 4pm. Check out before10.30am
- **Number of beds** - Cowshed 10:1x6,1x4 Barn 8:1x6,1x2
- **Booking** - Provisional booking taken by phone and confirmed by deposit.
- **Price per night** - £15.00pp (includes bed linen). Minimum of 6 people guarantees exclusive use of a lodge. Minimum of 2 nights stay on weekends (3 nights on Bank Holidays).
- **Public Transport** - Trains and coaches at Milford Haven. Buses at Herbrandston (approx 1/4 mile). Puffin coastal shuttle passes the farm. www.traveline-cymru.org.uk
- **Directions** - Follow A4076 through Milford Haven to roundabout by Docks. Take first exit (signed Hakin). Follow for 2 miles, look for first farm on left (next to layby).

CONTACT: Sean or Mandy Tilling
Upper Neeston Farm, Dale Road, Herbrandston, Milford Haven, SA73 3RY
Tel: 01646 690750
mail@upperneeston.co.uk www.upperneeston.co.uk

CAERHAFOD
LODGE

Ideally situated between the famous cathedral city of St Davids and the Irish ferry port of Fishguard, the Lodge overlooks the spectacular Pembrokeshire coastline. It is within easy walking distance of the well known Sloop Inn at Porthgain and the internationally renowned Coastal Path. The Celtic Trail cycle route passes the bottom of our drive making it an ideal stopover for cyclists.

The Lodge is a good base for all outdoor activities. Boat trips around Ramsey Island or to Grassholm to see the gannets can be arranged, as well as surfboard, wetsuit and cycle hire. The lodge is centrally heated and sleeps 23 in 5 separate rooms (4,4,4,5,6) all en-suite with great showers! There is a modern fully equipped kitchen/diner with patio and picnic tables and glorious sunsets. On site washing/drying room and secure storage area. Dogs welcome by prior arrangement. Smoking outdoors. Wales Tourist Board 4 star. Bike hire.

DETAILS

- **Open** - All year, 24 hours
- **Number of beds** - 23: 3x4 : 1x5 : 1x6.
- **Booking** - Advised in high season. 50% deposit.
- **Price per night** - Adult £15 Under 16 £12. Group rates.
- **Public Transport** - Trains at Fishguard (9m) and Haverfordwest (15m). Fishguard/Rosslare ferry. National Express Haverfordwest. 411 Bus Haverfordwest-St Davids-Fishguard 50yds from Lodge. Seasonal coastal shuttle service for walkers.
- **Directions** - GR Landranger 157, SM 827 317. A40 from Haverfordwest, left at Letterston (B4331) to Mathry. Left onto A487 to St Davids, right in Croesgoch for Llanrhian, at crossroads right for Trefin. After ½ mile turn into our drive.

CONTACT: Carolyn Rees.
Llanrhian, St Davids, Haverfordwest, Pembrokeshire, SA62 5BD
Tel: 01348 837859
Caerhafod@aol.com www.caerhafod.co.uk

OLD SCHOOL HOSTEL
FORMERLY YHA TREFIN

WALES

Escape to this wonderful, wild and rugged corner of the Pembrokeshire Coast National Park. We are in the centre of Trefin, an attractive village just a quarter of a mile from the famous coastal path and only 15 minutes from the cathedral city of St Davids and the popular beach at Whitesands Bay. The village has a pub and an award winning café/gallery. Stunning wild beaches and small harbour villages can be reached in a few minutes by car, or visited as part of a days circular walk. Our friendly characterful 4 Star hostel offers comfortable accommodation at prices that are hard to beat. Shared rooms are from £11 per person and we also offer singles, twins and doubles from only £14 per person. Family rooms sleeping 3 to 6 are available from £36 peak season. We also offer the option of an organic breakfast if desired. Our electricity is supplied from renewable energy, we offer 'eco' discounts and plant a tree for every booking. Help create a forest for the future – come and stay!

DETAILS

■ **Open** - All year, check in from 5pm. All day access.
■ **Number of beds** - 23: 1x6, 2x5, 1x3, 2x2
■ **Booking** - Advance booking recommended
■ **Price per night** - £11/£12 shared rooms, private rooms from £14 per person, family rooms from £36, exclusive use of hostel £200 per night.
■ **Public Transport** - Train/National Express to Haverfordwest then Richards Brothers bus 411 via St Davids to Trefin. For times phone Traveline 0870 6082608
■ **Directions** - From the A40 turn left onto the B4331 at Letterston then left onto the A487. After 2.5 miles turn right just after the Square and Compass pub for Trefin.

CONTACT: Sue or Chris
Ffordd-yr-Afon, Trefin, Haverfordwest, Pembrokeshire, SA62 5AU
Tel: 01348 831 800
oldschoolhostel@btconnect.com www.theoldschoolhostel.co.uk

PEMBROKESHIRE
ACTIVITY CENTRE

On the banks of the River Cleddau, a stones throw from the UKs only coastal national park, Pembrokeshire Activity Centre is the perfect venue for outdoor pursuits with an unrivalled choice of land and water activities from coasteering to kayaking, power boating to cliff climbing and much more. With our own on-site accommodation it is an ideal place to come and visit for a day or stay for a week! Activities available for all from 8-80, families, youth groups, team building, schools etc. Our large free car park means coaches are no problem and with three slip ways, neither is getting on the water. Facilities include a climbing wall, a cafe with balcony looking out over the river and a floodlit play area. Activity residentials or accommodation-only stays available all year round. Rooms sleep 4 or 2 in adult sized pine bunks. There are hand basins in each room and separate toilet and shower facilities. Common rooms have optional TV and tea & coffee making facilities. There are kitchens for self catering or meals can be provided for a wide range of dietary requirements. Bedding is provided but please bring your own towels.

DETAILS

- **Open** - All year, all day
- **Number of beds** - 80: 2 houses of 6 x 4 beds; 2 other floors of 8 x 2 beds.
- **Booking** - Booking is essential
- **Price per night** - From £13pp. Group discounts available.
- **Public Transport** - Pembroke Dock Train station 1 mile, Irish ferry Port 2 miles.
- **Directions** - From Pembroke, head north on A4139, then onto A477. On A477 take 3rd right, just before the bridge. Turn right at roundabout, the Center is 1/2 mile.

CONTACT:
Cleddau Reach, Pembroke Dock, Pembrokeshire, SA72 6UJ
Tel: 01646 622013
pac@princes-trust.org.uk www.pembrokeshire-activity-centre.co.uk

Hamilton Backpackers Lodge is an excellent overnight stop on the stunning Pembrokeshire Coast Path. It is also an ideal overnight stay five minutes from the ferries to Rosslare in Ireland. Pembrokeshire has a wealth of natural beauty and local history and many beautiful secluded beaches.

The Backpackers Lodge is a very comfortable and friendly hostel with small dormitories and double rooms, all centrally heated. There is a dining room and TV lounge with Sky. The garden at the back of the hostel has a hammock, barbecue and picnic tables. We provide free tea, coffee and light breakfast. There is parking close by and the hostel is in the centre of town near to a number of pubs serving good meals. There is no curfew. Smoking is permitted only in the garden patio. To find out more see website.

DETAILS

- **Open** - All year, 24 hours
- **Number of beds** - 10: 2 x 4, 1 x 2
- **Booking** - Booking advised to confirm beds. 50% deposit required from groups.
- **Price per night** - £16pp(dorm), £20pp in double ensuite
- **Public Transport** - Fishguard ferry port has a train station and ferries to Rosslare in Ireland. The port is 1 mile from the hostel (approx taxi fare £7). National Express coaches call at Haverfordwest (15 miles). For local buses in Pembrokeshire phone Richard Bros (01239) 613756.
- **Directions** - From Haverfordwest (A40) to Fishguard Square, across first right by tourist office, 50 yds on left. From Cardigan A487 (North Wales Road) up hill and first left. From harbour 1 mile to Fishguard Square, left, first right, 50 yards on left.

CONTACT: Steve Roberts
21/23 Hamilton Street, Fishguard, Pembrokeshire, SA65 9HL
Tel: 01348 874797 / 07813 687570
hamiltonbackpackers@yahoo.co.uk www.hamiltonbackpackers.co.uk

TYCANOL FARM
CAMPING BARN

Tycanol Farm offers accommodation for four in a camping barn close to the beautiful Pembrokeshire coast. For larger groups there is a camp site for tents and caravans which overlooks the whole of Newport Bay. Showers are available for the barn and camping and the hot water is free. There are no meals provided on the site but the camping barn has self-catering facilities and there are pubs and restaurants within a 10 minute walk. Laundry facilities are available on the site and there is also access to a drying room. There are many activities to enjoy in the surrounding area. Pony trekking and a golf club are within a mile of the site. The area is also ideal for canoeing and sailing. The site is a five minute walk to the coastal path and ten minutes to Newport itself. There is also a nature trail which contains badger setts. Free barbecue every night at 6.30pm. Everybody greeted with a warm welcome.

PLEASE CONTACT THIS HOSTEL BY PHONE OR POST.

DETAILS

- **Open** - All year, 24 hours
- **Number of beds** - 4 in the barn plus camping.
- **Booking** - Booking not always necessary.
- **Price per night** - £12pp per night (camping barn), £7pp per night (camping).
- **Public Transport** - Nearest train station is at Fishguard (7 miles away). Nearest National Express coaches are at Haverfordwest (18 miles away). Local buses pass the farm drive every hour; call (01239) 613756.
- **Directions** - Tycanol Farm is near beach a mile outside of Newport, Pembrokeshire on the A487 towards Fishguard. Turn right at milk-stand signpost.

CONTACT: Hugh Harries
Tycanol Farm, Newport, Pembrokeshire, SA42 0ST
Tel: 01239 820264

THE LONG BARN

The Long Barn is a traditional stone barn providing comfortable and warm bunkhouse accommodation. It is situated on a working organic farm in beautiful countryside, with views over the Teifi Valley. The stunning Ceredigion Coast and the Cambrian Mountains are both an easy drive away and the busy small town of Llandysul (1.5 miles away) has all essential supplies.

The barn's location is ideal for exploring, studying or simply admiring the Welsh countryside. Activities enjoyed by guests in the surrounding area include: fishing, swimming, climbing, abseiling, canoeing, farm walks and cycling. The barn is open all year, having adequate heating with a lovely warm Rayburn, log fire, roof insulation and double glazing throughout.

DETAILS

- **Open** - All year, all day
- **Number of beds** - 34
- **Booking** - Essential, deposit required
- **Price per night** - £10.00pp (adult), £8.00pp (under 18s). Discount of 10% for groups of 20 or more.
- **Public Transport** - Carmarthen (16 miles) has a train station and National Express service. Taxi fare from Carmarthen is approximately £20. Llandysul (1.5 miles away) has a local bus service, phone 0870 6082608 for details.
- **Directions** - OS map 146, GR 437 417. In Llandysul, at the top of the main street, take right hand lane. Turn sharp right down hill. After 100 yds turn sharp left. Another ½ mile turn first right. Continue for 1 mile Long Barn is on your right.

CONTACT: Tom or Eva
Penrhiw, Capel Dewi, Llandysul, Ceredigion, SA44 4PG
Tel: 01559 363200, Fax: 01559 363200
cowcher@thelongbarn.co.uk www.thelongbarn.co.uk

The hostel is a basic but nice old stone building on a small working farm in the hills near the West Wales coast. Our closest beach is about 7 miles away. The hostel has two floors, the top floor splitting into two rooms of 8 or two family rooms. The sleeping is basic on comfortable camp beds. There is a fully equipped kitchen, nice sized lounge, log burning stove and TV. There are 2 toilet shower rooms and a small drying room. We are close to one of the 7 top Welsh mountain bike areas (Brechfa Forest). Also as Adventure Beyond we offer a number of packages for stag and hen groups, schools, etc for team building or just a laugh. Activities (subject to availability) include canoeing, kayaking, raft building, climbing, fishing, farm fun, assault course, clay shooting, zorb ball, hill walking, orienteering courses, coasteering and surfing.

DETAILS

- **Open** - All year, all day
- **Number of beds** - 10: 2x8, 1x2 (Family rooms on request)
- **Booking** - Booking is essential, deposit required if booking more then 1 week.
- **Price per night** - £10pp (bring your own bedding)
- **Public Transport** - Train and bus stations at Carmarthen. Bus stop at Croeslan.
- **Directions** - From Carmarthen follow the A485, At Windy Corner Garage take left turn A4459 to Pencader, After Pencader take the next left (at top of hill) to Llandysul, Follow the road over the river on the A486 to the village of Croeslan. Take the left turn to Maesllyn, a very small road. Follow the road down a large hill and up the other side. At the village of Coed-y-Bryn there will be a dead end road in front of you. Go down to the yard and you are there.

CONTACT: Jethro, Glenis or Stuart
Nant Y Pobty Farm, Coed Y Bryn, Llandysul, Ceradigion, SA44 5LQ
Tel: 01239 858852, Mob 07787 123761
fun@adventurebeyond.co.uk www.adventurebeyond.co.uk

BWTHYN Y BUGAIL
SHEPHERD'S COTTAGE

Croeso, failte, degemer, bienvenue, wilkommen, bienvenida, witamy, welkom.

Welcome, to remote Bwthyn y Bugail, on a farm at 1265ft in the Elenydd. Panoramic views and no other buildings in sight. Escape from traffic noise, and modern distractions. The stars are breathtaking.

Trail walk or ride in the footsteps of the drovers who stayed here. See Blaen Brefi Nature Reserve, the Pysgotwr gorge, Soar y Mynydd chapel or nearby lakes. Defnyddiwch eich Gymraeg. For an extra dimension, dip into the culture and try a course in Welsh or local history.

The Bwthyn has wood/peat central heating, cast iron radiators, clean spring water, bathroom, kitchen/drying area. There is a cosy sitting room, dining room/ bilingual library, bike lock-up and emergency telephone. Winters by the Rayburn are magic when the cattle are in the byre and snow dusts the forest.

Why not try Ty'n Cornel and Dolgoch hostels or the New Inn, Foelallt Arms and shop Brefi.

DETAILS

- **Open** - All year from 1st May 2009, reception 4pm-7pm, 8am-10am
- **Number of beds** - 6: 1x4, 1x2 (1x 6 soon)
- **Booking** - Cash on arrival. To book send cheque 2 weeks prior (essential Xmas)
- **Price per night** - £14pp, double room £30. Courses extra.
- **Public Transport** - Trains: Llandovery 14m. Bus stop Llanddewi 6m.
- **Directions** - From Llanddewi go east for 4½m. After cattle grid take track to right for 1½m. No vehicular access. GR. SN 708515. Lifts possible.

CONTACT: Welsh Paul
Draenllwyn Du Farm, Llanddewi Brefi, Tregaron, Ceredigion SY25 6PG
Tel: 01974 298891 or write.
sam@backpackerspress.com

TY'N CORNEL
TYNCORNEL HOSTEL

Ty'n Cornel Hostel is an isolated old farmhouse in the hills, with a cosy open fire. Favoured by walkers, cyclists, bird-watchers and lovers of solitude it is in the beautiful Doethie valley on the Cambrian Way long distance footpath. There are comfortable wooden bunk beds and good self-catering facilities.

You can enjoy the wild open moorlands and lakes of the Elenydd uplands. Other attractions include the Cors Caron National Nature Reserve, red kite feeding station, the Welsh Gold Centre at Tregaron, Teifi Pools, Elan Valley reservoirs, Dolaucothi Roman gold mines, Strata Florida Abbey and Llanerchaeron country house (National Trust).

DETAILS

- **Open** - All year, 24 hours, Reception 5pm -11pm & 7am -10am
- **Number of beds** - 16: 2x8
- **Booking** - Booking advisable; essential mid Nov-mid March. Book online at www.yha.org.uk. or ring YHA booking office on 0870 770 8868. For bookings within a week of your stay, ring 01980 629259.
- **Price per night** - £10 per adult, £7.50 (under 18s). Block bookings negotiable.
- **Public Transport** - Trains: Aberystwyth 28 m; Llanwrtyd Wells 16m. Coach: x40 (Cardiff – Aberystwyth) Lampeter 15 m. Bus: 585 (Lampeter – Tregaron) Llanddewi-Brefi 7m.
- **Directions** - Road from Llanddewi-Brefi, near Tregaron: follow hostel signs SE 7m (last mile track) Bridle path N. up Doethie valley on the Cambrian Way (Llandovery 15 m) or byway 2m NW from Soar y Mynydd chapel.

CONTACT: YHA booking office or www.yha.org.uk
Llanddewi Brefi, Tregaron, Ceredigion, SY25 6PH
Tel: YHA booking office 0870 770 8868 or within a week of stay 01980 629259.
Fax: 0870 7706081
tyncornel@yha.org.uk www.elenydd-hostels.co.uk

DOLGOCH
HOSTEL

Come and experience the peace of this unique location in the remote Tywi valley. A stay in this 17th century farmhouse will take you into an era before electricity, with gas for lighting and a large open fire for heat. Dolgoch is a traditional simple hostel now owned by the Elenydd Wilderness Trust. It has hot showers, a self catering kitchen/dining room and 21 beds in 3 dormitories. The Lôn Las Cymru (Welsh National Cycle Route) and the Cambrian Way pass nearby and there are many other mountain tracks to explore on foot, by mountain bike or pony. The location is also ideal for bird-watchers and lovers of solitude. The hostel is close to an old drovers track which leads over the heathy Cambrian mountains for 5 miles to the equally remote and simple Ty'n Cornel Hostel. Why not stay a night in each hostel and follow in the treads of the old drovers through a countryside which has changed little since their day ?

DETAILS

- **Open** - All year, 24 hours, Reception 5pm -11pm & 7am -10am
- **Number of beds** - 21: (in 3 rooms)
- **Booking** - Booking information is available on the YHA website: yha.org.uk
- **Price per night** - £10 per adult £7.50 (under 18).
- **Public Transport** - Train to Aberystwyth,Carmarthen or Llanwrtyd Wells. Bus X40: Cardiff/Carmarthen to Lampeter/Aberystwyth, Bus 585: Lampeter/Aberystwyth to Tregaron. Postbus 287: Llandovery to Rhandirmwyn.
- **Directions** - SN 806 562. You can walk to Dolgoch over the hills from Tregaron or take the winding Abergwesyn mountain road. The hostel is ¾ mile south of the bridge, along an unsurfaced track.

CONTACT: YHA Booking Office or Chris Mason
Dolgoch, Tregaron, Ceredigion, SY25 6NR
Tel: 0870 770 8868. For bookings within 5 days call 01782 253274
dolgoch@yha.org.uk www.elenydd-hostels.co.uk

Stonecroft Lodge, our self-catering guest house, is situated in Llanwrtyd Wells, 'The Smallest Town in Britain '. Surrounded by the green fields, mountains and glorious countryside of Mid-Wales, Llanwrtyd is renowned Red Kite country and is the centre for mountain biking, walking, pony trekking etc. The town hosts many annual events such as the Man V Horse Marathon, World Bog Snorkelling Championships and the Mid-Wales Beer Festival.

The Hostel offers a warm welcome and a comfortable stay. We are Wales Tourist Board Star Graded and have private or shared rooms with fully made up beds. There is a fully equipped kitchen, TV, video, free laundry and drying facilities, central heating, large riverside garden and ample parking. The Hostel adjoins our Good Beer Guide pub, Stonecroft Inn (where great food is available), and is truly your 'home away from home', offering the best of everything for your stay.

DETAILS

■ **Open** - All year, all day - phone on arrival
■ **Number of beds** - 27: 1 x 1 : 3 x 4 : 1 x 6 : 4 x (dbl + 1 sgl)
■ **Booking** - Welcome, 50% deposit.
■ **Price per night** - £16. Discounts for 3+ nights. Phone for exclusive-use rates.
■ **Public Transport** - Llanwrtyd Wells Station on the Heart of Wales line is a few minutes walk from the hostel.
■ **Directions** - GR 878 468. From Llanwrtyd town centre (A483) take Dolecoed Road towards Abergwesyn. Hostel is 100 yds on left. Check in at Stonecroft Inn.

CONTACT: Jane Brown
Dolecoed Road, Llanwrtyd Wells, Powys, LD5 4RA
Tel: 01591 610327, Fax: 01591 610304
party@stonecroft.co.uk www.stonecroft.co.uk

MAESBRYNCOCH
BARN

Maesbryncoch Barn is set in a peaceful spot near Builth Wells with lovely views of Mid Wales Hills. Ideal for families and small groups to get away from it all. The open-plan living, sleeping and kitchen area has 6 fold out beds (pillow and pillowcase provided), heater, large dining table, cooking facilites, fridge/freezer and sink unit. There's a separate washroom with shower (free hot water) and WCs. There is also storage for bikes and a pony paddock. The local area is excellent for paragliding, walking, mountain biking, riding, canoeing and fishing. Less than 2 miles from the Wye Valley, 3 miles from Royal Welsh Showground and 3½ miles from Builth Wells with shops, pubs, a theatre, cinema, leisure centre and golf course. Nearest pub serving food is 2½ miles away in Hundred House village. We can provide breakfast and supper with a little notice. Bring your own sleeping bags or order a bedding and towel pack for your stay. Visit Wales rated 2* bunkhouse. Member of ABO. Sorry, no dogs.

DETAILS

- **Open** - Open all year, all day
- **Number of beds** - 6: 1x6
- **Booking** - By email or phone
- **Price per night** - On a sliding scale from £10 each for 6 people sharing, up to £15 for one person. Bedding and towel pack £5pp.
- **Public Transport** - Nearest trains at Builth Road (4½ miles). Daily buses to Builth from Newtown, Brecon, Cardiff, Abergavenny, Aberystwyth. Pick up from Builth /Builth Road may be possible or local taxi. More info: 0871 200 2233, www.traveline.org.uk
- **Directions** - Just to the south of the A481, 3½ miles from Builth Wells, half way between Llanelwedd and Hundred House. Grid reference SO079527.

CONTACT: Louise and Tim
Maesbryncoch, Llanfaredd, Builth Wells, Powys, LD2 3TE
Tel: 01982 551116 or 07709 202355
louise.mbc@virgin.net www.maesbryncochbarn.co.uk

Stay at the 16th century New Inn on the River Wye and discover the forgotten countryside of Mid-Wales. The New Inn has a bunkhouse ideal for parties of walkers and cyclists as well as double, twin and family B&B rooms. The bunkhouse has its own entrance and a large lobby which can be used for boots and waterproofs. Secure storage is available for cycles and motor-cycles. The bunkhouse is self contained with toilets and showers. There are no self catering facilities but the Inn specialises in serving imaginative home-cooked local-grown food and a Welsh breakfast of home-made sausages and dry cured bacon is available for £5.

Explore the surrounding countryside, inhabited by red Kites, or relax in the secluded beer garden. There is plenty of parking and a large function room for parties.

DETAILS

- **Open** - All year, all day, Pub closed 3pm - 5pm some days.
- **Number of beds** - Bunkhouse 10: 1x6, 1x4; B&B 11: family rooms, double & twin
- **Booking** - Book by phone.
- **Price per night** - £10 pp (Bunkhouse), £60 sole use of 6 bed room, £40 sole use of 4 bed room. Breakfast £5pp. Ensuite B&B in Inn £50 double/twin. Family rooms also available from £70.
- **Public Transport** - Trains at Llandrindod Wells 5 miles away. Infrequent bus service.
- **Directions** - Newbridge-on-Wye is on the A470 between Builth Wells and Rhayader. Travelling north on the A470 take a right turn in Newbridge and the New Inn is on the right.

CONTACT: Debbie and Dave
New Inn, Newbridge-on-Wye, Llandrindod Wells, Powys, LD1 6HY
Tel: 01597 860211
dave@pigsfolly.orangehome.co.uk   www.pigsfolly.co.uk/bunkhouse.htm

BEILI NEUADD
BUNKHOUSE

Beili Neuadd Bunkhouse is a converted 16th-century stone barn beautifully positioned in quiet, secluded countryside with delightful views, its own paddocks, stream, pools and woodland. The centrally heated barn sleeps 16 in 3 en-suite bunkrooms and includes a fully equipped kitchen/dining room, drying room and facilities for wheelchair users. The bunks have a standard mattress, bed linen is included, towels can be hired. Accommodation for 4 is also available in the adjacent Chalet and there is space to camp in the paddock behind. There are picnic tables and BBQ in the paddock and ample parking in the yard. The barn is 2.5 miles from the small market town of Rhayader - the gateway to the Elan Valley reservoirs, known as The Lakeland of Wales. It is adjacent to the Upper Wye Valley and the Cambrian Mountains. This spectacular countryside offers a wide range of activities including cycling, mountain biking, fishing, pony trekking, canoeing and of course bird watching and walking.

DETAILS

- **Open** - All year, all day access.
- **Number of beds** - 16: 2 x 6, 1 x 4. Chalet: 1 double, 2 singles
- **Booking** - Booking preferred (with deposit).
- **Price per night** - £14 per person. £200 sole occupancy.
- **Public Transport** - Nearest trains at Llandrindod Wells -12 miles. Some buses from Rhayader. Taxi from Rhayader about £4. Assistance with transport available.
- **Directions** - OS Explorer 200/OS147 GR 994698. Take the A44 east bound from Rhayader town centre (clock). After 0.4 miles turn left on unclassified road signposted Abbey Cwm-hir with Beili Neuadd sign. Take 1st left after 1.5 miles. Beili Neuadd 2nd farm on right after 0.4 miles.

CONTACT: Gillian and Richard Marks
Beili Neuadd, Rhayader, Powys, LD6 5NS
Tel: 01597 810211
rhayaderbreaks@yahoo.co.uk www.midwalesfarmstay.co.uk

PLAS DOLAU

Plas Dolau is set in quiet countryside just 3 miles from the popular coastal town of Aberystwyth. Ideal for exploring West Wales, walking, cycling, riding, fishing and golf etc. The holiday centre includes a warm country mansion (WTB 4 star hostel) with mainly dormitory style accommodation and an adjoining Scandinavian style farmhouse (WTB 3 star guesthouse) set in 22 acres.

Plas Dolau includes meeting rooms, dining rooms, games room, outdoors areas and walks. The centre can accommodate groups of up to 45 people. Various options for accommodation, provision of food, cooking facilities, etc are available. We are ideally suited for youth groups, field courses, retreats, house parties and many other groups or individuals. Phone to discuss your requirements.

DETAILS

■ **Open** - All year, 24 hours
■ **Number of beds** - 45: + cots etc. Plus 16 in farmhouse.
■ **Booking** - Recommended.
■ **Price per night** - Ranges from £16 (including basic breakfast) to £30 (private room, en-suite with full breakfast). From £500 per night for the whole mansion.
■ **Public Transport** - Nearest train station is in Aberystwyth. Taxi from the station will cost around £5. National Express coaches and local buses (525 and 526) will set down at the end of the hostel drive.
■ **Directions** - GR 623 813, OS map 135. On the A44, 3 miles from Aberystwyth, 1 mile from Llanbadarn railway bridge, 0.6 miles from turning to Bow Street. Sign on roadside says 'Y Gelli', B+B. Reception in 'Y Gelli'.

CONTACT:
Lovesgrove, Aberystwyth, Ceredigion, SY23 3HP
Tel: 01970 617834
pat.twigg@virgin.net   www.dolau-holidays.co.uk

MAES-Y-MOR

Maes-y-Mor offers superior accommodation at a budget price. Ideally situated near the town centre, 80m from the beach and 40m from the bus station. Accommodation at the hostel is room-only. There is a large kitchen diner with fridge freezer, hob oven, microwave and toaster enabling guests to prepare their own food. Bedrooms have TV, tea/coffee making facilities and beds of a superior quality to ensure a good nights sleep. Towels are provided. Halls and landings are themed in welsh history pictures. There is a car parking area at rear and secure shed for bikes.

Aberystwyth is an ideal base for north and south Wales. Visit Devil's Bridge with its dramatic waterfalls or Vale of Rheidol narrow guage railway, The National Library of wales, the Castle and the Harbour. Aberystwyth is a university town so there is plenty of night life. We offer a personal and helpful service.
Croeso Cymraeg Cynnes i bawb / a warm welsh welcome to all!

DETAILS

- **Open** - All year, 8am to 10pm
- **Number of beds** - 20: 8x 2, 1 x 4 (en-suite)
- **Booking** - Booking advisable
- **Price per night** - £19 per person, en-suite £22 per person. Single £22.
- **Public Transport** - Bus and Train Stations are within approximately 400 mts.
- **Directions** - From Bus and Train Stations follow Terrace Road in a straight line towards beach. Turn right at Tourist Board Shop, you will find us approx 30 mts along next to the cinema.

CONTACT: Gordon or Mererid
25 Bath Street, Aberystwyth, Ceredigion, SY23 2NN
Tel: 01970 639270 or 07966 502715
maesymor@hotmail.co.uk www.maesymor.co.uk

Maesnant is set in the remote hillsides of the Plynlimon mountain, an ideal location for hillwalking and mountain biking. The Centre is designed for use by youth groups, but family and other groups are welcome. Inside the centre there are 3 bunk rooms, two wash rooms (each with shower, wcs etc), kitchen and a large common room with dining facilities.

Accommodation in the Centre is limited to 16 persons, though camping is possible in the 12 acres of grounds. Maesnant is hired out on a self-catering basis. Groups under 16 years of age must include 2 adults. There are many attractions in the area; Devils Bridge waterfalls and steam powered railway, Llywernog Mine Museum, Bwlch Nant Yr Arian Forest Centre and the Powergen Rheidol Hydro Electric Power Scheme visitor centre.

DETAILS

■ **Open** - March to November, no restrictions
■ **Number of beds** - 16: 2 x 6 : 1 x 4
■ **Booking** - Telephone booking essential. Deposit (£30) required 4 weeks in advance.
■ **Price per night** - £5 pp
■ **Public Transport** - Nearest mainline railway station Aberystwyth, bus services to Ponterwyd.
■ **Directions** - A44 from Aberystwyth to Ponterwyd, take scenic route to Nan y Moch via mountain road, (east end of village by 30mph sign). After 6 cattle grids and before 7th take a right turn, Maesnant is 1.5 miles at the end of the road.

CONTACT: Julie Bellchambers
Maesnant, Ponterwyd, Aberystwyth, Ceredigion, SY23 3AG
Tel: 07747 017371
info@maesnant.org.uk www.maesnant.org.uk

BRAICH GOCH
BUNKHOUSE & INN

The Braich Goch is a 16th-century coaching inn situated 3 miles from Cadair Idris. There are stunning views of the Dulas valley and Dyfi Forest. The Braich has been specifically set up with outdoor enthusiasts in mind. Facilities include drying room, secure bike storage and large well equipped self-catering kitchen. There are 6 bedrooms, 4 en-suite and a further two bathrooms. The location is ideal for walking, mountain biking, cycling, climbing and canoeing at all levels as well as bird watching or simply chilling out. Dyfi Forest mountain bike trails on doorstep.

The Braich is also a pub with pool table, darts and other games to keep you entertained in the evening! Also available are activity packages with qualified instructors suitable for all levels. In the area are King Arthur's Labyrinth and Corris Craft Centre, Centre for Alternative Technology, Coed-y-Brenin Forest Park and the coast. WTB 4 star. Walkers & Cyclists Welcome Awards.

DETAILS

- **Open** - All year, all hours by arrangement
- **Number of beds** - 26: 5 x 4 : 1 x 6
- **Booking** - Essential for groups. 20% deposit, balance 2 weeks before arrival.
- **Price per night** - From £16pp
- **Public Transport** - Nearest train station to Corris is Machynlleth. Bus stop outside the 'Braich Goch' Inn. Taxis can be hired from Machynlleth.
- **Directions** - GR 754 075 On A487 between Machynlleth and Dolgellau at Corris turning. 2.5 miles north of Centre for Alternative Technology.

CONTACT: Ann or Andy
Corris, Machynlleth, Powys, SY20 9RD
Tel: 01654 761229 mobile 07881 626734
AnnBottrill@aol.com www.braichgoch.co.uk

CORRIS
HOSTEL

Nestled in the foothills of Cadair Idris, this award winning hostel enjoys splendid views over the Dyfi Valley. Corris Hostel is renowned as a spiritual haven with its caring, easy going atmosphere, friendly staff, cosy wood fires and collection of books, games and artefacts. Outdoors the evolving landscaped gardens provide a serene, relaxing environment.

Environmental awareness is promoted through the hostel's vegetarian focus, recycling, composting, gardens and energy efficiency. Visitors can find more about Green lifestyle at the nearby Centre for Alternative Technology (celebrated worldwide as Europe's leading Eco-Centre). Down river are national Biosphere nature reserves and miles of golden beaches at Aberdyfi. Wide range of countryside and environmental activities with workshops run by local people.

DETAILS

- **Open** - All year, all day access.
- **Number of beds** - 42/44
- **Booking** - Phone to check.
- **Price per night** - Adult £15.00, child £12.00, Breakfast £3.30.
- **Public Transport** - Buses 30, X32, 34 and Trawscambria 701 pass Machynlleth train station on the Cambrian Coast line with connection to Aberystwyth and Birmingham.
- **Directions** - GR 753 080. We are in the mountain village of Corris 6 miles north of Machynlleth. At Braich Goch turn off A487 into Corris. At Slaters Arms pub turn left, hostel is 150m uphill beyond a small carpark.

CONTACT: Anne, Michael or Debbie
Old School, Corris, Machynlleth, Powys, SY20 9TQ
Tel: 01654 761686
mail@corrishostel.co.uk www.corrishostel.co.uk

Ty'n y Berth is a former school at the foot of Cadair Idris on the southern edge of the Snowdonia National Park. Surrounded by mountains, valleys and crystal clear rivers, yet only 12 miles from the coast, it's a great location for outdoor activities and family holidays. The spacious accommodation sleeps up to 36. The main room is divided into dining and lounge areas; there is a commercial kitchen with large oven, hob and microwave; plenty of toilets & showers; drying room; pay phone; lockable storage for boats & bikes and parking for 10 cars.

Corris is within walking distance and has two pubs: the Slaters Arms, which does bar meals, and the Braich Goch Inn, which regularly has live music. Courses are also available in climbing, mountain walking, abseiling, gorge scrambling, mine exploration, ropes courses, orienteering, and team building. Accommodation for a further 35 is available at the Bryn Coedwig Centre (also run by Wide Horizons), four miles from Tyn Y Berth in the village of Aberllefenni.

DETAILS

- **Open** - All year , all day
- **Number of beds** - 36: 1x8, 3x6, 1x4, 1x2, 1xdbl, 2x1
- **Booking** - Book by phone or email.
- **Price per night** - Sole use £380, 12-14 beds £130, 10 beds £120.
- **Public Transport** - Trains run from London to Machynlleth with a change at Birmingham New Street. Our minibuses can meet your group at Machynlleth Station.
- **Directions** - On entering Corris Uchaf from north on A487. you will enter a 30 mph speed limit. Ty'n y Berth is the old school on the right, just inside the 30mph signs.

CONTACT: Jane or Dave
Corris Uchaf, Machynlleth, Powys, SY20 9RH
Tel: 01654 761678
tynyberth@widehorizons.org.uk www.widehorizons.org.uk/tyb

Caban Cader Idris is a listed building in a secluded wooded valley within walking distance of Cader Idris and the Mawddach Estuary in Snowdonia National Park. It is in an ideal setting for field work and outdoor pursuits with wonderful unspoilt mountain, valley and estuary walks from the doorstep. Local activities include climbing, hill walking, pony trekking, biking, canoeing, rafting and fishing. The area is also ideal for the study of geology, geography, local history, industrial archaeology and ornithology (RSPB woods adjoin grounds). Nearby are slate mines, dry ski slope, narrow gauge railways and beaches.

There is a large kitchen/dining room, two dorms sleeping 6 and 10, a lounge (with 3 beds), toilets, hot showers and a drying room. It is heated and has a payphone, car park and fire safety certificate. Camping by arrangement. This self-catering bunkhouse is ideal for groups but also open to individuals.

DETAILS

- **Open** - All year, no restrictions
- **Number of beds** - 19
- **Booking** - Booking is essential. Always phone before arrival. £20 per night deposit. Last minute enquiries welcome from individuals or groups.
- **Price per night** - Sole use:- £100 midweek, £125 Fri, Sat, Bank Holidays and New Year. Reduced rates for whole week bookings. Individuals £8 pp when available.
- **Public Transport** - Nearest train station is Morfa Mawddach (4 miles). Nearest bus stop is Abergwynant (¼ mile). For local bus info call 01341 422614.
- **Directions** - GR 682 169. From Dolgellau take the A493 to Fairbourne. 1 mile after Penmaenpool turn left just before Abergwynant Bridge. Bunkhouse 300yds on left

CONTACT: Dafydd Rhys
Islawrdref, Dolgellau, Gwynedd, LL40 1TS
Tel: 01766 762588, Mobile 07887 954301
dafydd.rhys@virgin.net

Crown Lodge, in Snowdonia National Park, sleeps 19 and is ideal for groups who require twin and single bedrooms. It is owned by Coleg Harlech WEA and is often used for educational purposes. It offers good basic no-frills accommodation (VisitWales 2 star) with ample parking and views over the miles of sandy beach at Tremadog Bay.

There is a kitchen for self catering and meals can be provided with prior notice. All bedding is provided but bring your own towels. The area is a haven for anyone who enjoys walking, climbing, sailing, fishing, pony trekking or cycling. Crown Lodge is within ¼ mile of Harlech town centre with its pubs, cafes, small shops, Harlech Castle and Theatr Ardudwy. The prestigious Royal St David's links golf course, considered to be the most difficult par 69 in the world, is nearby.

DETAILS

- **Open** - All year, key provided
- **Number of beds** - 19: 8 x 2, 3 x 1
- **Booking** - Booking is essential, non-refundable deposit of £60 required, full payment due 6 weeks prior to start date.
- **Price per night** - Sole use of property £470 - £2,100 / week – shorter periods available on request
- **Public Transport** - Harlech train station ¼ mile, limited bus service passes the property.
- **Directions** - Please apply for directions when booking.

CONTACT: Valmai Owen
Ffordd Isaf, Harlech, Gwynedd, LL46 2PR
Tel: 01766 781927
accom@fc.harlech.ac.uk www.harlech-holidays.com

BALA
BACKPACKERS

For Outdoor Adventures within the Snowdonia National Park, Bala Backpackers is Hostel-Style Good-Value Self-Catering Accommodation offering 32 Comfy SINGLE BEDS, 3 Private TWIN ROOMS and a Double Holiday-Let, in 1800's Character Buildings, located in a quiet, sunny chapel square, in the bustling market town of Bala, Mid North Wales. It is clean, safe and nice for the price with a careful, old, arty, homely atmosphere, with hints of Luxury, now called Flash-Packing! Bala boasts a five-mile-long Lake, a white-water River, ever popular for Raft Rides, and nestles beneath three 900metre Peaks. The hostel is equipped with Dining Room, Dripping Room and Guest Kitchen. Catering is available. A Leisure Centre, with fun pool, is at the lakeside, 5mins walk away. Plan your activities or just soak up the atmosphere by day or evening, in Town.

DETAILS

■ **Open** - All year, by prior arrangement (midweek especially). Reception 5pm-10pm and 8am-10am. Lock-Out 12pm
■ **Number of beds** - Hostel 32: 3x4, 4x5. + 3 Twin Rooms + 1 Double Holiday-Let.
■ **Booking** - On-line or by phone or email.
■ **Price per night** - Hostel: Sun-Thurs £12.50pp, Fri £14pp, Sat £15pp, Weekly £80pp. Twin room: £45, £55 ensuite. Holiday-Let: £325/week or £65/night, ONE-Night-Stay supplement at proprietor's discretion. All prices Include Bedding.
■ **Public Transport** - Trains: Wrexham (30 miles) or Barmouth (30miles). Bus no 94 every 2 hours Daily from Wrexham and Barmouth.
■ **Directions** - GR 926 358. Bala is on A494. Turn in the middle of Bala High Street, opposite the White Lion Royal Hotel, down Tegid Street to see HOSTEL Sign. Unload outside Hostel, but park round corner, in FREE overnight Pay & Display.

CONTACT: Stella Welch
32 Tegid Street, Bala, LL23 7EL
Tel: 01678 521700
info@Bala-Backpackers.co.uk www.Bala-Backpackers.co.uk

BALA
BUNK HOUSE

The coach house is a converted 200-year-old Welsh stone building. It carries WTB two star approval and is set back from the road in over an acre of picturesque grounds with a river and stream. Modernised to provide accommodation for outdoor activity groups, it is light, airy and comfortable with night storage heating and drying facilities. There is a large lounge/dining area and bunk rooms for 2, 4 and 8 plus annexe for 6. Separate ladies' and gentlemen's toilets have washing areas and hot showers. Fully equipped self-catering kitchen. The Little Cottage, a newly converted self-contained bunkroom sleeping 6, with kitchenette, shower and toilet/washing area, is ideal for smaller groups & families. Sheets & pillowcases are provided - bring a sleeping bag. There is a splendid view of the Berwyn Hills; together with the Aran and Arenig hills they provide superb walking. Bala Lake and the National White Water Centre are brilliant for water sports. Good pubs, restaurants and shops in Bala.

DETAILS

- **Open** - All year, no restrictions
- **Number of beds** - 26 : 1x2 : 1x4 : 1x6 : 1x8. 1x6 self-contained
- **Booking** - Book if possible, ring or write with 20% deposit. Weekends are busy.
- **Price per night** - Single night £16 pp, two or more nights £15 pp.
- **Public Transport** - Trains at Wrexham (30 miles). National Express at Corwen (10 miles). Local buses call at Bala (1.6 miles from hostel). Call hostel for a taxi.
- **Directions** - GR 950 372. From England take M6, M54, A5 through Llangollen then A494 for Bala. We are on the A494 1.5 miles before Bala.

CONTACT: Guy and Jane Williams
Tomen Y Castell, Llanfor, Bala, Gwynedd, LL23 7HD
Tel: 01678 520738, Fax: 01678 520738
thehappyunion@btinternet.com www.balabunkhouse.co.uk

Opening in March 2009, Llangollen's independent hostel is a fully refurbished town house with plenty of charm and character. In the centre of town, it is an ideal spot to explore the magnificent Vale of Llangollen, which offers walking, climbing, canoeing, paragliding, mountain biking and many other activities. The hostel provides comfortable and clean accommodation with cosy twin/ double rooms, family rooms, and great value 6 bed dorms. Continental breakfast is available, or you can prepare your own food in the fully equipped self-catering kitchen. There is a lounge with log-burner, book exchange and internet, plus a dining room, drying room and secure bike storage. Llangollen offers a great choice of restaurants and traditional pubs and is home to many cultural events, including the Fringe music festival and the annual International Eisteddfod. Other attractions include Valle Crucis Abbey, Telford's aqueduct, steam railway, Dinas Bran Castle, plus miles of superb scenery.

DETAILS

- **Open** - All year , all day (opening March 2009)
- **Number of beds** - 32
- **Booking** - Internet, e-mail or phone.
- **Price per night** - £14.50 (dorm), or from £16 (private room and/or en-suite).
- **Public Transport** - Daily National Express from London. Trains Ruabon (5 miles) – buses all day (every 15 mins until 6pm).
- **Directions** - From the A5 heading west, the hostel is located 50 yards past the main set of traffic lights on the right. Parking is at the rear of the hostel on Market Street – at the main traffic lights, turn right then first left.

CONTACT:
Isallt, Berwyn Street, Llangollen, LL20 8NB
Tel: 01978 861773, Mob: 07783 401894
info@llangollenhostel.co.uk www.llangollenhostel.co.uk

TYDDYN BYCHAN

Tyddyn Bychan is an 18th-century traditional Welsh farmhouse complex, set in two and a half acres of private grounds surrounded on all sides by farmland with a large parking area well away from the road. Situated in an excellent location for cycling, walking, climbing, fishing and numerous watersports including whitewater rafting.

The main bunkhouse sleeps 18 in two en-suite rooms. All the bunks are handmade and of a very high standard. The smaller bunkhouse sleeps 12 in two en-suite rooms and has its own kitchen and conservatory. All bedding, heating and electricity are included. We can provide delicious pre-booked, homemade food in the farmhouse and make up packed lunches. The bunkhouses are also very well equipped for self-catering with a well equipped kitchen / dining room..

DETAILS

- **Open** - All year, all day
- **Number of beds** - 30:- 1x10 1x8 2x6
- **Booking** - Booking is advisable
- **Price per night** - £12pp including bedding.
- **Public Transport** - Nearest train station is at Betws-y-Coed. Nearest National Express service at Llandudno. Phone 01492 575412 for details.
- **Directions** - GR 931 504. Turn off A5 at Cerrig y drudion. Take B4501 out of village for Llyn Brenig, take the turning on left for Cefn Brith. After about 2 miles you will see a phone box on left, chapel on right and the road widens for a layby. The gate for Tyddyn is on the left directly opposite junction on the right.

CONTACT: Lynda
Cefn Brith, Conwy, LL21 9TS
Tel: 01490 420680
lynda@tyddynbychan.co.uk www.tyddynbychan.co.uk

HENDRE ISAF
BASECAMP

Hendre Isaf is a 400-year-old converted farm building of stone and slate construction situated on the Ysbyty Estate. The 8,000 hectare estate takes in 51 Hill Farms, 31 cottages, forested valleys and high open moorland known as the Migneint. The Basecamp, set in a peaceful part of Snowdonia 6 miles from Betws-y-Coed, is available for private hire by groups and by negotiation is free for volunteers undertaking conservation work for the National Trust.

Local attractions include the dry ski slope and Plas y Brenin National Mountain Centre at Capel Curig, shops, leisure centre and swimming pool at Llanrwst, seaside resorts of Rhyl, Prestatyn and Llandudno.
The centre may be able to accommodate one person with special mobility needs - telephone for details of access. No pets permitted.

DETAILS

- **Open** - All year, 24 hours
- **Number of beds** - 17 in two dormitories on two floors
- **Booking** - Early booking recommended (March to October is very busy). A non returnable deposit of £100 paid with booking (cheques payable to the National Trust).
- **Price per night** - £12pp (£15 bank holidays). Minimum of 8 people.
- **Public Transport** - Trains at Betws-y-Coed (6 miles), Llandudno Junction (20 miles) and Llanrwst (10 miles); National Express bus station at Llandudno. Some local buses to Betws-y-Coed, but we advise bringing your own transport.
- **Directions** - Situated 6 miles SE of Betws-y-Coed near the junction of the A5 and the B4407 (signposted Ysbyty Ifan and Ffestiniog). GR855511 (OS sheet 116).

CONTACT: Dilys Jones
National Trust Ysbyty Estate Office, Dinas, Betws-y-Coed, Conwy, LL24 0HF
Tel: 01690 713321 / 710636, Fax: 01690 710678
dilysw.jones@nationaltrust.org.uk

CONWY VALLEY
BACKPACKERS BARN

Conwy Valley Backpackers is situated on a peaceful working farm that has organic status, in the heart of the beautiful Conwy Valley with excellent access to Snowdonia. Centrally heated with fully equipped self-catering kitchen, log fires, hot showers and a fire alarm system. We have three separate dorms sleeping 4, 6 and 10, two of which have their own toilet facility. We can also provide secure bike / canoe storage, grazing for horses & tourist information.

Beside the barn is a small stream and guests may picnic and BBQ on the river bank. An ideal space for restoration, relaxation and retreat. Continental breakfast (£3.50) / packed lunch (£5) / and buffet suppers (£10) are available by arrangement. Local activities range from fishing and hiking to white water rafting and mountain biking, and there are some great pubs and eating places within walking distance. Groups are welcome. Dogs only by prior arrangement.

DETAILS

- **Open** - All year, all day
- **Number of beds** - 20: 1 x 4 : 1 x 6 : 1 x 10
- **Booking** - Not essential but recommended
- **Price per night** - From £12.50pp. Sole use from £200. £1.50pp duvet hire.
- **Public Transport** - Train stations and coaches at Llandudno Junction and Conwy. Local bus 19 or 19a runs every 20 minutes from Conwy and Llandudno Junction, ask driver to drop you at Pyllau Gloewon farm gate.
- **Directions** - GR 769 697. Six miles south of Conwy on the B5106, look for Backpackers sign just before entering Talybont.

CONTACT: Claudia or Helen
Pyllau Gloewon Farm, Tal-y-bont, Conwy, Gwynedd, LL32 8YX
Tel: 01492 660504
claudia.bryan@btconnect.com www.conwyvalleybarn.com

LLANDUDNO
HOSTEL

James and Melissa would like to invite you to their charming Victorian 4 star hostel. We are a friendly hostel where individuals, families and groups (including schools) are welcome all year. Some of the guests comments "friendliest hostel we've ever stayed in", "Wow isn't it clean", "these bathrooms are fabulous as good as any hotel". Come and try us, we love to meet new people and look forward to getting to know you. Set in the heart of the Victorian seaside resort town of Llandudno, an ideal place to shop or explore the many varied local attractions. Excellent blue flag beaches, dry slope skiing, toboggan run, ten pin bowling, Bronze Age copper mine, traditional pier and many museums, fishing trips etc. Llandudno is within easy travelling distance to Snowdon, Bodnant Gardens and local castles. We are able to book local attractions for groups and secure some discounts.

DETAILS

■ **Open** - All year. Telephone in winter prior to arrival , All day
■ **Number of beds** - 46: 2x8 : 2x6 : 4x2 : 1x4 : 1 x family
■ **Booking** - Essential April to July
■ **Price per night** - From £17 per person, £40 per private twin room, £44 per private twin en-suite. Group and family rates on request.
■ **Public Transport** - Trains at Llandudno. Turn right as you exit station, cross road, turn left down Vaughan Street (towards the beach), left into Charlton Street.
■ **Directions** - From the A55 take A470 and follow signs to Llandudno town centre, straight through all roundabouts, after Asda turn 3rd left into Vaughan Street (signed train station), then 1st right into Charlton Street. Hostel is No 14.

CONTACT: James
14 Charlton Street, Llandudno, LL30 2AA
Tel: 01492 877430
info@Llandudnohostel.co.uk www.llandudnohostel.co.uk

CABAN CYSGU
GERLAN BUNKHOUSE

Caban-Cysgu offers comfortable, purpose-built accommodation at the foot of the Carneddau in the Welsh-speaking village of Gerlan. Being a community-run bunkhouse, a warm welcome is guaranteed. This is an ideal location for walking in Snowdonia, and provides an obvious base for the '14 3000ft Peaks' long-distance challenge. Cyclists are welcome too, the hostel being within a mile of Sustrans route 'Lôn Las Ogwen'. Rock-climbing at Idwal is close at hand, as well as the Carneddau crags. The nearby Afon Ogwen provides a popular venue for canoeists.

For more leisurely pursuits, try visiting Coed Meurig, Penrhyn Castle or the Greenwood Centre. Shops, pubs and cafés in Bethesda are within walking distance.

DETAILS

■ **Open** - All year, all day
■ **Number of beds** - 16 : 1x5, 1x2, 1x1, 1x8
■ **Booking** - Not essential, but recommended (with 20% non-returnable deposit).
■ **Price per night** - From £12.50 - £15 (with concessions for group bookings and children).
■ **Public Transport** - Bangor train station is 6 miles. Catch a bus from Bangor bus station to Gerlan (66), or Bethesda (fare £1.40). Taxi from Bangor approx. £10.00.
■ **Directions** - GR 632665. Travelling South on the A5, turn left in the centre of Bethesda just before Spar. Bear right, go up the hill over 2 cross-roads. Caban-Cysgu is the old school on the left, about ½ mile from the A5.

CONTACT: Dewi Emyln, Manager
Ffordd Gerlan, Gerlan, Bethesda, Bangor, LL5 3TL
Tel: 01248 605573
dewi@cabancysgu-gerlan.co.uk www.cabancysgu-gerlan.co.uk

BRYN TIRION FARM
BUNKHOUSE

Bryn Tirion is a traditional hillside farm set in the shadow of the imposing tower of Dolwyddelan Castle, with magnificent views over the upper reaches of the Lledr Valley. The farm has a campsite, bed and breakfast accommodation and bunkhouse. The bunkhouse occupies the first floor of a traditional farm building and is a non smoking area. It consists of one room with a fully equipped kitchen area and 4 bunks (sleeps 8). A second unit of 2 bunks (sleeps 4) on the ground floor has its own kitchen. Both units have mattresses, pillows, sheets and duvets. The toilet block (shared with the campsite) has hot showers, basins with hot & cold water, and shaving points. Situated at the foot of the mountain of Moel Siabod, Bryn Tirion is an ideal base for walking in the Snowdonia National Park. The farm is convenient for travelling to the popular village of Betws-y-Coed (6 miles), Llechwedd Slate Mines & Ffestiniog Railway at Blaenau Ffestiniog (5 miles), the Italianate village of Portmeirion (10 miles), Porthmadog (11 miles) and Bodnant Gardens (18 miles). The tranquil village of Dolwyddelan is a short stroll away with many paths to explore.

DETAILS

- **Open** - All year, by arrangement
- **Number of beds** - 8: 1x8 and 4: 1x4
- **Booking** - Recommended (with deposit). CONTACT BY PHONE OR POST.
- **Price per night** - From £13pp. Camping £3pp. B&B from £30pp.
- **Public Transport** - Dolwyddelan train station ¾ mile away.
- **Directions** - On the A470, ¾ mile on the Ffestiniog side of Dolwyddelan at the foot of the prominent castle, and 6 miles from Betws-y-Coed.

CONTACT: Mrs Caroline Price
Bryn Tirion Farm, Dolwyddelan, Nr Betws-y-Coed, Sir Conwy, LL25 OJD
Tel: 01690 750366
sam@backpackerspress.com

Nestled alongside the River Lledr in the heart of Snowdonia National Park, this former Quarry Manager's house is popular with travellers, walkers, schools, D of E and families. There is a large self-catering kitchen, dining room and television lounge, all centrally heated and with Wifi access. All bedding is provided in single, twin and family rooms plus a nine-bed dorm. We also offer a luxury self-contained cedarlog cabin, sleeping 5, in the grounds.
Lledr House has a private riverside garden, bicycle shed and plenty of parking. It is surrounded by woodland walks and cycle trails. Betws-y-Coed (4 miles) and stunning Llyn Elsi are popular tourist sites. Within walking distance of a pub, one mile from a SPAR shop (open daily until 9pm), and 25 minutes drive to Mount Snowdon. Just 2 miles from Moel Siabod.

DETAILS

- **Open** - All year (except Christmas week), check in from 5pm till 10.30pm.
- **Number of beds** - 31: 1x9, 2x4,1x6, 3x2, 2x1
- **Booking** - Bookings by phone or email held till 6pm. First nights deposit for larger groups.
- **Price per night** - £12.50 per person, £10 for children under 16. Sole use of hostel £295.
- **Public Transport** - Pont-y-Pant Station on the Conwy Valley Line is ¾ mile away. On Sunday there are 2 buses a day instead of the train.
- **Directions** - On the A5 from Llangollen to Bangor turn left just before Betws-y-Coed onto the A470 (signposted Dolgellau). The hostel is 4 miles, just after the large playing field. Walking from Pont-y-Pant station, turn left and left again after stone road bridge.

CONTACT: Brian or Melanie Quilter
Pont-y-Pant, Dolwyddelan, North Wales, LL25 0DQ
Tel: 01690 750 202. Mobile 07915-397-705 or 07915-397-660
Lledrhouse@aol.com   www.ukyh.com

THE EAGLES

The Eagles is a traditional inn offering real ales, and a very friendly atmosphere. Wales Tourist Board 4 star graded. The private accommodation (no sharing with strangers) consists of 6 rooms sleeping 4 and 2 rooms sleeping 2. All rooms are centrally heated and with tea and coffee making facilities; duvets, pillows and sheets are supplied. A fully equipped guest kitchen, secure bike storage and drying room are available. Bar meals are available Friday and Saturday evenings. The Eagles is situated on the edge of the peaceful village of Penmachno, in a secluded valley 4 miles south of Betws-y-Coed, within the heart of the Snowdonia National Park. The world class Penmachno Mountain Bike Trail is half a mile away. Snowdon itself is about 15 miles away. Surrounded by mountain scenery, this is ideal accommodation for groups or individuals walking, climbing, cycling or canoeing. Self-catering cottages are also available.

DETAILS

- **Open** - All year, totally flexible
- **Number of beds** - 28: 6 x 4 : 2 x 2.
- **Booking** - Recommended, essential for groups
- **Price per night** - £16pp. Groups of 10 plus £14.50pp. Whole bunkhouse £350.
- **Public Transport** - Betws-y-Coed Station 3.5miles. Bus 64 from Betws-y-Coed to Penmachno. From Ireland or London and points between London to Holyhead main line change at Llandudno Junction for Betws-y-coed.
- **Directions** - From A5, 2 miles east of Betws-y-Coed, at Conwy Falls Café, turn onto B4406 to Penmachno, cross bridge, The Eagles is in front of you.

CONTACT: Gerry or Linda McMorrow
Penmachno, Betws-y-Coed, Conwy, LL24 0UG
Tel: 01690 760177
inn@eaglespenmachno.co.uk www.eaglespenmachno.co.uk

Wonderfully situated in 7 acres of an Area of Outstanding Natural Beauty, 300m from a beach at south end of Holy Island, Anglesey. Nearby Holyhead has rail links and ferries to Ireland. The centre is an excellent base for so much in the outdoors and is immediately adjacent to the Anglesey Coastal Path. There is spectacular geology, a range of habitats and species of marine life, birds and plants. There are prehistoric remains and good walking on a varied and accessible coast. Kayakers have classic sea tours, overfalls, playwaves, surf and rockhopping. Climbers have Gogarth nearby and Rhoscolyn offers all grades in an attractive setting. Divers can beach launch for wrecks and scenic marine life. Birdwatching is excellent. There are two self-contained units and camping with toilets and showers. We encourage careful energy use, composting & recycling. Walking distance to pub.

DETAILS

- **Open** - All year, 24 hour access
- **Number of beds** - 20: 2x2, 1x4, 2x6. 16: 1x3, 2x4,1x5.
- **Booking** - Essential
- **Price per night** - £15.36
- **Public Transport** - Trains at Holyhead (10km) (London direct 4.5 hrs) or Valley (5km). National Exp Valley (6km). Bus 23/25 Holyhead Rhoscolyn (1km) or 4 & 44 Holyhead-Four Mile Bridge (3km). Ferry: Holyhead - Dublin or Dun Laoghaire.
- **Directions** - GR SH 278 752. From A5 traffic lights at Y Fali/Valley take B4545 Trearddur. In 2km at Four Mile Bridge fork left at sign Rhoscolyn 2miles. After 2km sharp left at camping symbols. In 800m fork right at large white gatepost.

CONTACT: Jacqui or Andy
Cerrig-yr-Adar, Rhoscolyn, Holyhead, Anglesey, LL65 2NQ
Tel: 01407 860469
enquiries@outdooralternative.co.uk www.outdooralternative.org

Totters is situated in the heart of the historic castle town of Caernarfon. Sheltered by the castle town wall, we are only 30 metres from the shores of the Menai Straits and get to see some fantastic sunsets. The town not only offers the visitor a huge selection of pubs and restaurants to choose from, but also acts as the perfect base for trips into the Snowdonia National Park. There is very good public transport in and out of the National Park.

The hostel is a 200-year-old, five floored town house, which is fully heated with all the comforts of home.We have a common room with TV and games, drying room, book exchange, dining room and a secure left luggage facility. The bedrooms sleep either 4 or 6 and can be arranged as mixed or single sex dorms. We also have what we call our 'Penthouse', a huge double en-suite with views over the Straits. This can be arranged as a family room

DETAILS

- **Open** - All year, all day access. Book in by 10pm.
- **Number of beds** - 30 : 4 x 6, 1 x4, 1 x 2 (en-suite)
- **Booking** - Booking is essential for groups in June, July, August and September.
- **Price per night** - £16 per person. £45 double room. Discounts for groups.
- **Public Transport** - Bangor train station is 7 miles from the hostel. Catch a bus from outside the station to Caernarfon. National Express coaches drop off in Caernarfon 200m from the hostel.
- **Directions** - Coming by road:- follow signs for town centre, turn right 200m after the big Celtic Royal hotel, keep going and Totters is the last house on the left.

CONTACT: Bob/Henryette
Plas Porth Yr Aur, 2 High Street, Caernarfon, Gwynedd, LL55 1RN
Tel: 01286 672963, Mob 07979 830470
totters.hostel@googlemail.com www.totters.co.uk

Pentre Bach provides alpine style bunkhouse accommodation, outdoor activities and a campsite. The camping barn has two floors. The ground floor has tables with benches and a cooking area with gas burners, 2 microwaves, fridge and freezer. Upstairs are alpine sleeping platforms with mattresses for 16. Toilets with washing facilities and showers, shared with the campsite, are just across the yard. Based between Waunfawr and Betws Garmon, Pentre Bach is surrounded by the superb scenery of Moel Eilio and Mynydd Mawr and has views towards Mount Snowdon. There are great walks from the barn or take a short car journey to the Nantlle ridge and the main footpaths up Snowdon (Ranger and Rhyd Ddu). Bach Ventures provide a variety of outdoor activities, whether you wish to be guided around the hills, try kayaking, climbing, or have an adventure gorge-scrambling.

DETAILS

- **Open** - All year, enquiries 9am until 10pm. Arrival after 4pm.
- **Number of beds** - 16: 1x16
- **Booking** - One night's deposit, balance payable on arrival. Short notice bookings accepted by phone or email.
- **Price per night** - £8.50 per person (inc gas / electric / showers). Sole use bookings negotiable according to group size.
- **Public Transport** - Train station at Bangor. S4 bus from Caernarfon to Beddgelert stops at the bottom of the drive on request.
- **Directions** - GR 531 579. At Pentre Bach just south of Waunfawr on the Caernarfon to Beddgelert road (A4085). Look for Camping Barn sign.

CONTACT: Karen Neil
Pentre Bach, Waunfawr, Caernarfon, Gwynedd, LL54 7AJ
Tel: 01286 650643
info@bachventures.co.uk   www.bachventures.co.uk

STONE
BARN

The Stone Barn and Studio are converted farm buildings at Tyddyn Morthwyl Farm and Caravan Park near Criccieth on the fringe of Snowdonia.

The farm provides a good centre for climbing and walking in Snowdonia and the Lleyn Peninsula. Tremadog Rocks (an all year rock climbing venue) is only 7 miles away. Canoeing and wind surfing nearby.

The Barn has an alpine style sleeping platform. Hot showers and toilets are shared with the caravan park. There is a wood burning stove for heating and clothes drying (wood provided free) and a kitchen area with fridge and water.

There is also The Studio, a small stone building with two single beds and washbasin, and a static caravan to let. Several pubs in the locality serve good bar meals.

DETAILS

- **Open** - All year, flexible
- **Number of beds** - 12
- **Booking** - 48 hrs advanced booking required, with one night's fee as deposit.
- **Price per night** - £7 per person in the Stone Barn including wood (discount for groups). £8 per night the Studio.
- **Public Transport** - Criccieth has a train station and National Express coach service. The hostel is 1.25 miles from Criccieth and a taxi service is available.
- **Directions** - 1.25 miles from Criccieth on B4411 Caernarfon road.

CONTACT: Mrs Trumper
Tyddyn Morthwyl, Criccieth, Gwynedd, LL52 0NF
Tel: 01766 522115
trumper@yrhenstabal.freeserve147.co.uk

Yr Helfa is a traditional bunkhouse situated in the heart of the Snowdonia National Park. This former farmhouse has been carefully restored and will sleep up to 18 people in 3 comfortable rooms. It has underfloor heating, 3 shower rooms with toilet and sink and a coal fire in lounge. All bedding is supplied. It uses sustainable energy, has a wind turbine, solar panels and a wood pellet boiler. Yr Helfa nestles directly at the foot of Moel Gynghorion with panoramic views from the Llanberis path around to Bwlch Masgwn (Telegraph Pass). It is in a mountain environment with direct access to a number of routes up Snowdon and yet only 20 minutes walk (1 mile) from Llanberis. The area is ideal for climbing, walking, fell running, horse riding and mountain biking. Award winning attractions include The Slate Museum, Electric Mountain, Dolbadarn Castle, Llanberis waterfall, Lake Railway and Snowdon summit railway. Llanberis has several restaurants and plenty of pubs for a night out.

DETAILS

- **Open** - All year, all day
- **Number of beds** - 18: 3x6
- **Booking** - Availability and booking form on website. Book by post, 30% deposit.
- **Price per night** - Whole Bunkhouse - £150 per night, 7 nights £1,000. Shared occupancy - Smaller groups £12 per person per night, each room sleeps six.
- **Public Transport** - Trains at Bangor (10 miles). Buses from Llanberis to Caernarfon and Bangor every half hour.
- **Directions** - The bunkhouse is on the road to the beginning of the Llanberis Snowdon track. Carry on past the track and it is the first gate on your right. Park in the parking area then walk ten minutes down another track.

CONTACT: Jane O'Donnell
Grove House, 18 High Street, Llanberis, Gwynedd, LL55 4EN
Tel: 0790 0087692
yrhelfa@hotmail.co.uk www.snowdonbunkhouse.co.uk

CRAFLWYN
BASECAMP

The historic Craflwyn Estate dates back to 1200 AD. Having been part of a monastery, a family residence and a Victorian hunting lodge, it is now a fully resourced conference and activity centre. The bunkhouse, located in the old stables, accommodates 12 people and can be divided into 2 self-contained units of 7 and 5 beds which can be hired individually. There is a dining/lounge area and a large kitchen. Craflwyn is set in a stunning location at the foot of Snowdon, in the Nantgwynant valley, with dramatic views and a magical atmosphere. The village of Beddgelert can be reached on foot via a riverside footpath. The village has pubs, bistros, cafés, shops and an information centre. Snowdon and the legendary Dinas Emrys are both on the doorstep and a wide range of beaches, historic houses, gardens and archaeological sites are all within easy reach. The hall offers en-suite accommodation and sleeps 14 people.

DETAILS

- **Open** - All year, all day. Office hours 9am-5pm Mon-Fri.
- **Number of beds** - 12: (2 self-contained units of 7 and 5 beds)
- **Booking** - 33% non-returnable deposit to secure the booking. Full payment due 10 weeks in advance.
- **Price per night** - Check website for latest prices. Two night minimum stay. Bank holidays 15% extra.
- **Public Transport** - Trains at Bangor and Porthmadog. Local buses stop nearby.
- **Directions** - Craflwyn Hall is approximately ¾ mile outside Beddgelert on the A498 towards Capel Curig.

CONTACT: Eirian Jones
The National Trust, Craflwyn, Beddgelert, Gwynedd, LL55 4NG
Tel: 01766 510120
eirian.jones@nationaltrust.org.uk www.craflwyn.org

SGUBOR UNNOS
BUNKHOUSE

Croeso Welcome Sgubor Unnos provides luxury bunkhouse accommodation on a Welsh speaking, traditionally run, family farm in the village of Llangian, one mile from Abersoch, famous for it's watersports and surfing beaches, Hell's Mouth and Porth Ceiriad. Centrally located, it is the ideal centre for outdoor activities including walking the newly opened Llyn Coast Path, surfing, cycling, golf, fishing and sailing. The farm also offers hovercraft cruising, a new experience in outdoor activities. Situated a few miles from Llangian at the tip of the Peninsula lies Bardsey Island where 20,000 saints are buried!! Why not pay them a visit? Trips around the island for it's wildlife and heritage can be arranged and sometimes accommodation on the island itself. The modern bunkhouse offers 3 bedrooms ideal for individuals or groups. Fully equipped kitchen/lounge, disabled facilities, covered BBQ area, secure storage, private parking, traditional village shop, post office and phone 500m away.

DETAILS

- **Open** - All year, all day
- **Number of beds** - 14: 2 x 4 : 1 x 6
- **Booking** - Not essential but recommended.
- **Price per night** - £16 (adult), £7 (under 10 years), including a light breakfast. Discount for more than 2 nights.
- **Public Transport** - Nearest train station is Pwllheli (7 miles). Good local bus and taxi service to Llangian. Public transport details on web site.
- **Directions** - GR 296 288 On entering Abersoch from Pwllheli, take the right hand turning up the hill signed to Llangian (follow brown signs). On left on leaving village.

CONTACT: Phil or Meinir
Fferm Tanrallt Farm, Llangian, Abersoch, Gwynedd, LL53 7LN
Tel: 01758 713527
tanrallt@btconnect.com   www.tanrallt.com

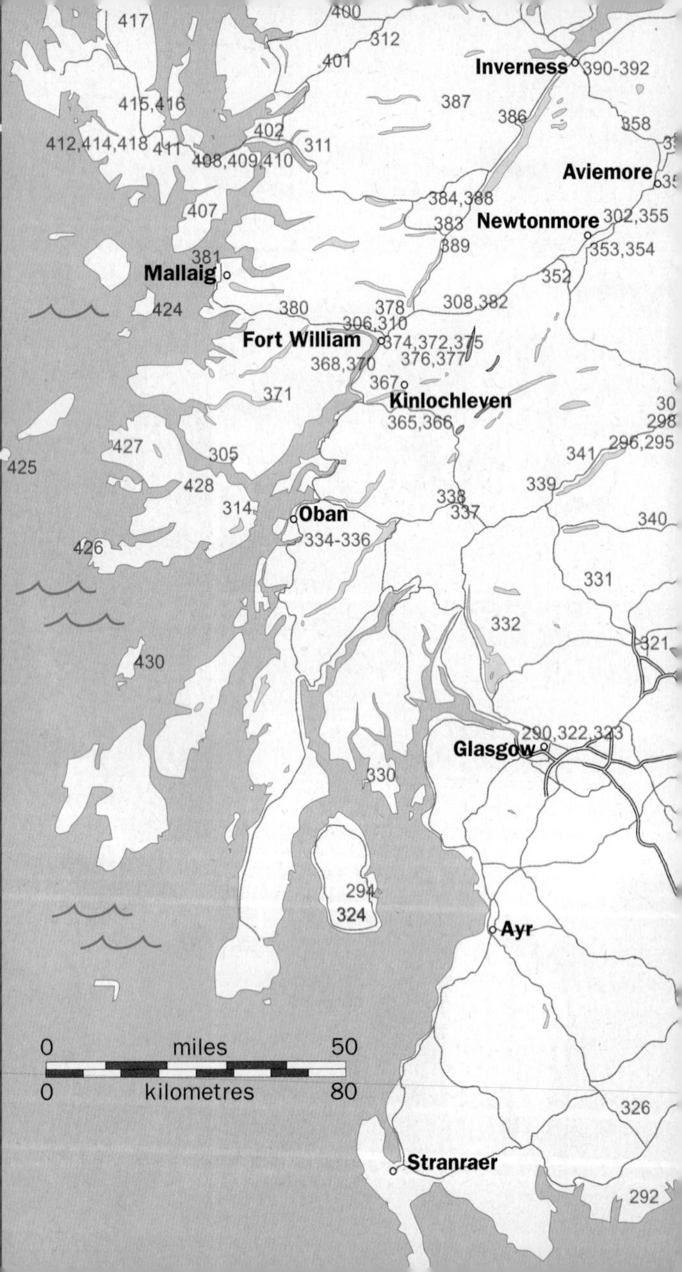

South Scotland

417
490
312
401
Inverness 390-392
387
386
858
415,416
402
412,414,418 411
408,409,410 311
Aviemore
635
407
384,388
383 **Newtonmore** 302,355
389
353,354
381
Mallaig
352
424
380
378
308,382
306,310
Fort William
874,372,375
368,370
376,377
371
367
Kinlochleven
365,366
30
298
296,295
427
341
339
425
428
305
314
Oban
338
340
334-336
337
426
331
430
332
321
330
290,322,323
Glasgow
294
324
Ayr

0   miles   50

0   kilometres   80

326

Stranraer

292

South Scotland

Peterhead

361
357,360

364

362,363   303,304
Ballater
Braemar

Aberdeen

345   350

344

342

Montrose

Dundee

Perth

KEY

45 - **Hostel page number**

45 - **Page number of group
only accommodation**

Edinburgh
291,318-320

293

328

E N G L A N D

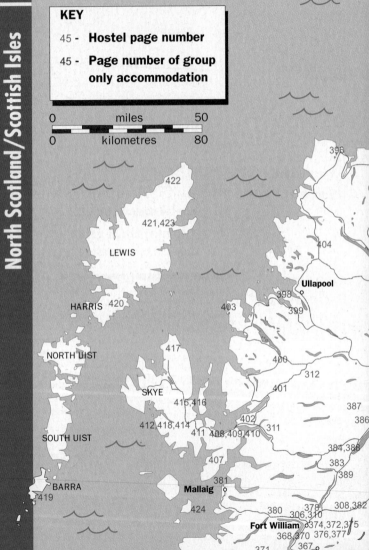

KEY

45 - **Hostel page number**

45 - **Page number of group only accommodation**

0   miles   50
0   kilometres   80

396

422

421,423

LEWIS

404

Ullapool

398

HARRIS 420

399

403

NORTH UIST

417

400

SKYE

312

401

415,416

387

386

412,418,414

402

411 408,409,410

311

384,388

SOUTH UIST

383

389

407

BARRA

381

419

Mallaig

378   308,382

424

380   306,310

Fort William 374,372,375

368,370 376,377

367

371

Kinlochleven

365,366

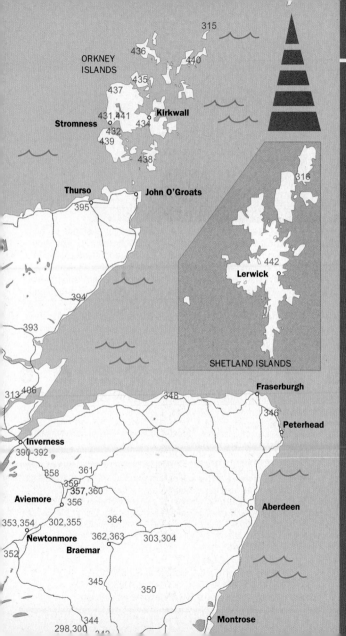

ORKNEY
ISLANDS

315

436

440

435

437

431,441

Stromness

434 **Kirkwall**

432

439

438

Thurso

John O'Groats

395

394

393

316

442

Lerwick

SHETLAND ISLANDS

313 406

348

Fraserburgh

346

Peterhead

Inverness

390-392

858

361

359

357,360

356

Aviemore

353,354

302,355

364

Newtonmore

362,363

303,304

352

Braemar

345

350

344

298,300

Montrose

North Scotland/Scottish Isles

CAIRNCROSS HOUSE
SCOTLAND UNIVERSITY OF GLASGOW

Cairncross House is in an excellent location within walking distance of the trendy West End and City Centre and is close to public transport. The West End is great for pubs and restaurants and has lots of good value places to eat. Nearby you will find some of Glasgow's top visitor attractions: Art Gallery and Museum, Transport Museum, University of Glasgow and its Visitor Centre, Hunterian Museum and Art Gallery. The City Centre offers great shopping, clubs and pubs.

The Hostel is part of the University of Glasgow's student residence and offers great value for money. Modern, well equipped with bed linen, wash basin in room, cooking facilities, showers, free laundry facilities and common room. Awarded the silver award for green tourism.

DETAILS

- **Open** - June to September, 8.00 am - 10.00 pm
- **Number of beds** - 242
- **Booking** - Advised but not essential, Booking address: Residential Services, University of Glasgow, 73 Great George Street, Glasgow, G12 8RR
- **Price per night** - £18.55 (inc. VAT) per person
- **Public Transport** - Buchanan Street Bus Station, Central Station and Queen Street Station are all 2 miles away. The nearest underground station is Kelvinhall (half mile) From George Square take buses 6 or 16, ask for Kelvinhaugh/Radnor St.
- **Directions** - From George St take St Vincent St, which becomes Argyle St after 1 mile. Through traffic lights take third left into Kelvinhaugh St, Cairncross House is on the right. From M8 J19 take A814 to Finnieston. Turn right into Finnieston St, continue to traffic lights and turn left into Argyle St. Kelvinhaugh St is third on the left.

CONTACT:
20 Kelvinhaugh Place, Glasgow, G3 8NH
Tel: 0141 330 4116/2318 or 0141 221 9334
vacationaccom@gla.ac.uk   www.glasgow.ac.uk/cvso

Looking for a hostel in Edinburgh? Do the smart thing and choose SmartCityHostels, the newest Edinburgh hostel. We're a purpose-built five-star city centre hostel, great for anyone visiting Edinburgh, whether for the Festivals, Hogmanay or just backpacking on a budget. Our location is right in the heart of Edinburgh's Old Town - one minute from the Royal Mile and only a few minutes from Edinburgh Castle, the Scottish Parliament, many more of Edinburgh's visitor attractions, and night-life. All our rooms are en suite with the biggest and most comfortable hostel beds in Edinburgh. Fantastic showers, towels and bedlinen included in the price. Our Smart City Café serves food and drinks all day every day with Wi-Fi access throughout the café. If you are looking for cheap hostel accommodation in Edinburgh then do the smart thing and make your hostel in Edinburgh Smart City Hostels.

DETAILS

- **Open** - All year , 24 hours
- **Number of beds** - 620
- **Booking** - Not essential, but recommended in summer
- **Price per night** - From £13.50 per person per night. Group rates available on request.
- **Public Transport** - Airport transfer and Waverley train station 5 minutes walk; St Andrews Bus Station 5-10 minutes walk.
- **Directions** - From Waverley bridge turn left into Market Street, then turn right into Jeffrey Street. At first set of traffic lights at the Royal Mile turn right. Blackfriars Street is first left and smartcityhostels is on your right.

CONTACT: Reservations
50 Blackfriars Street, Edinburgh, EH1 1NE
Tel: 0870 892 3000, Fax: 0131 524 1988
info@smartcityhostels.com www.smartcityhostels.com

CASTLE CREAVIE
HAY LOFT

Castle Creavie Hayloft has recently been converted to a comfortable, family friendly, camping barn. The ground floor has utility sinks, small area for kettle and microwave, shower room and toilet. Upstairs is the carpeted loft with 4 single beds and balcony doors opening to spectacular unspoiled views of the Galloway countryside. Bring your own sleeping bag, or hire the bed-linen/duvets at £3.00 p.p.per stay. Breakfast available at the farmhouse pre booked. Guests are welcome to enjoy the farm footpaths and observe the daily life on this working sheep farm. Enjoy freshly baked bread and cakes, honey, and our own home reared lamb, pork and bacon.

CastleCreavie is named after the two Iron Age forts and is situated 4 miles from the popular harbour town of Kirkcudbright which has a good range of pubs, cafes and restaurants. Galloway is famed for its many castles, abbeys, first class walking, long sandy beaches, and the Stanes.

DETAILS

- **Open** - All year, all day
- **Number of beds** - 4: 1x4
- **Booking** - Book by phone. Deposit required by post.
- **Price per night** - £12 pp. £3 to hire bedding.
- **Public Transport** - 4 miles from Kirkcudbright citylink services.
- **Directions** - From the A75 take the A711 to Kirkcudbright. In the town centre turn left at the Royal Hotel onto the B727 (Gelston), pass the cemetery and at the next road junction go straight on (Auchencairn / Dundrennan). Follow for approx 4 miles.

CONTACT: Charlie and Elaine Wannop
Castle Creavie, Kirkcudbright, Dumfries and Galloway, DG6 4QE
Tel: 01557 500238, Fax: 01557 500238
info@castlecreavie.co.uk www.castlecreavie.co.uk/

The Well Road Centre is a large Victorian house set in its own grounds in the charming spa town of Moffat. The centre is ideal for youth groups, adult groups, conferences, residential workshops, sports events, multiple family gatherings and outdoor activity clubs. All rooms are fully carpeted and centrally heated. There are two spacious meeting rooms, a large bright self-catering kitchen fully equipped for 65, games hall for indoor sports, table tennis room and snooker room. The are 13 bedrooms of various sizes, two of them with en-suite facilities. Two separate toilet/shower areas for mixed groups. Bring your own sleeping bags or duvets. Ample parking for cars, minibuses and equipment trailers and the nearby park can be used for football matches. Moffat is in the Southern Uplands, an hour from Edinburgh and Glasgow. Ideal area for golfers, bird watchers, walkers and cyclists. All groups have sole use.

DETAILS

- **Open** - All year, all day
- **Number of beds** - 65: in 13 rooms (2 en-suite)
- **Booking** - Check availability and send £100 deposit to secure booking.
- **Price per night** - £10pp (based on 2 nights), £8.30pp (based on 3 nights). £7.50pp (based on 4 nights), £5.71pp (based on 1 week). Fuel extra. Minimum group size is 25. Smaller groups are welcome but must pay for 25.
- **Public Transport** - Trains at Lockerbie(16m). Citylink bus to Glasgow/Edinburgh.
- **Directions** - From A74 take Moffat turning and enter the High Street (town square). Turning to the right around the shops on the south side of the square, follow Holm St to the T-junction. Turn left into Burnside, following up and right into Well Rd.

CONTACT: Ben Larmour
Huntly Lodge, Well Road, Moffat, DG10 9JT
Tel: 01683 221040
Ben8363@aol.com www.wellroadcentre.co.uk

ALDERSYDE
BUNKHOUSE

Aldersyde Bunkhouse is a purpose built bunkhouse on the beautiful island of Arran (Scotland in miniature). Lamlash is a haven for golfers, there are 3x18 hole, 1x12 hole and 3x9 hole golf courses all very reasonably priced. Arran has lovely coastal and forestry walks and Goatfell at 874 metres. Both loch and sea fishing are available with boats for hire or organised trips. Bird life is plentiful and varied. We are a short sail from the Holy Island which has been bought by Same Ling as a retreat, visitors are welcomed. The 'Waverley', the only remaining sea-going paddle steamer in the world, calls at Arran twice weekly during the summer for trips on the Clyde. Arran offers a unique geology formation and is well used by universities. Brodick Castle and gardens are well worth a visit. There are standing stones at various sites, the most popular are at Machrie Moor. Crafts are part of island life and are varied, with visitor participation welcomed. A distillery and brewery are also very interesting. Food is available to suit all tastes, while the bunkhouse has self-catering with a new kitchen. Wheelchair friendly - electric wheelchair available.

DETAILS

- **Open** - All year, all day
- **Number of beds** - 21: 1 x 11 : 1 x 7
- **Booking** - Advisable
- **Price per night** - From £12.50pp - group reduction and for length of stay
- **Public Transport** - Bus meets the ferry at Ardrossan.
- **Directions** - Due south from the ferry at Ardrossan. The Hostel is in Lamlash behind the Aldersyde Hotel.

CONTACT:
Lamlash, Arran, KA27 8LS
Tel: 01770 600959
jpricelamlash@hotmail.com www.aldersydebunkhouse.co.uk

Wade House and the Bunkhouse are at the foot of a south facing slope with beautiful walks and climbs in Tayside (Weem) Forest Park.   Built in the 1700s Wade House is a listed building where General Wade stayed while building his roads. The adjoining old barn has been converted to a 4* luxury bunkhouse, with underfloor heating and log fired stoves.   There are also two self-contained cottages.

Home of the National Kayak School, ideal for whitewater kayaking and sea kayaking. Superb mountain biking also on cycle route #7 and Rob Roy Way. Instruction available for rock climbing, ice climbing, hill walking, mountaineering, whitewater rafting and canyoning.
Bar meals next door at Weem Hotel. Midge free and sheltered sunny front garden and courtyard.

DETAILS

- **Open** - All year, flexible but generally all day
- **Number of beds** - Wade House 9 : 1x5, 1x4. Bunkhouse 25: 2x4/5, 1x2/3, 1x8/9, Two beautiful cottages 1x9, 1x4/5
- **Booking** - Advisable, book by phone or email
- **Price per night** - From £15 per person. Long stay rates available.
- **Public Transport** - Buses from Aberfeldy connect to trains at Pitlochry & Perth.
- **Directions** - North from traffic lights in Aberfeldy, over General Wade's bridge over the River Tay for 1km, the Adventurer's Escape is next to the Weem Hotel on the B846.

CONTACT: Stuart Wagstaff
Weem, Aberfeldy, PH15 2LD
Tel: 01887 820498 or 07774 644 660
info@adventurers-escape.co.uk www.adventurers-escape.co.uk

DUNOLLY
SCOTLAND ADVENTURE OUTDOORS

Dunolly House comprises two units, the first is a 48-bed Victorian house, the other is a smaller 15-bed cottage. All rooms are fully carpeted and centrally heated with modern pine beds (linen and duvets provided). The complex can be taken together or as separate units for groups and individuals with catering to suit.

We have a fantastic range of activities on site which can be booked by groups and individuals. They include river rafting, duckying, kayaking, gorge ascent, archery, mountain biking, high ropes challenge and climbing wall. We have our own qualified instructors and we are licensed to run activities for children under the regulations of the Adventure Activities Licensing Authority.

Come and enjoy !!

DETAILS

- **Open** - All year, 24 hours
- **Number of beds** - 63
- **Booking** - Booking is normally necessary
- **Price per night** - From £11.00
- **Public Transport** - Nearest train station is in Pitlochry (14 miles away). Citylink coaches stop at Ballinluig (11 miles away) and Pitlochry. Local buses to Aberfeldy.
- **Directions** - Turn off the A9 Road at Ballinluig. Travel for 5 miles. Turn right at the T junction. Travel 6 miles until Aberfeldy. Continue through the main street and we are the last house on the right as you exit Aberfeldy.

CONTACT: Booking Office
Taybridge Drive, Aberfeldy, Perthshire, PH15 2BP
Tel: 01887 820298
info@dunollyadventures.co.uk   www.dunollyadventures.co.uk

THE BUNKHOUSE
GLASSIE FARM

Situated 1,000 feet above sea level on a south facing mountain-side. The steading has been converted into two high standard units. They are perfect for relaxing after a busy day out on the local munroes / hills and lochs. Fantastic location for group gatherings, stag and hen parties, outdoor activity weekends or just a place to re-charge and take in the amazing views. There are 2 totally separate units which can be hired individually or as a whole. These units both have fully equipped kitchens and a dining area / seating area. There are extra tables / chairs and B-B-Q`s for outside eating and even a spit-roaster for that special occasion. Plenty of parking spaces and a large drying room. Bunks come with fitted sheets / pillow + case / duvet with cover. Activities in area include W/W/Rafting, Clay Shooting, Paintball, Quad Biking and many others.

DETAILS

- **Open** - All year, phone enquiries between 9am and 9pm
- **Number of beds** - 39: Original Unit 25:1x6, 1x8,1x4, 1x7. Newer Unit 14; 2x4,1x6
- **Booking** - Groups ONLY for Fri / Sat Weekends. Individuals / groups for Sun to Thur nights. Booking in advance essential and securing deposits required.
- **Price per night** - Whole Place for a Fri + Sat weekend = £1,329 or Original Unit (25) = £881, or Newer Unit (14) = £494. Individuals/small groups are £17pppn from Sun to Thur nights. Check own website for Special Deals.
- **Public Transport** - Trains at Pitlochry (12 miles), bus at Aberfeldy (2.5 miles)
- **Directions** - See website to print directions. From the x-roads at The Black Watch in Aberfeldy, follow the B846 over River Tay at Wades Bridge. Turn right at the Aileen Craggan Hotel (signed Strathtay), approx 50mtrs after foot bridge on RH side over the Tay turn left (bunkhouse sign on RH side). Follow track for 1.5 miles.

CONTACT: Julian Rickard
Glassie Farm, Aberfeldy, Perthshire, PH15 2JN
Tel: Office; 01887 820265 or Mobile; 07849 689386
j_j_rickard@hotmail.com   www.thebunkhouse.co.uk

THE GRANDTULLY

SCOTLAND

The Grandtully is perfectly situated about 40 metres from The River Tay, which makes it a brilliant base for canoeists / kayakers, with rapids and a slalom course on the doorstep. Munroe baggers / walkers have approximately 30 Munroes within sensible travelling distance, while there's plenty of other local walks for all abilities. Also ideally situated for mountain biking and golf with 20+ great golf courses nearby. The accommodation has 8 twin bedded rooms and 2 family rooms sleeping 4. The Grandtully has its own cafe / bar 'The Tully'. We cater for larger groups, including stag / hen weekends and family gatherings etc. We can arrange for your own themed chocolate party or casino night There's an amazing selection of activities available for your whole group (w/w rafting, canyoning, quad biking, paintballing, etc). 10% discount for SCA members hiring whole facility.

DETAILS

- **Open** - all year, phone enquiries between 9am and 9pm.
- **Number of beds** - 24
- **Booking** - Advanced booking is highly advised, deposit required.
- **Price per night** - A weeks exclusive use is £2796, or £998 for Fri & Sat nights. Weekday (Sun to Thur) £18 pp (inc.ensuites). 10% discount for SCA members hiring whole facility.
- **Public Transport** - Trains at Pitlochry (6 miles), bus stops outside the front door.
- **Directions** - See website for printable directions. The village of Grandtully is on the A827 5 miles from Aberfeldy and 4 miles from junction with the A9. The Grandtully is just on the main road with its car park around the back.

CONTACT: Wez or Claire
The Grandtully, Grandtully, By Aberfeldy, Perthshire, PH9 0PL
Tel: Wez 07736 212617, Claire 07595 894582
info@thegrandtully.com www.thegrandtully.com

INSH HALL
LODGE

Situated between Loch Insh and the foothills of Glenfeshie, Insh Hall Lodge provides comfortable double, twin and family rooms on a room only, B&B or full board basis. Rooms are equipped with bed linen and TVs.

Facilities include self catering kitchens, large meeting room, laundry/drying room, sauna and mini gym, outdoor volleyball and basketball, as well as private car parking.

FREE WATERSPORTS OFFERED TO GUESTS STAYING TWO OR MORE NIGHTS (SET TIMES.)

Meals are available in the Boathouse Restaurant situated by the shore, 120 yds from the lodge. Loch Insh is the starting point for many local walks, lochside trails and cycle routes (located on Sustrans Cycle Way, Route 7).

DETAILS

■ **Open** - All year, all day
■ **Number of beds** - 28: double, twin and family rooms
■ **Booking** - Booking is recommended but not always required. Deposit taken.
■ **Price per night** - From £16-£35 per person.
■ **Public Transport** - Trains at Aviemore and Kingussie (7 miles from Loch Insh). Nearest airport is Inverness, approximately one hour north of Loch Insh.
■ **Directions** - Situated near Kincraig, 7 miles south of Aviemore, 7 miles north of Kingussie on the B9152, follow signs for Loch Insh Watersports. Local bus routes from Aviemore to Kincraig, approx 1 mile from the lodge.

CONTACT: Receptionist
Insh Hall, Kincraig, Inverness-shire, PH21 1NU
Tel: 01540 651272
office@lochinsh.com www.lochinsh.com

Exceptional accommodation in the Scottish highlands for families, friends, couples and groups. Guests from all over the world have been delighted by this refreshingly stylish base in Royal Deeside, in the dramatic surroundings of the Cairngorm Park. The owners Alan and Cathy Low are committed to meeting the highest standards. Cathy is a professional storyteller and both speak French and German and teach English. For details of English programmes, please visit www.schoolhouse-english.eu. There's a large lounge with giant sofas and open fire, a bright dining room and a choice of family, double or twin rooms. The beds are superkingsize and all rooms have excellent ensuite showers. There's a large garden with BBQ hire, outdoor eating facilities and car park. Schoolhouse can provide excellent accommodation for groups of up to 24 in 3 ensuite dorms with up to 8 bunks in each. Bed linen and towels are supplied and breakfast is included. In-house catering can be provided, delicious meals and lunches being freshly prepared often using ingredients straight from the garden.

DETAILS

- **Open** - All year, all day
- **Number of beds** - 22
- **Booking** - Booking essential for groups
- **Price per night** - From £18 per person, includes breakfast.
- **Public Transport** - From Aberdeen Bus Station (bus enquiries 01224 212266).
- **Directions** - From Aberdeen follow the A93 to Ballater (43 miles). From Inverness follow Grantown-on-Spey then A939 to Ballater (70 miles). From Perth follow A93 to Blairgowrie, then continue to Ballater (65 miles).

CONTACT: Alan or Cathy Low
Anderson Road, Ballater, Aberdeenshire, AB35 5QW
Tel: 013397 56333
info@school-house.eu www.school-house.eu

HABITAT
@ BALLATER

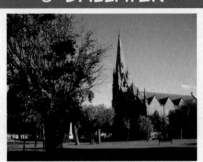

Set in the village of Ballater, with a range of shops, pubs and restaurants, this is a recently completed, purpose built hostel, ideal for families, groups and independent travellers. Within the Cairngorms National Park it is a great position for enjoying a variety of outdoor activities.

All rooms are ensuite, ranging from 8 bed dorms to 4 bed rooms suitable for families. Bedding is included.

There's a large kitchen /dining / lounge area with wood burning stove and under floor heating throughout.

The hostel has been built adhering to environmentally sound principles including the installation of a ground source heat pump.

Ballater is an ideal location for exploring the Cairngorms, Royal Deeside and Aberdeenshire.

DETAILS

- **Open** - All year, opening Jan 2009, all day
- **Number of beds** - 37: 2x8, 1x7, 3x4, 1x2. All ensuite.
- **Booking** - Book by phone or email.
- **Price per night** - £15 per person.
- **Public Transport** -   From Aberdeen Bus Station (phone 01224 212266)
- **Directions** - On A93 just west of bridge over river in centre of Ballater.

CONTACT: Harry and Claudia Leith
Bridge Square, Ballater, Aberdeenshire, AB35 5QJ
Tel: 013397 53752
info@habitat-at-ballater.com www.habitat-at-ballater.com

Lochaline on the shores of the Sound of Mull has two bars, a café and a shop. There are lovely coastal, woodland walks close to the village and challenging hill walks on Mull. Diving and sea, river and loch angling are available locally and it is an ideal location for trips to the Ardnamurchan peninsula, the mountains of Glencoe, Fort William and Mull. The Dive Centre overlooks the Sound of Mull and provides self-catering accommodation for individuals and groups in twin rooms with underfloor heating and full ensuite facilities. There are ample supplies of hot water, an efficient drying room, a fully equipped kitchen and a lounge with TV and video. Catering is also available. The Old Post Office, a stone's throw from the pier and bar, provides self-catering accommodation for groups of 10. Return from your day to a roaring log fire in the comfy lounge and cooking on a range stove. The bedrooms offer sea views (3 twin rooms, and one family room). All you need are towels. There is a dive vessel which can be charted for wildlife watching day trips and winter wildlife breaks are available.

DETAILS

- **Open** - All year, 24 hours
- **Number of beds** - Centre 24: 12x2, Old Post Office 10: 1x4, 3x2
- **Booking** - Advisable, with 50% deposit
- **Price per night** - Dive Centre: £20 pp per night. Old post Office: £200 per night.
- **Public Transport** - Caledonian MacBrayne ferry runs daily 0745 to 1900 from Fishnish on Mull. Buses run from Corran Ferry, 8 miles outside Fort William.
- **Directions** - As you descend into the village of Lochaline on the A884, look out for signposts. The Centre is just beyond the shop, up a steep drive.

CONTACT: Mark and Annabel Lawrence
Lochaline, Morvern, Argyll, PA34 5XT
Tel: 01967 421627
dive@lochalinedivecentre.co.uk www.lochalinedivecentre.co.uk

SMIDDY
BUNKHOUSE

A friendly welcome at our comfortable, family run, mountain hostels in a loch-side location overlooking the Caledonian Canal. Pine clad interior gives a cosy, friendly atmosphere. Stunning mountains and water at the doorstep with the meeting of the West Highland Way and Great Glen Way. Hot showers. Fully equipped kitchens available at all times (food available from local shop until 10pm daily). Use of 2 efficient drying / laundry rooms. Bedding provided. Fully heated for all year round use. Outdoor information / daily snow and avalanche reports. Advice/instruction available from resident mountain and water based instructors and guides for: winter and summer walking/climbing; river,loch and sea kayaking; dinghy sailing. Hire for sea and river of kayaks/open canoes, dinghy and other equipment. AALA licensed outdoor centre. Group and family accommodation. Meeting / lecture room facilities available by arrangement.

DETAILS

- **Open** - All year, all day (with key). Key deposit required.
- **Number of beds** - 26 : 3x4, 1x6, 1x8
- **Booking** - Telephone to pre-book.
- **Price per night** - £11.50 - £14.00 (seasonal) pp (incl. bedding).
- **Public Transport** - Two minutes walk from Corpach Railway Station on the Mallaig Line. Three miles from Fort William (trains from Glasgow and London).
- **Directions** - Take A82 north out of Fort William towards Inverness. After one mile take A830 north towards Mallaig and follow for 2 miles to village of Corpach. Turn left immediately opposite "Key" stores, signposted 'Snowgoose Mountain Centre'. The hostel is 30yds on left.

CONTACT: John or Tina
Snowgoose Mountain Centre, Station Road, Corpach, Fort William, PH33 7JH
Tel: 01397 772467, Fax: 01397 772467
ihg@highland-mountain-guides.co.uk www.highland-mountain-guides.co.uk

Àite Cruinnichidh, 15 miles north east of Fort William, occupies a unique sheltered spot adjacent to the Monessie Gorge; explore remote glens, mountain passes and lochs. Numerous easy walks within minutes of the hostel and seven magnificent canoeing rivers within 20 miles. The location is also ideal for climbing (rock & ice), mountain biking, skiing or just relaxing. A warm, peaceful, friendly, country hostel in a converted barn. Àite Cruinnichidh has been renovated to high standards and sleeps 32 in five rooms of four, one of six, one twin and one double/family room en-suite. All bedding supplied. A fully equipped kitchen/dining room, sitting room, excellent showers. Additional facilities:- sauna suite, garden, seminar room, dark room, use of maps, advice on walking/cycling routes. Groups and individuals welcome. We do not have wheel chair access but we are glad to accommodate people with all forms of disability whenever we can, and know some sign language.

DETAILS

- **Open** - All year, 24 hours
- **Number of beds** - 32: 1x6,5x4,1x twin, 1 x family / double en-suite
- **Booking** - Booking advised, 50% deposit.
- **Price per night** - £12 per person, discounts for groups
- **Public Transport** - Roy Bridge train station and bus stop (2 miles) has several trains and buses to and from Fort William daily. Pick up available from Roy Bridge.
- **Directions** - From Fort William follow A82 for 10 miles to Spean Bridge, turn right onto A86 for 3 miles to Roy Bridge. Pass though village and continue for 2 miles. The hostel is on right 100m after Glenspean Lodge Hotel on left.

CONTACT: Gavin or Nicola
1 Achluachrach, By Roy Bridge, Near Fort William, PH31 4AW
Tel: 01397 712315
gavin@highland-hostel.co.uk www.highland-hostel.co.uk

FARR COTTAGE
LODGE

Farr Cottage is situated in Corpach, just 3 miles from Fort William town centre, with a breath-taking view of Ben Nevis and across Loch Linnhe, in the outdoor pursuits capital of Scotland. We specialise in whisky evenings and there is a full range of in-house facilities including satellite television, video lounge, licensed bar, self-catering facilities, email, laundry and drying facilities, central heating and hot showers. We also organise outdoor pursuits which comprise white water rafting, canyoning, climbing, abseiling, skiing, snowboarding, fishing, golf and many many more! We can provide evening meals, breakfast, picnic lunches and we will ensure you have the break or holiday of a lifetime with us. Our professional team are geared to meet your needs and requirements. The FULL Scottish Experience!!

DETAILS

■ **Open** - All year, 24 hours
■ **Number of beds** - 30: in cottage 2 x 2 : 2 x 8 : 1 x 10. 18: in lodge 1 x 2 : 1 x 4 : 2 x 6. Both buildings fully self-contained.
■ **Booking** - Advance booking advised
■ **Price per night** - £16pp, from £17pp in double room. Group rates available.
■ **Public Transport** - Corpach train station is 200m from the hostel. The nearest Citylink service is three miles away at Fort William. Taxi fare from Fort William centre is approximately £7.50.
■ **Directions** - Follow the A82 north from Fort William centre towards Inverness for 1.5 miles. Turn left at the A830 to Mallaig. Follow this road for 1.5 miles into Corpach. We are on the right.

CONTACT: Cliff or Dee
Corpach, Fort William, PH33 7LR
Tel: 01397 772315
mail@farrcottage.com www.farrcottage.com

KINTAIL LODGE
BUNKHOUSES
SCOTLAND

Kintail Lodge stands at the foot of the Five Sisters of Kintail, right on the shores of Loch Duich. It is an ideal base for touring Skye and the Western Highlands or for bagging some of the 30 Munroes in the area. In the grounds of the hotel there are two budget accommodation units which are especially popular with walkers, climbers and fishermen. The Wee Bunk House has a cosy room with bunks to sleep 6 people and a snack kitchen containing fridge, hot rings, kettle, microwave and basic cooking utensils. There is a shower room with a toilet and the building is wheelchair friendly. The Trekkers' Lodge sleeps 6 people in two twin rooms and two single rooms, each with their own washbasin. There are 2 shower rooms with toilets and a snack kitchen equipped as in the Wee Bunkhouse. After a long day in the hills you can unwind in the relaxed atmosphere of the traditional Kintail Bar, where good food is served and beer is plentiful. Or enjoy the lochside garden and patio. Packed lunches are available if ordered the night before.

DETAILS

- **Open** - All year, all day (restricted winter hours)
- **Number of beds** - Trekkers Lodge 6: 2x2,2x1, Wee Bunkhouse 6:1x6
- **Booking** - Book by phone or email.
- **Price per night** - £13.50pp, 3+ nights £12.50pp, Sole use of Trekkers lodge £75 per night. Sole use of Wee Bunkhouse £65 per night.
- **Public Transport** - See Citylink website
- **Directions** - Kintail Lodge is situated on the A87 between Invergarry and the Skye Bridge.

CONTACT: Reception
Kintail Lodge Hotel, Glenshiel, Kyle of Lochalsh, Ross-shire, IV40 8HL
Tel: 01599 511275
kintaillodgehotel@btinternet.com www.kintaillodgehotel.co.uk

LEDGOWAN HOTEL
AND BUNKHOUSE

Ledgowan Lodge is a traditional country house hotel with cosy log fires, original features and friendly bar open to residents and non-residents. The bunkhouse is adjacent to the hotel and bunkhouse guests have full use of the hotel's facilities. Ledgowan Lodge is perfectly situated for the hill walker, climber or anyone wanting low cost basic overnight accommodation. It is within easy driving distance of the Torridon and Fannich Mountain ranges and Fionn Bheinn Mountain is on the door step. The lodge sleeps twelve adults in six separate rooms, each with a set of bunk beds, wash hand basin, chest of drawers and thermostatically controlled heating. There is a one off charge for providing towels and linen. The two bathrooms contain large baths with shower facilities and a toilet. There are basic cooking facilities and a refrigerator for self catering, but it is recommended that guests socialise within the hotel where the welcome provides a restaurant, bar meals, real fires and lively conversation. There is ample car parking in the grounds and an excellent drying room within the hotel. Camping available.

DETAILS

- **Open** - All year, all day
- **Number of beds** - 12: 6 x 2
- **Booking** - Book by phone or email
- **Price per night** - £12pp. £24 for sole use of 2 bed bunkroom. Linen £5 (one off charge). Camper vans and tents (with use of bunkhouse) £5pp.
- **Public Transport** - Achnasheen Station is one mile from the bunkhouse.
- **Directions** - On the A890, 1 mile south of Achnasheen

CONTACT: Reception
Legowan Lodge Hotel, Achnasheen, Ross-shire, Scottish Highlands, IV22 2EJ
Tel: 01445 720252
info@ledgowanlodge.co.uk www.ledgowanlodge.co.uk

Situated in beautiful Glenglass, sheltered by Ben Wyvis, this comfortable bunkhouse is named after the breathtaking Black Rock Gorge. It is an ideal base for touring the highlands and seeing wildlife, including seals in the Cromarty Firth and dolphins at Cromarty. Highland Games are held throughout the area. It is sited at the eastern end of a hikers' route across Scotland and on the Lands End to John O'Groats route for walkers and cyclists. The village has a general shop, Post Office, bus service and an inn (serving good bar meals and breakfasts) 250m away.

Available to groups or individuals, accommodation is in four rooms of four and one room for 1. Blankets are available and sheet sleeping bags can be hired. There is a self-catering kitchen and dining area with TV, showers and launderette facilities. There is also a camping ground. All areas of the bunkhouse are easily accessible by wheelchair and suitable for the disabled.

DETAILS

- **Open** - April 1st to October 31st, 24hr access. New arrivals 9am - 9pm
- **Number of beds** - 17 : 4 x 4, 1 x 1
- **Booking** - Not always essential. Deposit of 1 night's fee to secure booking.
- **Price per night** - £12- £14 per person. 10% off for groups of 8+.
- **Public Transport** - Nearest train station Dingwall (6 miles) Nearest Citylink drop off Inverness (15 miles). There are local buses hourly.
- **Directions** - Follow A9 north from Inverness, 2 miles north of Cromarty Firth bridge take left turn for Evanton. Follow camping signs.

CONTACT: Lillian
Evanton, Dingwall, Ross-shire, IV16 9UN
Tel: (01349) 830917
enquires@blackrockscotland.co.uk www.blackrockscotland.co.uk

SHIELING
HOLIDAYS

We're right on the sea, with views to Ben Nevis. There are regular sightings of seals and otters, and sometimes of porpoises, dolphins and eagles. Stroll to the ferry, pub, shops, swimming pool and miniature steam railway. Walk to Torosay and Duart Castles. Catch the bus for Tobermory; for Iona (where Columba brought Christianity to Scotland) and for Staffa (home of puffins, and inspiration for Mendelssohn's overture 'Fingal's Cave').

Your accommodation is in Shielings, unique carpeted cottage tents, made by us on Mull, which are clean, bright and spacious, and have real beds for 2, 4, or 6. There are super showers, and communal Shielings with woodburner, TV, payphone and launderette. Our campsite is rated '5 stars, exceptional, World Class' by the Scottish Tourist Board.

DETAILS

- **Open** - April to October, 24 hours (Reception 0800 - 2000)
- **Number of beds** - 18:   6 x 2 : 1 x 6.
- **Booking** - Please email a booking enquiry from our website www.shielingholidays.co.uk
- **Price per night** - £12.00 pp, Under 15's £8.50 pp, bedding £3.00pp
- **Public Transport** -   From Glasgow, rail (08457 484950) or bus (08705 505050) at 12.00, ferry (01680 812343) at 16.00 from Oban, arrive Mull 16.40; back by 11.00 ferry, arrive Glasgow 15.45.   Please check times before travel.
- **Directions** - GR 724 369 From ferry, left on the A849 to Iona. After 400 metres, left opposite church past old pier to reception - 800 metres in all.

CONTACT: David Gracie
Craignure, Isle of Mull, Argyll, PA65 6AY
Tel: 01680 812496
info@shielingholidays.co.uk www.shielingholidays.co.uk

HOSTEL

The North Ronaldsay Bird Observatory is situated at the south west corner of the island with outstanding views and an adjacent shell sand beach. Seals and the unique seaweed-eating sheep are abundant along the coast which skirts the 34 acres of croft managed by the observatory. The observatory sees spectacular bird migration through the island in Spring and Autumn. It offers a special attraction for those interested in wildlife, but welcomes all visitors. The Observatory Hostel consists of three dormitories and a self-catering kitchen in a converted barn and byre of the croft. The Byre sleeps four in two bunks and has en-suite washing, shower and toilet facilities. It is particularly suitable for family use. The Barn also sleeps four and shares facilities with the Bøl which has a single bunk sleeping two. Adjacent is the Observatory Guest House (3 star) which has a lounge bar and meals which are available to hostellers.

DETAILS

- **Open** - All year, 24 hours, open all day, no curfews.
- **Number of beds** - 10 : 2x4, 1x2 House:8 :2x4 and private rooms
- **Booking** - Advance booking essential
- **Price per night** - Hostel £12-£13. Half board in hostel from £27. Guest House private rooms £40-£53 half board
- **Public Transport** - Loganair flights from Kirkwall (Orkney) leave daily. Ferry from Kirkwall on Fridays and between May-Sept also on Tuesdays(subject to tides and weather). Small boats may be chartered. Orkney can be reached by vehicle ferries from Aberdeen, Thurso (Scrabster) and Gill's Bay, and a passenger summer service from John O'Groats.
- **Directions** - Situated at the south west corner of the island

CONTACT: Duty Warden
NRBO, North Ronaldsay, Orkney Islands, KW17 2BE
Tel: 01857 633200, Fax: 01857 633207
bookings@nrbo.prestel.co.uk www.nrbo.f2s.com

GARDIESFAULD
HOSTEL

Gardiesfauld Hostel is on Unst, the most northerly of the Shetland Isles. The island has spectacular cliffs, sculpted by the Atlantic Ocean on the west and secluded, golden, sandy beaches on the east with rocky outcrops where seals and otters appear. The Gulf Stream provides a moderate climate and the clean peaceful setting offers an invigorating chance to relax in a community where crime is unknown. During the summer enjoy long hours of daylight and the twilight of the "simmer dim" while in winter the long nights provide the backdrop for a vibrant cultural life. Situated on the picturesque shore at Uyeasound, this refurbished hostel combines superb facilities with a relaxed atmosphere. There is a kitchen, dining room, lounge, conservatory, coin operated laundry, showers (coin operated) and rooms with ensuite facilities. Caravans and tents welcome.

DETAILS

- **Open** - April to September, Open in winter for prebooked groups, all day
- **Number of beds** - 35: 1 x 11, 2 x 6, 2 x 5, 1x 2
- **Booking** - Book by phone or email
- **Price per night** - Adults £12pp, children (under 16) £8pp. Camping from £6 a tent.
- **Public Transport** - Ferry from Aberdeen to Shetland (Northlink Ferries). The bus meets the ferry and continues to Unst. Ask for Uyeasound. Flights to Lerwick (BA). From Fetlar catch 7:55am ferry from Oddsta (Bus meets ferry)
- **Directions** - Take the A970 north from Lerwick to Voe then the A968 north to Toft . Take the ferry from Toft to Ulsta in Yell. Take the A968 north to Gutcher. Take the ferry from Gutcher to Belmont. Follow the A968 north and head into Uyeasound (B9084). Follow the road to the pier and look out for the hostel sign board.

CONTACT: Warden
Uyeasound, Unst, Shetland, ZE2 9DW
Tel: 01957 755279
enquiries@gardiesfauld.shetland.co.uk www.gardiesfauld.shetland.co.uk

www.hostel-scotland.co.uk

The hostels in the following section are all members of Scottish Independent Hostels. Each hostel is unique in its character and quality assured by Scotland's national tourist body, VisitScotland. This ensures that however widely SIH hostels may differ in character and location, they all share similar high standards of cleanliness and comfort.

 VisitScotland Quality Assured

 Member of Scottish Independent Hostels

Members of Scottish Independent Hostels :-
- Have fully equipped self catering kitchens
- Provide all bedding required
- Adhere to SIH minimum Standards
- Provide plenty of local information
- Look forward to your visit

While in Scotland pick up the famous FREE SIH Blue Hostel Guide. Available from all tourist offices and SIH member hostels. Or order your free copy from the SIH website
www.hostel-scotland.co.uk

CASTLE ROCK
HOSTEL

In a wonderful location, facing south with a sunny aspect and panoramic views over the city, Castle Rock Hostel is just steps away from the City Centre with the historic Royal Mile, the busy pubs and late-late nightlife of the Grassmarket and Cowgate and of course the Castle. Most of the rooms have no traffic noise, there are loads of great facilities, 24 hour reception and no curfew. With its beautiful and dramatic skyline Edinburgh is truly one of the world's great cities. The cobbled streets of the Old Town lead past mysterious gothic buildings up to the magnificent castle. Below the castle's rocky pinnacle lies the New Town's 200 year old Georgian splendour.

DETAILS

- **Open** - All year, 24 hours
- **Number of beds** - 235
- **Booking** - Booking not always essential. First nights payment needed to book
- **Price per night** - From £13 per person. I.D. required for check-in.
- **Public Transport** - 5/10 minute walk from Edinburgh Bus St'n and Waverley Train St'n. (Taxis £3-£5). Airport bus goes to train station so it's easy to get to the hostel.
- **Directions** - From St Andrews Sq bus station go to Princes Street, turn right and then first left. From Waverley Bridge (with Princes Street behind you) take the right up the mound, at the junction go left, then at cross roads go right towards the Castle. Continue till road forks,Johnston Terrace will be on left. From railway station turn right onto Market Street and then straight ahead up the Mound, at the junction go left, then at cross roads go right towards the Castle. Continue till road forks,Johnston Terrace will be on left. From airport take bus 100 to last stop, Waverley Bridge (same instuctions from Waverley Bridge).

CONTACT: Receptionist
15 Johnston Terrace, Edinburgh, EH1 2PW
Tel: 0131 225 9666
castlerock@scotlandstophostels.com www.castlerockedinburgh.com

The High Street Hostel has become a hugely popular destination for world travellers since opening in 1985 and is one of Europe's best regarded and most atmospheric hostels.

Located just off the historic Royal Mile in a 400 year old building it is the perfect base for exploring all the city's attractions – and of course its wonderful nightlife!

Providing excellence in location, ambience and facilities, the hostel is highly recommended by more than ten of the world's top backpacker travel guides.

DETAILS

- **Open** - All year, 24 hours
- **Number of beds** - 152
- **Booking** - Booking in advance not always essential, 1 nights payment for booking.
- **Price per night** - From £13 pp
- **Public Transport** - Only a 5/10 minute walk from Edinburgh bus station or Waverley train station. Taxis cost between £3-£5 from each. The airport bus also stops outside the train station on the last stop so it is very easy to get to the hostel.
- **Directions** - From the bus station (St Andrews Square) turn left onto Princes Street then first right onto Northbridge. At top turn left onto the High Street on the Royal Mile and hostel is on Blackfriars St. on right. From railway station turn right then straight ahead up the Mound, at the junction go left, then at cross roads left again going down hill. After the traffic lights Blackfriars St is second on the left. From airport take bus 100 to last stop, Waverley Bridge (same instuctions from Waverley Bridge).

CONTACT: Reception
8 Blackfriars Street, Edinburgh, EH1 1NE
Tel: 0131 557 3984
highstreet@scotlandstophostels.com www.highstreethostel.com

ROYAL MILE
BACKPACKERS

Royal Mile Backpackers is a small and lively hostel with its own special character. Its size means that you will quickly come to make friends with which to explore the town and swap travelling tales. Step outside and be on the doorstep of one of the most vibrant and exciting cities in Scotland! Enjoy the benefit of access to the lively bustling High Street with its wide range of facilities. Guests who stay with us can join our free walking tour of the Old Town which leaves from our sister hostel High Street Hostel on weekends. Only a few minutes walk from the castle and handy for just about everything!

DETAILS

- **Open** - All year, all day, Reception 7am – 3am (24hrs during August)
- **Number of beds** - 48
- **Booking** - Booking not always essential, first nights payment required for booking.
- **Price per night** - From £13 per person. I.D. required for check-in.
- **Public Transport** - Only a 5/10 minute walk from both Edinburgh bus station and Waverley train station. A taxi costs between £3-£5 from each. The airport bus also stops out side the train station on the last stop so is very easy to get to the hostel.
- **Directions** - From main bus station turn left onto Princes Street then take first right onto Northbridge. At top turn left onto the High St. on the Royal Mile. From train station take the Princes Street exit (up Waverley Steps), at top go right then right again up Northbridge, then left at cross roads, hostel's on the left above the Oxfam Shop. From airport take bus no.100 to city centre, get off at Waverley Bridge. Walk away from Princes St. towards the roundabout, go over roundabout onto Cockburn Street. At the top of Cockburn Street turn left onto the High St. on the Royal Mile. Cross traffic lights at Northbridge and hostel is on left above the Oxfam Shop.

CONTACT: Receptionist
105 High Street, Edinburgh, EH1 1SG
Tel: 0131 557 6120
royalmile@scotlandstophostels.com www.royalmilebackpackers.com

The Willy Wallace Hostel is the only independent backpackers accommodation in Stirling. This historic town, midway between Glasgow and Edinburgh, has an important medieval castle which has guarded the "Gateway to the Highlands" since ancient times. Willy Wallace is a friendly well-run hostel in an attractive Victorian building right in the town centre and next to the train and bus stations. It offers discount accommodation for families, groups and touring backpackers visiting historic Scotland. The hostel is well-known for its friendly staff, large comfortable common room and clean well equipped kitchen. The bedrooms are warm, bright and spacious. There are twin and double rooms, family rooms and dormitories. The specially built bunks are adult size and robust. The mattresses are comfortable and all bed linen is provided. Relax and make friends in the grand common room where tea and coffee are free. Or keep in touch with your friends using our Internet facilities. Come and stay at Willy Wallace Hostel in the heart of historic Scotland.

DETAILS

- **Open** - All year, all day - no curfew
- **Number of beds** - 64: 1x18, 1x12, 1x10, 1x8, 3x4(family), 1x 2(bunks), 1x2 (dble)
- **Booking** - Book online or by phone
- **Price per night** - £11 to £15 per person (dorm), Family rooms from £35. Doubles from £35. Twin in bunks £30.
- **Public Transport** - Next to Stirling train and bus stations.
- **Directions** - From train station walk to the top of Station Road and turn right onto Murray Place. Hostel is at the end of Murray Place above Oxfam.

CONTACT: Reception
Willy Wallace Hostel, 77 Murray Place, Stirling, FK8 1AU
Tel: 01786 446773
contact@willywallacehostel.com www.willywallacehostel.com

BUNKUM
BACKPACKERS

Bunkum is a family-run backpackers hostel situated in a 150 year old Victorian town house in the city's West End It is surrounded by parks, gardens and trendy cafes, bars and clubs. It has beds in twin rooms and dormitories (very spacious!) There is a large self catering kitchen, laundry, telephone, a small library, free showers, free lockers, and an adjacent car park. Prices start at £8.50 per person per night (weekly rate).

We are very near Glasgow University, Botanic Gardens, Rennie Mackintosh House, Kelvingrove Museum, Scottish Exhibition Centre and Ohran Mhor venue. More details can be found on the website -www.bunkumglasgow.co.uk. Student card or passport required to stay

DETAILS

- **Open** - All year, all day
- **Number of beds** - 36: 2x2, 4x6, 1x8
- **Booking** - Advisable – Visa/Mastercard to guarantee bed.
- **Price per night** - £8.50 (weekly rate). Otherwise From £12 (dorm), £16 (twin). There is a surcharge for payments by card.
- **Public Transport** - Take the Subway (metro) from the city centre to Hillhead station. Exit right and take first street on the right (Great George Street). At the end of Great George Street turn left into Hillhead Street. Bunkum is on the left at number 26.
- **Directions** - From the city centre on the A82 (Great Western Road) turn into Byres Road opposite the Botanic Gardens . On Byres Road take second left into Great George Street. At the end of Great George Street turn left into Hillhead Street (number 26).

CONTACT: Reception
26 Hillhead Street, Glasgow, G12 8PY
Tel: 0141 581 4481
Bunkumglasgow@hotmail.com www.bunkumglasgow.co.uk

'Glasgow's Only City Centre Hostel' providing budget en-suite accommodation in Glasgow City Centre, only 2 minutes walk from Central Station. Ideally suited for international visitors to discover the city's cultural heritage and vibrant nightlife or convenient for guests to stay over after a concert or night out clubbing. We welcome groups of all sizes throughout the year and make an ideal choice for sports teams, concertgoers and school/college parties. Facilities include the 'Osmosis' bar, games room, chill-out lounges with Big-screen TV and SKY, 24hr reception, internet access, self-catering kitchen, guest laundry, luggage storage and free bike storage.

There are TVs in all the twin and double rooms and FREE Wi Fi.

DETAILS

- **Open** - All year, all day
- **Number of beds** - 364: Singles, 2, 4, 8 and 14 person all en-suite
- **Booking** - Individuals with credit card. Groups - 20% deposit required. Book on-line at www.euro-hostels.co.uk
- **Price per night** - From £13.95 B&B pp en-suite. Discount for mid-week bookings and long stays. Apply for group discounts.
- **Public Transport** - Central Railway Station 2 mins, Queen Street Railway Station 7 mins, Buchanan Bus Station 10 mins, Glasgow Airport 8 miles.
- **Directions** - From the bus station turn right into North Hanover St and right into West George St (past Queen St Rail Station). Turn left into Buchanan St and right down Argyle Street (left if arriving from Central Rail Station). Go down Jamaica St and the hostel is on the corner joining Clyde St.

CONTACT: Reception
318 Clyde Street, Glasgow, G1 4NR
Tel: 0141 222 2828, Fax: 0141 222 2829
glasgow@euro-hostels.co.uk www.euro-hostels.co.uk

KILMORY LODGE
BUNKHOUSE

This bunkhouse in a tranquil, rural setting is ideal for your group accommodation. The Isle of Arran is one of the most accessible Scottish islands; it's only a one hour ferry trip from the mainland. It offers the visitor hill-walking, mountaineering, golf, fishing, cycling, pony trekking and a bewildering choice of extreme sports. The bunkhouse is affordable, modern, comfortable and able to sleep up to 23. We supply all the bed linen, so no need to bring anything except your towels and of course, your food! We have a great, contemporary kitchen with all you'll need. Attached to the bunkhouse is the village hall which can provide extra rooms and an auditorium at extra cost. Ideal for educational groups, weddings, music workshop groups, clubs or any group needing extra facilities. We look forward to welcoming your family, club, group, school or any combination of these except stag parties! Phone or email with your queries. Registered Scottish Charity SC028200.

DETAILS

- **Open** - All year, 24 hours
- **Number of beds** - 23: 2 x 8, 1 x 4 (en-suite) 1 x 3 (en-suite)
- **Booking** - Book ahead, 40% deposit. £100 security deposit on arrival.
- **Price per night** - £15 per person for groups of 15+. £20 per person for smaller groups.
- **Public Transport** - Buses stop on demand directly outside the Hall and Bunkhouse. These buses meet all the ferries that arrive and depart from the main ferry terminal at Brodick.
- **Directions** - Bunkhouse attached to Kilmory Public Hall located in village centre.

CONTACT:
Kilmory, Isle of Arran, KA27 8PQ
Tel: 01770 870345, Fax: 01770 870345
kilmory.hall@btinternet.com www.kilmoryhall.com

Whether you require a fully residential activity holiday or just a self catering base while you explore the Southern Upland Way or tackle the 7 Stanes, we offer accommodation to suit all requirements. Our Lodge has all the creature comforts you require after a hard day outdoors including fully self catered kitchen, hot shower rooms, dining area and TV sofa area for relaxing. There are launderette facilities on site and a drying room for wet kit.

We offer a range of activities from sailing, windsurfing, power boating, kayaking, canoeing, outdoor laser quest, archery, fishing, mountain biking and climbing, From instructor training to family fun days out. Our aim is to give you a memorable holiday experience in a safe friendly family atmosphere

DETAILS

- **Open** - All year, 0900 – 1800 (late arrivals catered for)
- **Number of beds** - 20: 5 x 4
- **Booking** - Preferable – the more notice the more likely we can take you. Last minute avaialabilty if space permits.
- **Price per night** - £14.50 pp or £13.00 for four or more people. Blankets or duvets provided at £5 pp for duration of stay.
- **Public Transport** - Just 1.5 hours from Glasgow and Carlisle and 1 hour from Prestwick and Dumfries. Public transport buses (limited!) are available from Castle Douglas to the centre.
- **Directions** - Located on the A713 at the North East end of Loch Ken, in Dumfries and Galloway (SW Scotland).

CONTACT: Richard or Kieran
Parton, Loch Ken, Castle Douglas, Dumfries and Galloway DG7 3NQ
Tel: 01644 420626
gsc@lochken.co.uk   www.lochken.co.uk

MARTHROWN
OF MABIE BUNKHOUSE

Marthrown is set in the heart of Mabie Forest, about 6 miles south of Dumfries. It has a traditional sauna, a wood burning spring water hot tub, a large BBQ, garden areas and plenty of room for groups. The forest itself has newly developed mountain bike routes, ranging in length and difficulty. Bike hire is nearby as is the 7 Stanes mountain bike trails. Although we are a self-catering hostel meals are available to order.

Marthrown is suitable for all age groups. Facilities include secure dry store for bikes and equipment and a large dining area suitable for meetings. For something a little different why not try staying in the Roundhouse or the Tipi. For more info see our web site below.

DETAILS

- **Open** - All year, 24 hours
- **Number of beds** - 24: 1x8:1x7:1x6:1x5 + Roundhouse, Yurt and Tipi
- **Booking** - Telephone a few days in advance.
- **Price per night** - £16-£17.50. Duvet £3.00. Sole use on request.
- **Public Transport** - From Dumfries (White Sands) take the Stagecoach bus service 372 to Mabie Forest. It is best to arrive in daylight. 1.5 mile walk from road.
- **Directions** - From Dumfries take A710 (west) to Mabie Forest passing through the village of Islesteps. Turn right signposted Mabie Forest and Mabie House Hotel. Follow tarmac road over speed bumps to the end of the Hotel and Forest Rangers Office, through courtyard and onto forest track, Marthown is signposted and is exactly one mile into the forest.

CONTACT: Mike or Pam Hazlehurst
Mabie Forest, Dumfries, DG2 8HB
Tel: 01387 247900
mike@marthrown.com   www.marthrown.com

BUTE
BACKPACKERS

Bute Backpackers, your friendly independent hostel, has 40 beds with a mixture of single, twin, double & family rooms. Some rooms are ensuite and there are separate male and female shower facilities and also toilets on each level. There is also a separate self contained cottage dorm with its own fully equipped kitchen and bathroom and shower facilities. In the main house the self catering kitchen is equipped to the highest standard and there is a large seafront dining room. There is also a 40ft seafront lounge with woodburner and open fire, Sky TV, internet and wi fi access. Also a drying room, laundry facilities, private car park for twelve cars and secure bike racks. There are regular live music sessions which includes open mike for any budding muso's to join the fun.

DETAILS

- **Open** - All year, 24hr access, no curfew. Reception 10am - 10pm,
- **Number of beds** - 40: Main House 32: in 14 rooms   Cottage 8:
- **Booking** - Deposit only required for group bookings.
- **Price per night** - From £15 to £25 per person.
- **Public Transport** - Take train to Wemyes Bay Station and Ferry Port (40 mins from Glasgow Central). Then ferry to Rothesay, Isle of Bute. Hostel 900m from ferry or take a taxi (taxi rank adjacent to port) which costs approximately £2.50.
- **Directions** - Turn right as you leave ferry footpath and walk straight ahead for five hundred metres past the discovery centre and putting green. Continue straight ahead for another three hundred metres and Bute Backpackers is on your left. By car turn right on to main road. Continue for three hundred yards to the mini roundabout . Head straight on for a further three hundred yards and the hostel and access to the private car park is adjacent to the main road on your left .

CONTACT: Reception
The Pier View, 36 Argyle Street, Rothesay, Isle of Bute, PA20 0AX
Tel: 01700 501876
butebac@butebackpackers.co.uk www.butebackpackers.co.uk

Trossachs Tryst has been purpose-built on its own 8 acre site, set amidst beautiful scenery (on Sustrans route 7c) just outside the bustling tourist town of Callander. The hostel, which is the only one in the Trossachs area, opened in August 1997 and is finished to a very high standard, hence its nickname 'Poshtel' The rooms are all en-suite and are either 8, 4 or single. The 4 bed family rooms have their own private kitchen / dining facilities and can be used as twin rooms on request. There is a spacious dining / common room, well equipped kitchen, a laundry and drying room. A large meeting / recreation room is also available and may be booked separately for conferences, parties, etc. We have an on-site Cycling Centre, which also sells basic provisions. Other activities available locally include hill walking, pony trekking, canoe hire / instruction, fishing and sailing.

DETAILS

- **Open** - All year, Nov to Feb advanced bookings only, reception 8am - 11pm
- **Number of beds** - 30
- **Booking** - Booking advised at all times. Groups must book with deposit.
- **Price per night** - £15 to £25 including linen & continental breakfast. Group and family discounts on request.
- **Public Transport** - Nearest train station is at Stirling (15 miles). Nearest Citylink coach stop is at Callander (1.5 miles). Pick up from Callander can usually be arranged.
- **Directions** - GR 606 072. The hostel is situated one mile up Invertrossachs Rd from its junction with the A81 (Glasgow Rd) in Callander.

CONTACT: Mark or Janet
Invertrossachs Road, Callander, Perthshire, FK17 8HW
Tel: 01877 331200, Fax: 01877 331200
mark@scottish-hostel.co.uk www.scottish-hostel.co.uk

LEDARD FARM
BOTHIES

Ledard Farm is a working hill farm and the centre for the Scottish Sheepdog School. It faces the Queen Elizabeth State Forest (25,000h), Ben Lomond and Loch Ard. Highland Adventure outdoor activity centre is also sited on the farm and offers clay pigeon shooting, fishing, sailing, canoeing, mountain bikes, quad biking and hill walking. Ledard Farm has beautiful views across Loch Ard. The main path to the twin summits of Ben Venue passes through the farm and there are numerous forest paths for walking and cycling all within easy reach.

Four Ledard Bothies each sleep 2 people. They are fully heated and also have fans. Guests can use their own sleeping bags or hire them for £5 (beds have quilt, sheet and pillow slip). The toilets and showers are in an adjacent building as are the self catering facilities. There is ample secure parking. Cars can be left safely when walking climbing or cycling in the area.

DETAILS

■ **Open** - Apr–Oct (inc), all day. Arrive between 4pm and 8pm, depart before 11am
■ **Number of beds** - 8: 4 x 2
■ **Booking** - Booking essential – deposit for groups only.
■ **Price per night** - First night £20pp, thereafter £15pp. Sleeping bag hire £5.
■ **Public Transport** - Bus services to Aberfoyle from Stirling (adjacent to train station) or Glasgow (Buchanan Street Bus Station). We will pick you up from Aberfoyle or you can get a local taxi.
■ **Directions** - Located in the middle of the Loch Lomond and The Trossachs National Park. From Aberfoyle take B829 in the direction of Kinlochard and Inversnaid for 5 miles (8kms). The farm is on the right 300m after Forest Hills Hotel.

CONTACT: Ferg or Fra
Ledard Farm, Kinlochard, Stirling, Stirlingshire, FK8 3TL
Tel: 01877 387219
ferg@ceilidh-band.demon.co.uk www.highland-adventure.co.uk

CORRAN
HOUSE

Corran House is part of a Victorian terrace with magnificent sea-scapes across the bay to the Isle of Kerrera and the hills of Mull. There is a warm welcome for visitors and reasonably priced accommodation for singles, couples, families and groups. The house has a large self-catering kitchen, spacious TV lounge, comfortable, commodious, well appointed guest rooms and 4 bed dormitories with generous size beds - most rooms have en-suite facilities. Corran House is well situated for exploring Argyll and visiting the inner Hebrides. It is only a short walk along the sea front to the bus, train and ferry terminals.   Downstairs is Markie Dans bar with patio and spectacular views. The pub offers great highland hospitality, tasty meals, live entertainment, wide screen TV, pool table and a late licence all year round to enable the discerning drinker to sample the best range of malt whiskies on the west coast. Pony trekking trips now available - prior booking advisable. Photos courtesy of Highland Photos.

DETAILS

- **Open** - All year, reception 10am-9pm. Check in after 3pm.
- **Number of beds** - 36 : 7x4 : 1x2 : 1x6. plus Guest rooms : 11.
- **Booking** - Advisable. Credit card secures bed. Early / late arrival with notice.
- **Price per night** - Bunk room from £14pp. Guest rooms from £25pp.
- **Public Transport** - Oban train, bus and ferry terminals are 900m from the house.
- **Directions** - Corran House overlooks Oban Bay to the west of the town centre. From the Tourist Information and all the Oban transport terminals, with the sea on your left, walk along George Street past the Columba Hotel into Corran Esplanade. Follow the seafront for 300m. Corran House is on your right above Markie Dans Bar.

CONTACT:
1 Victoria Crescent, Oban, Argyll, PA34 5PN
Tel: 01631 56 6040, Fax: 01631 56 6854
enquiries@corranhouseoban.co.uk www.corranhouseoban.co.uk

Jeremy Inglis Hostel is only 150 yards from the station and the bus terminus in Oban.

Prices include a continental breakfast with muesli, toast and home made jams, marmalade and Vegemite, etc.
Tea and coffee are available at any time.

The rooms are mostly double and family size so you have some privacy, all linen is included in the price.

Kitchen facilities are provided and the hostel is heated by meter.

Smoking is not allowed in the hostel.

DETAILS

- **Open** - All year, no curfew, access with a key
- **Number of beds** - 37
- **Booking** - Booking preferred. Deposit in certain circumstances.
- **Price per night** - From £12-£14 per person (in a shared room), including continental breakfast. Single rooms (when available) £18.00-£22.00
- **Public Transport** - Nearest train and Citylink drop off 150 metres from hostel. Ferries to Islands 350 metres. For ferry enquiries phone 01631 566688.
- **Directions** - The Hostel is in Airds Crescent, one of the streets off Argyll Square. The Hostel is on the second floor, pink door.

CONTACT: Jeremy Inglis, Katrin or Michael
21 Airds Crescent, Oban, Argyll, PA34 5SJ
Tel: 01631 565065, Fax: 01631 565933
jeremyinglis@mctavishs.freeserve.co.uk

OBAN
BACKPACKERS

Oban Backpackers has become many people's favorite hostel thanks to its friendly atmosphere, excellent facilities and beautiful seaside town setting. There's an enormous self catering kitchen, a pool table and lots of information about things to do in Oban and Argyll. Oban is a picturesque town possessing spectacular views across to the islands - the view at dusk from McCaig's Tower provides a sunset you are unlikely to forget. The bustle of fishing boats, ferries, yachts and seabirds make the waterfront a lovely place to be. Boat trips leave Oban to the many beautiful Scottish Isles and more remote areas of Scotland. Ancient standing stones, medieval castles and whisky distilleries all in the area, with seal colonies, hairy coos and the best fish and chips in Scotland all within walking distance. Minibus available for transfers and custom made tours.

DETAILS

- **Open** - All year, reception open 5:00pm-10:30pm and 7am-10:30am
- **Number of beds** - 48: 3 x 6, 1 x 8, 1 x 10, 1 x 12
- **Booking** - Booking is strongly recommended but not essential – deposit equivalent to first night's accommodation to be paid in full to confirm the booking.
- **Price per night** - From £13.50 per person
- **Public Transport** - Close to Oban Train Station and Citylink buses.
- **Directions** - From A85 turn left onto Deanery Brae as you are coming into Oban. Follow the road onto Breadalbane Street. A pub with green lights is on the right, we are a little further on the left. Parking is usually available out the front. If arriving by bus or train, walk along the waterfront through town, keeping the ocean on your left. Continue straight on up George Street, past a cinema on the right, then the Taj Mahal Indian restaurant. We are a few doors further, a white building on the same side.

CONTACT: Receptionist
Breadalbane Street, Oban, Argyll PA34 5NZ
Tel: 01361 562 107
oban@scotlandstophostels.com www.scotlandstophostels.com

On a working farm within the Loch Lomond and Trossachs National Park this is an ideal location for a single night, weekend or a week's let for families or groups. An ideal base for hill walking with Munros, the West Highland Way, canoeing, fishing, and skiing nearby. The Wigwams are comfortably equipped with mattresses, electric lights and heating etc (not metered). Large wigwam sleeps 4/5 on benches. Small wigwam sleeps 4 with mattresses on the floor. Each has own car park, picnic bench and campfire. Beaver is a deluxe wigwam sleeping 5 with kitchen, toilet, shower & TV. Also available: five self catering lodges, some with separate bedrooms, lounge, kitchen, shower and toilet; space for camping and caravans; Kirkton Farmhouse for groups up to 12; and a yurt sleeping 5. Logs,kindling and peat available in the shop, also our own sausages to cook on your camp fire. Site has toilet /shower block, hot and cold water and a fully equipped kitchen. Bedding & towels can be hired @£3/set.

DETAILS

- **Open** - All year, , all day
- **Number of beds** -
- **Booking** - Book by phone or email.
- **Price per night** - Small wigwam £25 for 2. Large wigwam £30 for 2. Yurt £50 for 2. £10/extra adult, £8/extra child. From £175 per week with £20/extra person. Lodges from £190/week.Short breaks in some lodges eg £40/night for 2 in Apache Lodge.
- **Public Transport** -
- **Directions** - Situated on Scottish Agricultural College's research farm on the A82 three miles north of Crianlarich, thirty minutes south of Glencoe Ski-Centre.

CONTACT:
Tyndrum, Crianlarich, Perthshire FK20 8RU
Tel: 01838 400251
wigwam@sac.ac.uk www.sac.ac.uk/wigwams

BY THE WAY
HOSTEL AND CAMPSITE

By The Way Hostel and campsite can be found in the Loch Lomond National Park halfway between Arrochar's peaks and the grandeur of Glencoe. The site, run by experienced hillwalkers, is aimed primarily at outdoor enthusiasts and with great walking (the West Highland Way passes by the hostel), climbing, white water paddling and gold-panning nearby, there is lots to be enthusiastic about (Munro-baggers can find 50 Munros within 20 miles). Accommodation options range from camping (with an indoor cooking/dining area and campers drying room), through basic trekker huts, to a purpose built four star hostel with twin and double rooms as well as dormitory accommodation, great self catering facilities and drying room. For more comfort still, a three bedroom centrally-heated timber holiday chalet. By The Way is in Tyndrum with the village pub, shops, café and Tourist Information Centre nearby. The Glasgow to Fort William road is 250m from the site (far from the madding traffic noise) and both the Glasgow Oban and Glasgow Fort William trains stop in Tyndrum.

DETAILS

- **Open** - Hostel open all year. Camping from Easter to October, 24 hours
- **Number of beds** - 26 in hostel; 24 in huts; 50 camping.
- **Booking** - Always phone in advance. Deposit (Visa/Access) guarantees bed.
- **Price per night** - Hostel dorms from £15pp. Huts from £9pp. Camping £6pp
- **Public Transport** - Intercity coach and rail service pickup points in Tyndrum to Edinburgh, Glasgow, Fort William and Oban. Sleeper service to London.
- **Directions** - GR NN 327 302. Travelling on A82 follow sign in village for Tyndrum Lower Station. Hostel is immediately before station.

CONTACT: Jim or Jean Kinnell
Lower Station Road, Tyndrum, FK20 8RY
Tel: 01838 400333, Fax: 01838 400243
info@tyndrumbytheway.com www.TyndrumByTheWay.com

Braveheart Backpackers is a cosy cottage with private, shared and ensuite bedrooms. A real 'home from home' hostel with open log fire, well equipped kitchen, cd player, tv, video, musical instruments, BBQ. Situated in the scenic village of Killin ('one of Scotland's prettiest villages') by beautiful Loch Tay. Great hillwalking and 'munro bagging' location with Ben Lawers very nearby. Bikes, canoes and kayaks available to rent from the hostel and guided tours arranged too.

This is a great place to chill out or be active within the Loch Lomond and Trossachs National Park. There is much to do and see in the area with ancient castles, whisky distilleries, stone circles, early Celtic Christian & Druidic standing stones, crannogs (Bronze age loch dwellings), ancient woodlands, Fortingall Yew Tree 'the world's oldest tree' and Glen Lyon 'Scotland's loveliest glen', all a short distance away. The area is steeped in history & mystery, so come & catch it whilst it is still a secret!

DETAILS

- **Open** - All year, all day
- **Number of beds** - 12
- **Booking** - Please book by phone or email.
- **Price per night** - Dorms £15.00 - £20.00 pp. Twin Room £20 pp. Special Rate: £12.50 pp for groups of 8 staying 1 week.
- **Public Transport** - 100m from nearest public transport. Buses to Callander and Stirling. Nearest train station Crianlarich (12 miles)
- **Directions** - Located next to Killin Hotel in a small courtyard behind the church.

CONTACT: Peter or Reception
Lochay Lodge & Cottage, Killin, Perthshire, FK21 8TP
Tel: 01567 829 089, Mob: 07796 886 899
peter@secretscotland.co.uk www.cyclescotland.co.uk

COMRIE
CROFT

Situated in a 200-year-old farmstead, Comrie Croft offers an attractive, great value escape amongst the Scottish hills. Just over one hour's drive from Edinburgh or Glasgow, the Croft is ideal for individuals, families or groups. There are endless things to see and do. Explore the mountains, have a go at adventure sports like quad-biking or white-water rafting, hold a team-building meeting or seminar, tour Scotland's Oldest Distillery, discover Loch Lomond National Park at Loch Earn, swim in our own mill pond, walk on the estate, hire a bike, find ruined castles, or simply read a book on the sofa.

Among the facilities are a choice of standard or en-suite private rooms, a cosy living room with books, games and movies and full self-catering facilities. We also have an eco campsite (tents only), shop, bike hire, indoor and outdoor games facilities, conference facilities, and our own 230 acre estate offering walks and mountain bike trails.

DETAILS

- **Open** - All year, all day
- **Number of beds** - 56 + 14 (2 units)
- **Booking** - Recommended
- **Price per night** - £16pp - £18 pp en-suite. Group and family discounts.
- **Public Transport** - Train stations: Dunblane, Stirling, or Perth. Our own bus stop is served by no. 15 from Perth (approx. every hour). Summer only Citylink service to Oban and Fort William. Ask for Comrie Croft.
- **Directions** - Signposted from the A85 between Crieff (5 miles) and Comrie (2 miles).

CONTACT:
Comrie Croft, By Crieff/Comrie, Perthshire, PH7 4JZ
Tel: 01764 670140
info@comriecroft.com www.comriecroft.com

CULDEES
BUNKHOUSE
SCOTLAND

Culdees offers an independent hostel and B&B accommodation in the heart of a caring community which aims to live at one with the natural environment. Whether you're a motorist, a cyclist or a Munro bagger, you'll find it a homely place for just a night or for all your holiday. The bunkhouse has a well equipped kitchen with dining area for 16 people. Four bedded bunk rooms with digital locks, individual reading lights, duvets, fresh linen, towels, and an extra pillow. The Bed and Breakfast accommodation in the house has two family rooms and one double room. Also available to guests is a living room with television area and a wide range of movies. Large music room with baby-grand and other instruments. Big open barn, ideal for barbecues, gatherings, great when it's raining! Drying room with washer and dryer. Lockable bike shed. Toys, play area, plenty of space for outdoor games. Goat milk and eggs when available. Tourist Board 3 star recommended. Gold Award for Green Tourism.

DETAILS

- **Open** - All year, 24 hours
- **Number of beds** - Bunkhouse 16: 4x4, B&B 10: 2x4, 1x2
- **Booking** - Book with credit card.
- **Price per night** - £15pp (bunkhouse), £24.50 Bed and Breakfast
- **Public Transport** - Train Pitlochry 25 miles. Coach Aberfeldy 9miles. Local bus four days a week and the school bus will drop at hostel track. Collection from Aberfeldy's bus stop if stuck.
- **Directions** - GR 716 447 From A827 Killin to Aberfeldy road turn left at the hotel in Fearnan. At top of hill turn left (Dalchiaran) signposted Culdees.

CONTACT: Maryse
Culdees, Boreland Farm, Fearnan, nr Aberfeldy, Perthshire, PH15 2PG
Tel: 01887 830519, Mobile 07904 954116, Fax: 01887 830664
contact@culdeesbunkhouse.co.uk www.culdeesbunkhouse.co.uk

WESTER CAPUTH
LODGE

Wester Caputh Lodge sits on the outskirts of the village by the River Tay in beautiful rural Perthshire. Four miles from Dunkeld, at the heart of Scotland, it is just over an hour's travel from Edinburgh and Glasgow. There are quiet roads for cycling and excellent woodland and river walks. The river offers some of the best rafting, canoeing and fishing in the country. Five castles and four distilleries are within an hour's drive. Dunkeld is an unspoilt town of antiquity with places to eat and drink and plenty to see and do. We offer five very comfortable rooms with bunk-beds. The kitchen is equipped for serious cooking. The living room has a piano, games, and a log stove. There is a garden with BBQ. Enjoy music and good conversation - or simply the deep peace of green Perthshire.

DETAILS

- **Open** - Closed winter mid-week, check-in from 4pm
- **Number of beds** - 17: 2x2, 1x3, 1x4, 1x6
- **Booking** - Booking advisable
- **Price per night** - Prices will change to £16 per adult, £10per child, babies free
- **Public Transport** - Train station at Birnam (5 miles). Hourly Stagecoach bus from Perth (Mill St), ask for Caputh Village. Infrequent buses from Dunkeld. Local taxis available.
- **Directions** - From north: From A9 take A923 to Dunkeld. After Dunkeld bridge turn right onto A984 to Caputh (4.5 miles). After church on right turn right (B9099) then 1st right at foot of hill. A few hundred yards on right (long white building). From south: From A9 take B9099 through Luncarty and Murthly. Cross river into Caputh. Turn left at foot of hill (signed Dunkeld). A few hundred yards on right (long white building).

CONTACT: Catherine Boot
Manse Road, Caputh, By Dunkeld, Perthshire, PH1 4JH
Tel: 01738 710449
info@westercaputh.co.uk www.westercaputh.co.uk

PITLOCHRY
BACKPACKERS HOTEL
SCOTLAND

Pitlochry Backpackers Hotel provides what is without doubt some of the most luxurious backpacker's accommodation in Scotland.

Set in the heart of beautiful rural Perthshire, it makes a terrific first stop for any trip into the Highlands. Historic Dunkeld, Blair Castle and numerous whisky disilleries are just a few of the attractions within easy reach, and some of Scotland's finest walking and cycling trails are right on the doorstep of this very special hostel

It provides all the comforts of a hotel plus the ambience and facilities of a hostel. Twin, double and dorm rooms are available plus a wonderful sunny lounge, overlooking the main street.

DETAILS

- **Open** - March to October, 7.30am-12pm 4pm-11pm (please check at reception as times may vary)
- **Number of beds** - 79
- **Booking** - Booking in advance not always essential. First nights payment required.
- **Price per night** - From £13 per night. I.D. required for check-in.
- **Public Transport** - Buses will drop you off on Atholl Road and the hostel is only 1min walk. The train station exits onto Atholl Road also, only 5 mins walk.
- **Directions** - If coming from the south, follow the A9 until you see signposts for Pitlochry. Once in the town you'll reach Atholl Road and the hostel is just on the right-hand side, with a customer car park behind the building – you can get to this by taking the immediate right after the hostel entrance. If coming from the north, once on Atholl Road hostel is on your left, with parking just before the entrance to the left. .

CONTACT: Receptionist
134 Atholl Road, Pitlochry, PH16 5AB
Tel: 01796 470044
pitlochry@scotlandstophostels.com www.pitlochrybackpackershotel.com

GULABIN
LODGE

Gulabin Lodge is beautifully situated in the heart of Glenshee at the foot of Beinn Gulabin offering the nearest accommodation to the Glenshee ski slopes. We offer nordic, alpine, telemark skiing and snowboarding and have a dry ski slope where lessons are available. Gulabin is an ideal base for climbing, walking or mountain biking, whether you are a beginner or an expert. Other activities available include rock climbing, gorge walking, abseiling, archery, rifle shooting, orienteering, canyoning, kayaking. Nine-hole golf course, 85m aerial runway and pony trekking nearby. Five minutes walk from the hostel are the Spittal of Glenshee Hotel and Dalmunzie Hotel both with friendly bars and excellent meals. The lodge offers comfortable accommodation for individuals, families and groups with two cosy lounges with log fires. Free hot showers. All rooms have wash basins and linen. Packages for groups. Ski, Snowboard & Nordic hire equipment, and Mountain bike hire with guided trips available.

DETAILS

- **Open** - All year, 24 hours, arrive by 9pm
- **Number of beds** - 37 :- 9 rooms available
- **Booking** - Booking advisable with 20% deposit
- **Price per night** - From £15pp (bed only). From £20.00pp B&B, Family rooms from £45. Full board available. Sole use available.
- **Public Transport** - Train and bus stations at:- Pitlochry (22 miles), Blairgowrie (20 miles), Glasgow (100 miles), Edinburgh (70 miles). Post bus calls half a mile away.
- **Directions** - Gulabin Lodge is on the A93 road at Spittal of Glenshee - 20 miles north of Blairgowrie and 19 miles south of Braemar. Transport can be arranged.

CONTACT: Darren and Tereza
Spittal of Glenshee, By Blairgowrie, PH10 7QE
Tel: 01250 885255 Mobile: 07799847014
info@gulabinlodge.co.uk www.gulabinlodge.co.uk

RATTRAY HEAD
ECO-HOSTEL

Rattray Head Eco-Hostel is a former lighthouse shore station among huge dunes on an isolated 11 mile long beach. Come and relax in this gorgeous most easterly part of mainland Scotland, and enjoy one of its driest, sunniest, midge-free areas. The 1892 granite building has been renovated to form a modern, non-smoking, dog-friendly coastal retreat.

The hostel has a self-catering kitchen, a double bedroom, and three bunkrooms with four beds in each. It is part of the SIH network and has Visit Scotland 2-star grading. 3 stars, Cyclists Welcome, Walkers Welcome, and Green Business awards are all pending. The North Sea Cycle Route (Sustrans 1) is 17 miles inland and passes through historic Aberdeenshire with stone circles, castle ruins and golf courses.

DETAILS

■ **Open** - All year, phone in winter, , Check-in 4–8pm, check-out 11am. No curfew.
■ **Number of beds** - 14: 1x2, 3x4
■ **Booking** - Booking is available with first night as deposit.
■ **Price per night** - £13 which includes tea, coffee, squash, bedding. A private double room is available at £20pp.
■ **Public Transport** - Airport, coach and train stations at Aberdeen (43 miles). Buses 260, 263 run frequently between Aberdeen and Peterhead. Bus 269 runs hourly between Peterhead and Fraserburgh. Taxi from Peterhead about £17.
■ **Directions** - NK103577 Rattray is signed from the A90 Peterhead to Fraserburgh road. The hostel is at the end of the lane near the lighthouse, about 3 miles from the A90.

CONTACT: Rob and Val
Lighthouse Cottages, Rattray Head, Peterhead, Aberdeenshire, AB42 3HA
Tel: 01346 532236
hostel@rattrayhead.net www.rattrayhead.net/hostel

CULLEN HARBOUR
HOSTEL

This special location on the shores of the Moray Firth offers our guests a relaxing break with the sound of the sea at night, and lovely coastal walks by day. Accommodation at the hostel is spacious and uncluttered with the best solid single beds, power shower, and separate bathroom.

The facilities include a Rayburn solid fuel cooker and comfortable dining and sitting areas. There is a large laundry area and drying room.
Children enjoy the sandy harbour beach and many rockpools. Pubs and food are readily available.

DETAILS

- **Open** - All year, all day but please check in initially by 21.30
- **Number of beds** - 10: 2x5
- **Booking** - Not essential for individuals. For groups and advanced bookings a deposit is required.
- **Price per night** - £15 pp
- **Public Transport** - Cullen village is easily reached by buses from Inverness or Aberdeen, or trains to Elgin or Keith and then by bus to Cullen. Car journeys from Inverness or Aberdeen take 1 and a half hours.
- **Directions** - The hostel is found immediately adjacent to the harbour a 5 min walk downhill from Cullen village square. Go under the viaduct and turn off to your right downhill (as the main road curves to the left), keep on following the road down to the sea and harbour, keeping the sea on your left proceed beyond the harbour and turn in to your left opposite "Cullen Joiners". You will see our stone cottages and the red painted hostel.

CONTACT: Ruth or Howard
The Sailors Store, Portlong Rd, Cullen, AB56 4AG
Tel: 01542 841997, Mob:07912 079416
ruth@hyde-owens.com www.cullenharbourholidays.com

PROSEN HOSTEL

SCOTLAND

Glenprosen is the most intimate of the Angus Glens on the southernmost edge of the Cairngorm National Park. Two Munros, the Mayar and Driesh, link Glenprosen to the Cairngorms plateau. The Minister's Path leads over to Glen Clova, whilst a new footbridge and path along the prettiest stretch of the river Prosen connects to Glenisla and the Cateran Trail in Perthshire. Prosen Hostel was recently converted from an old school to provide accommodation for those using the upgraded East Cairngorms footpath network. Converted to the latest and greenest specification, the living room has a wood burning stove, internet connection, and raised area for admiring the view (& red squirrels) through the school's huge windows. A drying room and laundry facilities complete the cosy welcome. It sleeps a total of 18 in 3 bunkrooms, sleeping 4, 4 &6 and a family room sleeping 4. The nearby village hall is available to rent for ceilidhs, music sessions, parties and celebrations. STB 4 star. Green Tourism Bronze Award.

DETAILS

- **Open** - All year, all day
- **Number of beds** - 18:1x6, 3x4
- **Booking** - Book by phone or email
- **Price per night** - £18 pp, £14pp if whole hostel is taken. Minimum periods apply for Christmas and New year
- **Public Transport** - Trains Dundee; buses Kirriemuir (regular to Dundee & Forfar)
- **Directions** - From Kirriemuir follow B955 signed to Prosen, Clova and Cairngorms National Park. At Dykehead fork left. Carry on for 7 miles until public road ends at telephone kiosk. Turn acute right and follow tarmac 200m uphill to hostel.

CONTACT: Hector or Robert
Prosen Hostel, Balnaboth, Kirriemuir, Angus, DD8 4SA
Tel: 01575 540238/302
hectormaclean@compuserve.com   www.prosenhostel.co.uk

The Pottery Bunkhouse is situated within the new Cairngorm National Park, in the valley of the river Spey looking onto the Monadhliath mountains to the North. Laggan is a working Highland village with a reputation for adventurous rural initiatives, such as the Laggan Forestry Project, which now boasts a full-on mountain biking centre. It provides an ideal base for day trips to many places including Loch Ness, or for local exploration of the Monadhliath mountains, Strathmashie forest, Loch Laggan, Creag Meagaidh Nature Reserve, the Corrieyairack Pass, Ben Alder and many tracks and paths. The Bunkhouse is a purpose built timber building nestling at the rear of the Caoldair pottery and coffee shop. The facilities include two en-suite family rooms and three bunkrooms, disabled shower/toilet, lounge and TV room, kitchen, drying room, central heating throughout and hot-tub-spa for hire. The on-site coffee shop has excellent home-baking and a range of clothing and artefacts (summer season only). The nearby pub (400m) provides meals and a lively local bar.

DETAILS

- **Open** - All year, All day. No curfew
- **Number of beds** - 34
- **Booking** - Telephone to check availability especially for weekends and groups.
- **Price per night** - £12pp in a 8 bed Dorm. Family rooms £55 per night (sleeping 5) with own sleeping bags. Linen available for hire.
- **Public Transport** - Nearest trains and Citylink coaches are in Newtonmore (7 m).
- **Directions** - You will find us on the A889, 8 miles from the A9 at Dalwhinnie heading west to Fort William and Skye.

CONTACT: Lynda
Caoldair Pottery, Laggan Bridge, Inverness-shire, PH20 1BT
Tel: (01528) 544231
lynda@potterybunkhouse.co.uk www.potterybunkhouse.co.uk

Newtonmore, a traditional village in the Cairngorms National Park, is a great base for outdoor activities, relaxing or touring. The village has shops, a petrol station and several hotels which serve good value food and drink. See where Monarch of the Glen was filmed, visit the Highland Folk Museum, the MacPherson Museum and Waltzing Waters! Walk, climb, ski, canoe, windsurf, cycle, fish, golf, birdwatch or sail.

Our purpose built hostel has showers, a brilliant drying room, a well equipped kitchen, central heating and a lounge/dining area with wood burning stove. No meters.

Inverness 46 miles, Fort William 50 miles, Glasgow/Edinburgh 110 miles

Come and stay in our hostel, the area is unique.

DETAILS

- **Open** - All year, all day, no curfew
- **Number of beds** - 10: 1 x 2, 2 x 4
- **Booking** - Phone to check availability (20% deposit) or book online.
- **Price per night** - From £13 (adult), £10 (under 12) and £5 (under 5). Private rooms £34(twin), £48(triple), £64(quad).
- **Public Transport** - Newtonmore train station + bus stops nearby.
- **Directions** - GR 713 990. The hostel is behind Craigellachie House in the centre of the village at the junction of the A86 and B9150. Look for blue signs.

CONTACT: Kathryn or Peter
Craigellachie House, Main Street, Newtonmore, Inverness-shire, PH20 1DA
Tel: (01540) 673360
pete@HighlandHostel.co.uk www.HighlandHostel.co.uk

STRATHSPEY
MOUNTAIN HOSTEL

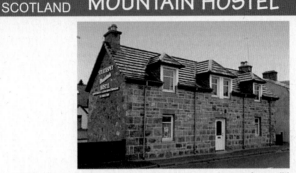

Our attractive accommodation is in the very heart of a traditional highland village. Newtonmore is an excellent central location with hills, mountains, rivers, ski slopes, crags, lochs, golf courses and brilliant walking all on the doorstep. The village is well served with hostelries serving fine ales and good bar food.

Strathspey Mountain Hostel is a refurbished Victorian villa and has excellent facilities. There are 3 power showers, 4 toilets, comprehensive cooking facilities, a bike shed, 2 TV lounges, coal fires and parking on-site for 10 cars. A 6 bed self-catering cottage is also available. What more could you hope for in the heart of the Highlands? The comments in our guestbook reinforce the overall quality throughout. You will not be disappointed by your visit.

DETAILS

- **Open** - All day, 24 hours
- **Number of beds** - Hostel 18: 2x6, 2x3 Cottage 6: 1x4, 1x2
- **Booking** - Recommended but not essential
- **Price per night** - £12.50 per person.
- **Public Transport** - The nearest railway station is half a mile away. Buses from Inverness and Perth stop 200 metres away on the main street.
- **Directions** - The hostel is in the very middle of the village main street next to the police station, zebra crossing, school and post office. The main street through the village is the A86.

CONTACT: Laurie
Main Street, Newtonmore, Inverness-shire, PH20 1DR
Tel: (01540) 673694
strathspey@newtonmore.com www.newtonmore.com/strathspey

Set in beautiful Glen Feshie with immediate access to the Cairngorm National Nature Reserve, this hostel is ideally placed for walking, climbing and cycling.

In winter Glen Feshie is the perfect base to try cross-country ski touring. Watersports and pony trekking are nearby for those with transport.

The hostel has three bunkrooms each with four beds, and a double room (duvets and linen provided). Hot showers, and good drying facilities are available.

The kitchen is fully equipped for self-catering and there is a wood burning stove in the common room/dining area.

DETAILS

- **Open** - All year, all day
- **Number of beds** - 16: 4 x 4
- **Booking** - Booking advised at weekends.
- **Price per night** - £202 sole use of whole hostel
- **Public Transport** - Trains at Kingussie (15km) and Aviemore (15km). Citylink stop at Kingussie, Aviemore and Kincraig (7km). Collection possible with notice.
- **Directions** - GR 849 009. From Kingussie take B9152 to Kincraig. Turn right at Kincraig, down unclassified road, after 2km turn left onto the B970 towards Feshiebridge. After crossing the River Feshie in 1.5km, turn right onto a road signposted Achlean and hostel, follow for 4km.

CONTACT: David Phimister
Balachroick House, Kincraig, Inverness-shire, PH21 1NH
Tel: (01540) 651323
info@glenfeshiehostel.co.uk www.glenfeshiehostel.co.uk

AVIEMORE
BUNKHOUSE

Nestling in the wooded valley of Strathspey beneath the often snow covered granite mass of the Cairngorm plateau, is the village of Aviemore. Local attractions include the Cairngorm funicular railway, Strathspey steam railway, fishing in the River Spey (or Rothiemurcus fish farm if you are hungry), dog sledding, off road driving, swimming pools, golf courses, clay pigeon shooting, mountain bike trails and pony trekking.

Aviemore Bunkhouse is the place to stay for friendly, cheap self-catering accommodation in Aviemore.

We offer en-suite accommodation comprising bunk and family rooms, for mountaineers, cyclists, walkers, individuals, groups, families and tourists travelling towards Skye, Loch Ness,and Orkney or as a base to explore the Cairngorms National Park

DETAILS

- **Open** - All year, 24 hours
- **Number of beds** - 44: 3 x family (4), 4 x 6 bunk, 1 x 8 bunk
- **Booking** - Advance booking required with a deposit.
- **Price per night** - From £16.50 pp.
- **Public Transport** - Aviemore train station and bus stop for Citylink and National Express coaches are 10 minutes walk from the hostel.
- **Directions** - GR 894117, O.S. Landranger 35/36. Arriving in Aviemore from A9 take right turn at junction signposted Cairngorms. Dalfaber Road is next left.

CONTACT:
By the Old Bridge Inn, Dalfaber Road, Aviemore, PH22 1PU
Tel: 01479 811181
sales@aviemore-bunkhouse.com www.aviemore-bunkhouse.com

ABERNETHY BUNKHOUSES SCOTLAND

Sharing a car park with the Speyside Way and just yards from the river, the converted Nethy Station offers all that a group could expect from a bunkhouse. It is well-equipped, fully central heated and has two public areas. Most rooms have triple bunks. We now have 2 bunk rooms with outside access and no store room. We call it Narnia, as you can reach them through a wardrobe!

Whether you self-cater or we cook for you as a group you will have access to the kitchen at all times. We never ask people to share the building so you may sleep, walk, ski, board, hike, ride, fish etc…. at your own convenience!

The station is only 200 yards from the centre of Nethy Bridge with its shop, butcher, pub and interpretive centre and half way between two wintersports areas. Dogs are welcome but please do not let them sleep on the beds!

DETAILS

- **Open** - All year, anytime
- **Number of beds** - 24: 2 x 9 :3 x 2.
- **Booking** - Essential (with deposit)
- **Price per night** - £11.50pp May-Sep. £12.50pp Oct–Apr. Minimum of 7 people.
- **Public Transport** - Take train or Citylink coach to Aviemore. Local buses are available from Aviemore to Nethy Bridge Post Office, phone 01479 811566.
- **Directions** - GR 002 207. Hostel is adjacent to the Speyside Way. From the B970, with Post Office on your right, go over the bridge and turn left immediately. Past the butcher turn second right.

CONTACT: Patricia or Richard
Nethy Bridge, PH25 3DS
Tel: 01479 821370
info@nethy.org www.nethy.org

SLOCHD MHOR
LODGE

Slochd Mhor Lodge is perfectly situated in the spectacular Strathspey in the Cairngorm National Park and halfway between the villages of Carrbridge and Tomatin.   The Lodge is on an 'off road' section of the No 7 Sustrans cycle route and surrounded by hills and forests.   This is also perfect walking country and in winter there are nordic ski trails from the doorstep.   All other outdoor pursuits are within easy reach. Slochd Mhor Lodge offers a genuine welcome in warm cosy surroundings. Fully equipped kitchen with wood burning stove and a spacious dining area together with large lounge/lecture room with woodburner. Other facilities include a drying room and laundry facilities, some en-suite rooms, a room suitable for wheel-chair user, an on-site cycle shop/workshop, MT bike hire, and in winter nordic ski hire. We have basic provisions for sale and there is an outside seating and BBQ area. Ample parking.
Visit Scotland 4 star graded. Silver Green Business Award. Cyclists Welcome and Walkers Welcome members.

DETAILS

- **Open** - All year, 24 hours
- **Number of beds** - 28: 1x10 : 1x6 : 2x5 : 1x2
- **Booking** - Booking recommended
- **Price per night** - From £15.00pp. Sole use rates available.
- **Public Transport** -   Nearest bus and train station Carrbridge (4miles). City Link London/Edinburgh and Glasgow/Inverness stop at Carrbridge.
- **Directions** - From south on A9, after mileage board 'Inverness 23' travel 1.5 miles north, take first opening on left marked 'Slochd'. Then first opening on right (¼ mile)

CONTACT: Liz or Ian
Slochd, Carrbridge, Inverness-shire, PH23 3AY
Tel: 01479 841666
Slochd666@aol.com www.slochd.co.uk

Your hosts at Fraoch Lodge are Andy & Rebecca. The house is of a traditional Edwardian design, made of granite. Artefacts from travels through Asia & Africa adorn the walls as do mountain pictures. Comfortable accommodation is provided in six twin rooms. Two of these rooms are the only rooms on the top floor with a shared shower and toilet, so are ideal for use by families. Each bedroom has its own hand basin and there is 1 toilet & shower for every 4 beds. Catering is available at Fraoch Lodge with meal times to suit your group. We cater for all kinds of groups and can tailor our menu to your requirements including for those who may have special dietary needs. Will Hide's article in The Guardian on 7.5.05 said "we spent the first night enjoying Rebecca's cooking, which would have passed muster in any hotel. Home-made fishcakes, curries, white chocolate & pecan brownies, and raspberry & basil ice cream make up just a small part of her repertoire..."

DETAILS

- **Open** - All year, closed for cleaning from 10am – 5pm except by prior arrangement
- **Number of beds** - 12: 6 x 2 (twin rooms)
- **Booking** - Booking advised – essential late Dec, Feb, Easter, Jul & Aug.
- **Price per night** - £16 - £20 depending on length of stay.
- **Public Transport** - Trains at Aviemore (5 miles away). Follow Speyside Way North to reach hostel on foot. Bus No.36 (Grantown on Spey) and No.15 (Inverness) both stop in Boat of Garten. Hostel is 50m from bus stop at north end of village.
- **Directions** - Follow signs for Boat of Garten from A95. We are at north end of village, opposite village green.

CONTACT: Andy or Rebecca
Deshar Road, Boat of Garten, Inverness-shire, PH24 3BN
Tel: 01479 831 331
sih@scotmountain.co.uk www.scotmountain.co.uk/hostel

LAZY DUCK
HOSTEL

One Scotland's smallest, the 8 bed Lazy Duck Hostel nestles neatly amongst ancient Caledonian pine trees looking south across a 100 acre heather moor to Cairngorm summit. Together with its 4 lightweight tent camping ground, sauna and natural waterfowl ponds it has been a magnet to travellers since the beginning of the last century.   The pristine, snug, colourful mountain style hostel accommodates both parties and individuals, and when individuals have booked we stop at 6 in number to be sure everyone is comfortable. The extensive covered garden, allows visitors to stretch out in basket chairs in front of a baronial open log fire & BBQ. Bike hire, horse riding and watersports are nearby as are The Lecht and Cairngorm Mountain facilities. Lazy Duck is an elemental award winning hostel where the code of "You do a bit; we do a bit" is alive and well. It's the sort of place you thought didn't exist any more.........

DETAILS

- **Open** - All year, all day
- **Number of beds** - 8: (2 x 4 beds) when booked by groups, otherwise 6 beds.
- **Booking** - Booking recommended, - for weekends essential to be well in advance
- **Price per night** - £13 per person
- **Public Transport** - Train or intercity coach to Aviemore (10miles). Local bus (except Sundays) or taxi from train station £15. Ask for 'Causar Crossroads' in Nethy Bridge and for local guidance (¼ mile walk) to Lazy Duck Hostel.
- **Directions** - From Aviemore take A95 and B950 via Boat of Garten to Nethy Bridge. Cross river bridge and take 1st right at sign 'Lazy Duck Hostel 1 mile' in hotel garden and look for our green hostel sign on RHS in the forest.

CONTACT: David or Valery
Lazy Duck Hostel, Nethy Bridge, Inverness-shire,PH25 3ED
Tel: 01479 821642
lazyduckhostel@googlemail.com www.lazyduck.co.uk

BUNKHOUSE

Ideal accommodation for groups and families visiting the stunning Cairngorms National Park, near Aviemore, in the Highlands of Scotland!

Four family/group rooms with private/en-suite shower rooms. Two fully equipped kitchen/dining rooms with televisions, stereos. Large, enclosed garden, BBQ, campfire area, play equipment. Ample off road parking, discount card and free wireless broadband.

A superb location for year round activities! Summer/winter mountaineering, skiing/snowboarding. rock climbing & abseiling, kayaking & canoeing, Bountain biking, gorge swimming, orienteering, sailing, windsurfing, golf. Many other local attractions, ideal for families / rest days.
VisitScotland 3* Hostel, Hospitality Assured.

DETAILS

- **Open** - All year, all day
- **Number of beds** - 24 : 1x4 : 2x6 : 1x8
- **Booking** - In advance to avoid disappointment.
- **Price per night** - From £15.50 (dorm). Private rooms from £46.50
- **Public Transport** - Nearest train station Aviemore. Nearest airport Inverness. Good bus services from both to Grantown Square. Ardenbeg is 2 minutes walk.
- **Directions** - From the A9 approach Grantown on the A95 passing Dulnain Bridge. At first roundabout turn left into Grantown, just before traffic lights turn left into Chapel Road. Turn right at the end of road into Grant Rd. Ardenbeg is 2nd house on left.

CONTACT: Rebecca
Grant Road, Grantown-on-Spey, Moray, PH26 3LD
Tel: (01479) 872824
enquiries@ardenbeg.co.uk www.ardenbeg.co.uk

RUCKSACKS
BRAEMAR

Rucksacks Braemar is an excellent base for those who enjoy the outdoors. There are 30 Munros in the surrounding Cairngorms, with access to the more remote areas via a large network of mountain bike trails. Deeside is ideal for pleasant walks with a variety of landscapes and remnants of ancient Caledonian Forest. Canoeists enjoy the Dee and Clunie on the doorstep and skiing is available in season.

Groups and individuals are welcome all year in the three self contained buildings. Linen and duvets are provided for the Cabin and Cottage. Sleeping bags are required for the Alpine Hut where you sleep on foam matresses on two alpine platforms.

All rooms are heated and the kitchens are fully equipped. Drying facilities included with no meters. Food, mountain bike and ski hire are available locally. Dogs welcome by prior arrangment.

DETAILS

- **Open** - All year, all day
- **Number of beds** - Alpine Hut 10: 1x10. Cottage 10: 1x8,1x2. Cabin 6: 1x4,1x2.
- **Booking** - Booking advisable (phone or write). Deposit of £2 per person per night.
- **Price per night** - From £7 to £15 per person.
- **Public Transport** - Service No 201 from Aberdeen operates all year. From May to Sept Heather Hopper travels from Braemar north to Strathdon and south to Perth.
- **Directions** - Situated in the centre of Braemar village, 200 metres from bus stop by shops. Turn left at red telephone boxes, then first right and Rucksacks is facing you.

CONTACT: Kate Muirhead
15 Mar Road, Braemar, Aberdeenshire, AB35 5YL
Tel: 013397 41517
sam@backpackerspress.com

Surrounded by the beauty of Deeside, Braemar Lodge is in a quiet setting only a two minute walk from the village itself. Braemar Lodge Hotel was formerly a Victorian shooting lodge and is set in extensive grounds two minutes from the centre of Braemar in the heart of Royal Deeside.

Our great value Bunkhouse provides comfortable accommodation for up to 12 people within the hotel grounds. The bunkhouse is equipped with two shower rooms, one of which is suitable for wheelchair access. The bunkhouse also has excellent drying and laundry facilities, excellent for damp clothes and ski boots. A generous fully equipped kitchen is also available for all your self catering needs. Guests are also welcome to use the hotel's excellent dining facilities if a rest from self catering is required. All bed linen and towels are supplied for the duration of your stay.

DETAILS

- **Open** - All year, all day
- **Number of beds** - 12: 3x4
- **Booking** - Book by phone or email
- **Price per night** - From £13 per person
- **Public Transport** - Aberdeen airport 59 miles. Railway stations at Perth (50 miles) and Aberdeen. Buses to Braemar from Aberdeen where the bus and rail station are side by side. Two minute walk to hotel from Braemar village bus stop.
- **Directions** - The hotel is situated on the A93 on the left if you are arriving form the south. Two minutes walk from the village centre.

CONTACT: Reception
66 Glenshee Rd, Braemar, Aberdeenshire, AB35 5YQ
Tel: 013397 41627
mail@braemarlodge.co.uk   www.braemarlodge.co.uk

JENNY'S BOTHY
CROFTHOUSE

The Bothy has an airy feel with whitewashed stone walls, carpeted floor and simple furnishings. In the main room a futon, single and two bunkbeds create a cosy sitting area around the woodburning stove with space for rainy day activities. There is an electric cooker and fridge, eating area, tiled work surfaces and an upright drier and pulley for drying clothes. An adjoining family room has a double and single bed with electric heater and cot available. Apart from the excellent hot shower, water is heated by a large kettle! Situated 3/4 mile along a track, with nearby river, scots pine and open rolling hills, the bothy offers complete peace and is in the habitat of deer, mountain hare and alpine plants. Some of the lowest UK figures for upland rainfall make it an excellent base for birdwatching, hillwalking and exploring Upper Donside with castles, galleries, distilleries, Pictish and standing stones.   Nearest hotel 1.5 miles. Other local activities include riding, mountain biking, fishing (with permit) and skiing.

DETAILS

- **Open** - All year, All day
- **Number of beds** - 10
- **Booking** - Booking is recommended. Please ring before arrival.
- **Price per night** - Children half price. For packages and sole-use please enquire
- **Public Transport** - Buses at Ballater (14 miles) and Strathdon (8 miles). Heatherhopper bus (with free cycle carriage on some journeys) runs through the Glen twice daily May to Sept (Tel. 01224 664584.)
- **Directions** - From south, about 2 miles into Corgarff tale left turn after Rowantree Cottage signposted Old Military Road. Bothy is 2nd house along.

CONTACT: Jenny Smith
Dellachuper, Corgarff, Strathdon, Aberdeenshire, AB36 8YP
Tel: 019756 51449
jenny@jennysbothy.co.uk www.jennysbothy.co.uk

GLENCOE
INDEPENDENT HOSTEL SCOTLAND

Glencoe Independent Hostel (signed Glencoe Bunkhouse), is centred around an historic west highland croft in the heart of beautiful Glencoe, offering great value accommodation for groups, families and individuals. It is set in a secluded and peaceful woodland midway between Glencoe village and the Clachaig Inn with immediate access to world class cycling, walking, climbing and kayaking and 20 mins from White Corries ski centre. Relax and enjoy the beautiful surroundings or explore further afield to Ardnamurchan, Mull, Fort William and Skye. The hostel has 3x6 and 1x8 bed rooms, a lounge with open fire in winter, cooking and dining facilities. The self catering Alpine bunkhouse sleeps 20 in a large open plan barn ideal for outdoor activity and school groups. There are also caravans for 4 to 6 people and a log cabin for 2-3 people. Drying room, small shop and bike storage.

DETAILS

- **Open** - All year (phone in Nov and Dec) , 9am - 9 pm
- **Number of beds** - Hostel: 26, Bunkhouse: 20, 4 caravans of 4/6, Log cabin: 2/3
- **Booking** - Booking advised in summer. 30% non refundable deposit required.
- **Price per night** - From £9.50 to £18 per person
- **Public Transport** - 1.5miles from bus stop in Glencoe Village (crossroads). Citylink buses 914, 915 and 916 from Skye, Fort William and Glasgow. Local bus 44 from Fort William and Kinlochleven. For West Highland Way take White Corries near Kingshouse Hotel to Glencoe Crossroads (20 mins).
- **Directions** - Sign posted Glencoe Bunkhouse. From A82 south, take right turn for Clachaig Inn, 1 miles after pub on left. From north, take left turn for Kinlochleven, then immediate right to Glencoe Village. 1 mile out of village on right .

CONTACT: Keith or Davina
Glencoe Independent Hostel, Glencoe, Argyll, PH49 4HX
Tel: 01855 811906
info@glencoehostel.co.uk www.glencoehostel.co.uk

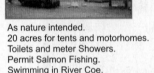

BLACKWATER
HOSTEL & CAMPSITE SCOTLAND

Blackwater Hostel is in the centre of the scenic village of Kinlochleven surrounded by the Mamore mountains midway between Glencoe and Ben Nevis. An ideal stopover for families, cyclists, walkers, climbers and those who are walking the West Highland Way. There are high and low-level, half-hour to full-day walks, all with great views, or if you prefer there is a regular bus service from the village to Glencoe, Ballachulish and Fort William. Water sports are available nearby. Ice Factor, Europe's first indoor 14 metre ice/climbing wall is only 200 metres away. This is comfortable, high-quality STB 4 star bunkhouse accommodation. All rooms have en-suite facilities, TV and central heating. Facilities include self-catering kitchens, lounge, dining conference area and drying room. There are supermarkets, pubs & restaurants within two minutes walking distance. Campsite has drying room, showers & covered area.

DETAILS

- **Open** - All year, 24 hours
- **Number of beds** - 39 - 2,3,4,8 bedded rooms
- **Booking** - Essential (between 8am-8pm)
- **Price per night** - From £14pp including bed linen. £32 for twin.
- **Public Transport** - The nearest train station is Fort William and National Express travels from Glasgow to Glencoe and Fort William. Regular bus service to Kinlochleven all day from Glencoe, Ballachulish and Fort William.
- **Directions** - GR 188 618. OS sheet 41. From A82 Glasgow to Fort William road at Glencoe turn right to Kinlochleven. The hostel is situated near the centre of Kinlochleven. Just past the Co-op a large sign with an arrow will point you to Hostel.

CONTACT: Caroline
Lab Road, Kinlochleven, Argyll, PH50 4SG
Tel: 01855 831253 or 0791 9366116
black.water@virgin.net www.blackwaterhostel.co.uk

CORRAN
BUNKHOUSE

Corran Bunkhouse 4 star accommodation is situated in a stunning loch side location surrounded by mountains in the magnificent Highlands of Scotland, 8 miles south of Fort William and 7 miles north of Glencoe. The Corran Bunkhouse is made up of two fully equipped self catering bunkhouses which between them can offer comfortable accommodation for up to 32 people. One bunkhouse sleeps 12 and the other sleeps 20 making Corran Bunkhouse an ideal base for small and large groups. Individual travellers are welcome and the room sizes make the bunkhouse ideal for family groups. All bedrooms have a TV and ensuite facilities. There are fully equipped kitchen / dining areas, drying room, central heating, laundry facilities, private parking and a steam room situated in the smaller bunkhouse. Children and pets welcome. Group discounts. Come and enjoy the many outdoor activities available in the area such as Climbing, Walking, Canoeing, Kayaking, Cycling and Mountain Biking.

DETAILS

■ **Open** - All year, all day (reception 9am -10pm)
■ **Number of beds** - 32: 8x2 1x3 2x4 1x5
■ **Booking** - Advisable but not necessary - major credit cards accepted.
■ **Price per night** - £16 per person, £14 per person for block bookings of 12 or more. £24 for single occupancy. Prices included bedding and power
■ **Public Transport** - Trains at Fort William (8 mile bus or taxi ride to hostel). Regular busses to Fort William from the south and from Inverness stop 100m from hostel (ask for Onich). Check the Citylink web site for bus details.
■ **Directions** - Corran Bunkhouse lies on the Onich side of the Corran/Ardgour Ferry 8 miles south of Fort William on the A82 trunk road from Glasgow to Inverness .

CONTACT:
Onich, Fort William, PH33 6SE
Tel: 01855 821 000
corranbunkhouse@btconnect.com www.corranbunkhouse.co.uk

INCHREE LODGE

SCOTLAND

Inchree is perfectly located for West Highland touring and walking, being midway between the Ben Nevis and Glencoe mountains. (15 minutes to each.) The Corran Ferry, which provides access to the beautiful Ardnamurchan Peninsula, is just 500 metres away. You can explore forest, waterfall, beach and hill walks from the door. All accommodation is self-catering, (breakfast available) with family / group, double & twin rooms available in Lodge, Hostel and Chalet accommodation. Larger groups can book any of the facilities for their exclusive use if required. Relax in our Pub-Restaurant, which serves Good Food, Real Ales and Malt Whiskies. Group and club functions / dinners fully catered for. Other facilities include efficient wet-gear drying rooms, barbecue area & climbing wall. Walking and touring guides provided. Internet access and WI-FI hotspot available.

DETAILS

- **Open** - All year, all day and evening
- **Number of beds** -   95:   Lodge 36 beds, Group Hostel 19 bunks, 8 Chalets with 4-6 beds in each.
- **Booking** - Pre-booking recommended but not essential. All major credit and debit cards accepted
- **Price per night** - From £14 to £25 per person.
- **Public Transport** - Long distance and local buses drop-off 200 metres away.
- **Directions** - Situated on A82 7 miles north of Glencoe and 7 miles south of Fort William, at the north end of Onich village. Turn off A82 (signposted Inchree) up a minor road for 200 metres.

CONTACT: David Heron
Onich, Nr. Fort William, Highlands, PH33 6SE
Tel: (01855) 821287 , Fax: (01855) 821287
stay@inchreecentre.co.uk www.inchreecentre.co.uk

ARIUNDLE
BUNKHOUSE

The Ariundle Centre is located at the beginning of the Ariundle Oakwoods, close to glorious walks, bird song, climbing, cycling, canoeing and fishing. It is a friendly family run business with a licensed restaurant, tea room, craft shop and bunkhouse. The 4 star Bunkhouse was completed in February 2006 and sleeps 26 people. The rooms are large and airy and there is a drying area and self catering facilities. Linen is supplied and towels can be hired for 50p. The Bunkhouse is ideal for walkers and climbers. Groups, individuals and families are all welcome and family rooms are available. Individually cooked breakfasts, morning coffee, light lunches and scrumptious home baking are available in the restaurant and the sandwiches and baking make ideal packed lunches. In the evening candlelit suppers are served using local products, sometimes with a local musician to entertain. The centre can cater for your party or wedding and your guests can sleep in the bunkhouse. The small village of Strontian has a petrol station and a well stocked shop. Camping available if bunkhouse is full.

DETAILS

- **Open** - All year,
- **Number of beds** - 26: 2x8, 2x4,1x2
- **Booking** - Advance bookings accepted all year
- **Price per night** - From £13pp. Group discount for advance payment.
- **Public Transport** - 1 mile from the nearest public transport.
- **Directions** - If travelling from north, east or south the quickest way to arrive at the Centre is to take the A82 to the Corran Ferry and then follow the road to Strontian. (Turn left when you come off the ferry).

CONTACT: Kate Campbell
Ariundle Centre, Strontian, PH36 4JA
Tel: 01967 402279
ariundle@aol.com www.ariundle.co.uk

Situated within fifteen minutes walk of Fort William High Street, Calluna is ideal for short or long stays. The modern accommodation consists of one flat, an alpine loft and two apartments. Bedding is supplied, along with a spacious kitchen, comfortable lounge and efficient drying rooms. On the spot advice from Alan Kimber (Mountain Guide) and an on-site indoor bouldering wall, with over 60 problems set by David Macleod (Britain's best rock and ice climber), make this an ideal all weather climbing venue. Waterproofs, boots, axes, crampons and mountaineering courses are also available (see website for details). Calluna is well known for peace, quiet and fine views over Loch Linnhe to the hills of Ardgour. A popular base for climbing and canoeing groups, families and individual globe trotters. Plenty of parking for mini-buses and trailers. Lecture room available for groups

DETAILS

- **Open** - All year, 24 hours (keys supplied)
- **Number of beds** - 26: 5 x 2 (twin beds), 4 x 4
- **Booking** - Phone up beforehand
- **Price per night** - £13.00 - £17.00 per person
- **Public Transport** - Fort William train and coach/bus stations are 20 mins walk away. Alan & Sue offer a free lift from the stations when available - just phone.
- **Directions** - By vehicle: From roundabout (West End Hotel) go uphill on Lundavra Rd and take third on left (Connochie Rd) between four-storey flats. Follow Connochie Rd (do not take right turns) and arrive at our back door! On foot: Ask for directions to the West End Hotel and follow the route above (15/20 mins on foot).

CONTACT: Alan or Sue
Heathercroft, Fort William, Inverness-shire, PH33 6RE
Tel: 01397 700451, Fax: 01397 700489
info@fortwilliamholiday.co.uk www.fortwilliamholiday.co.uk

BANK STREET
LODGE

Bank Street Lodge is situated 100 metres from Fort William High Street which has numerous shops, pubs, restaurants, banks etc. There is a fully equipped kitchen with cooker, fridge, microwave, cutlery and crockery provided.

Our common room / lounge has a TV, it also provides tables and chairs for eating self prepared meals, and a snack vending machine. All bedding is provided, we also have en-suite rooms available (twins, doubles and family).

The Stables Restaurant, at the front of the building, serves fine food for lunches and dinners - treat yourself. Fort William is an ideal base from which to enjoy walking, climbing, cycling or mountain biking.

The new world-renowned Nevis Range mountain bike trails and ski centre are only a short distance from the town centre. Three star STB rating

DETAILS

- **Open** - All year, 24 hour reception
- **Number of beds** - 42: 6 x 4 : 3 x 3 : 1 x 7 : 1 x 2
- **Booking** - Booking advised. Deposit required for long stays or groups.
- **Price per night** - £14, £15 or £17.50 per person. Group rates available.
- **Public Transport** - Train and Bus stations at Fort William, 500 metres from Lodge.
- **Directions** - Head for Town Centre via the underpass, turn left after Tesco supermarket on Bank Street, then head up the hill for 150 metres, we are above the Stables Restaurant. Car parking is available.

CONTACT: Kenny/John/Linda
Bank Street, Fort William, PH33 6AY
Tel: 01397 700070
bankstreetlodge@btconnect.com www.bankstreetlodge.co.uk

Deep in the Highlands, surrounded by spectacular mountain scenery lies Fort William, a mecca for those with a spirit of adventure. You can start (or end) the 'West Highland Way' in Fort William, hike or bike along mountain trails, go for a boat trip on the sea loch or just take it easy amidst the wonderful scenery. Even in winter Fort William stays busy with skiing, snow-boarding, mountaineering and ice-climbing. Nestling on a hillside above the town, with wonderful views, our characterful and comfy hostel provides everything you'll need after a day in the hills. In the evening put your feet up in our elegant lounge in front of a real fire or stroll down to the choice of local pubs. Ben Nevis, Britain's highest mountain, is just around the corner and below it, Glen Nevis, perhaps Scotland's prettiest glen, with wonderful waterfalls and ancient pine forest. Dramatic and eerie, Glencoe awaits a few miles away for an excellent day trip.

DETAILS

- **Open** - All year, all day. Reception 7am-12pm and 5pm-10.30pm (times may vary)
- **Number of beds** - 38:00:00
- **Booking** - Booking not always essential, first nights payment required for booking.
- **Price per night** - From £13 per person. ID required for check-in.
- **Public Transport** - Train and bus stations are only 5/10 minute walk from hostel.
- **Directions** - From north on the A82 go right at roundabout towards town centre. Turn left onto Victoria Road, then left at fork onto Alma Road, From south on the A82 go straight over first roundabout. At second roundabout go right onto Belford Road following Inverness signs, then turn right up Victoria Road then into Alma Road at left fork. From stations walk past supermarket, turn left before the underpass, heading onto the Belford Road. The hostel is just a bit further up, on Alma Road on the right.

CONTACT: Receptionist
Alma Road, Fort William, PH33 6HB
Tel: 01397 700 711
fortwilliam@scotlandstophostels.com www.fortwilliambackpackers.com

ACHINTEE FARM
HOSTEL

Achintee Hostel offers a friendly, relaxing stay with plenty of walking right from the door. The Ben Nevis footpath starts from the door and the West Highland Way passes within half a kilometre. This small country hostel is attached to the side of a farm house in Glen Nevis, just across the river from the Glen Nevis Visitor Centre.

The hostel has twin rooms, a triple and a 4/5 bed dorm. It has a self catering kitchen, good drying rooms and has wifi. Laundry is done for £1.50 a carrier bag (wash & dry). The Ben Nevis Inn serves meals and is just 50m away. Larger groups are not catered for.

DETAILS

- **Open** - All year, 24 hrs
- **Number of beds** - 14: 3x2, 1x3, 1x4/5
- **Booking** - Booking advised, credit card to secure booking
- **Price per night** - Dorm £14.50pp, Twin £16pp.
- **Public Transport** - Train/bus stations in Fort William (2km). In Summer bus #41 comes up Glen Nevis close to hostel (ask for Visior Centre stop). Taxi approx £6.
- **Directions** - Walking: Take the A82 north out of Fort William, then up Glen Nevis for one mile to the Glen Nevis Visitor Centre (Ionad Nebhis). The hostel is across the river from here. Cross the foot bridge, turn right for 50 mtrs and come through our garden gate and up to the farmhouse front door. Driving: From the south; take A82 north out of Fort William to the Glen Nevis roundabout, turn left (do not take Glen Nevis exit), turn right in front of traffic lights onto Claggan Rd, Right at Spar shop onto Achintee Rd, drive to end of rd (2km), right turn at Ben Nevis Inn and down the hill.

CONTACT:
Achintee Farm. Achintee, Glen Nevis, Fort William, PH33 6TE
Tel: 01397 702240
info@achinteefarm.com   www.achinteefarm.com

BEN NEVIS INN
BUNKHOUSE
SCOTLAND

The Ben Nevis Inn is located in one of the most beautiful and famous areas of Scotland, at the very foot of Ben Nevis, Britain's highest mountain. The Inn sits in Braveheart country at the start of the Ben Nevis path and a mile from the end of the West Highland Way. The bunkhouse offers everything that walkers and mountaineers will need, with self catering facilities including a large kitchen, comfortable bunks, and a separate drying area. All bunks have a duvet and all bed linen (no sleeping bags allowed). The bunkroom sleeps 24 divided into three sections and has some great views onto Glen Nevis.

The Inn offers an extensive menu with plenty of local produce and something to suit all tastes. There is frequent live music, check out events on the Inn's website . The bunkhouse is 20 minutes walk from the centre of Fort William which has cafes, provisions shops, outdoor-ware shop, pubs, and a well-equipped and recently refurbished leisure centre with swimming pool.

DETAILS

- **Open** - All year, all day
- **Number of beds** - 24: 3x8
- **Booking** - Strongly recommended. Book online with full payment.
- **Price per night** - £14.00 to £15.00 per person per night.
- **Public Transport** - Train station and bus stop in town centre, 2 miles (30 mins walk) from bunkhouse. There is a taxi rank outside the station.
- **Directions** - From A82 in Fort William take road to Inverness. Just before lights turn right onto Achintee Rd towards Claggan. At Spar shop turn right and follow road.

CONTACT:
The Ben Nevis Inn, Claggan, Achintee, Fort William, Inverness-shire, PH33 6TE
Tel: 01397 701227
info@ben-nevis-inn.co.uk www.ben-nevis-inn.co.uk

CHASE THE
WILD GOOSE HOSTEL

Chase The Wild Goose Backpackers' Hostel is located on the Great Glen Way and cycle route in the village of Banavie, near Fort William and at the end of the West Highland Way. You can be sure of a warm welcome, a comfortable bed and the company of like-minded travellers in a pleasant out-of-town environment.

Chase The Wild Goose is ideal accommodation, whether you are on a relaxing holiday break with family or friends, enjoying the adventure of a lifetime, travelling the world or living life in the extreme.
Take time out in the Scottish Highlands. The scenery is breath-taking! The hospitality is second to none!

DETAILS

- **Open** - All year, 7.00am - 10.00pm (late keys)
- **Number of beds** - 48 : 2x8, 3x6, 2x5, 1x4
- **Booking** - Pre-booking is advised. Credit or debit card secures booking.
- **Price per night** - From £9.95 per person. Reductions for under 16s and groups. Exclusive use is available to groups at excellent rates.
- **Public Transport** - The hostel is located just 100m from Banavie train station. The Fort William-Mallaig-Isle of Skye bus stop is nearby on the A830.
- **Directions** - Travel north from Fort William on the A82, signed Inverness. After 1.5 miles, turn left on the A830 'Road to the Isles' for Mallaig. After 1 mile, cross the canal and take a right turn, then 2nd left. Expect to see a large building with flags on the roof. If walking, take a short-cut to Banavie along the Great Glen Way.

CONTACT: Fergus
Great Glen Way, Lochiel Crescent, Banavie, Inverness-shire, PH33 7LY
Tel: 07979 407980 or 01397 772531
enquiries@great-glen-hostel.com www.great-glen-hostel.com

GLENFINNAN
SLEEPING CAR

Glenfinnan sleeping car provides unique, comfortable accommodation in an historic railway carriage adjacent to Glenfinnan Station. It is an ideal location for the mountains of Lochaber, Rough Bounds, Moidart and Ardgour. It makes a good starting point for bothy expeditions and is a useful stopping off point on the route to Skye.

Why not use it also for extended stays using road or rail for trips to fishing, golf, ferries, cruises, and beach locations?

There is a fully equipped kitchen, showers, a drying room and total hydro-electric heating.

The adjacent dining coach provides excellent meals to give you a break from self catering

DETAILS

- **Open** - All year, 24 hours
- **Number of beds** - 10
- **Booking** - Booking preferred and advisable to avoid disappointment.
- **Price per night** - £12 pp.
- **Public Transport** - Site is adjacent to Glenfinnan Railway Station on the West Highland Line (Glasgow-Fort William-Mallaig) and is 100m from a bus stop.
- **Directions** - On the A830, 15 miles from Fort William and 30 miles from Mallaig.

CONTACT: John or Hege
Glenfinnan Station, Glenfinnan, nr Fort William, PH37 4LT
Tel: 01397 722295, Fax: 01397 722495
susanjohnson75@tiscali.co.uk   glenfinnanstationmuseum.co.uk

SHEENAS
BACKPACKERS LODGE SCOTLAND

The Backpackers Lodge in Mallaig offers a homely base from which you can explore the Inner Hebrides, the famous white sands of Morar and the remote peninsula of Knoydart. Mallaig is a working fishing village with all the excitement of the boats coming in. You can see the seals playing in the harbour waiting for the boats and whale watching trips are available from the harbour.

The hostel provides excellent budget accommodation with two rooms each with six beds, a drying room, full central heating and fully equipped kitchen/common room. It has three star plus grading with the Scottish Tourist Board.

On site is the Tea Garden Cafe open 9am-6pm serving quality meals, snacks, speciality coffee and home baking. In the evening The Garden Restaurant (open from 6pm to 9pm) serves home cooked bistro style seafood. Meals available from April to October. See website for pictures of our food and the beautiful countryside around.

DETAILS

- **Open** - All year, 24 hours
- **Number of beds** - 12: 2 x 6
- **Booking** - Telephone ahead for availability and bookings.
- **Price per night** - £14.50 per person.
- **Public Transport** - Mallaig has a train station and services by Citylink coaches. For information on local buses phone 01967 431272.
- **Directions** - From railway station turn right, hostel is two buildings along.

CONTACT:
Harbour View, Mallaig, Inverness-shire, PH41 4PU
Tel: 01687 462764
sam@backpackerspress.com www.mallaigbackpackers.co.uk

GREY CORRIE
LODGE

Roy Bridge is an ideal base for outdoor activities – canoeing, hill walking, mountain biking, fishing – and for studying the fascinating local geology & history.
The Grey Corrie Lodge provides bunkhouse style accommodation for up to 28 people. Facilites include a self-catering kitchen & common room with wood burning stove, communal showers/toilets, drying room & washing machine.

Meals are available in the bar/hotel on site and we have ample car parking. The tariff is £12.50 per person per night; bedding is provided.

DETAILS

- **Open** - All year, check in after 4pm or by prior arrangement
- **Number of beds** - 28: 1x8, 2x4, 6x2
- **Booking** - Booking is recommended for large groups. £10 per person deposit required. Last minute bookings are often available.
- **Price per night** - £12.50 per person. Groups of 20 or less can book sole occupancy for £250 per night.
- **Public Transport** - Roy Bridge train station is on the main Glasgow – Fort William line. The station is a short walk from the hotel. Local buses run from Roy Bridge to Fort William via the Nevis Range.
- **Directions** - From Fort William take the A82 to Spean Bridge, turn right onto the A86 and continue 3 miles to Roy Bridge. Roy Bridge Hotel & Grey Corrie Lodge are on the right and are well signposted. Going north on the A9 turn on to the A889 at Dalwhinnie. At the T-junction turn left onto the A86 and carry on 24 miles to Roy Bridge. We are on the left on entering Roy Bridge.

CONTACT: Becky
Grey Corrie Lodge, Roy Bridge, Inverness-shire, PH31 4AN
Tel: 01397 712236
info@roybridgehotel.co.uk www.roybridgehotel.co.uk

INVERGARRY
LODGE

SCOTLAND

Invergarry Lodge is a 4-star self-catering hostel located in the Great Glen, surrounded by mountains, glens, rivers and lochs. Ideally situated for most outdoor pursuits, it also provides a great base for exploring the Highlands. We are a short drive from Loch Ness and are ideally placed for day trips to Fort William, Fort Augustus, Inverness and the Isle of Skye.

The lodge is spacious and comfortable, accommodating up to 24 in 5 dormitory-style bedrooms. Facilities include a large kitchen, spacious lounge and dining areas and free wireless internet access and broadband. The hostel also has provision for bike and kayak storage and has a large drying room if required. The hostel is open all year round to individuals, families and groups.

DETAILS

- **Open** - All year (phone first November to March), all day
- **Number of beds** - 24:- 2x6 : 1x4 : 2 x family (double + 3 single) subject to availability rooms can be booked as doubles/twins
- **Booking** - Recommended. Same and next day bookings, card number secures. Advance bookings 25% deposit please.
- **Price per night** - From £15.00 per person
- **Public Transport** - Citylink buses 915, 916 (Glasgow-Fort William-Skye) and 919 (Fort William-Inverness) serve Invergarry.
- **Directions** - Take the A82 to Invergarry. From the south, Mandally Road is on the left, before the village, just past St Finnans Church. From the north, take the first turning on the right after the A87. From the village, the hostel is a 10min walk. Go south on the A82 towards Fort William. After the bridge, take the first road on the right.

CONTACT: Matt or Jenny
Mandally Road InvergarryPH35 4HP
Tel: (01809) 501412
mail@invergarrylodge.co.uk www.invergarrylodge.co.uk

MORAG'S
LODGE

Morag's Lodge is set in wooded grounds just minutes walk from the centre of Fort Augustus. The village, situated at the southern end of Loch Ness, is ideally located for hill walking, cycling and kayaking. It's an ideal stop on The Great Glen Way. The hostel offers the best quality budget accommodation for backpackers and independent travellers. Rooms hold a maximum of six people in huge comfy beds and most have en-suite facilities. There are private rooms available including doubles. You can relax in the sun lounge, watch the television with a selection of great Scottish movies, or enjoy a drink beside the open fire in the bar. A drying room and bike hire are also available. We offer a well equipped self-catering kitchen and dining room. Breakfast and dinner are available on request. Parking is available in the hostel grounds. The hostel is graded 4 stars by VisitScotland and has the Green Tourism Silver Award.

DETAILS

- **Open** - All year, all day. Check-in from 5pm (earlier by arrangement)
- **Number of beds** - 85: 6x6, 1x5, 8x4, 4x3
- **Booking** - Booking recommended. Credit card details or cheque required to confirm.
- **Price per night** - £17.00 pp bunk. £45 double or twin.
- **Public Transport** - Bus stop for Fort William and Inverness 300 mtrs from Morag's Lodge.
- **Directions** - From Inverness, arrive at Fort Augustus, turn first right up Bunoich Brae. Morag's Lodge 100mtrs on left. From Fort William, go through village past petrol station and car park. Take next left up Bunoich Brae.

CONTACT: Rebecca
Bunoich Brae, Fort Augustus, Inverness-shire, PH32 4DG
Tel: 01320 366289
info@moragslodge.com www.moragslodge.com

Loch Ness Backpackers is a warm and friendly little hostel with a relaxed atmosphere, good music and no curfew. It has grown from an 18th-century farm cottage and barn and provides a warm open fire to greet you on cold nights. The house forms the main area of the hostel with reception, lounges, dining room, kitchen and toilets / showers on the ground floor, and two dormitories and one double room in the upstairs area. A converted barn (the bunkhouse) contains four more dormitories, toilets / showers and a kitchen / dining area. There is also a great BBQ area, garden & car park.

Loch Ness Backpackers is within easy walking distance of Loch Ness, Urquhart Castle, three pubs, restaurants, a supermarket, a fish & chip shop, post office, bank, gift shops and bus stops. A perfect location for activity or relaxation amongst spectacular scenery. Horse riding, fishing on the loch and mountain biking can all be arranged locally (great bikes available for hire).

DETAILS

- **Open** - All year, all day
- **Number of beds** - House 16: Bunkhouse 24: (1x2, 2 x family room, 6 x dorms).
- **Booking** - Check availability on website or by phone.
- **Price per night** - From £14 per person.
- **Public Transport** - Nearest trains at Inverness. Rapsons, Megabus and Citylink buses all pass close to the hostel.
- **Directions** - Near the A82 Inverness to Fort William road. Turn off is next to the stone bridge in Lewiston near the Smiddy pub.

CONTACT: Wendy and Neil MacIntosh
Coiltie Farm House, East Lewiston, Drumnadrochit, Inverness, IV63 6UJ
Tel: 01456 450807
info@lochness-backpackers.com www.lochness-backpackers.com

BCC LOCHNESS
HOSTEL
SCOTLAND

BCC Lochness Hostel is a top quality purpose built-hostel (graded 5 star by VisitScotland) with superb facilities. All rooms are en-suite and offer the very latest in facilities for the discerning traveller. It lies in the heart of one of Scotland's most stunning glens, enabling you to escape from modern life.

This is an excellent base from which you may explore the world famous Loch Ness, Urquhart Castle, Glen Affric (National Nature Reserve) and Glen Strathfarrar which are renowned for their stunning beauty and variety of wildlife. From the hostel there are 6 golf courses all within 30 minutes drive. Also it is ideally placed for hill walking, Munro bagging, mountain biking, cycling, fishing and horse riding. Also as a stop off point for those travelling to Skye etc and yet is only twenty minutes drive from the historic new City of Inverness. The hostel is situated near the main bus route and is within easy walking distance of the nearby tearoom/shop.

DETAILS

- **Open** - All year, all day
- **Number of beds** - 30: 5 x 6/4
- **Booking** - Book by phone or email.
- **Price per night** - From £12 per person. From £30 for twin room.
- **Public Transport** - Buses from Inverness, Drumnadrochit and Fort William stop nearby.
- **Directions** - We are midway between Drumnadrochit and Cannich on the A381 which leads to Glen Affric National Nature Reserve.

CONTACT: Donald MacLean
Bearnock, Glen Urquhart, Drumnadrochit, Inverness-shire, IV63 6TN
Tel: 01456 476296 Mob:07780 603045
info@bcclochness.co.uk www.bcclochnesshostel.co.uk

STRAVAIGERS
LODGE

Stravaigers Lodge is an independent, purpose-built, family-run hostel with 30 private rooms sleeping 60 people (no dorms). It offers comfortable, low priced accommodation for individuals, families and groups.

Situated in Fort Augustus on the shores of Loch Ness, our hostel is only five minutes walk from the Caledonian Canal, Loch Ness and the Great Glen Way. Pubs, restaurants and shops are also within 5 minutes walk.

The lodge provides a warm welcome, friendly service and an excellent place to stay. situated in the beautiful village of Fort Augustus at the southern end of Loch Ness.

DETAILS

- **Open** - April to New year, 10am onwards
- **Number of beds** - 60: 30x2
- **Booking** - Notice required for bookings in off peak season.
- **Price per night** - £12 to £15 per person.
- **Public Transport** - Regular air links from London to Inverness and daily bus service from airport via Inverness and Loch ness to Fort Augustus.
- **Directions** - From white canal bridge head towards B862 (Whitebridge) and follow for 100metres, hostel on your right

CONTACT:
Glendoe road, Fort Augustus, Inverness-Shire, PH32 4BZ
Tel: 01320 366257
stravaigerslodge@aol.com

GREAT GLEN
HOSTEL
SCOTLAND

Nestled between mountains and lochs in the heart of the "Outdoor Capital of the UK", 20 miles north of Fort William and 10 miles south of Loch Ness, the Great Glen Hostel is an ideal location whether you're touring the Highlands, bagging Munros or paddling rivers and lochs, and we are only a few minutes' walk from the Great Glen Way.

We provide comfortable accommodation in dormitories and family rooms. Hostel facilities include a self-catering kitchen, drying room, laundry, bike and canoe storage, free internet access, hot showers and a hostel store.
The whole hostel is available for exclusive rental for groups throughout the year.

DETAILS

- **Open** - Open all year , all day
- **Number of beds** - 54: 1x2, 2x5, 1x6, 3x8, 1x12
- **Booking** - Booking recommended. Please telephone in advance or book online
- **Price per night** - Dorm beds £14-15. Family rooms from £65. Whole hostel available for exclusive hire from £350 per night
- **Public Transport** - Citylink bus services between Glasgow and the Isle of Skye, and between Fort William and Inverness will stop nearby. Nearest railway station: Spean Bridge. Nearest airport: Inverness.
- **Directions** - We are located 11 miles north of Spean Bridge and 3 miles south of Invergarry on the A82 in a small settlement called South Laggan. Citylink buses stop 100m north of the hostel on the A82. If you are walking the Great Glen Way, stay on the Way until you see signs directing you to the hostel.

CONTACT: Clem or Kirsty
South Laggan, Spean Bridge, Inverness-shire, PH34 4EA
Tel: 01809 501430
bookings@greatglenhostel.com   www.greatglenhostel.com

EASTGATE
BACKPACKERS

Eastgate Hostel is a perfect base for backpackers, walkers and cyclists to explore the Highland capital and surrounding area. Loch Ness is only a short drive away, as is Urquhart Castle and Culloden battlefield. Day trips to Skye, Orkney and the north are possible and tours are available to Culloden & Loch Ness. Inverness boasts an excellent choice of pubs, clubs and restaurants to suit all tastes, while a large modern shopping centre is located directly opposite us. We are a 5 minute walk from the train and bus stations. Find us on the second floor, opposite the "Eastgate Shopping Centre". Enjoy your stay in a cosy, relaxed atmosphere with friendly staff, who will advise you on travel arrangements, bookings etc. Make full use of all our facilities: large kitchen, lounge/dining room, beer garden (only hostel in Inverness with this facility), barbecue, ample showers, 2 twin rooms, 1 quad room, 5 six-bedded rooms, free tea and coffee, no curfew, cycle hire, free WiFi. Book-a-bed-ahead service. Children and groups most welcome. A Visit Scotland 3* hostel.

DETAILS

- **Open** - All year, 8am-1.30pm and 3.30pm-11pm. No curfew.
- **Number of beds** - 47
- **Booking** - Booki 2/3 weeks in advance in summer. 20% deposit for groups.
- **Price per night** - From £11pp. Discounted rates during off peak season.
- **Public Transport** - Inverness has a train station and is served by Citylink buses.
- **Directions** - Turn left outside train/bus stn, cross at traffic lights next to taxi rank. Walk to High St, turn left, in 50m you will see Eastgate Shopping Centre. We are opposite on the right. Enter between Chinese takeaway and Celtic shop.

CONTACT:
38 Eastgate, Inverness , IV2 3NA
Tel: 01463 718756 Mob: 07504 913706 Fax: 01463 712006
jazzy2908@live.co.uk www.Eastgatebackpackers.com

HIGHLANDER
HOSTEL

SCOTLAND

The Highlander Hostel is a new hostel in the heart of the city of Inverness providing an excellent base to explore the Highlands and Islands of Scotland.

The city has many attractions, including the museum and art gallery, Inverness castle (with the Castle Garrison Encounter Exhibition) and Loch Ness (of legendary monster fame).
This capital of the Scottish Highlands has much to offer during the day and great nightlife at night.

The hostel has a self catering kitchen and TV lounge. There is also a laundry, internet facilities, safe luggage store and bike shed (bring your bike lock). Rooms come in a variety of sizes including family rooms and private rooms. All the bedding and linen is provided and towels can be hired.

There is a public car park in front of the hostel.

DETAILS

- **Open** - All year, all day. Reception 8:00am - 11:00pm.
- **Number of beds** - 79: 1x12, 3x10, 2x6, 1x4, 1x2, 1dbl, 1 x1
- **Booking** - Book online, by email or by phone.
- **Price per night** - From £12 per person.
- **Public Transport** - Hostel is directly beside the main bus terminal and only five minutes from the train station.
- **Directions** - In the heart of the city of Inverness.

CONTACT: Alex
23a High Street, Inverness, Inverness-shire, IV1 1HY
Tel: 01463 221225
highlanderhostel@highlanderhostel.com www.highlanderhostel.com

INVERNESS
STUDENT HOSTEL

Inverness, capital of the Highlands, is set amongst some of Scotland's most fascinating attractions. The bustling town centre soon gives way to lochs, hills, forests and glens. Close to Inverness Castle, the intimate and lively Student Hostel enjoys wonderful panoramic views of the town and the mountains beyond. After a hard day's Nessie hunting, our hostel provides a friendly cosy place to unwind, just yards from the city's varied nightlife and a few minutes walk from the bus and train stations. Visit the beautiful ancient pine forest of Glen Affric, tranquil but deeply historic Culloden Battlefield, the 4,000-year-old standing stones at Clava Cairns or stroll down the river bank to the waterfront to try to glimpse the wild dolphins in the nearby Moray Firth. Famous Loch Ness lies just a few miles upstream and of course has its own special wild animal.

DETAILS

- **Open** - All year, all day, reception 7am-11pm (times may vary)
- **Number of beds** - 57
- **Booking** -   Booking not always essential. First nights payment needed to book.
- **Price per night** - From £13 per person, I.D. required for check-in.
- **Public Transport** - Inverness Train Station and Bus Station are a mere 10 minute walk from the hostel. Alternatively jump in a taxi for around £5.
- **Directions** -   Head to the city centre and the castle. Hostel is up from Castle Terrace past the castle. Where road forks take the left onto Culduthel Road. Hostel is second building on right. From Train/Bus Station turn left onto Academy St. When you see the Marks and Spencers ahead of you, cross at the traffic lights and go down Inglis St. At the end turn right along the High Street, and then left at the bottom going up Castle St past the castle. Continue up Culduthel Road and hostel is on right.

CONTACT: Receptionist
8 Culduthel Road, Inverness, IV2 4AB
Tel: 01463 236556
inverness@scotlandstophostels.com www.invernessstudenthotel.com

Stay on a first class train in Rogart in the heart of the Highlands halfway between Inverness and John O'Groats. The three railway carriages have been tastefully converted, with many original features. Two sleep 8, one is subdivided to sleep 4 and 2. There are two beds per room, and a kitchen, dining room, sitting room, showers and toilets. They are heated and non-smoking. All bedding is included. We also have a cosy showman's wagon which sleeps two. Four trains per day in each direction serve this small crofting community which has a shop, post office and pub with restaurant. Glenmorangie and Clynelish distilleries, Dunrobin Castle and Helmsdale's Heritage Centre are easy to reach by train or car. See the silver salmon leap at Lairg and the seabirds and seals in Loch Fleet. Or just enjoy the peace of Rogart.

The climate is good and the midges are less prevalent than in the west! Families welcome. Free use of bikes for guests.

DETAILS

- **Open** - March to November inclusive, 24 hours
- **Number of beds** - 24:   8 x 2 : 1 x 4 : 2x 2.
- **Booking** - Booking is not essential.
- **Price per night** - £14 per person, 12yrs and under £9 person. (10% discount if you arrive by bike or train).
- **Public Transport** - Wick to Inverness trains stop at the door.
- **Directions** - We are at the railway station, 4 miles from the A9 trunk road, 54 miles north of Inverness.

CONTACT: Kate or Frank
Rogart Station, Sutherland, Highlands, IV28 3XA
Tel: 01408 641343   Mobile/Text 07833 641226
kate@sleeperzzz.com www.sleeperzzz.com

HELMSDALE
HOSTEL

This small friendly hostel was recently upgraded. Although now privately run, it is affiliated to the SYHA and a member of VisitScotland (4 Stars). Set in the small scenic village of Helmsdale, halfway between Inverness and John O'Groats, it is ideal for cycling, coastal walks, hill walks and birdwatching. Backpackers, birdwatchers and families are welcome. Accommodation (all with en-suite showers): 1 female dorm with 8 beds; 1 male dorm with 8 beds; 2 family bedrooms (sleep 4) with a double bed and bunks.

FACILITIES Bed linen provided, towel hire available, fully equipped kitchen, large dining area, comfortable lounge area, solid fuel heating, drying cupboard, internet access, cycle shed, garden / barbecue area.

4 star Scottish Tourist Board graded.

DETAILS

- **Open** - Easter to Sept (inc) other dates by request, not open during the day.
- **Number of beds** - 24: 2x8, 2x4
- **Booking** - Book in advance
- **Price per night** - Dorm £16.50pp, children from £7.50 (family room).
- **Public Transport** - Helmsdale is served by the City Link bus service and is on the railway line from Inverness to Thurso.
- **Directions** - The hostel is situated on the corner of the A9 and Old Caithness Road (park in Rockview Place). Arriving by bus: Walk up the slope for 100 metres. The Hostel is after the old church on your left. (200 metres). Arriving by train: Cross over the old bridge, turn right along Dunrobin Street, then left up Stafford Street. Hostel is at the top of the slope on the left (half a mile).

CONTACT: Irene Drummond
Stafford Street, Helmsdale, Sutherland, KW8 6JR
Tel: 01431 821636 or 07971 516287
Irene.Drummond@btinternet.com www.helmsdalehostel.co.uk

Thurso is the northern-most town on the UK mainland. Caithness has a rich history which can be traced back to its Viking roots. The cliffs are spectacular and every narrow rock ledge is alive with guillemots, kittiwakes, fulmars and posing puffins. The wildlife off shore is equally fascinating where seals and porpoises haunt the surf. A great way to experience both the coast and the wildlife is to take one of the boat trips around the coast.

The Hostel has been upgraded and is a Visit Scotland 4 Star hostel with all rooms ensuite. Using their own backpacking experience the owners have developed a level of comfort and service which ranks it amongst the top places to stay for families, individuals and couples wanting privacy in the twin / double rooms. The hostel is also affiliated to the SYHA. Surfing, pony trekking, fishing, quad biking and coastal walks are all available in the area.

DETAILS

- **Open** - All year, 24 hours
- **Number of beds** - 30: 4 x 4 - 1 x 6 - 3 x 2 (or 3) beds
- **Booking** - Advisable, deposit please for groups.
- **Price per night** - Dorm £14pp Double/Twin £34. Family room £50. Breakfast is included in the price.
- **Public Transport** - Train station 10 minutes walk. Bus stop 2 minutes walk.
- **Directions** - From Train station follow Princes Street downhill to Sandras. Buses stop on St George Street. Walk uphill (2 mins) 1st right, 1st left and 1st right again to Princes Street. By car or bike follow A9 to Olrig St, take junction opposite Bank onto bottom end of Princes Street.

CONTACT: George or James
24-26 Princes Street, Thurso, Caithness, KW14 7BQ
Tel: (01847) 894575
sandras-backpackers@ukf.net www.sandras-backpackers.co.uk

LAZY CROFTER
BUNKHOUSE

The Lazy Crofter is a small hostel, traditional yet modern with a cosy and informal atmosphere. It offers self-catering accommodation to groups, families and individuals at unbeatable prices. Set between magnificent mountains and stunning seascapes it enjoys wonderful views over the North Atlantic Ocean. It is owned and managed by Robbie and Fiona Mackay, who pride themselves on the warm atmosphere and genuine highland hospitality and invite you come, relax and enjoy a slower pace of life.

The Bunkhouse sleeps 20 in a mix of dorms and two-man bunkrooms. The bedrooms are warm, bright and airy; linen is provided and all rooms are fully made-up for your arrival. There's a modern, fully equipped self-catering kitchen, drying room with American-style washing machine, powerful hot showers, ample parking, bike storage, and secure lockers.

A well stocked village store and Post Office are 100 metres away and it's only a short walk to pubs / restaurants / tourist information and amazing golden beaches.

DETAILS

- **Open** - All year, check in after 12 noon
- **Number of beds** - 20: 2x8, 2x2
- **Booking** - Booking is preferred. Deposits required for group bookings.
- **Price per night** - £14 per person
- **Public Transport** - Nearest trains at Lairg, just over an hours drive away. A daily bus service (May- September) leaves Inverness in the morning, driving via Ullapool.
- **Directions** - Grid reference NC 406 679 OS sheet 9.

CONTACT: Fiona
Durine, Durness, Sutherland, Scotland, IV27 4PN
Tel: 01971 511202
fiona@durnesshostel.com www.durnesshostel.com

BADRALLACH
BOTHY

On the tranquil shores of Little Loch Broom overlooking An Teallach, one of Scotland's finest mountain ranges, Badrallach Bothy and Camp Site with its welcoming traditional buildings offers a fine base for walking and climbing in the hills of Wester Ross, Caithness and Sutherland. You can fish in the rivers, hill lochs and sea, or simply watch the flora and fauna including many orchids, golden eagles, otters, porpoises, pine martens, deer and wild goats. Guests often sit around the peat stove in the gas light (there is now electric here too) and discuss life over a dram or two. Hot showers, spotless sanitary accommodation (STB graded 4 star excellent), an unbelievable price (thanks to S.N.H), and the total peace makes our Bothy and camp site (12 tents only) one that visitors return to year after year. We also have a caravan, 4 star cottage and dinner, b&b. Hire canoes, kites, bikes, boats and blokarts.

DETAILS

- **Open** - All year, all times
- **Number of beds** - 12 plus bedspaces (Alpine style platforms). We have had 20 at a squeeze, mats & sleeping bags required.
- **Booking** - Recommended
- **Price per night** - £5 pp £1.50 per vehicle. £60 sole use (£100 Xmas & New year).
- **Public Transport** - Westerbus (01445 712255) operate Mon/Wed/Sat between Inverness/Gairloch and drop at road end Dundonnell, 7 miles from hostel. Pick-up can be arranged.
- **Directions** - GR 065 915 Located on the shore of Little Loch Broom 7 miles along a single track road off the A832, one mile east of the Dundonnell Hotel.

CONTACT: Mr/Mrs Stott,
Croft No 9, Badrallach, Dundonnell, Ross-shire, IV23 2QP
Tel: 01854 633281
mail@badrallach.com www.badrallach.com

Sail Mhor Croft is a small rural hostel which is situated at Dundonnell on the shores of Little Loch Broom. The mountain range of An Teallach, which has the reputation of being one of the finest ridge walks in Great Britain, is right on our doorstep and the area is a haven for walkers of all experience as well as for photographers.

Whether you wish to climb the summits, walk along the loch side, visit a beautiful sandy beach or just soak up the tranquillity of the area, you know the scenery cannot be beaten anywhere in the country. The hostel offers accommodation for up to 16 persons in three dorms which are fitted with anti-midge screens. Guests have a choice of using our self-catering facilities or we can provide a full breakfast. It is advisable to ring in advance in order to book yourself a bed, the next self-catering hostel is many miles away.

DETAILS

- **Open** - All year, except Xmas, New Year and January, flexible
- **Number of beds** - 16:- 2 x 4 : 1 x 8
- **Booking** - Always phone in advance. Groups should book as soon as possible.
- **Price per night** - £13 per person, self-catering. £170 sole use.
- **Public Transport** - Nearest train station is Inverness (60 miles). Nearest City Link bus drop off is Braemore Junction (15 miles). Wester bus passes the hostel 3 times a week; Mon, Wed and Sat. It also provides a service between Gairloch and Ullapool on Thursday afternoon.
- **Directions** - GR 064 893 (sheet 19) 1.5 miles west of Dundonnell Hotel on A832.

CONTACT: Dave or Lynda
Camusnagaul, Dundonnell, Ross-shire, IV23 2QT
Tel: 01854 633224
dave.lynda@sailmhor.co.uk www.sailmhor.co.uk

KINLOCHEWE
BUNKHOUSE

Kinlochewe Bunkhouse is part of the Kinlochewe Hotel. The accommodation consists of one dormitory with 12 bunks and individual lockers for each bunk. There are central heating, hot showers, toilets, drying room and a well equipped kitchen. The Bunkhouse is ideally placed for walking and climbing in the Torridon Mountains and the many Munros that they have to offer, indeed there are over 20 Munros within 20 miles of Kinlochewe.

The Hotel Bar is open all the year round, and serves excellent home-made food at affordable prices and it also has a selection of real ales and 50 malt whiskies. We provide pillow and pillow case but ask that you bring your own sleeping bags and towels (and a padlock for the locker). For cyclists we are able to provide secure housing for bicycles.

DETAILS

- **Open** - All year, 8am - midnight
- **Number of beds** - 12
- **Booking** - Essential for groups, deposit required. Advisable for individuals.
- **Price per night** - £12 per person.
- **Public Transport** - Nearest train station is in Achnasheen (10 miles away). Trains run three times a day and the postbus meets the lunchtime train and also comes to Kinlochewe. On Tuesdays, Thursdays and Fridays the 5pm Westerbus from Inverness to Gairloch stops outside the hostel around 6.45pm.
- **Directions** - Kinlochewe is situated at the junction of the A832 Garve to Gairloch road and the A896 north from Torridon.

CONTACT: Andrew and Gail Staddon
Kinlochewe by Achnasheen, Wester Ross, IV22 2PA
Tel: 01445 760253
bookings@kinlochewehotel.co.uk www.kinlochewehotel.co.uk

Gerrys Hostel is situated in an excellent mountaineering and wilderness area on the most scenic railway in Britain.

The photo shows the hostel, looking North West. The hostel has a comfortable common room with log fire and library.

Come and go as you please. No smoking inside or out.

Accommodation for non-smokers.

PLEASE CONTACT THIS HOSTEL BY PHONE OR POST

DETAILS

■ **Open** - All year (check by phone), book in 5pm to 8.30pm. Later by arrangement only.
■ **Number of beds** - 20: 1 x 10 : 2 x 5. Double and twin also.
■ **Booking** - Prepay to secure bed, or phone.
■ **Price per night** - From £13 pp, discount for long stay large groups.
■ **Public Transport** - Achnashellach Station is 4km west of the hostel. Nearest Citylink coaches drop off at Inverness. Local Bus between Inverness and Lochcarron: Wednesday and Saturday 3pm.
■ **Directions** - GR 037 493. 95 miles north of Fort William, 50 miles west of Inverness on A890.

CONTACT: Gerry Howkins
Craig, Achnashellach, Strathcarron, Wester-Ross, Scotland, IV54 8YU
Tel: 01520 766232
sam@backpackerspress.com www.gerryshostel-achnashellach.co.uk

PLOCKTON STATION
BUNKHOUSE
SCOTLAND

Plockton Station Bunkhouse is adjacent to the railway station, only six miles from Kyle of Lochalsh. It is ideal for those travelling by train or bus. For hill-walkers with cars Plockton is well situated for trips to Torridon, Kintail mountain range and the Cuillins on Skye. There are nearly 50 Munros within an hours drive.

The bunkhouse has 4 bedrooms, 2 sleeping 4 people and 2 sleeping 6 people. All rooms have solid pine bunks (3' wide) and bed-linen is included (13.5 tog quilts, pillows and sheet sleeping sacks). There are two shower rooms and toilets downstairs with a further toilet upstairs.

The spacious open-plan living kitchen and dining area is fully equipped with cooker, microwave, fridge and kitchen utensils. The living area has comfortable seating and a colour T.V.

There is full central heating throughout, and a washing machine and tumble-dryer are available.

The bunkhouse is only 600 yards from shops and pubs.

DETAILS

- **Open** - All year, all day
- **Number of beds** - 20: 2x6, 2x4
- **Booking** - Book by phone or email.
- **Price per night** - £11.00 - £12.00 per person
- **Public Transport** - Close to Plockton train station. Citylink coaches drop off at Kyle of Lochalsh. Postbus from Kyle to Plockton.
- **Directions** - Adjacent to the train station in the village of Plockton.

CONTACT: Michael or Gillian
Nessun Dorma, Burnside, Plockton, Ross-shire, IV52 8TF
Tel: 01599 544 235
mickcoe@btinternet.com   www.hostel-scotland.co.uk

Perched on the cliff tops 12 miles north of Gairloch, Rua Reidh Lighthouse must have one of the most dramatic settings of all the Scottish Hostels. The lighthouse still beams out its light over the Minch to the Outer Isles and Skye, but since its automation the adjoining house, no longer needed for keepers, has been converted into a comfortable independent hostel. The centrally heated house has two sitting rooms with log fires, a self-catering kitchen, a drying room, three private rooms and four dorms (each sleeping four), some rooms with en-suite shower. Meals are available from the main dining room and guided walking and rock sports sessions are also offered. The area of the lighthouse is unspoiled and makes a perfect place to watch for whales, dolphins etc. For an away from it all experience travel to the 'edge of the world' and Rua Reidh Lighthouse.

DETAILS

- **Open** - All year (except last 3 weeks in Jan), 9am - 11pm
- **Number of beds** - 26: 3 x 4; 2 x 3; 4 x 2
- **Booking** - Pre-booking advisable.
- **Price per night** - From £10pp (dorm) to £20pp (private with en-suite facilities)
- **Public Transport** - Nearest train station Achnasheen (40 miles). Nearest Citylink coaches Inverness (80 miles). Westerbus 01445 712255 and Scotbus run a daily connection between Inverness/Gairloch (12 miles from hostel).
- **Directions** - From Gairloch take the road signed Big Sands and Melvaig, follow this road for 12 miles to the lighthouse. The last 3 miles is a private road with 20mph limit.

CONTACT:
Melvaig, Gairloch, IV21 2EA
Tel: 01445 771263
ruareidh@tiscali.co.uk www.ruareidh.co.uk

INCHNADAMPH
LODGE

Situated at the heart of the dramatic Assynt mountains, Inchnadamph Lodge has been tastefully converted to provide luxury hostel accommodation at a budget price. Twin, family and dormitory (4-8 people) rooms are available and a continental-style breakfast is included. We have a large self-catering kitchen, a lounge and a dining room (both with real fires), and a games room. Packed lunches are available on request and bar meals are served at the Inchnadamph Hotel. At the foot of Ben More Assynt, and overlooking Loch Assynt, you are free to explore one of the wildest areas in the Highlands. Mountains can be climbed from our door! The Inchnadamph Nature Reserve is right by us - home to a wide diversity of birds, plants, animals and full of exciting geological features. Nearby lochs are popular for trout fly fishing. Details and photos on our website.

DETAILS

- **Open** - All year - phone November-March inclusive, 24 hours
- **Number of beds** - 38: 8x2 : 7x2 : 4x2 (dormitory) 12 (twin/double)
- **Booking** - Advised, required Nov-March.
- **Price per night** - £16.00-£17.00 (dormitory) £22-£26 (twin room) inc continental breakfast and linen. Group discounts.
- **Public Transport** - Transport is available to our door from Inverness 6 days a week, either by train to Lairg and then postbus, or by coach to Ullapool and minibus to Inchnadamph. Times vary - please call us for details.
- **Directions** - Inchnadamph is 25 miles north of Ullapool on the Lochinver/Durness road. The lodge is the big white building across the river from the hotel.

CONTACT: Chris
Inchnadamph, Assynt, Nr Lochinver, Sutherland, IV27 4HL
Tel: 01571 822218, Fax: 01571 822232
info@inch-lodge.co.uk www.inch-lodge.co.uk

BALINTRAID HOUSE
SCOTLAND HIGHLAND RETREAT

Balintraid House is a rambling house in a beautiful location looking directly out onto historic Cromarty Firth. It offers a comfortable alternative to staying in Inverness when driving north or west, or an ideal location to base your Highland holiday. Locally you can see dolphins, seals, swans and migrating birds in the firth. Take a short drive to Shin Falls or Rogie Falls and see salmon leaping up the waterfalls. Explore the Pictish Trail, sample whisky at nearby Glenmorangie or Dalmore Distilleries and enjoy walks to the Fyrish monument, Ben Wyvis and numerous others. Discover original Caledonian forests at Glen Affric. Visit a castle or two. Relax to traditional feis or other music at local venues and hotels.

Facilities include a well-equipped kitchen, central heating, warm duvets and comfy beds, internet access, table tennis, musical instruments and small library. Free range eggs available, and tea/coffee. Please note: we have cats.

DETAILS

- **Open** - All year, please phone for access times.
- **Number of beds** - 9: flexible, single/double/family/group dorm.
- **Booking** - Recommended, please advise if arrival time changes.
- **Price per night** - From £14
- **Public Transport** - Stagecoach stop at house. Trains from Inverness (Thurso / Wick) will stop at Invergordon. Phone for pick up, 3 miles away (charge).
- **Directions** - 26 miles north of Inverness. Turn off A9 for Invergordon and follow coastal road (B817) northwards for 2 miles, passing through small village of Saltburn. After the last house there are two big fields then a clump of trees with two drives on left leading to house.

CONTACT: Anita
Balintraid House, Balintraid, by Invergordon, Ross-shire, IV18 0LY
Tel: (01349) 854446 Mob: 07917710279
balintraid.house@virgin.net www.balintraidhouse.co.uk

FLORA MACDONALD
HOSTEL
SCOTLAND

Flora Macdonald Hostel offers clean, comfortable accommodation in the magnificent surroundings of the Sleat Peninsular in the south of the Isle. In this region, also known as the Garden of Skye, visitors may see golden eagles, sea eagles, red and roe deer, otters and lots of other wildlife. It is also of enormous interest to geology students.

The owner Peter Macdonald, a direct descendent of the Lords of the Isles, the Macdonald Chiefs and Robert the Bruce, is a local historian happy to share his knowledge of the area and breeds rare Eriskay ponies on the family croft.

The hostel has solid pine bunks and is fully centrally heated. It has a modern well equipped kitchen, a drying room with washer and tumble dryer, and a conservatory to sit in and enjoy the views.

DETAILS

- **Open** - All year, 9am to 9pm.
- **Number of beds** - 24: 1x10, 3x4, 1x2
- **Booking** - Booking is not essential but strongly advised. Deposits required with all bookings, at least 1 week in advance.
- **Price per night** - £14 dorm beds, private rooms £30 to £60. 20% reduction for block bookings and individual stays in excess of 7 nights.
- **Public Transport** - Regular bus service between Broadford and Armadale (bus stop at end of hostel road by the church).
- **Directions** - 3 miles from Armadale opposite Kilmore church, 22 miles from Skye bridge on the A851.

CONTACT: Peter Macdonald
Kilmore Sleat, By Armadale, Isle of Skye, IV44 8RG
Tel: 01471 844272/440
peter.macdonald@cillemhor.freeserve.co.uk

DUN CAAN
HOSTEL

This warm and friendly hostel, set on the harbour front in the romantic fishing village of Kyleakin, is the ideal base for your Isle of Skye visit. Overlooking the ancient ruins of Castle Moil (once home of a Viking princess known as Saucy Mary) you'll be enjoying beautiful sea and mountain views from every room.

We provide you with a well-equipped self-catering kitchen, free teas and coffees, hot showers, a cosy common room with TV, freshly laundered bed linen, a drying room for wet outdoor clothing, lots of books to read, games to play and advice on what to see and do on this truly magnificent island. Also available at the hostel: laundry services and bike hire. Please note that this is a non smoking hostel. Local facilities include a coffee shop, bars, restaurants and a general store and post office. Let's Go recommended and STB 4-star.

DETAILS

- **Open** - 1st March to 1 Oct, all day
- **Number of beds** - 14: 1 x 6 (dorm): 2 x 4 (quad)
- **Booking** - Booking advisable in June, July and August. All major credit cards accepted. Secure on-line booking.
- **Price per night** - From £14 inc. bedlinen, teas and coffees. No hidden costs.
- **Public Transport** - Kyle of Lochalsh Train station arrivals connect with Skye Bridge bus to Kyleakin (last stop Dun Caan Hostel). City Link coaches stop near to Hostel. Ferries Armadale, Kylerhea (summer only).
- **Directions** - After crossing the Skye Bridge turn left at the roundabout for Kyleakin. Through village towards harbour and old ferry pier.

CONTACT: Terry or Laila
The Pier Rd, Kyleakin, Isle of Skye, IV41 8PL
Tel: 01599 534087
info@skyerover.co.uk www.skyerover.co.uk

Saucy Mary's offers many rooms with sea or mountain views and is situated close to the Skye Bridge right on the major transport links from Inverness and Glasgow.

The hostel is in the centre of the village of Kyleakin which is a good base for exploring Skye and the Outer Hebrides.

Accommodation starts from just £16 per person and comprises rooms of 3 to 6 persons. Single rates are available off-season and there are many private rooms for two persons as twins and doubles. There are also some private en-suite rooms for up to 4 persons.

Saucy Mary's has a cosy bar serving local drinks and a full menu. There are self-catering, laundry, and drying facilities. Wifi access is free

DETAILS

- **Open** - All year, 24 hours (except Christmas Day)
- **Number of beds** - 70: including 5 doubles (2 en-suite) and 4 twins
- **Booking** - Credit card details required for advance booking.
- **Price per night** - From £16 per person. Prices include VAT.
- **Public Transport** - Buses run direct to Glasgow and Inverness. Trains run to Kyle (on the other side of bridge) from Inverness.
- **Directions** - Cross the toll free Skye Bridge, turn left and Saucy Mary's is 500m on the right.

CONTACT:
Saucy Mary's Lodge, Kyleakin, Isle of Skye, IV41 8PH
Tel: (01599) 534845
saucymarys1@btconnect.com www.saucymarys.com

SKYE
BACKPACKERS

Skye Backpackers sits in the picturesque fishing village of Kyleakin, skirted by mountains and sea. A real 'home away from home', the hostel is a sanctuary for any weary traveller. Curl up by the open fire with a good book, or in the summer enjoy the hostel's large garden. Whatever you're looking for - hillwalking, sightseeing or the legendary faeries, this island will not disappoint. Our lovely hostel staff can also help arrange bus tours and hiking treks!

Kyleakin is on the main bus route and is also easily accessible by boat or from the train station at Kyle on the mainland. The village offers a shop, café, choice of pubs and spectacular scenic views. One of Europe's most dramatic and haunting lands, words can do little justice in describing the awesome beauty of the Isle of Skye. The majestic Cuillin Mountains dominate the rugged landscape, which is peppered with lochs, glens and tiny fishing villages.

DETAILS

- **Open** - All year, all day. Reception 7am-12pm and 5pm-10.30pm (times may vary)
- **Number of beds** - 39
- **Booking** - Booking in advance not always essential, first nights payment required for booking.
- **Price per night** - From £13 per person. I.D. required for check-in.
- **Public Transport** - Kyle of Lochalsh train station is the closest train station and is only a short bus ride (approx 5/10mins) from the hostel. The bus drops you just opposite the hostel.
- **Directions** - From Kyle of Lochalsh go over the Skye Bridge then take first exit at roundabout, which takes you into Kyleakin. The hostel is on the right hand side after the Kings Arms Hotel. Park in the car park opposite hostel or on the hostel grounds.

CONTACT: Receptionist
Kyleakin, Isle of Skye, IV41 8PH
Tel: 01599 534510
skye@scotlandstophostels.com www.skyebackpackers.com

Sligachan Bunkhouse overlooks the 'Black Cuillins' and is an ideal base for exploring the magnificent mountains of Skye. Several routes up the peaks pass the Bunkhouse and the path to 'Loch Coruisk' can be seen from the verandah. The Bunkhouse is surrounded by peaceful mountain scenery on a track easily accessible by car. It is only a 5 minute walk from the bus stop at Sligachan, which sees a regular bus service from the mainland and Portree. The Sligachan Hotel can be seen from the Bunkhouse, about a 5 minute walk, and will provide a hot meal from breakfast through to dinner. The bar is a great place to relax after a long day's trekking and has a great display of malt whiskies and we make our own real ale at the Cuillin Brewery. The Bunkhouse has 4 bedrooms, full kitchen facilities and a lounge with open fire.

DETAILS

- **Open** - March 1st to October 31st, all day
- **Number of beds** - 20
- **Booking** - Booking essential for large groups. Deposit required.
- **Price per night** - £15pp. Linen Hire £3. Block bookings £260 per night or £1600 per week.
- **Public Transport** - Train - 1) Fort William to Mallaig, crossing by ferry to Armadale, buses to Sligachan (30m). 2) Inverness to Kyle of Lochalsh, catch bus over Skye Bridge to Kyleakin, connect with bus to Sligachan.
- **Directions** - Inverness: A82 Invermoriston take A887 then A87 to Kyle of Lochalsh, cross Skye Bridge, continue on A87. Fort William: A830 to Mallaig, cross to Skye on ferry, take A851 to Broadford, then A87

CONTACT:Sligachan Hotel
Sligachan, Isle of Skye, IV47 8SW
Tel: 01478 650204
reservations@sligachan.co.uk www.sligachan.co.uk

We offer a variety of accomodation, including a fully equipped bunkhouse, self-contained family units, twin rooms and heated wooden wigwams.

Situated on a 12 acre croft in Portnalong beside Loch Harport, we are ideally situated for all outdoor activities. The Cuillins are easily accessible via nearby Sligachan and Glenbrittle, there is a pier and slipway for launching boats 500m down the road, and the pub is 500m up the road.

It is possible to block book all of our accommodation for large groups, and it is also possible for smaller parties to exclusively book our self-contained units (bothies), each of which have their own kitchens, toilets & showers.
Visit Scotland Quality Assurance Grading –
4 Star Hostel. "The best value hostel on Skye"

DETAILS

- **Open** - All year, 24 hours
- **Number of beds** - 40 + camping.
- **Booking** - Deposit or credit/debit card details required to confirm bookings.
- **Price per night** - Dorm £10. Twin £12.50. For Bothies & Wigwams see website.
- **Public Transport** - Cross Island Citylink coaches from mainland pass through Sligachan. Two buses daily (excl. Sun) from Portree via Sligachan to Portnalong.
- **Directions** - GR 348 353. From Sligachan take the A863 for 4 miles then left onto B8009 for 6 miles through Carbost and Fernilea to Portnalong. Follow signs for Croft Bunkhouse & Loch Harport Gallery, it is 500yds past the pub.

CONTACT: Dave
Portnalong, Isle of Skye, IV47 8SL
Tel: 01478 640254. Mobile 07841 206 157, Fax: 01478 640254
skyehostel@lineone.net   www.skyehostels.com

WATERFRONT
BUNKHOUSE

Waterfront Bunkhouse has been purpose built to provide a high degree of style and comfort. Twenty feet from the edge of Loch Harport, the accommodations command breathtaking views of the Cuillins. The bunkhouse is an ideal base for the hill walkers or sightseeing touristS, with spectacular scenery and abundant wildlife in the surrounding hills and glens. The hostel sleeps 24 and consists of dormitory type rooms with 6 or 4 beds and one en-suite room. Upstairs there is the kitchen and common room with a balcony overlooking the loch. Full laundry facilities and showers are available (also open to visiting yachtsmen). The waterfront bunkhouse is about 40 mins from Broadford, 25 mins from Portree and next to The Old Inn, a traditional highland pub providing breakfast, lunch and dinner if required. Live traditional music every weekend and a welcoming open fire.

DETAILS

■ **Open** - All year (please ring for availability), 24 hours
■ **Number of beds** - 24: 2 x 6 bed & 3 x 4 bed
■ **Booking** - In peak season booking 4 weeks or more in advance is advised (deposit required).
■ **Price per night** - £14 per person, £16pp for en-suite room. Sole use £270.
■ **Public Transport** - The nearest railway station is Kyle of Lochalsh. Citylink coaches (from the mainland and north Skye) drop off at Sligachan. Two local buses run each weekday, from Portree via Sligachan to Fiskavaig
■ **Directions** - From Sligachan take the A863 for 4 miles then left onto B8009 for 4 miles to Carbost The Waterfront Bunkhouse is in the center of the village next to the Old Inn public house and opposite the school

CONTACT: Angus or Spencer
The Old Inn, Carbost, Isle of Skye, IV47 8SR
Tel: (01478) 640205, Fax: (01478) 640325
waterfront@oldinn.f9.co.uk   www.carbost.f9.co.uk

PORTREE
INDEPENDENT HOSTEL SCOTLAND

Centrally situated in Portree, the capital of Skye, this hostel provides quality inexpensive self-catering accommodation with a fully equipped kitchen/dining area (continental breakfast is available on request).

Originally the island's main post office it has been converted to an independent hostel sleeping 60 in small family rooms and dormitories. All bedding is provided free. There is also a well-equipped launderette on site. Only 50 metres from the bus terminus it is an ideal base for touring the island. Within easy walking distance there is a wide variety of shops, pubs, eating places, three national banks and post office. From the hostel there are pleasant coastal and woodland walks. Bike and car hire are available locally. Portree holds an annual Folk Festival in July and the Highland Games are in August.

DETAILS

- **Open** - All year, no curfew
- **Number of beds** - 60
- **Booking** - Phone booking held to 5pm. Advance payment guarantees bed. Visa/ Mastercard/Switch accepted.
- **Price per night** - £12.50 to £14 per person.
- **Public Transport** - Cross island buses from the mainland to Uig pass through Portree.
- **Directions** - Situated 50 metres from the main square in the town. Approaching Portree on the A850/A87 road from the mainland the hostel is between the long stay car park and the town centre.

CONTACT: Matti and Iain
The Old Post Office, The Green, Portree, Isle of Skye, IV51 9BT
Tel: 01478 613737, Fax: 01478 613758
skyehostel@yahoo.co.uk www.hostelskye.co.uk

BAYFIELD
BACKPACKERS

Bayfield Backpackers is located in the centre of Portree, Skye's main town. With views of the Cuillins towering in the distance and the sparkling waters of Portree Bay opposite, the hostel is ideally situated for mountaineers and walkers. It is also the perfect base for those wanting to explore the islands attractions at a more leisurely pace. Accommodation consists of one 8 bed en-suite dorm and four 4 bed rooms. One of the 4 bed rooms is en-suite and has full disabled facilities. The state of the art kitchen will help you prepare those all-important meals. The comfortable lounge/dining area can accommodate 16 people and has spectacular views over Portree Bay to the Cuillin Hills beyond. The deck terrace has the same views. VisitScotland 4 stars.

DETAILS

- **Open** - All year, all day, reception 07.45 - 22.00
- **Number of beds** - 24: 1x8, 4x4
- **Booking** - Booking advisable but not required.
- **Price per night** - £13.00 to £15.00 per pseson
- **Public Transport** - Citylink buses from Glasgow, Fort William and Inverness. Trains at Kyle of Lochalsh, last train misses the bus to Portree by 5 mins.
- **Directions** - The hostel is only 1 min from the bus station. When you get off the bus look for the police station then to your right you will see some phone boxes, walk past them and turn left, cross the road and then to your right there is a set of steps. We are at the bottom of the steps overlooking the bay. Travelling by car head for the village centre, turn right when you see the signs for the long stay car park and we are 50m on the left. If you are travelling by car from Fort William and using GPS be careful that you are not routed via Mallaig.

CONTACT: Murdo
Bayfield Backpackers, Bayfield, Portree, Isle of Skye, IV51 9EW
Tel: 01478 612231
info@skyehostel.co.uk www.skyehostel.co.uk

The hostel is set in the beautiful Trotternish peninsula of North Skye. The area is famous for the distinctive cliffs and rock formations of the Quiraing and enjoys spectacular views of both the Western Isles and Wester Ross. Pursuits from the hostel - without a car - include Hiking, Hill Walking, Rock Climbing, Painting and Photography. Boat Trips, Fishing, Sea Kayaking and Pony Trekking are available locally. Present day wildlife regularly seen are Otters, Dolphins, Whales and Eagles, whilst the past has left Dinosaur Footprints and Fossils. The hostel is centrally heated and fully equipped with all bedding and sheets provided. Phone the hostel for travel information outwith the public bus service times. There is a hotel with a restaurant just 100 metres from our door. Groups are welcome and there is camping available.
VisitScotland graded 3 star.

DETAILS

- **Open** - All year, but phone from November to March as we may be closed . All day
- **Number of beds** - 40: 3 x 2 : 3 x 6 : 2 x 8.
- **Booking** - Booking is essential for groups and suggested for individuals during the summer.
- **Price per night** - £13.00pp - £17.50pp. Small charge for payment by credit card or cheque with bank card.
- **Public Transport** - Buses come from Portree daily, except Sunday and stop 100 metres from the hostel.
- **Directions** - GR464 720. 34 kilometres north of Portree, 5 kilometres north of Staffin on coast road. Adjacent to the Flodigarry Hotel. Landranger map 23.

CONTACT: Bryan
Flodigarry By Staffin, Isle of Skye, IV51 9HZ
Tel: 01470 552212
hostel.flodigarry@btinternet.com www.hostelflodigarry.co.uk

SKYE WALKER
SCOTLAND INDEPENDENT HOSTEL

Come and visit the Skywalker Hostel on the Isle of Skye and experience a warm welcome and true Scottish hospitality.

Skyewalker Hostel is ideally situated as a base for exploring the island and offers real value for money. Our campsite is situated at the rear of the hostel and campers are welcome to use hostel facilities.

Skyewalker Hostel hosts regular Scottish folk music sessions and it is also possible to book the whole place for special occasions such as birthdays, Munro completion parties, family get-togethers etc.

DETAILS

- **Open** - 1st March to 31st Oct (all year for groups), reception open till 10pm
- **Number of beds** - 40: (plus 10 tents)
- **Booking** - Book early to save disappointment. On-line booking available via our website.
- **Price per night** - From £13.50 per person.
- **Public Transport** - Two local buses run each weekday, running from Portree via Sligachan to Portnalong (hostel) and back. Citylink coaches (from the mainland and north Skye) drop off at Sligachan. No public transport on Sundays.
- **Directions** - The Hostel is easy to get to once you have reached Skye. Simply get to Sligachan which lies roughly in the centre of Skye. From there take the A863 for 5 miles to the turn off for Carbost which takes you onto the B8009. Proceed through Carbost to Portnalong and you have arrived! GR 348 348.

CONTACT: Brian or Lisa
Old School, Portnalong, Isle of Skye, IV47 8SL
Tel: 01478 640 250, Fax: 01478 640 420
enquiries@skyewalkerhostel.com www.skyewalkerhostel.com

DUNARD HOSTEL

Dunard is a warm, friendly, family run hostel on the beautiful island of Barra in Scotland's Outer Hebrides. The hostel has a cosy living room with a lovely fire, hot showers and spacious kitchen. There are bunk, twin and family bedrooms. Situated in Castlebay the hostel has views over the castle to beaches and islands beyond. We are close to the ferry terminal, a handful of shops, and bars which often fill with live music. During the summer the island is alive for 'Feis Bharraidh' a gaelic festival of music, song and dance. Take time and explore this truly beautiful island with stunning white beaches, quiet bays where otters hunt and seals bask on rocks, dunes and meadows carpeted in flowers, and wild windswept hills home to golden eagles. Join one of our friendly guided sea kayaking trips and paddle amongst sheltered islands for really close-up wildlife encounters (no experience needed) www.clearwaterpaddling.com

DETAILS

- **Open** - All year, except Christmas and New Year , all day
- **Number of beds** - 16: 3 x 4 : 2 x 2.
- **Booking** - Booking advised, especially during the summer. Booking essential for groups.
- **Price per night** - £13 per person. £34 twin room. £48 family room (sleeps 4). £180 - £220 sole use.
- **Public Transport** - The hostel is a 3 minute walk from the Ferry Terminal in Castlebay. If using a local bus ask to be dropped at the hostel.
- **Directions** - From Ferry terminal in Castlebay head up hill, turn left and we are the third house past the old school. (200m from Terminal)

CONTACT: Katie or Chris
Dunard, Castlebay, Isle of Barra, Western Isles, HS9 5XD
Tel: 01871 810 443
info@dunardhostel.co.uk www.dunardhostel.co.uk

DRINISHADER
HOSTEL

Drinishader Hostel is a traditional crofters cottage situated 5 miles from Tarbert ,8 miles from the white sandy beaches. It is located on the Golden Road,above Drinishader Harbour, overlooking the beautiful East Loch Tarbert.

A cottage with character in warm atmosphere, it has a cosy lounge with open fire, a well-equipped kitchen,comfortable orthopaedic bunks,Hot shower and Laundry facilities are available.Pick-up services from Tarbert can be arranged if there are no bus services.

There is a shop-cum-post office nearby & you can pre-order fresh,delicious homemade bread, cakes to be delivered to your breakfast table.

Among the activities guests enjoyed are: coastal/hill walking, cycling, sightseeing, birds/wild life watching or simply chilling out.

If you're not fresh when you arrive, you will be when you leave! We hope it will be a home from home for you, So come and discover the magic of Drinishader!

DETAILS

- **Open** - All year, 10.00-22.00
- **Number of beds** - 12
- **Booking** - Advisable to confirm beds, may require deposit.
- **Price per night** - From £11.00 per person.
- **Public Transport** - Caledonian MacBrayne ferries (01876 500337) from Ullapool to Stornoway or from Uig (Skye) to Tarbert. Drinishader is a 15 min bus journey from Tarbert (01851-705050). Bus stop is just by hostel. There are 5 buses each day.
- **Directions** - From Tarbert follow the A859 south. After 3.5km turn left along the Golden Road. The hostel is located just above the harbour in Drinishader.

CONTACT:Roddy or Warden
Drinishader, Isle Of Harris, HS3 3DX
Tel: 01859 511 255
drinishaderhostel@gmail.com

Laxdale Bunkhouse is contained within Laxdale Holiday Park which is a small family-run park set in peaceful tree lined surroundings. Located 1.5 miles away from the town of Stornoway, this is an ideal centre from which to tour the islands of Lewis and Harris. Built in 1998, the bunkhouse consists of four bedrooms with four bunks in each room and caters for backpackers, families or larger groups looking for convenient, low cost accommodation. There is a spacious fully equipped dining kitchen which provides two cookers, fridge and microwave, and a comfortable TV lounge in which to relax. There is also a drying room. Toilets and showers are located within the building and are suitable for the disabled. Outside there is a covered veranda, picnic table and BBQ area.

DETAILS

- **Open** - All year, 8am - 10pm
- **Number of beds** - 16: 4 x 4
- **Booking** - July and August booking advisable one week in advance.
- **Price per night** - £13pp (high season), £12pp (low season). £185 sole use (high season), £162 sole use (low season).
- **Public Transport** - Buses every 30mins stop close to hostel. Taxi fare from town centre approximately £2.50.
- **Directions** - From Stornoway Ferry Terminal take the A857. Take the second turning on the left past the Hospital. Follow camping signs for one mile out of town. The Bunkhouse is located inside the holiday park. From Tarbert or Leverburgh take A859 for 40 miles to Stornoway. Turn left at the roundabout and 2nd left after hospital then as above.

CONTACT:
Laxdale Holiday Park, 6, Laxdale Lane, Stornoway, Isle of Lewis, HS2 0DR
Tel: 01851 706966 / 01851 703234
info@laxdaleholidaypark.com www.laxdaleholidaypark.com

GALSON FARM
HOSTEL

Our comfortable, cosy, fully equipped hostel provides the perfect haven from which to explore the crofting townships of Ness and the west side of Lewis, with sandy beaches, wildlife, historic sites and culture on the doorstep. Situated within a cobbled stone courtyard enjoying stunning views of the Atlantic Coast towards the Butt of Lewis Lighthouse.

A short walk through our croft, with its network of footpaths, takes you to the shore and river, with otters regular visitors.

Comprising of one dormitory with up to 8 beds, two shower / toilets and a kitchen / dining room. Bedding can be supplied if required as can meals by order. Bus service to Stornoway, shop within 2 miles. Visit Scotland 4star hostel. Stay a while, for memories of a lifetime.

DETAILS

- **Open** - All year, 24 hours
- **Number of beds** - 8
- **Booking** - Always phone in advance. Deposit (Visa/Access) guarantees bed.
- **Price per night** - £15pp. Sole use : 2 people £48, up to 8 people £75.
- **Public Transport** - The nearest ferry runs from Ullapool on the mainland to Stornoway which is 20 miles from the hostel. Local buses run from Mondays to Saturdays. Enquire at Stornoway Bus Station.
- **Directions** - GR 437 592. Follow A857 Stornoway to Ness(Nis) road for 20 miles. At Galson (Gabhsann) turn left at phone box. Bunkhouse is ¼ mile.

CONTACT: David and Hazel Roberts
Galson Farm House, South Galson, Isle of Lewis, HS2 0SH
Tel: 01851 850492, Fax: 01851 850492
GalsonFarm@yahoo.com www.galsonfarm.co.uk

The Heb Hostel is a family run backpackers hostel in the heart of Stornoway on the enchanting Isle of Lewis. It is an ideal stop/stay for travellers visiting the Hebrides & welcomes surfers, cyclists, walkers, families & groups.

Clean, comfortable, friendly and relaxed - Heb Hostel aims to provide you with a quality stay at budget prices.

There are many facilities, including a common room with TV, peat fire, local guides & information.

DETAILS

- **Open** - All year, all day. New arrivals phone to get access code.
- **Number of beds** - 26: 1x8, 2x7,1x4
- **Booking** - Booking is not essential but may be advisable at busier times. Deposits are only required for groups. Payment is due on arrival by cash or cheque.
- **Price per night** - £15 per person per night. 10% discount on booking the whole hostel for more than one night
- **Public Transport** - By plane- From Glasgow, Edinburgh or Inverness(British Airways) Aberdeen(Eastern Airways) Inverness & Benbecula(Highland Airways). By Ferry (Caledonian McBrayne) Ullapool to Stornoway(Lewis), Uig(Skye) to Tarbert(Harris) or Berneray(Uists) to Leverburgh(Harris)
- **Directions** - From Bus station – Exit front door, cross South Beach St & walk up Kenneth St. Pass 1st intersection & we are 2nd on the right. From ferry terminal – come out main exit, turn left, follow pedestrian walk-way to the bus station. From Airport – take bus to Stornoway bus station.

CONTACT: Christine Macintosh
25 Kenneth St, Stornoway, Isle of Lewis, HS1 2DR
Tel: 01851 709889
christine@hebhostel.com www.hebhostel.com

GLEBE BARN

SCOTLAND

The Glebe Barn has charm and character whilst providing comfortable accommodation with magnificent views. You can enjoy breathtaking scenery along numerous walks; study fascinating geological formations, or explore varied natural habitats with incredible varieties of plant and animal species. Relax on beautiful sandy beaches, listen to the famous singing sands and watch the eagles soar above the spectacular Sgurr of Eigg. Just a mile away there is a well-stocked shop and café/restaurant with regular traditional music sessions. Facilities at the Barn include a well-equipped kitchen, spacious lounge/dining room (polished maple floor, log fire), a combination of twin, triple, family and dormitory rooms, each with wash hand basins (linen provided), central heating, hot showers, Wi-F, plus laundry facilities.
There is also a lovely new annexe offering self contained facilities for 2.

DETAILS

- **Open** - Individuals April to October, Groups all year, all day
- **Number of beds** - 24: 1 x 2 : 2 x 3 : 1 x 6 : 1 x 8 + annex for 2.
- **Booking** - Booking essential prior to boarding ferry. Deposit required.
- **Price per night** - £16 (1/2 nights), £14 (3+ nights). Twin room £36 (1/2 nights), £32 (3+ nights). Sole Use (min 14 persons) £15pp (1/2 nights), £12.50pp (3+ nights).
- **Public Transport** - Fort William is the nearest National Express Coach stop. The early train from Fort William to Arisaig and Mallaig meets the ferry. Daily summer sailings from Arisaig or Mallaig.
- **Directions** - One mile from pier. Follow tarmac road around the bay over the cattle grid and up the hill. Luggage transport for groups and taxi service on request.

CONTACT: Karen or Simon
Isle of Eigg, PH42 4RL
Tel: 01687 482417
simon@glebebarn.co.uk www.glebebarn.co.uk

Tiree is an idyllic Hebridean Island, perfect for outdoor pursuits, wildlife enthusiasts, and those yet to experience the total tranquility of stunning white beaches and crystal clear seas.

A warm welcome and excellent facilities await you at Millhouse. Bikes are for hire to explore the island, visit the thatched cottage and lighthouse museums, find the standing stones, wonder at the machair flowers or watch the seals. Watersports take place on adjacent Loch Bhasapol, and the secluded Cornaig beach is a ten minute walk away. There is a resident RSPB warden on the island and a bird hide near the hostel.

For walkers, Millhouse is on the Tiree Pilgrimage route linking the ancient chapels and monuments around the island. STB 4* Hostel

DETAILS

- **Open** - Mar-Oct, open in winter by arrangement, open all day (quiet after 11.30pm, check out 10am)
- **Number of beds** - 16/18 : 2 x 2/3 : 2 x 6 plus 3 family rooms : 12 beds: 3 x 4
- **Booking** - Advisable, please check vacancies before boarding the ferry
- **Price per night** - Twin £17pp. Dorms £14pp. Family £42-£56 per room.
- **Public Transport** - Caledonian MacBrayne ferry from Oban to Tiree or Flybe flight from Glasgow. Local Ring and Ride bus 01879 220419.
- **Directions** - From ferry turn right at T junction, then left at next fork. Continue for 4 miles to Millhouse Hostel

CONTACT: Judith Boyd
Cornaigmore, Isle of Tiree, Argyll, PA77 6XA
Tel: 01879 220435
tireemillhouse@yahoo.co.uk www.tireemillhouse.co.uk

IONA
HOSTEL

Tucked into the rocky outcrops at the north end of the island, Iona Hostel has spectacular views to Staffa and the Treshnish Isles, and beyond Rhum to the Black Cuillins of Skye. The hostel is situated on the working croft of Lagandorain (the hollow of the otter). This land has been worked for countless generations, creating the familiar Hebridean patchwork of wildflower meadow, crops and grazing land, home to an amazing variety of plants and birds. We offer quiet sanctuary for those that seek it, in easy reach of island activities.

Iona Hostel is new, well-reviewed and recommended. Whether travelling on your own, with friends, or as part of one of our many visiting groups, Iona Hostel offers you a warm welcome - with the best views and duck eggs this side of heaven. 4 star STB. Green Tourism Gold Award. We regret no dogs are allowed.

DETAILS

- **Open** - All year, Closed 11am-1pm for cleaning - no curfew
- **Number of beds** - 21: 1 x 2 : 2 x 4 : 1 x 5 : 1 x 6.
- **Booking** - Is strongly advised, 50% deposit.
- **Price per night** - £18.50 adult £12.50 under 10s (bedding included).
- **Public Transport** - Caledonian Macbrayne ferry service from Oban or Mull 08705 650000. For buses on Mull 01546 604695. Taxi service on Iona 0781 0325990.
- **Directions** - You cannot bring your car onto Iona, but there is free parking in Fionnphort on Mull at the Columba Centre. Iona Hostel is the last building at the north end of the island, 2 km from the pier and up beyond the abbey.

CONTACT:
Iona Hostel, Iona, Argyll, PA76 6SW
Tel: 01681 700781
info@ionahostel.co.uk www.ionahostel.co.uk

A warm welcome awaits guests at the community run village Bunkrooms. Dervaig is a pretty village on the edge of a sheltered sea loch, seven miles from Tobermory in the beautiful northwest of Mull. There are lovely walks along Loch Cuin and to nearby standing stones, while the sparkling sands and turquoise waters of Calgary Bay are 5 miles away. It has 2 good little shops and the oldest inn on the island (serving great pub food!). It makes a perfect base from which to explore the area – local wildlife tours, sea eagle hide and rewarding hill-walking, hidden beaches and coves. Bunkrooms are comfortable with a well equipped kitchen and separate dining and sitting area. Each room has ensuite facilities. The Dervaig Village Hall is used through the year for various events such as producers' markets, weddings and ceilidhs. Bunkroom guests are welcome to attend the ceilidhs and enjoy local music.

DETAILS

- **Open** - All year, all day
- **Number of beds** - 10: 1x6, 1x4
- **Booking** - Remote location so booking is advised (walk-in bookings welcome too!)
- **Price per night** - From £12 per person.
- **Public Transport** - Train Glasgow to Oban. Ferry (www.calmac.co.uk) to Craignure. Bus to Tobermory connects with bus to Dervaig. (See www.mict.co.uk)
- **Directions** - From ferry terminal drive to Salen. Take Dervaig road 2 miles north of Salen. At T junction (after 8 miles) turn right. Pass the pub and up the hill for 15 yards. Dervaig Hall and bunkrooms is 2nd left after the pub, down a slope over a cattle grid.

CONTACT: Emma Leigh Murtagh
Dervaig Village Hall, Dervaig, Isle of Mull, PA75 6QN
Tel: 01688 400 491
dervaigbunkrooms@phonecoop.coop www.bunkrooms.mull-scotland.co.uk

GLENAROS
LODGE

A warm welcome awaits you at this unique house on the magical Isle of Mull. There are wonderful views over the sea and to the ruins of ancient Aros Castle. It is an ideal central location for hikers, cyclists and motorists wishing to see the whole island, view its wildlife and special geology whilst also being near Tobermory. Red deer can be glimpsed in the early morning grazing in front of the Lodge. Bird watchers can spot heron, mallard, puffins and sea eagles amongst many other birds. Seals are common off the shore and dolphins, whales and the occasional otter may also be seen in the bay right outside the house. Glenaros Lodge is a traditional, homely, cosy house with much information on the island's history and wildlife. For those visitors who just want a holiday away from it all then here is that special, peaceful oasis with extensive grounds & woodlands. There are five private, family and shared rooms, three of which have magnificent sea views. Also two yurts and camping in the grounds. Meals are available on request. There is a self-catering kitchen, guest lounge & log fire. Bikes and canoes for hire. Tours of Mull and Iona can be arranged too.

DETAILS

- **Open** - All year, all day
- **Number of beds** - 18
- **Booking** - Book by phone or email.
- **Price per night** - Dorm £15pp, twin room £25pp.
- **Public Transport** - Ferry from Oban to Craignure is generally met by a Bowman's Bus which goes to Glenaros (not on Sundays). Ask for Glenaros Lodge.
- **Directions** - Approximately 1 mile north of Salen on A848. Hostel is on the left.

CONTACT: Peter
Glenaros Lodge, Aros, Salen, Isle of Mull, PA72 6JP
Tel: 01680 300301 Mob: 07796 886899
peter@hostel-mull.co.uk www.glenaroslodge.net

COLONSAY
KEEPER'S LODGE

The Lodge is located on a peaceful and idyllic Inner Hebridean island to the south of Mull which boasts magnificent sandy beaches, ancient forests and beautiful lochs. The place is teeming with wildlife which includes dolphins, seals, otters and many rare species of bird. There are ancient standing stones and a 14th-century priory with exceptional carved Celtic tombstones, and the famous Colonsay House gardens and café are open to visitors to enjoy twice a week. We offer for hire mountain bikes to tour the area and tennis racquets to use on the free court. The pub, café, shop and village hall, where there are regular Ceilidhs, are all within three miles. Fresh lobster, crab and langoustines can be bought from the fishing boats in the harbour and don't forget the best oysters in the world are grown on Colonsay. The lodge is a refurbished former gamekeeper's house and bothies. It is centrally heated and has 3 large twin, 3 small twin and 1 family room. It has a huge dining/cooking/sitting area and a separate sitting room with a log fire. Bed linen provided.

DETAILS

- **Open** - All year, 24 hours
- **Number of beds** - 16   6 x 2 : 1 x 4.
- **Booking** - Required 24 hours in advance.
- **Price per night** - £16pp twin, £12pp bothy, £14pp 4 bed dorm.
- **Public Transport** - Train and coach in Oban. Ferry to Colonsay takes 2.5 hours.
- **Directions** - Ferry departs Oban 5 times a week April to October, Sun, Mon, Wed, Thurs, Fri (rest of year Mon, Wed, Fri). From Kennacraig and Port Askaig, Islay on Weds. Transport for hostellers can be arranged if required.

CONTACT: Rhona Robinson
Colonsay Estate Cottages, Isle of Colonsay, Argyll, PA61 7YP
Tel: 01951 200312
colonsaycottages@dial.pipex.com www.colonsay.org.uk

BROWNS
HOSTEL AND HOUSE SCOTLAND

Stromness - a small friendly town where both the hostel and house are centrally situated in Victoria Street, near shops, pubs, restaurants, Post Office, bank. museum and the Pier Art Centre. An ideal base for the tourist as it is also within walking/cycling distance of the wildlife, high cliffs, beaches, beautiful sunsets, the historical sites of Skara Brae, Standing Stones, the Palace and Brough of Birsay etc., and for fishing, golfing, bowling, surfing, to dive on the many wrecks in Scapa Flow, or (for the beginner) to book a Scuba-dive course. Free internet access available. Hostel - very popular with all ages, is praised for its cosy well equipped kitchen, seating all guests at one sitting. In the evenings, the big table is a great gathering place and many enjoyable times have been had. Sleeps 14. House - self-catering, has kitchen, sitting room, en-suite bedrooms and laundry room. Let as a whole or per room. Sleeps 12-14

DETAILS

- **Open** - All year, all day. No curfew, keys provided.
- **Number of beds** - Hostel 14: 3 x 1 :2 x 2 : 1 x 3: 1 x 4. House 12-14:
- **Booking** - Booking advisable during March to October. Pre-paid bookings secure (send sae for receipt). Telephone bookings kept only for limited time.
- **Price per night** - From £11(inc linen), special rate for groups.
- **Public Transport** - Train or bus to Thurso, bus 2 miles to Scrabster then boat to Stromness. Alternatively from Gills Bay to St Margarets Hope by boat or John O'Groats by boat to Burwick then bus to Stromness via Kirkwall.
- **Directions** - Browns accommodation is near to the harbour in Stromness, just two minutes along street. Next door to Royal Hotel.

CONTACT: Sylvia Brown
Stromness, Orkney, KW16 3BS
Tel: 01856 850661
info@brownshostel.co.uk www.brownsaccommodation.co.uk

HOY CENTRE

Surrounded by magnificent scenery the Hoy Centre is ideally situated for a peaceful and relaxing holiday. The centre was completely refurbished in 2005 and offers high quality, four star accommodation. All rooms are en-suite (with shower) and each room has twin beds and a bunk bed, seats, lockers and all bedding. One room is equipped for wheelchair access. There is a well equipped kitchen, comfortable lounge area with TV and a separate spacious dining hall. Underfloor heating ensures a comfortable temperature. Washing and drying facilities are also available. Much of North Hoy is owned and managed by the RSPB. The reserve comprises 3,500 ha of upland heath and cliffs with a large variety of birds. Off the west coast is The Old Man of Hoy, a 137m sea stack, perhaps Orkney's most famous landmark and a great place to see puffins. The dramatic hills of North Hoy and stunning sea cliffs offer excellent walking. The nearest shop is 16km away.

DETAILS

- **Open** - All year, all day
- **Number of beds** - 32: 8x4
- **Booking** - Preferred. Groups send 25% deposit, balance 28 days prior to arrival
- **Price per night** - 13pp, £10 (juniors), £3.25 (under 3's). Family room (4 beds) £31.40. Private rms:- 2 adults £35.70, 3 adults £42.40, 4 adults £51.95. Sole use £270, £1453 a week.
- **Public Transport** - Short walk from Moaness Pier (pedestrian ferry from Stromness). Ferry details www.orkneyferries.co.uk (01856 872044). Taxis and minibuses are available on the island.
- **Directions** - Car ferry arrives from Houton to Lyness, which is 16km from centre.

CONTACT: Recreation Department
Hoy Centre, Hoy, Orkney, KW16 3NJ
Tel: 01856 873535 ext 2415
recreation@orkney.gov.uk   www.hostelsorkney.co.uk

PEEDIE
HOSTEL

The Peedie Hostel is a quaint hostel situated in the heart of the town of Kirkwall, and within walking distance of the Main Steet and many local attractions.

It has a prime waterfront location on Ayre Rd, Kirkwall, and is within 200m of the Shapinsay and North Isle ferry terminals and within 300m of the island's main bus station, making it ideal for islanders and island hoppers alike.

It is close to all local amenities, including the only Orcadian nightclub, Fusion. Numerous pubs, restaurants and shops are all extremely close at hand.

The Peedie Hostel has 3 rooms; two with a single bunk bed and one with a pair.

Shared facilities include a kitchen and shower/bathroom.
Rooms are complete with sinks, TVs and enjoy views over the bay.
All rooms are heated.

DETAILS

- **Open** - All year, all day
- **Number of beds** - 8 : 2x2,1x4
- **Booking** - Bookings can be made by phone, email or letter.
- **Price per night** - £12 pp.
- **Public Transport** - 200m to North Isle & Shapinsay ferries. 300m to main bus station.
- **Directions** - Situated on the sea front on Ayre Road.

CONTACT:
1 Ayre Houses, Ayre Road, Kirkwall, Orkney, KW15 1QX
Tel: 01856 875477
kirkwallpeediehostel@talk21.com davidwild.co.uk/peediehostel/

Rousay Hostel is situated on a working orqanic farm within easy walking distance of shops, restaurant, pub, bike hire and the pier. Modern, purpose built and well equipped, the hostel has two dormitories and one single room, showers, kitchen and laundry facilities. There's a camp site adjacent to the hostel and campers have use of the hostel facilities.

Organic produce may be available to buy from the farm and bike hire is available at the hostel.

The island of Rousay is a walker and birdwatcher's paradise with many footpaths and a nearby bird reserve. Often called "the Egypt of the North" Rousay contains some of the best preserved archaelogical sites in the north of Scotland, set in spectacular scenery rich in wildlife, plants and flowers. The small friendly community creates a unique welcome for the visitor to this beautiful island.

DETAILS

- **Open** - All year, all day
- **Number of beds** - 11
- **Booking** - Book by phone or email.
- **Price per night** - £10.00 (£12 with linen), £5 camping,
- **Public Transport** - Travel to Orkney via a choice of four ferry routes from John O'Groats (summer only), from Scrabster, from Aberdeen or from Gills Bay. Once on mainland Orkney travel from Kirkwall to Tingwall Pier to cross by frequent ferry to Rousay. Easy walk from the pier to the hostel.
- **Directions** - Ask directions from the pier.

CONTACT: Carol or Eric
Trumland Organic Farm, Rousay, Orkney, KW17 2PU
Tel: /Fax: 01856 821 252
trumland@btopenworld.com

THE BARN
CHALMERSQUOY

The Barn offers four star quality hostel accommodation and camping facilities, all year round, in Westray (The Queen O' The Isles), Orkney.

The Barn has excellent kitchen and lounge facilities and offers twin and family rooms, all with a sea view. It is in a great location to explore the many cliffs, beaches, seabirds and walks that our island has to offer. You can also explore the Heritage Centre, craft businesses and well stocked local shops. If you don't want to cook in, the Pierowall Hotel is 3 minutes walk from the Barn and offers excellent food and bar facilities.

DETAILS

- **Open** - All year, if we're in, we're open.
- **Number of beds** - 13: 1x4, 1x3, 3x2
- **Booking** - Booking advisable. No deposit required.
- **Price per night** - £16 pp or £160 per night for exclusive use . Special winter rates available for exclusive use if two nights booked.
- **Public Transport** - There is a bus service available from Rapness Ferry Terminal to The Barn from mid-May to mid-September. This bus service is available on request during the winter season. The number to phone to request the bus is 01857 677758 (Kenneth Harcus).
- **Directions** - Westray is one of the north isles of Orkney. Travel to Westray with Orkney Ferries (Tel: 01856 872044 to book car) or Loganair (Tel: 01856 872494). From Rapness Ferry turn right and drive north for 7 miles. You will then see Pierowall Village. The Barn is on the outskirts of Pierowall Village. It is well signposted and central to all facilities.

CONTACT: The Harcus family
Chalmersquoy, Westray, Orkney, KW17 2BZ
Tel: 01857 677214
johnharcus@btinternet.com www.thebarnwestray.co.uk/

The Birsay Outdoor Centre is situated in the northwest corner of the Orkney mainland, in close proximity to spectacular and varied coastline, scenery and beaches. Nearby at the Brough of Birsay you can see the remains of early Christian and Norse settlements on a tidal island. The Centre is also conveniently placed to visit Orkney's 5,500 year old Neolithic Heartland which was granted World Heritage status by UNESCO in 1999, and includes the Ring of Brodgar. Close by are the Standing Stones of Stenness, the tomb of Maeshowe and, in Sandwick, the well-preserved village of Skara Brae. The Centre has been recently refurbished and offers comfortable accommodation, with all new furniture, beds and appliances. It sleeps up to 30 in 5 bedrooms, family rooms are available and all linen is provided. It has a well equipped kitchen, dining area and small lounge, a drying room and disabled access.

DETAILS

■ **Open** - April to Sept (available for group bookings outside this period).
■ **Number of beds** - 28: 2x4, 1x2, 1x6, 1x12 plus camping.
■ **Booking** - Bookings preferred. If it's a group booking 25% deposit required with balance payable 28 days prior to arrival
■ **Price per night** - £11.90pp/£9 juniors/£3.25 under 3s. £29.20 per night excusive/ family use of 4-bed room. Exclusive use of Centre (32 beds) £216/£1190 per week.
■ **Public Transport** - For buses from Kirkwall and Stromness contact Orkney Coaches (01856 870555). Ferries from Scrabster, (Northlink Ferries 01856 872044), from Gills Bay, (Pentland Ferries 01856 831226). Foot passenger ferries from John O'Groats, summer only (John O'Groats Ferry 01955 611353)
■ **Directions** - OS sheet 7 GR253267

CONTACT: Recreation Department
Birsay, Orkney, KW17 2LY
Tel: 01856 873535 ext. 2415
recreation@orkney.gov.uk www.hostelsorkney.co.uk

St. Margarets Hope Backpackers is a traditional stone building. It has two family rooms, one single room one four bedded room and one dorm with eight beds. It also has a fully equipped kitchen, laundry room and shower room. St. Margarets Hope Backpackers is situated in one of the prettiest villages in Orkney. There are three well stocked shops, a Post Office, three pubs serving good beer & food, an award-winning restaurant and a craft shop.

During the summer the passenger-only ferry Pentland Venture sails three times a day and docks seven miles from the village. Pentland Ferries docks in the village, she sails all year three trips a day and takes vehicles.
The bus stop is just across the road from the hostel which goes to Kirkwall four times a day.

DETAILS

- **Open** - All year, arrival up until 21:00 (unless otherwise arranged) and checkout by 10:00
- **Number of beds** - 17: 1x8, 1x4, 2x2, 1x1
- **Booking** - Not essential, payment on arrival.
- **Price per night** - £12 per person
- **Public Transport** - The hostel is a 10 min walk from Pentland Ferries and across the road from the bus stop for Kirkwall, which goes 4 times a day (except Sundays). 50yds from Bus stop.
- **Directions** - Situated in the centre of St Margaret's Hope village in South Ronaldsay, the most southerly of the Orkney Isles.

CONTACT:
Back Road, St Margaret's Hope, Orkney, KW17 2SP
Tel: 01856 831225
orkneybackpackers@hotmail.co.uk

Rackwick Hostel is in the scenic Rackwick Valley in the north of Hoy. Much of North Hoy is owned by the RSPB, where a large variety of birds live and breed. Off the west coast of the reserve towers The Old Man of Hoy, a 137m sea stack and is, perhaps, Orkney's most famous landmark and a great place to see puffins. Local wild flowers and bird life make this a must for naturalists to visit. The remainder of the island is a fascinating variety of hills, dramatic coastal scenery and low-lying fertile land. The hostel sleeps 8 in two rooms, two pairs of bunks per room. All bedding is provided. There's a small kitchen with a good range of utensils, and a seperate eating area. Camping and free car parking is available. The nearest shop to the hostel is 21km away so bring provisions!

DETAILS

- **Open** - April to September, Signing in by arrangement with warden.
- **Number of beds** - 8: 2x4
- **Booking** - Booking is preferred. 25% deposit required for groups with balance payable 28 days prior to arrival.
- **Price per night** - £10.25 / £9 juniors / £3.25 under 3s. Family room / exclusive use (4 beds) £27. Sole use of Centre (32 beds) £53 / £286 per week.
- **Public Transport** - Passenger ferry from Stromness to Moaness Pier (about 10 km away). Private hire and taxis are normally available at the pier, or alternatively the walk to the hostel is via the scenic Rackwick valley which takes approximately 2 hours. Car ferry from Kirkwall to Lyness, about 21 km away. (Orkney ferries 01856 872 044/www.orkneyferries.co.uk).
- **Directions** - In Rackwick village on the NW coast, OS sheet7 GR199998.

CONTACT: Recreation Department
Rackwick, Hoy, Orkney, KW16 3NJ
Tel: 01856 873535 ext. 2415
recreation@orkney.gov.uk www.hostelsorkney.co.uk

AYRES ROCK
HOSTEL

Sanday is the perfect place to take time out. You'll find long stretches of unspoilt sandy beaches, an abundance of birds, seals and other wildlife, glittering seas, clear air and spectacular skies. Those of us lucky enough to live here enjoy a rare quality of life in a small, friendly and safe community. Ayre's Rock Hostel has accreditation by Visit Scotland and is rated at four stars. There are two twin rooms and one family ensuite room. Our brand new lounge area with expansive views over the Holms of Ire offers a comfortable place to relax after a day's exploration of our beautiful island. A further visitors' sitting area is provided in the conservatory of the main house. A kitchen is available for self-catering, or guests can have B&B. Evening meals can be provided by arrangement. Takeaways are also available from the Ayre's Rock Chip Shop when open.

DETAILS

- **Open** - All year, 8.00 am to 10.00pm
- **Number of beds** - 8 : 2x2 1x4
- **Booking** - Book by phone or email
- **Price per night** - From £12 per per night shared room or £16 per night single occupancy. Group booking from £50 per night
- **Public Transport** - The direct ferry from Kirkwall Pier to the Loth terminal in Sanday takes an hour and twenty minutes. Passenger fares are about £13 return (Orkney Ferries 01856 872044 www.orkneyferries.co.uk). Flying direct from Kirkwall airport to Sanday takes 11 minutes and a return flight costs about £65. There are usually two flights per day and they are well used by the islanders (LoganAir - 01856 872494 - www.loganair.co.uk). For local buse and taxi phone 01857 600410.
- **Directions** - 6 miles from Loth ferry Terminal and 3 miles from Sanday air field.

CONTACT: Julie or Paul
Ayre , Coo road, Sanday, Orkney KW17 2AY
Tel: 01857 600410
paul_allan1967@hotmail.co.uk www.ayres-rock-sanday-orkney.co.uk

On the Stromness waterfront, a short distance from the ferry terminal, Hamnavoe Hostel makes an ideal base for your visit to Orkney. It has single, twin and family rooms with one recently-upgraded to en-suite. The rooms have easy access to the shower, bathroom and toilet on each floor. They are fitted with wash hand basins, pine bunk beds and have stunning views out across Hamnavoe. The light and airy kitchen has two cookers, microwave, double fridge, freezer, toasters, kettle and sandwich toaster. The large dining table has fantastic views over the harbour and marina. The lounge has comfortable seating, freeview TV, video, stereo and a stock of books, cards and games. There is a small laundry room with coin operated washing machine, tumble drier and iron. There's is a pay phone and wi-fi internet connection. Entry is by a coded door lock and individual rooms have keys. Free long stay car park. Come and visit the nearby islands of Graemsay and Hoy, check out the World Heritage Sites or just relax in the tranquillity of island life.

    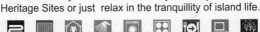 

DETAILS

■ **Open** - All year, all day, no curfew, check in from 2pm and check out by 10am., Reconfirm your booking by 7pm on the scheduled date of arrival.
■ **Number of beds** - 13: 1x4, 1x1, 4x2
■ **Booking** - Book with deposit of first night, re-confirm by 7pm on the arrival day.
■ **Price per night** - From £15pp. Private rooms £15 to £31. Family room £45.
■ **Public Transport** - Orkney Ferries run to Stromness Ferry terminal. There is a, regular bus service to and from the town of Stronmness from the terminal.
■ **Directions** - On the waterfront a short walk from Stromness ferry terminal.

CONTACT: Mr George Argo
10a North End Road, Stromness, Orkney, KW16 3AG
Tel: 01856 851202
info@hamnavoehostel.co.uk www.hamnavoehostel.co.uk

SHETLAND
SCOTLAND CAMPING BÖD NETWORK

The Shetland camping böd network offers low cost accommodation in nine historic buildings with fantastic scenery - giving the opportunity to tour these beautiful islands, staying in böds en route. Due to the böd's historic nature, no two buildings are the same and facilities vary. The smallest böd sleeps four and the largest sixteen. Electricity, hot water and showers are available in six of the nine buildings and solid fuel stoves and mains water in all. Each böd has a story to tell, for example Voe Sail Loft was once a knitwear workshop, where the jumpers for Sir Edmund Hillary's expedition to reach the peak of Mount Everest in 1953 were produced. 7 out of 9 have local meals available within 2 miles and 7 out have 9 have (variable) facilities for less able people. Under 16s must be accompanied by an adult. No pets allowed. Explore Shetland, bed down in a böd. For further info log onto: www.camping-bods.co.uk.

DETAILS

- **Open** - 1st March – 31st October, The böds are unmanned but a custodian is contactable until 9pm, please call to arrange entry
- **Number of beds** - 4 to 16 (depending on böd).
- **Booking** - Booking is not essential however, as böds are unmanned it is best to book in advance to ensure the custodian is available before arrival.
- **Price per night** - £6 to £8 pppn. Group discounts are also available.
- **Public Transport** - Information on public transport within Shetland: www.shetland.gov.uk/transport/ Information on cycle and car hire: www.visitshetland.com/getting-around/
- **Directions** - Ferry from Aberdeen to Shetland (NorthLink). Flights to Shetland from Orkney, Inverness, Aberdeen, Edinburgh and Glasgow (Flybe).

CONTACT: Reception
For info: Shetland Amenity Trust, Garthspool, Lerwick, Shetland, ZE1 0NY
Tel: (01595) 694688
info@shetlandamenity.org www.camping-bods.co.uk

KEY

45 - Hostel page number

miles

kilometres

446

Coleraine

Londonderry

Strabane

Ballymena

Larne

445

Omagh

Cookstown

Belfast

Enniskillen

Armagh

Craigavon

Downpatrick

Newry

Newcastle

Belturbet

Cavan

Dundalk

Navan

Mullingar

Dublin

Dun Laoghaira

Kildare

Imagine driving down a country lane, with flowery banks and ancient hedges, into a place that feels like home. Omagh Hostel, Northern Ireland's only EU Flower hostel, welcomes you with a big smile. It is a remote, peaceful, small family hostel, nestled at the edge of the Sperrin Mountains. Breath clean air, wander green valleys while buzzards soar overhead or cycle on deserted roads. Billy and Marella Fyffe have spread their green ethos throughout the hostel from composting to biomass heating. The hostel has single, twin and double rooms, rooms for 3 and 2 small dorms/family rooms. There is a conservatory ideal for drying wet gear. You are free to explore the gardens where vegetables and fruit are grown organically and are available to buy in season. Megalithic sites abound in the area. We are 20 miles from Beagmore stone circle, of enormous European importance, 20 miles from Devenish Island monastic site, 4 miles from Ulster American Folk Park and just 20 miles from the world renowned Janus Statues on Boas Island. We love children and families and children love it here. We have two friendly dogs and a cat called Tigger.

DETAILS

- **Open** - 1st March to 30th September, all day, please arrive before 10pm.
- **Number of beds** - 26:- 1 x 1 2 x 2 2 x 4 2 x 7
- **Booking** - Pre-booking essential for large groups.
- **Price per night** - £12.50 per adult, Euros accepted.
- **Public Transport** - Free pickup from Omagh bus station by arrangement.
- **Directions** - From Omagh take B48 towards Gortin. Turn right onto Killybrack Road before The Spar Shop. Keep on road and follow signs to hostel.

· CONTACT: Marella or Billy
Glenhordial, 9a Waterworks Road, Omagh, Co Tyrone, BT79 7JS
Tel: UK (02882) 241973, Fax: 241973
marella@omaghhostel.co.uk www.omaghhostel.co.uk

Situated on the Causeway Coast, this family run hostel is ideally situated for exploring this beautiful area including the famous Glens of Antrim.

The modern purpose built hostel offers large self-catering kitchen and communal room. Meals can be prepared for groups on request and there are rooms in a variety of sizes ~ all en-suite.

A ten minute walk takes you to the famous rope-bridge or Ballintoys picturesque harbour. The village has two pubs, both with restaurants and entertainment most nights of the week.

Often traditional sessions are on offer with everyone welcome to join in.

DETAILS

- **Open** - All year, all day
- **Number of beds** - 100 : variety of size rooms, all en-suite
- **Booking** - Booking is essential in high season
- **Price per night** - From £14pp (children under 2 free)
- **Public Transport** - Coastal bus from Belfast, twice a day No 252. Service No 172 Coleraine/Portrush 6 times a day. Free pick up from Bushmills, Giants Causeway and Ballycastle.
- **Directions** - Ballintoy on main coast road (B15) between Bushmills and Ballycastle. Hostel situated on main street in centre of village.

CONTACT: Seamus or Josephine
42A Main Street, Ballintoy, Ballycastle, Co Antrim, BT54 6LX
Tel: UK (028) 20762470 or 20769391
info@sheepislandview.com www.sheepislandview.com

Barholm is a Victorian House and can sleep up to 50 people. The house is tastefully furnished, overlooks Strangford Lough and is situated in an Area of Outstanding Natural Beauty. We can offer our guests a choice of single, double en-suite, family en-suite or group rooms at budget prices. As well as being fully equipped for self-catering we can provide meals on request. A conference room is available for seminars, functions etc and can seat up to 50 people. Portaferry offers natural interest and typical Irish charm and hospitality. It is the home of Exploris, one of Europe's finest aquaria to which our guests are offered concessionary tickets. Strangford Lough is a marine nature reserve offering exceptional wild life as well as sporting activities such as canoeing and diving. Visit our website for further details.

DETAILS

■ **Open** - All year, all day)
■ **Number of beds** - 45: 2 single, 4 double, 4 family (1x3,1x4,2x5). Groups 1x4, 2x8.
■ **Booking** - Advised for some rooms and groups
■ **Price per night** - From £14 in group room. Discounts for groups and long stays. Whole house from £500.
■ **Public Transport** - No 10 bus from Belfast to Portaferry - drop off point 'The Square' follow ferry signs - Barholm directly opposite ferry terminal.
■ **Directions** - By car from Belfast: follow directions to Newtownwards then sign posts to Portaferry - Barholm is opposite ferry terminal. By Car from Dublin / The South: drive via Downpatrick to Strangford, catch car ferry, Barholm is directly in front of you as you drive off the ferry.

CONTACT: Will Brown
11 The Strand, Portaferry, Co Down, BT22 1PF
Tel: UK (028) 427 29598, Fax: UK (028) 427 29784
info@barholmportaferry.co.uk www.barholmportaferry.co.uk

Located right downtown close to Chinatown and Gastown. You may walk to restaurants, nightclubs, buses (local for Vancouver Island), skytrain, north Vancouver Ferry, Stadium and Ice Hockey Arena.

This heritage listed building was built in 1911 by Henry Pybus, captain of the Canadian Pacific steamship 'Empress of Japan' which took the blue ribbon while setting the Trans-Pacific crossing record 1887. The hotel originally accommodated railway and ocean going travellers back to both Pacific and Atlantic.

A nautical theme is retained, 34 private rooms, 12 per floor, showers on each floor, no dorms, all linen provided, parking facilities in same block. City bus from airport one block at 'The Hudson Bay Department Store'.

DETAILS

- **Open** - All year, 24 hours. Check in 8-30am/10-30pm, no curfew
- **Number of beds** - 88: 3x4, 12x3, 20x2
- **Booking** - Book ahead if possible
- **Price per night** - C$44 double room, C$59 triple room, C$79 quad room. Weekly: double C$295, triple C$395, quad C$535. All private.
- **Public Transport** - Buses operate from local Airport, Greyhound and Rail Station.
- **Directions** - From train station or Greyhound take Sky Train to Granville Station, at The Hudson Bay Department Store. From Airport take bus #424 change at Airport station, board 98 B line to Granville Station (skytrain stop). Walk to Dunsmuire, turn right, first left into Richards Street.

CONTACT: Manager
577 Richards Street, Vancouver, British Columbia V6B2Z5, CANADA
Tel: +1 604 684-3713. Toll free (USACanada) 1-800-982-0220.
sourceentvan@telus.net www.stclairvancouver.com

KILLEANY LODGE PILGRIM HOSTEL	Aran Islands,	+353 99 61393	www.aislinglodge.com
ARAN ISLANDS MAINISTIR HOUSE	Aran Islands	+353 99 61169	www.mainistirhousearan.com
SHEEP ISLAND VIEW	Ballycastle	+44 28 20762470	www.sheepislandview.com
GARRANES FARMHOUSE HOSTEL	Beara	+353 27 73032	www.dzogchenbeara.org
URHAN HOSTEL	Beara	+353 27 74036,	
ARNIE'S BACKPACKERS HOSTEL	Belfast	+44 28 90 242867	www.arniesbackpackers.co.uk
HOMEFIELD BACKPACKERS	Bundoran	+353 719841288	www.homefieldbackpackers.com
CASHEL HOLIDAY HOSTEL	Cashel	+353 62 62330	www.cashelhostel.com
MOUNT BRANDON HOSTEL	Castlegregory	+353 66 7138299	www.mountbrandonhostel.com
MARINA INN	Dingle	+353 66 9151660	
THE BLUESTACK CENTRE	Drimarone	+353 74 97 35564	www.donegalbluestacks.com
ISAACS HOSTEL	Dublin	+353 1 8556215	www.dublinbackpacker.com
JACOBS INN	Dublin	+353 1 8555660	www.dublinbackpacker.com
LITTON LANE HOSTEL	Dublin	+353 1 872 8389	www.irish-hostel.com
SHIPLAKE MOUNTAIN HOSTEL	Dunmanway	+ 353 23 45750	www.shiplakemountainhostel.com
WOODQUAY HOSTEL	Galway	+ 353 91 562618	www.woodquayhostel.ie
GALWAY CITY HOSTEL	Galway	+ 353 91 566959	www.galwaycityhostel.com
SLEEPZONE GALWAY CITY	Galway	+353 91 566999	www.sleepzone.ie
INISHBOFIN ISLAND HOSTEL	Inishbofin	+353 95 45855	www.inishbofin-hostel.ie
FÁILTE HOSTEL	Kenmare	+353 64 42333	www.kenmare.eu/failtehostel/
KENMARE LODGE HOSTEL	Kenmare	+353 64 40662	
THE RITZ ACCOMMODATION	Killybegs	+353 74 9731309	www.theritz-killybegs.com
LEITRIM LAKES HOSTEL	Kiltyclogher	+353 72 54044	
MAYNOOTH CAMPUS ACCOM.	Maynooth	+ 353 1 708 6400	www.maynoothcampus.com
OMAGH HOSTEL AT GLENHORDIAL	Omagh	+44 2882 241973	www.omaghhostel.co.uk
BARHOLM	Portaferry	+44 28 427 29598	www.barholmportaferry.co.uk
PORTMAGEE HOSTEL	Portmagee	+353 66 948 0018	www.portmageehostel.com
RICKS CAUSEWAY COAST HOSTEL	Portstewart	+44 28 708 33789	
JAMAICA INN	Sixmilebridge	+ 353 61 369220	www.jamaicainn.ie
HARBOUR HOUSE HOSTEL	Sligo	+353 71 9171547	www.harbourhousehostel.com
OLD MILL HOLIDAY HOSTEL	Westport	+353 98 27045	www.oldmillhostel.com
BED & BREAKFAST	Paris,	+ 33 14 02 68 308	42ruepoissonniere.tripod.com/
ALOHA HOSTEL	Paris	+ 33 1 42 73 0303	www.aloha.fr
PASSAGE	Brugge,	+32 50 340232	www.passagebruges.com
CHARLIE ROCKETS	Brugge	+32 503 30660	www.charlierockets.com

SHELTER CHRISTIAN HOSTELS	Amsterdam	+31 20 624 4717	www.shelter.nl
COSMOS AMSTERDAM HOSTEL	Amsterdam	+31 206 252 438	www.hostelcosmos.com
ANKER HOSTEL	Oslo	+47 22 99 72 10	www.ankerhostel.no
GENERATOR BERLIN	Berlin	+ 49 30 417 2400	www.generatorhostels.com
HEART OF GOLD HOSTEL, BERLIN	Berlin	+49 30 2900 3300	www.heartofgold-hostel.de
PEGASUS HOSTEL	Berlin	+49 30 2977360	www.pegasushostel.de
A&O HOSTEL AM ZOO GMBH	Berlin	+49 30-8891360,	www.aohostels.com
A&O HOSTEL AND HOTEL MITTE	Berlin	+49-30-809470	www.aohostels.com
A&O HOSTEL FRIEDRICHSHAIN	Berlin	+49-30-29 77 810	www.aohostels.com
U INN BERLIN HOSTEL	Berlin	+49 30 3302 4410	uinnberlinhostel.com
LOLLIS HOMESTAY HOSTEL	Dresden	+49 35181084 58	www.lollishome.de
4 YOU MUNICH HOSTEL	Munich	+49 89 55 21 660	www.the4you.de
HAUS INTERNATIONAL	Munich	+49 89 12 00 60	www.haus-international.de
WOMBATS MUNICH	Munich	+49 89 59989 180	www.wombats-hostels.com
PENTHOUSE BACKPACKERS	Osnabrück	+49 541 600 9606	www.penthouseBP.com
JUGENDGASTEHAUS STUTTGART	Stuttgart	+49 711 241132	www.hostel-Stuttgart.de
GIMMELWALD MOUNTAIN HOSTEL	Gimmelwald	+41 033855 17 04	www.mountainhostel.com
DOWNTOWN LODGE	Grindelwald	+41 33 853 08 25	www.downtown-lodge.ch
GRINDELWALD MOUNTAIN HOSTEL	Grindelwald	+41 33 854 38 38	www.mountainhostel.ch
BACKPACKERS VILLA SONNENHOF	Interlaken	+41 33 826 71 71	www.villa.ch
LAUSANNE BACKPACKER	Lausanne	+41 21 601 8000	www.lausanne-guesthouse.ch
JEUNOTEL	Lausanne	+41 21 626 02 22	
BACKPACKERS LUCERNE	Lucerne	+41 41 360 04 20	www.backpackerslucerne.ch
LAGO LODGE BISTRO	Nidau b.Biel	+41 32 331 37 32	www.lagolodge.ch
LAZY FALKEN BACKPACKERS	Unterseen	+41 33 822 3043	www.falken-hotel.ch
RIVIERA LODGE	Vevey	+41 21 9238040	www.rivieralodge.ch
MATTERHORN HOSTEL	Zermatt	+41 27 968 1919	www.matterhornhostel.com
CITY BACKPACKER HOTEL BIBER	Zurich	+41 44 251 9015	www.city-backpacker.ch
YOHO INTERNATIONAL HOTEL	Salzburg	+43 662 879 649	www.yoho.at
WOMBATS VIENNA	Vienna	+43 1 897 2336	www.wombats-hostels.com
HOSTEL RUTHENSTEINER	Vienna	+43 1 893 4202	www.hostelruthensteiner.com
EMILE HOSTEL	Gibraltar, SP	+350 51106	
EDELWEISS YOUTH HOSTEL	Barcelona	+34 933575280	www.edelweissyouthhostel.com
BARCELONA MAR HOSTEL	Barcelona	+34 93 324 85 30	www.barcelonamar.com
JACINTO BENAVENTE UNIVERSITY	Malaga	+34 952657099	www.residenciajb.net

PURPLE NEST HOSTEL	Valencia	+34 963 532 561	www.nesthostelsvalencia.com
FATTORIA BASSETTO	Firenze	+39 0571 668 342	www.fattoriabassetto.com
RING HOSTEL	Island Ischia	+ 39 0 81987546,	www.ringhostel.com
HOSTEL OF THE SUN	Naples	+39 08142 06393	www.hostelnapoli.com
BELLA CAPRI HOSTEL AND HOTEL	Naples	+39 081552 9494	www.bellacapri.it
PENSIONE MANCINI HOSTEL	Naples	+39 081 553 6731	www.hostelpensionemancini.com
SANDY HOSTEL	Rome	+39 064 884585	www.sandyhostel.com
PENSIONE OTTAVIANO HOSTEL	Rome	+39 063 973 7253	www.ottavianohostel.com
BELLAROMA HOSTEL	Rome	+39 063975 0599	www.bellaromahostel.com
M & J PLACE HOSTEL	Rome	+39 06446 2802	www.mejplacehostel.com
ALESSANDRO PALACE HOSTEL	Rome	+ 39 06 4461 958	www.hostelsalessandro.com
YELLOW HOSTEL	Rome	+39 06 4938 2682	www.yellowhostel.com
VICTORIA HOSTEL IN ROME	Rome	+39 06 44 70 586	www.cristinahouse.com
YOUTH STATION HOSTEL	Rome	+39 06 4429 2471	www.youthstation.it
PAGRATION YOUTH HOSTEL	Athens	+30 210 7519530	www.athens-yhostel.com
ARPACAY HOSTEL	Prague	+42 0/251 552297	www.arpacayhostel.com
RITCHIE'S HOSTEL AND HOTEL	Prague	+420 222 221 229	www.ritchieshostel.cz
MELLOW MOOD CENTRAL HOSTEL	Budapest	+36 1 411 1310	www.mellowmoodhostel.com
HOSTEL FORTUNA	Budapest	+36-1 215 0660	www.fortunahostel.hu
MARCO POLO HOSTEL	Budapest	+36 1 413 2555	www.marcopolohostel.com
TANGO HOSTEL	Koycegiz	+90 252 262 2501	www.tangohostel.com
THE YOUNG TOURIST CENTRE	Vilnius	+ 3705 2611547;	www.vjtc.lt
BALACLAVA BACKPACKERS	Crimea	+38 067 398 7888	www.crimean-backpackers.org
YAROSLAV INT. HOSTEL	Kiev	+38-044 417 3189	www.HIHostels.com.ua
OLD PRAGUE HOSTEL	Prague	+420 224 829 058	www.oldpraguehostel.com
ATLANTIS HOSTEL	Krakow	+48 12 398 78 13	www.atlantishostel.pl
DIZZY DAISY DOWNTOWN HOSTEL	Krakow	+48 12 398 78 14	www.krakowhostel.pl
PRAGUE SQUARE HOSTEL	Prague	+420 224 240 859	www.praguesquarehostel.com
TAMKA HOSTEL	Warsaw	+48 22 213 29 53	www.tamkahostel.pl
VANA TOM HOSTEL	Tallinn	+372 6 31 32 52	www.hostel.ee
HOSTEL EOL 777	Constanta	+40 727 555556	
SAMESUNS LODGE BANFF	Banff Alberta	+403-762-5521	www.samesun.com
THUNDER BAY HOSTEL	Thunder Bay	+1 807 983-2042	www.backpackers.ca
HOSTELS CANADA ST CLAIR HOTEL	Vancouver	+1 604 684-3713.	www.stclairvancouver.com
SAMESUNS LODGE VANCOUVER	Vancouver	604-682-8226	www.samesun.com

Backpackers Hostels Canada
Auberges Backpackers Canada

Visit Canada!
Visit ... www.backpackers.ca

swiss ✛ backpackers

Hostels · Herbergen · Auberges · Ostelli

www.swissbackpackers.ch

Dear Backpacker,

at Swiss Backpackers hostels we offer you a home away from home. You receive a warm welcome, can enjoy a budget, yet comfortable bed, where you can let all the impressions, made every day while travelling, settle. In the self catering kitchens you will find a good atmosphere, not only to cook and eat, but also to get chatting with other travellers. There is no membership required. See for yourself that we provide the quality hostels of Switzerland.

32 hostels in 26 cities all over Switzerland

6677 Aurigeno, **Baracca Backpacker**, +41 (0)79 207 15 54

4008 Basel, **YMCA Hostel Basel**, +41 (0)61 361 73 09, info@ymcahostelbasel.ch

3011 Bern, **Backpackers - Hotel Glocke**, +41 (0)31 311 37 71, info@bernbackpackers.ch

3013 Bern, **Landhaus - Backpackers Paradise**, +41 (0)31 331 41 66, landhaus@spectraweb.ch

3992 Bettmeralp, **Backpacker Venus**, +41 (0)27 927 25 85, info@venustourist.ch

8784 Braunwald, **adrenalin backpackers hostel**, +41 (0)79 347 2905, info@adrenalin.gl

6558 Cabbiolo/Lostallo, **Humanita Backpackers**, +41 (0)91 830 1481, info@humanita.ch

7002 Chur, **JBN Hostel**, +41 (0)81 284 10 10, info@justbenice.ch

1202 Genève, **City Hostel Geneva**, +41 (0)22 901 15 00, info@cityhostel.ch

3826 Gimmelwald, **Mountain Hostel**, +41 (0)33 855 17 04, mountainhostel@tcnet.ch

3818 Grindelwald, **Downtown Lodge**, +41 (0)33 853 08 25, downtown-lodge@jungfrau.ch

3818 Grindelwald, **Mountain Hostel**, +41 (0)33 854 38 38, info@mountainhostel.ch

1882 Gryon, **Chalet Martin**, +41 (0)79 724 6374, info@gryon.com

7130 Ilanz, **Gasthof Mundaun**, +41 (0)81 925 45 55, info@mundaunpub.ch

3800 Interlaken, **Backpackers Villa Sonnenhof**, +41 (0)33 826 71 71, mail@villa.ch

3800 Interlaken/Matten, **Balmer's Herberge**, +41 (0)33 822 19 61, mail@balmers.com

3800 Interlaken/Unterseen, **Hotel & Backpacker Falken**, +41 (0)33 822 30 43, falken@quicknet.ch

3800 Interlaken, **Happy Inn Lodge**, +41 (0)33 822 32 25, info@happy-inn.com

3800 Interlaken, **River Lodge**, +41 (0)33 822 44 24, welcome@riverlodge.ch

3718 Kandersteg, **Gemmi Lodge**, +41 (0)33 675 85 85, info@gemmi-lodge.com

7031 Laax-Cons, **Backpacker Deluxe Capricorn**, 41 (0)81 921 21 20, info@caprilounge.ch

1007 Lausanne, **Guesthouse & Backpacker**, +41 (0)21 601 80 00, info@lausanne-guesthouse.ch

3822 Lauterbrunnen, **Valley Hostel**, +41 (0)33 855 20 08, info@valleyhostel.ch

6005 Luzern, **Backpackers Lucerne**, +41 (0)41 360 04 20, www.backpackerslucerne.ch

8212 Neuhausen am Rheinfall, **Zak Backpackers**, +41 (0)52 672 5521, info@zakzak.ch

2560 Nidau b. Biel, **Lago Lodge**, +41 (0)32 331 37 32, sleep@lagolodge.ch

6430 Schwyz, **Hirschen Schwyz**, +41 (0)41 811 12 76, info@hirschen-schwyz.ch

7554 Sent, **Backpacker Hotel Swissroof**, +41 (0)81 864 17 22, info@swissroof.ch

9657 Unterwasser, **Saentislodge**, +41(0)71 998 5025, saentis@beutler-hotels.ch

1800 Vevey-Montreux, **Riviera Lodge**, +41 (0)21 923 80 40, info@rivieralodge.ch

6484 Wassen, **Gotthardbackpacker**, +41 (0)79 306 54 23, www.gotthardbackpacker.ch

8001 Zürich, **City Backpacker/Hotel Biber**, +41 (0)44 251 90 15, sleep@city-backpacker.ch

Wake up in the (BEST) IRISH HOSTELS

{ Beds for all AGES! }

Book Online at
www.hostels-ireland.com

The network of IRISH TOURIST BOARD approved hostels all over IRELAND

INDEPENDENT HOLIDAY
HOSTELS
OF IRELAND

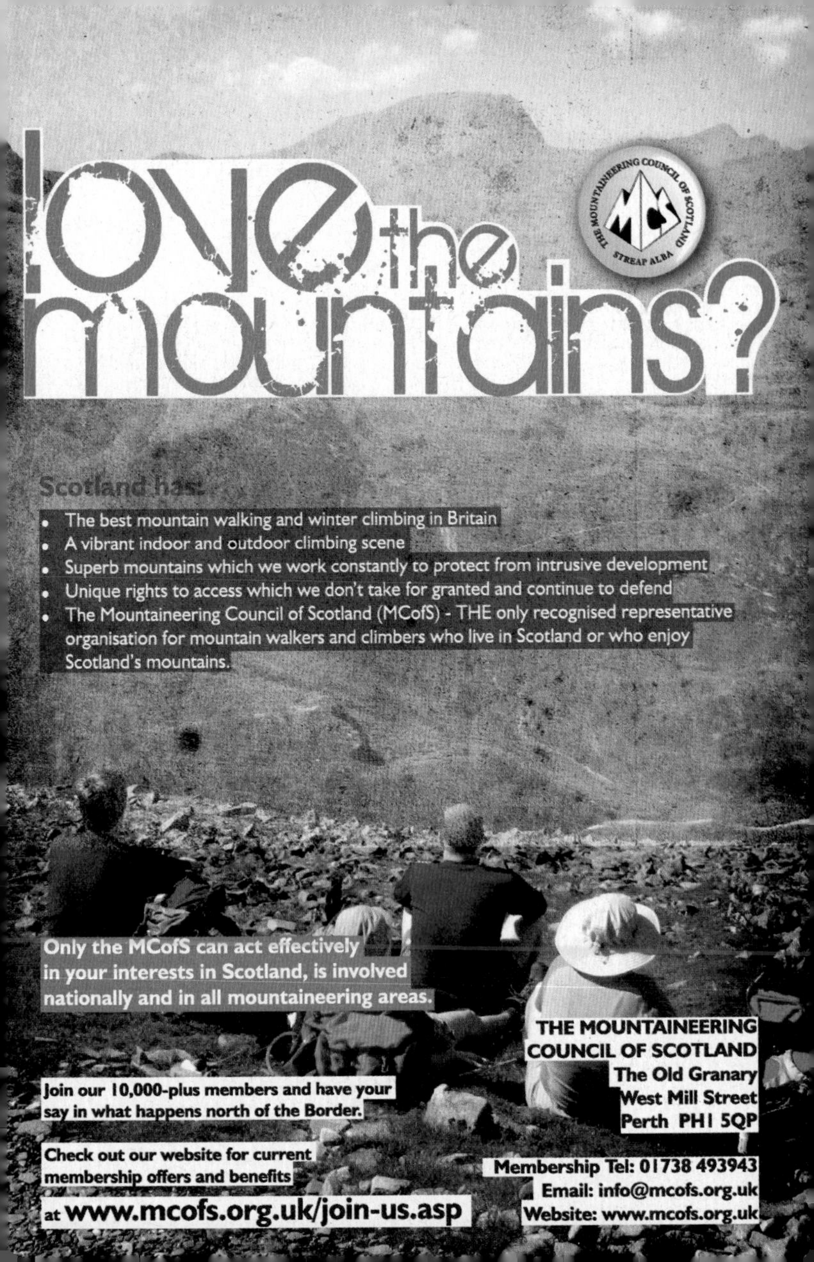

love the mountains?
THE MOUNTAINEERING COUNCIL OF SCOTLAND
MCS
STREAP ALBA
Scotland has:
• The best mountain walking and winter climbing in Britain
• A vibrant indoor and outdoor climbing scene
• Superb mountains which we work constantly to protect from intrusive development
• Unique rights to access which we don't take for granted and continue to defend
• The Mountaineering Council of Scotland (MCofS) - THE only recognised representative organisation for mountain walkers and climbers who live in Scotland or who enjoy Scotland's mountains.
Only the MCofS can act effectively in your interests in Scotland, is involved nationally and in all mountaineering areas.
THE MOUNTAINEERING COUNCIL OF SCOTLAND
The Old Granary
West Mill Street
Perth PH1 5QP
Join our 10,000-plus members and have your say in what happens north of the Border.
Check out our website for current membership offers and benefits
at www.mcofs.org.uk/join-us.asp
Membership Tel: 01738 493943
Email: info@mcofs.org.uk
Website: www.mcofs.org.uk

INDEX

3 PEAKS BUNK BARN	142
ACHINTEE FARM HOSTEL	376
ADVENTURERS ESCAPE	295
AIRTON QUAKER HOSTEL	140
ÀITE CRUINNICHIDH	308
ALBATROSS BACKPACKERS IN!	188
ALDERSYDE BUNKHOUSE	294
ALL STAR HOSTEL	65
ALL STRETTON BUNKHOUSE	97
AMBLESIDE BACKPACKERS	164
ARDENBEG BUNKHOUSE	361
ARIUNDLE BUNKHOUSE	371
ASHLEE HOUSE	80
AVIEMORE BUNKHOUSE	356
AVON TYRRELL ACTIVITY CEN.	52
AYRES ROCK HOSTEL	440
BADRALLACH BOTHY	398
BALA BACKPACKERS	262
BALA BUNK HOUSE	264
BALINTRAID HOUSE	406
BANK STREET LODGE	374
BARHOLM	447
BARN FARM BARNS	110
BARROWBURN CAMPING BARN	194
BASE LODGE	51
BATH YMCA	44
BAYFIELD BACKPACKERS	416
BCC LOCHNESS HOSTEL	387
BEILI NEUADD BUNKHOUSE	250
BEN NEVIS INN BUNKHOUSE	377
BENTS CAMPING BARN	148
BERROW HOUSE BUNKHOUSE	90
BERWICK-ON-TWEED BPS	202
BIRMINGHAM CENTRAL BPS	95
BIRSAY OUTDOOR CENTRE	437
BISHOP MASCALL CENTRE	89
BLACK ROCK BUNKHOUSE	313
BLACKWATER HOSTEL	367
BLUEBELL FARM BUNKBARN	198
BLYTHESWOOD HOSTEL	34
BRAEMAR LODGE BUNKHOUSE	363
BRAICH GOCH BUNKHOUSE	256
BRANSDALE MILL	134
BRAVEHEART BACKPACKERS	339
BRIDGES LONG MYND Y HOSTEL	96
BRIGHTON ROYAL HOTEL	57
BRISTOL BACKPACKERS HOSTEL	46
BROOK HOUSE BARN	128
BROWNS HOSTEL AND HOUSE	431
BRYN TIRION FARM BUNKHOUSE	274
BUNKUM BACKPACKERS	322
BUSHEY HEATH FARM BARNS	114
BUTE BACKPACKERS	330
BWTHYN Y BUGAIL	242
BY THE WAY HOSTEL	338
CABAN CADER IDRIS	260
CABAN CYSGU GERLAN	272
CAERHAFOD LODGE	232
CAIRNCROSS HOUSE	290
CALLUNA	372
CAMPBELL ROOM GROUP	41
CANAL BARN BUNKHOUSE	221
CANTREF FARM BUNKHOUSES	220
CARDIFF BACKPACKER	210
CARDIFF UNIVERSITY ACCOM	212
CASTLE CREAVIE HAY LOFT	292
CASTLE ROCK HOSTEL	318
CATBELLS CAMPING BARN	176
CAUSEWAY FOOT CAMPING BARN	178
CENTRAL BACKPACKERS OXFORD	88
CHASE THE WILD GOOSE HOSTEL	378
CHATTON PARK BUNKHOUSE	195
CHESTER BACKPACKERS	121
CLINK HOSTEL	72
CLYNGWYN BUNKHOUSE	224
COLDBLOW FARM BUNKBARNS	58
COLONSAY KEEPER'S LODGE	430
COMRIE CROFT	340
CONWY VALLEY BARN	268
CORRAN BUNKHOUSE	368
CORRAN HOUSE	334
CORRIS HOSTEL	258
COURT HILL CENTRE	84
CRAFLWYN BASECAMP	282
CRAGG BARN CAMPING BARN	173
CROFT BUNKHOUSE BOTHIES	412
CROWN LODGE GROUP ACCOM.	261
CULDEES BUNKHOUSE	341
CULLEN HARBOUR HOSTEL	348
DALESBRIDGE	136
DARTMOOR EXPEDITION CENTRE	30
DAVID DONALD FS BASE	47
DEEPDALE BACKPACKERS	102
DEEPDALE GRANARY GROUP HOS.	101
DEMESNE FARM BUNKHOUSE	191
DENTON HOUSE	179
DERVAIG BUNKROOMS	427
DINAH HOGGUS CAMPING BARN	172
DOLGOCH HOSTEL	246
DOVER CASTLE HOSTEL	68
DRINISHADER HOSTEL	420
DUDDON SANDS HOSTEL	155
DUN CAAN HOSTEL	408
DUN FLODIGARRY HOSTEL	417
DUNARD HOSTEL	419
DUNOLLY ADVENTURE OUTDOORS	296
EASTGATE BACKPACKERS	390
ELMSCOTT HOSTEL	25
EMBASSIE HOSTEL	124
EURO HOSTEL GLASGOW	323
EXETER GLOBE BACKPACKERS	37
EXMOOR BASECAMP	40
FALMOUTH BACKPACKERS	19
FARR COTTAGE LODGE	310
FELL END BUNKHOUSE	151
FELL END CAMPING BARN	157